Women in American History

Series Editors

Mari Jo Buhle
Nancy A. Hewitt
Anne Firor Scott

A list of books in the series appears at the end of this book.

Gendered Strife
& Confusion

Gendered Strife & Confusion

The Political Culture of Reconstruction

Laura F. Edwards

University of Illinois Press   Urbana and Chicago

© 1997 by the Board of Trustees of the University of Illinois
Manufactured in the United States of America

1 2 3 4 5 C P 5 4 3 2 1

This book is printed on acid-free paper.

Library of Congress Cataloging-in-Publication Data

Edwards, Laura F.
    Gendered strife and confusion : the political culture of
Reconstruction / Laura F. Edwards.
        p.   cm. — (Women in American history)
    Includes bibliographical references (p.) and index.
    ISBN 0-252-02297-1 (cloth : acid-free paper). — ISBN 0-252-06600-6
(pbk. : acid-free paper)
    1. Women—Southern States—History—19th century. 2. Sex role—
Southern States—History—19th century. 3. Reconstruction.
I. Title. II. Series.
HQ1438.S63E35   1997
305.3'0973'09034—dc20   96-25317
                                                              CIP

For John

Contents

Preface

On 3 October 1876, the local newspaper in Granville County, North Carolina, printed an open letter from H. C. Crosby, an African-American leader and prominent local Republican. Crosby was concerned about the recent county Republican convention, which he considered a disgrace to the party. The problem, he explained, was that self-interested office seekers had dominated the proceedings and used them "to carry out their own avaricious designs, regardless of the wishes of the people." More specifically, Crosby feared that the nominees would ignore the interests of African Americans. The result, he claimed, was "gendered strife and confusion" within the party's ranks. Of course, Crosby meant that the convention "*en*gendered strife and confusion." But in this slip, he hit upon one element of Reconstruction so deeply embedded within political thought and social relations of the time that it was rarely explicitly acknowledged then and is often overlooked by historians today. Crosby was unfamiliar with the term, but gender played a significant role in engendering the "strife and confusion" that plagued the Republican party in 1876. As I will argue, gender, in combination with race and class, shaped the political terrain not just in Granville County but across the South during Reconstruction. This gendered component changes our perspective on the issues, the actors, and the conflicts of this period. In this sense, "gendered strife and confusion" accurately describes the politics of Reconstruction as a whole.

The closer I looked at the people of Granville, the more difficult it was to come up with accurate terms to describe them. I use categories to describe groups of people with the assumption that they are not fixed, but relative, fluid, and overlapping. After southern surrender, for instance, wealthy white southerners were not as wealthy as they had been before the war, but they still controlled more economic, political, and cultural resources than either newly freed slaves or poor whites. They also managed to better their position over time.

Because the war and emancipation reduced many wealthy whites to relative poverty, I use "elite white" to describe a wider group of people who did not necessarily enjoy the same economic status, but who nonetheless shared key ideological premises and distinguished themselves from the poor of both races. "Elite," therefore, is not reducible to either economic class or political affiliation. In fact, not all "elites" were even white. Some African Americans embraced components of the elite outlook, although not those aspects that accentuated racial hierarchy. There were also elites in both the Republican and Democratic parties. Of course they differed on key points of public policy and political strategy, but they still shared many social and cultural precepts. By identifying individuals within both the Republican and Democratic parties as "elite" I realize that I invite criticism by blurring important political distinctions between these two groups. But I do so to emphasize important differences *within* the two parties that have been too often overlooked in the tendency to focus on divisions between leaders of the two parties and to identify these leaders as representative of party membership as a whole. To minimize the problem, I use the terms "conservative," "moderate," and "radical" to distinguish different political positions within and between the Democratic and Republican parties.

I open myself to the same kind of criticism by extending the term "elite" to those who were not wealthy and who may, in fact, have been no better off materially than the poor people next door. I have no intention of brushing aside the importance of material resources to the control of cultural and political power. To the contrary, I try to point out the places where the ideological positions of these people did not serve their economic interests. Still, I think it is important to acknowledge that many people shared elements of a cultural and political outlook, even if they did not share economic or even racial positions. Those who had recently fallen on hard times, young people who were attached to propertied families but did not own property in their own names, and those who aspired to climb up the economic and social ladder to become the successful "capitalists" promoted in the pages of the local newspapers could accept certain "elite" cultural and political ideals, even if they seemed at odds with the immediate material realities of their lives.

The term "common whites" encompasses those men and women from antebellum yeomen and propertyless white families who maintained reservations about the postwar "elite" vision. I do not see common whites as a self-contained group. To the contrary, their political interests and cultural concerns often overlapped with those of both elite whites and African Americans. When I refer to "poor whites" I usually mean propertyless whites, unless I am using the term in a comparative sense to refer to those—white, black, or both—who were poorer than their wealthier neighbors.

The term "African American" refers to the majority of poor blacks as well as more elite property-owning black farmers, artisans, and professionals. Class differences were not as pronounced among African Americans as they were among whites in the immediate postwar years, but they were important and became increasingly so over time. When these differences among blacks become important to the analysis, I mark them with class-related adjectives: poor, propertyless, working-class, middle-class, propertied, or elite.

Acknowledgments

Many people have helped me write this book. A Smithsonian Fellowship at the National Museum of American History and a Monticello College Foundation Fellowship at the Newberry Library gave me opportunities to finish writing. The University of South Florida generously gave me time off to take advantage of these fellowships. A Research and Creative Scholarship Award from the Research Council at the University of South Florida, an Albert J. Beveridge Research Grant from the American Historical Association, as well as a Dissertation Research Fellowship from the University of North Carolina at Chapel Hill provided research funds. The staff members at all of the archives I used made research possible. Those at the North Carolina Department of Archives and History in Raleigh and the North Carolina Collection at the University of North Carolina were particularly patient and helpful. I would also like to thank specifically the staffs of the Southern Historical Collection at the University of North Carolina, the Special Collections Department at Duke University, and the National Archives. Laurie Weakley and Edward Estock graciously opened up their home to me whenever I was in North Carolina, providing hospitality for which I will always be grateful and friendship I will always treasure.

Over the years, so many people have read and commented on this work that it is sometimes difficult to tell where my ideas end and theirs begin. Words fail to express my debt for their generosity with their thoughts and their time; I can only try to emulate their example. Conversations with Noralee Frankel and Hannah Rosen were instrumental in conceptualizing the book. Nell Painter's critique of my unrevised dissertation was influential in helping me shape it into a book. Her support and encouragement were also critical in bringing the project to this final stage. I was fortunate enough to have three other reviewers—Linda Kerber, Amy Dru Stanley, and Anne Scott—whose insightful readings greatly strengthened this work. So did thoughtful remarks of those who read all or part of the manuscript:

Peter Bardaglio, Ben Brown, Victoria Bynum, Peter Coclanis, Pete Daniel, Glenda Gilmore, Jacquelyn Hall, Dirk Hartog, Nancy Hewitt, Bob Ingalls, John McAllister, Jan Reiff, and Dave Roediger. Jim Anderson, John Blassingame, Carol Blesser, Elsa Barkley Brown, Catherine Clinton, Pat Cooper, Jim Grossman, Tera Hunter, Karen Leathem, Nancy MacLean, and Kathleen Paul commented on conference papers and drafts that eventually evolved into chapters. Discussions of my work at the Newberry Library Fellows' Seminar and Social History Seminar, the American Bar Foundation Lunch Series, and the Social History Workshop at the University of Chicago were also helpful in clarifying my analysis. Karen Hewitt has been a model editor. I am particularly grateful to her and Nancy Hewitt for their interest in this manuscript at a crucial moment. Giovanna Beradusi and Kirsten Fischer have given their time and, with Golpho Alexopolous and Fraser Ottanelli, have made the University of South Florida a congenial and stimulating place to work. Thanks also go to Sheila Cohen and Ana Varela-Lago for their research assistance. John McAllister has lived with this project the longest; it was he who first encouraged me to think that I could do scholarly work and then gave me the inspiration to proceed.

Parts of the introduction have appeared in *Feminist Studies* 22 (Summer 1996): 363–86. Parts of chapters 1 and 5 have appeared in *Law and History Review* 14 (Spring 1996): 81–124. Parts of chapter 5 have also appeared in the *North Carolina Historical Review* 68 (July 1991): 237–260.

Gendered Strife
& Confusion

Introduction: The Disappearance of Henderson Cooper and Susan Daniel: Redrawing the Political Terrain of the Postemancipation South

Late in 1864, Susan Daniel, the wife of a landless white man, accused two slaves, William Cooper and Henderson Cooper, of rape. A few months later, on the eve of southern surrender, the Granville County Superior Court convicted and sentenced both men to death. Only William Cooper, however, was hanged. Henderson escaped and fled to Washington, D.C., where he lived until the fall of 1866, when Granville officials captured him and brought him back to the county. Although the court then affirmed his sentence and rescheduled his hanging, the execution never took place. At the eleventh hour, the Freedmen's Bureau intervened, declaring the sentence void because it had been rendered by a Confederate court not recognized by the U.S. government. The bureau then directed the case to a court of inquiry for further investigation. Citing evidence that Susan Daniel had consented to the act and pointing out that Henderson Cooper was charged only with aiding and abetting, the court concluded that he had committed a crime, but not one that merited death. Based on this report, a U.S. military tribunal then tried Henderson Cooper, found him guilty, and, ignoring the court of inquiry's recommendation, sentenced him to death. But Cooper's luck held. At this point, the Freedmen's Bureau's assistant commissioner declared his latest death sentence void and ordered Cooper to be tried on a new indictment by local authorities. The decision could have resulted in Cooper's release, since he had already been tried and convicted on the same charge. This time, fortune failed Henderson Cooper. As he awaited his trial and possible acquittal, a fire burned the jail to the ground. None of the prisoners survived.[1]

The Cooper-Daniel case is only one of many incidents in Granville County that fit awkwardly within the usual narrative outlines of Reconstruction history that focus on the reorganization of the South's labor system and party politics. The documents relating to the case were among the first pieces of evidence I uncovered, but I set them aside for several years because they seemed irrelevant to the main issues of Reconstruction. I assumed that Confederate officials had fabricated a rape charge against two black men and then the Freedmen's Bureau had intervened to correct this miscarriage of justice. Beyond that, I saw Henderson Cooper's and Susan Daniel's story as a dramatic anecdote rooted in a unique set of local circumstances. While dismissing Henderson Cooper and Susan Daniel, I embraced Granville County's atypicality in a different way at this early point in my project, imagining that my study of this tobacco-producing area would provide a counterpoint to studies on the cotton South. Located in central North Carolina along the Virginia border, Granville County hardly seemed representative of anything but tobacco production. As the project developed, however, rich local records as well as new work in women's and African-American history drew me toward the people who lived in the county, instead of the locality itself. Reframing my questions, however, did not shake the typicality issue, which trailed doggedly only a few paces behind me, insisting that intensive work on this local area would always preclude the possibility of making any large claims. The parallels to other fields are striking. Facing similar questions, women's historians have argued that women's lives appear irrelevant only when the universal historical actor is assumed to be male. As scholars in African-American history have pointed out, that actor is generally white, leaving black men and women on the sidelines of history as well. These insights apply directly to the people in Granville County, the majority of whom were either female or black or both. Extending the analogy another way, Granville County residents also seem unrepresentative because of the common historical presumption that major cities form the centers from which history filters out to the hinterlands.

The subjects of my study, among them Susan Daniel and Henderson Cooper, challenged this notion. As is so often the case in local research, they stubbornly refused to fit the categories we historians laid out for them. At first, I trimmed off their ragged edges, muted their colorful cacophony, and dutifully forced them into their allotted conceptual spaces. I failed. They kept escaping to join a growing crowd on the fringes of my analysis that loudly mocked my efforts to control them. Finally, I began to listen more carefully to those on the borders. Their defiance of accepted categories reminded me that common historical presumptions, identifying certain people and

NORTH CAROLINA
AT THE BEGINNING OF
1870
Showing Approximate County Divisions
within Present State Boundaries
Map by
L. Polk. Denmark.

From David Leroy Corbitt, *The Formation of North Carolina Counties, 1663–1943* (Raleigh: State Department of Archives and History, 1950); reproduced with permission.

places as "central" and "significant" and others as "peripheral" and "irrelevant," were themselves products of a highly contested history. In the heady years following Henderson Cooper's escape, the residents of Granville County battled over these very boundaries. From this perspective, their conflicts provide a window on the process that shaped the analytical categories historians now use, often more uncritically than we should.

Private and Public, Social and Political

Susan Daniel's rape charge opened an era of conflict within Granville County that did not end until 1887. The evidence suggests that local conservative leaders seized on the case in the waning months of the Confederacy in a desperate bid to strengthen their hold on an increasingly unruly population. By convicting and hanging two black men for the rape of a white woman, local authorities could address the racial fears of many white residents and demonstrate their ability to maintain antebellum racial hierarchies even as the institution of slavery was crumbling around them. It is not surprising then that these same conservative officials resurrected the case by capturing Cooper in Washington in 1866, when the implications of the Confederacy's surrender were still unclear.[2] At this time, elite whites in the county faced the defiance of African Americans, who were trying to establish the terms of their newfound freedom. They also faced the resentment of many common whites, who were painfully putting their lives back together after a war they had never been enthusiastic about in the first place. Hanging Cooper would send a strong message to all Granville County residents about who held power. A black man dead at the end of a rope warned all African Americans not to push the limits of their freedom too far. Cooper's execution would deliver a different message to common whites. Because this particular case involved a poor white woman, conservative authorities could use it to ease the resentment of those whites who shared Susan Daniel's poverty and affirm their place as the legitimate representatives of all white residents. But the attempt to use the capture and execution of Henderson Cooper as a demonstration of the power and competence of conservative rule failed miserably. When the Freedmen's Bureau took Cooper into custody the day before his hanging, it summarily stripped county officials of their authority much as an errant son might be disciplined by his father. With conservatives left standing open-mouthed and empty-handed on the courthouse steps, their handling of the case appeared as little more than hollow posturing.

At this point, Governor Jonathan Worth entered the conflict. Although a former Whig and unionist, Worth stubbornly resisted any change in the racial and class hierarchies that had structured slave society. As President Andrew Johnson's conservative Reconstruction plan lost credibility with Congress and Worth's own term as governor drew to a close, Worth only dug in his heels further. Embittered and embattled, he saw in the Cooper-Daniel case all the dangers he believed federal policies posed to the people and the state of North Carolina. Supporting Granville County authorities, he tried to influence the Freedmen's Bureau's treatment of the case. Later, he used its handling as a central piece of evidence in a series of articles exposing what he considered to be the atrocities of northern occupation.[3]

Governor Worth equated the Cooper-Daniel case with the public power of propertied white men and the disastrous consequences that would result if these men no longer stood at the apex of power. Moving seamlessly between the rape and his concerns about the state's public institutions, he rarely bothered to distinguish between the two. In one passage, he graphically depicted the act itself: "This was a rape of peculiar atrocity. Two strong negroes enter the house of a poor but worthy woman and in the presence of her little daughter each of them commits a rape upon her." Then, without ending the sentence, he jumped from the dwelling house where the rape was committed to the statehouse: and the federal government "interposes its shield and allows one of the monsters to go unpunished. . . . If alienation to the government in this state is on the increase, as is often alleged to our prejudice, is it to be wondered at?"[4] The vulnerability of Susan Daniel became the vulnerability of the people of North Carolina, while the illegitimate power of Henderson Cooper became the illegitimate power of northern officials who meddled in state government. As long as the state's rightful leaders remained hamstrung by these interlopers, the people of North Carolina, like Susan Daniel, had no recourse. They could only hope that justice would prevail. No doubt, conservative leaders within Granville County agreed.[5]

Clearly the Cooper-Daniel case was staged at the intersection of social and political history, a juncture that allowed conservative leaders at both the state and local levels to use the figures of Susan Daniel and Henderson Cooper in a dramatic allegory of Reconstruction politics. Yet this tale revealed little about the social context that informed conservatives' rhetoric and drove their political concerns. Existing secondary literature provides few clues, since historians of Reconstruction have generally focused on either social or political history but not on their relationship to each other. Where political historians have examined the intricacies of party politics and the impact of public policy, social historians have questioned this institutional emphasis. Moving the focus away from the nation's statehouses to southern fields and households, they have argued that the outcome of people's daily struggles over economic resources and social relations is as pivotal to understanding the period as the decisions of political leaders. The best social history is inherently political; like traditional political history, it is about power. Yet, at the time I began this project, few historians had followed the lead of W. E. B. Du Bois in his epic *Black Reconstruction,* which placed conflicts staged in southern fields and households in an explicitly political context. Since then, a host of scholars have moved us further down this path, linking social and political history in innovative ways. Nonetheless, the relationship between the two remains difficult to tease out, because it is much easier to trace the effects of public policy on people's daily lives than the other way around.[6]

More recent work in women's history and African-American history suggests new ways to approach this dilemma. Exploring the position of women in society, feminist scholars have questioned the uncritical use of oppositional categories such as public/private. Arguing that "public" and "private" are not fixed categories, but ideological ones, these critics have shown how the boundaries have changed over time. They also have criticized the tendency of scholars to accept ideology as reality, thereby assuming a distinction between a public, male sphere and a private, female sphere, which obscures the relationship between the two. Race and class, as other critics have pointed out, also influence the shape of "private" and "public." Rooted in middle-class culture, notions of sharply differentiated spheres of life inevitably misrepresent the ways African Americans, other ethnic groups, and working-class whites organized their worlds.[7] These insights thus blur the distinction between political history, with its focus on public institutions, and social history, with its emphasis on the "private" matters of work and family.

Although concerned with these connections, other scholars of Reconstruction have used race and class to focus their analyses. This study adds gender to the mix. The result is a conceptual lens that brings new issues into view and allows us to see the connections between the private sphere and the public world much more clearly. Indeed, such an approach carries particular relevance for historians of emancipation, which remade southern households as thoroughly as it did the region's political institutions. Far more than a collection of people or a place of residence, the antebellum household defined private obligations and mediated the distribution of public power. In the slave South, men and women did not just live in households; they acquired formal legal identities through their relations to other household members as husbands and wives, fathers and mothers, parents and children, masters and slaves, and household heads and dependents. These identities and the households in which they were based then provided the framework that structured social and political relations in the South as a whole.[8]

Marking the boundaries between private and public space, the household also connected these two spheres in the figure of a white head of household. Before emancipation, household heads assumed economic, legal, and moral responsibility for a range of dependents, who included African-American slaves as well as white women and children. They also shouldered the duty of representing their dependents' interests in the public arena of politics. In this way, private authority translated directly into public rights and power. By contrast, law and social convention denied both private and public power to those who were supposed to be subsumed within the private sphere—wives, slaves, and children. All of these groups occupied distinctly different positions. Equating the subordination of slaves, which was absolute, with the subordination of white women and children would constitute a serious misrepresentation of southern society. But the status of these groups overlapped in the sense that the law defined them as dependents and relegated them to the private sphere, where they were subject to the governance of a household head. They could move in the physical space outside the household's borders, but they could not claim the requisite civil and political rights that would allow them to assume the same independent public personas that white male household heads did.

Thus, in the decades before the Civil War, the gender, racial, and class dimensions of private and public power converged. The figure of a household head was an adult, white, propertied male. To those who held the reins of power in antebellum North Carolina, these were the only people capable of the responsibilities of governance, whether private or public. Because women, children, and African Americans were considered to lack both self-control and the capacity for reason, they were thought to require the protection and guidance of white men. But white men claimed power on their ability to fulfill the duties of household head, not on the ascriptive basis of their race and sex alone. Not every man measured up. Dependency tainted all those who lacked sufficient property to control their own labor and maintain their own households. Nevertheless, all propertyless white men possessed the potential to head independent households. In this sense, their position was always different from that of white women and African Americans, who could step out of their proper place and even step into the role of household head, but could never fully embody the power of that role.

The anomalous position of unmarried white women and free black men and women in the antebellum period suggests how strongly gender and race shaped notions of independence and dependence. Even when these people headed their own households, the residue of dependency that clung to them made it difficult for them to fulfill their duties. None could participate directly in politics. Beyond that, free black men and women faced legal and customary restrictions that denied them a whole range of civil rights and economic opportunities and, as a result, made it that much more difficult for them to maintain independent households. Unmarried and widowed free women, both black and white, did exercise rights in the status of *feme sole,* but having individual rights to contract and own property did not mean that women could comfortably assume a place at the head of a household. Because southern law defined parental rights as the rights of fathers, mothers had only tenuous claims to their children. Without parental rights, women, particularly propertyless women, struggled against great odds to keep their families together. The task was almost impossible for unmarried free black women, whose children were routinely apprenticed as soon as they were old enough to be separated from their mothers and to carry on meaningful labor.[9]

War and emancipation shook the antebellum household to its foundations, destabilizing the configuration of private and public power it supported. Freed from their dependent position as slaves, African-American men could, theoretically, take on the role of household head with all its private and public privileges. Although African-American women would find it difficult to claim the same rights as their menfolk, they might well demand privileges previously reserved for white women as dependent wives and daughters. At the same time, many white men faced the loss of their property and, in the case of slaveholders, most of their dependents as well. Not only did the borders of their households shrink but the very basis of their mastery there was called into question, a situation that also undermined their exclusive claims to public power. Thus the household, in both its private and public forms, became a highly contested political issue. After all, political and civil rights still hinged on how households were defined, who qualified as household heads, and what rights they and their dependents could exercise. As early as 1864, at the time of Henderson Cooper and William Cooper's first trial, the answers to these questions were open to redefinition and contest in a way they had never been during slavery.

It was in this particular context that Susan Daniel's rape charge acquired such political resonance. Rape disrupted relationships within the household's borders. Both law and social convention defined the act as the raw exercise of power by a man over a woman. At the same time, rape was also an exercise of power by a man over another man, because the woman in question was assumed to be a dependent wife or daughter within a household headed by a white propertied man. In one sense, rapists committed a crime against property, by violently taking a woman's sexuality—that which she exchanged with men for material support and emotional companionship and which was, by law, her husband's or father's possession. Beyond that, rape cut through the web of social relations that knit family members together. A household head's authority over his dependents rested on his duty to provide and protect. In exchange, women surrendered themselves and their offspring to their husbands and male kinfolk. By compromising the ability of both the men and women involved to fulfill their appointed social roles, rape had the potential to shatter this entire arrangement.[10]

But the implications of rape were not confined within the household's borders. Both the act and its legal treatment reflected and reinforced the racial and class dynamics that determined which people could claim civil rights and political power. In the antebellum period, neither southern law nor most whites recognized the rape of female slaves as a crime. As property, they could not be raped, or so the logic went. Similarly, law and white social conventions did not consider rape to be a crime against a slave woman's menfolk. As property and as dependents who could never form households of their own, slave men did not have the same rights to women as men who were white and free. In practice, this legal fiction condoned not only the rape of slave women but also the hierarchies of power that subordinated all African Americans within slavery. The act of rape dramatized the gender oppression that made slave women vulnerable to sexual exploitation, while it simultaneously affirmed the racial and class hierarchies that defined all African Americans as merely slaves, not men and women.[11]

Slavery, however, was not the only divide in southern society. Even though southern law privileged all white people, not all whites received equal treatment. The law protected poor white women from rape in theory, but the courts often ignored these rapes in practice. Unlike elite white women, poor white women had to prove themselves worthy before the court accepted their charges—not an easy job given the class bias of elite court officials. The handling of these cases, then, revealed entrenched gender and class hierarchies that actually made poor white women far more vulnerable to sexual attack than elite white women were. These cases also underscored the class subordination of poor white men, whose poverty and relative powerlessness made them less able to protect their womenfolk from all outside threats—whether from rapists or crop failures—than elite white men. Yet, because the courts denied poor white women's rape charges on a case by case basis, they gave the appearance that decisions were based solely on the merits of individual women's complaints. The results upheld the fiction that all whites were equal under the law, just as they reproduced the class hierarchies that actually structured southern society.[12]

Poised between the private and public spheres, rape carried the potential to confirm or destabilize both simultaneously. But it only entered political discourse at moments of great change and uncertainty. Reconstruction was just such a time. To be sure, propertied white men in the antebellum period had considered black-male-on-white-female rape a serious offense that challenged larger social relations. But as long as the hierarchies of southern society were firmly grounded by the institution of slavery, such rapes did not seem to be as great a threat as they would be after emancipation and the Confederacy's defeat. It was then that the Cooper-Daniel case moved over the boundary separating private disputes from public conflicts. But illuminating this connection between private and public is only the first step in redrawing the political terrain. The next involves problematizing the connection, examining the ways different people used it for their own political ends.[13]

Politics from Above

The voices of Governor Worth and Robert Avery, a northern-born Freedmen's Bureau agent, dominated one strand of the debate over the Cooper-Daniel case. For all their differences, both worked from the understanding that the gendered lines of authority within private households provided the foundations for public power and positioned propertied white men as the primary political actors. Originating from these men, political power radiated from them to operate on those at the margins, in the private sphere. This rendering of the political terrain emerges with vivid clarity in Worth's and Avery's depictions of Susan Daniel and Henderson Cooper. Daniel's and Cooper's personas changed, chameleonlike, depending on the author. But their place as passive figures, incapable of fully participating in the events unfolding around them, remained constant in both men's accounts.

Jonathan Worth was so convinced that the interests of the state's propertied white men represented those of the population as a whole that it never occurred to him that African Americans might need the intervention of the military to protect their interests. The very idea was anathema to him, since African Americans had no political concerns or public existence in their own right. In fact, for Worth, any independent action on the part of those he considered dependents— ex-slaves, propertyless men, and white women—was subversive. Their proper place was within a household, the interests of which were represented by a white, propertied man. All these people were a threat. But then Governor Worth believed unruliness to be part of their nature. In his eyes, the new crisis and the real problem were northern policies that upset the southern social and political order. Consequently, he saw the Cooper-Daniel case not as a political conflict that involved common whites and African Americans, but one that centered on the interests of elite white men, northern and southern. In his writings about the case, he accentuated the strength of Henderson Cooper and William Cooper, but it was power of a particular kind. Drawing on racial beliefs that emphasized African-American men's uncontrollable hypersexuality, he described their power as the undirected rage of "monsters." This destructive power could be contained only if society was structured appropriately—that is, according to Worth's ideas of appropriate social relations, in which black men remained under the direct control of propertied white men.[14]

Worth was so incapable of envisioning an independent public role for African Americans or even propertyless whites, whom he termed "white negroes," that he identified white northern leaders as the real culprits. In his mind, only these men had the power to direct events and shape policy. The Coopers may have committed the crime, but it was northern leaders who allowed a dependent people to be given freedom and then refused to discipline them as necessary. Conservative officials within Granville County agreed. Frustrated in their attempts to control the outcome of the Cooper-Daniel case or the political conflict that followed in its wake, they, like Governor Worth, blamed the Freedmen's Bureau officials.[15]

Superficially, Robert Avery's reports provide a counterpoint to Governor Worth's version of the Cooper-Daniel case. He too represented the case as the inversion of legitimate power relations. But, unlike Governor Worth or Granville County's conservative leaders, Avery identified the crux of the problem as a corrupt society dominated by slavery and the interests of slaveholders. Questioning Henderson Cooper, he heard a very different story than the one in the court record. Cooper maintained that Susan Daniel had consented to sexual relations, a line of defense that local officials had silenced. Given the "popular feeling which then longed for the conviction" of the two accused men, no white witnesses had come forward to substantiate their story or attack the character of Susan Daniel. Even two years after the trial witnesses, both black and white, still feared retaliation. Based on this information, Avery determined the Coopers' trial to be little more than a cruel charade and questioned the ability of local authorities to uphold the rule of law: Henderson Cooper "was tried during a period of intense excitement, on him all the feelings of his times were enlisted against him." Agreeing with Avery's interpretation, Assistant Commissioner James V. Bomford followed up on his recommendation and put the case into the bureau's hands.[16]

Yet, for all the differences, Governor Worth's and Robert Avery's versions of the case shared a great deal. Where Worth supported local authorities and the antebellum social order, Robert Avery criticized both and worked to realize full civil and political rights for African Americans. Nonetheless, Avery envisioned the conflict as one between white northerners and elite white southerners, just as Governor Worth did. In his account, Henderson Cooper in particular and African Americans in general appear as worthy, but passive recipients of the privileges of citizenship, which had been denied them by white southerners until white northerners arrived on the scene to correct matters. This view of African Americans conformed to the racial ideology of many white northerners. At its best, as with Robert Avery, it took the form of a responsibility to bring the ways of free labor and political democracy to an oppressed people. At its worst, it took the form of a racism that rivaled any southern variety in its virulence. While there is a considerable difference between the two extremes, neither cast African Americans as political actors in their own right.[17]

Images of Susan Daniel restricted the public arena still further, eliminating women from its borders as well. To Governor Worth, Daniel was a gentle mother and a loyal Confederate wife. To Robert Avery and the bureau's assistant commissioner, she was an evil seductress, whose conscious debauchery represented the corruption that permeated private life and public institutions across the entire South. Yet the double-sided image of Susan Daniel stemmed less from divisions between North and South than from a bifurcated view of women common to both regions. From this perspective, women were either virtuous or not. Virtue, moreover, obtained its meaning in reference to racial and class assumptions that characterized poor white and black women as innately depraved and middle-class and elite white women as morally principled. Indeed, some elite whites in Granville County, including Henderson Cooper's former master, agreed with Robert Avery and believed Susan Daniel to be little more than a common prostitute. Whether pure or corrupt, her presence symbolized the disruption of public space in both Worth's and Avery's accounts. Indeed, she was the only woman who appeared in any public role at all. Women, from this perspective, belonged within the private sphere. Once they ventured outside and intruded in the public arena, they became unwitting pawns in conflicts beyond their control. Those judged "virtuous" deserved rescue. Everyone else would be abandoned.[18]

Worth's and Avery's vision of politics not only limited participation but also narrowed the scope of public debate. Both men constructed a discourse that revolved around the interests of propertied white men and silenced those of everyone else. Their concern with rape is particularly telling. For them, it was a metaphor that graphically communicated propertied white men's anxieties about their public power. As such, it became a convenient vehicle through which to debate the ways race and class would shape civil rights and the exercise of power through institutional channels. This metaphorical construction allows sexual assault into the public arena only through these issues. Otherwise, it fades into the background as a private matter of no consequence to public order. Other equally dramatic rape cases unfolded during this same time. Not only did they pass by with little notice or comment but readings of rape's political implications other than those of Worth and Avery failed to find their way into official reports or newspaper articles. In a broader sense, this same dynamic placed a whole host of issues outside the public arena, erasing all efforts by African-American and common white women and men to shape the course and content of political debate. For all these reasons, Governor Worth's and Robert Avery's accounts of the Cooper-Daniel case did far more than merely reflect their political visions; they also worked to maintain these visions, by actively containing the field of political conflict and limiting the very issues recognized as political.[19]

Politics from Below

Neither Governor Worth nor Robert Avery was entirely successful in imposing his political vision on the Cooper-Daniel case. Even in their written accounts, Worth and Avery found it very difficult to control Susan Daniel, Henderson Cooper, and others like them. Outside the confines of paper and pen, it was virtually impossible. In fact, the political meanings Worth and Avery attached to the case made sense only in relation to the actions of the people they were trying to erase from their narratives. Most immediately, the political conflicts the two men enacted through the case depended on the presence of Susan Daniel and Henderson Cooper. More broadly, the case became a political issue precisely because scores of African Americans and common whites refused to fill the roles allotted to them by men like Governor Worth and Robert Avery. Even as Worth and Avery rhetorically moved all of these people back over the line into private space, skirmishes were being fought on the border separating the two spheres. At issue was the placement of the line that Worth and Avery were so carefully policing.

Within Granville County, Henderson Cooper's recapture and re-sentencing apparently mobilized those, both black and white, who opposed the political domination of the local elite. As he sat in jail awaiting his execution for the second time, Republicans in Washington upped the political stakes by passing the Reconstruction Acts, which, among other things, increased the power of the Freedmen's Bureau and made ratification of the Fourteenth Amendment and its guarantee of African-American male suffrage mandatory for readmission into the Union. Back in North Carolina, the fledgling Republican party prepared for action, African Americans became ever more vocal in their political demands by the time of the 1868 elections, and the opposition began its reign of terror. Granville County was no exception. Violence there soon escalated into a pitched battle for political power.[20]

In 1867, the situation was already so volatile that a group of the "most respectable citizens," as they called themselves, approached the local Freedmen's Bureau agent for help. In a request buried amidst the local agent's correspondence and apparently ignored by Governor Worth and higher-level bureau agents, these "most respectable citizens" asked for a squad of U.S. soldiers to keep the peace at Henderson Cooper's execution. Noting that there had already been one attempt to rescue Cooper, they felt that federal troops would have a "wholesome effect on the Freedmen, and others, showing that the U.S. Authorities will sustain all efforts of the Civil Authorities to suppress and punish crime."[21] Considering the attitude of most elite white southerners toward the presence of federal troops, it was an interesting request. It also reveals the inability of Granville County's conservative elites to control public space, as "the Freedmen and others" defiantly demonstrated their unwillingness to remain on the political margins. The Freedmen's Bureau may have intervened on Henderson Cooper's behalf at an opportune time; but it was "the Freedmen and others" who drew the bureau's attention to the case and who drove the "respectable citizens" of Granville County to request federal intervention to prop up their own, increasingly shaky position.[22]

Like those who rallied on his behalf, Henderson Cooper refused to accept a passive role in the events unfolding around him. Awaiting retrial after the bureau returned him to local authorities, he took fate into his hands and, in the company of his fellow prisoners, set fire to the jail in an attempt to break out. All the evidence suggests they were unsuccessful, but doubts lingered. The heat from the blaze had been so intense that only a few bones remained, none of which were readily identifiable. Given the testimony at the inquest, it appears that some African Americans and common whites believed that Henderson Cooper had finally made his way to freedom. Needless to say, this interpretation carried a very different political lesson than those either Governor Worth or the Freedmen's Bureau desired.[23]

Appropriately enough, Cooper's fiery finale destroyed the jail, a building that symbolized to many the inequities of a political system designed to protect the power of a few. The jail—or rather the absence of one—soon became the source of acute embarrassment to the county's conservative leaders, who could not afford to rebuild it. Predictably, they blamed the Freedmen's Bureau. Since the bureau's prisoner had burned the jail down, they reasoned, the bureau should pay for a new one. The Freedmen's Bureau, however, unceremoniously declined, maintaining that Henderson Cooper was not its responsibility. No doubt Cooper would have added that he was not anyone's responsibility—or anyone's dependent. He acted as his own person. So did those around him who resisted conservative rule. These people were not provoked or duped by white northerners as Jonathan Worth and local officials believed; nor were their actions irrational outbursts, as the northern bureau agents thought. To the contrary, the "Freedmen and others" held their own visions of public life.[24]

Women stood among the "Freedmen and others," despite Governor Worth's and Robert Avery's attempts to deny their presence there. Even Worth's and Avery's descriptions of Susan Daniel suggest as much. If Worth managed to transform her into the flower of southern womanhood, he did so only with great difficulty. In fact, he could only maintain the image by writing the actual woman out of the story altogether. Not coincidentally, Worth rarely even bothered to mention her by name.[25] While not the chaste figure of Worth's imagination, neither was Susan Daniel the epitome of moral corruption, as Avery and his bureau superiors made her out to be. Instead, she lived in a world where poverty and necessity shaped the meaning of virtue and where the boundaries between black and white overlapped considerably. When her husband was conscripted into the Confederate army, she was left to fend for herself and her young daughter as best she could. Daniel continued to live on James C. Cooper's plantation, where her husband had worked as an overseer and where William Cooper and Henderson Cooper were enslaved. While there, she maintained close ties with several slaves, and with William Cooper in particular. Whatever the nature of these relationships, they were not all that uncommon. In Granville County, free blacks, poor whites, and slaves often mixed, sexually and otherwise. Whites tolerated such behavior, but only as long as it did not become too blatant. Apparently Susan Daniel crossed over that fine line. Convinced that she was too familiar with his slaves and believing her a bad influence on them, James C. Cooper turned her out.[26]

Sometime after that, Daniel charged William Cooper and Henderson Cooper with burglary and rape. It may have been as straightforward as that. There are other possibilities as well. Daniel may have been angry with William Cooper, and this was her way of punishing him. If her relationship had become too flagrant for whites in the community, she may have been covering her tracks. Had she been engaged in prostitution, she may have been retaliating for lost compensation. All of these possibilities appeared in other similar rape cases in the pre- and postemancipation years, but Susan Daniel might just as well have pursued the case for entirely different reasons.[27] After filing charges, she may have approved of the way local officials handled the case. But even if she did, it is likely that she attached somewhat different meanings to the proceedings than did Governor Worth, the Freedmen's Bureau, and county officials. Ultimately, we will never know why Susan Daniel made the case public or what she thought of its subsequent trajectory because her voice was so effectively excluded from the proceedings. For historians, the danger lies in allowing the silent female figure of this particular case to stand in for all women.[28]

There is no need to heroize Susan Daniel, whose actions not only played into conservative hands but also resulted in the deaths of two black men. Nonetheless, the complexity of her story suggests how hard Worth, Avery, and local officials had to work to keep women outside the public arena. Their success in this one instance was anything but representative. African-American and common white women formed a loud, visible, and vigorous public presence both during and after the Civil War.[29] These women spoke from their positions within communities, but they did not see themselves as mere appendages of their menfolk in the way that Governor Worth and bureau officials did. Often, they acted on their own interests, as women who were also poor or black or both. These women, for instance, considered not just rape, but excessive physical violence of any kind as a problem. Even as Governor Worth and the Freedmen's Bureau were debating the disposition of the Cooper-Daniel case, African-American and common white women began filing cases against their employers, men of a different race, men of a different class, men of their own race and class, men in their own families, and other women as well. Demanding a hearing for their concerns, they not only moved private issues onto the public stage but they also claimed speaking roles for themselves as political actors.[30]

Redrawing the Political Terrain

But what does all this commotion in Granville County have to do with anything else? To place Granville County's local conflicts within the history of Reconstruction is to stumble again over the line separating social history, which so often takes local areas as its focus, from political history, which looks to the state and national level for analytical direction. This disjuncture has been the subject of the most searing critiques of the historical profession. Targeting both the proliferation of local studies and of subfields generally, critics concede that work influenced by the "new" social history has uncovered significant information on people and places previously left out of the historical record. Nonetheless, they insist that this ever-expanding store of details has only fragmented traditional historical narratives without offering any positive alternatives. Similar calls for synthesis even issue from within the "subfields" themselves.[31] In response, other historians have questioned the utility of synthesis, arguing that traditional historical narratives achieve coherence only by focusing on party politics and national events to the exclusion of all else. Indeed, social historians have long maintained that certain people's absence from the nation's statehouses does not mean their concerns were unimportant or apolitical. Instead, the vast majority of people stated their positions in the arenas that were open to them, places as ordinary as the fields where they worked and the streets where they lived. Indeed, it is no accident that many "subfields" have employed local sources to revise traditional historical narratives. Those barred from institutional politics and public arenas at the national or even the state level only become visible to historians at the local level.[32]

Yet, within the terms of this debate, adding new people and places to existing historical narratives will never fully recast them. Those who critique social history often call for work that connects private life and interior worlds to public events and exterior realities. Yet the distinction itself reveals key assumptions that make synthesis problematic. First, it constructs the political and the social in isolation from each other, one as the weighty world of public issues, the other as the slippery subjectivity of private lives. No wonder the connection seems so illusive. This view of history then further obscures it, privileging those at the centers of power as public representatives of universal concerns while diminishing those on the periphery as particular groups with private interests. As such, the people of Granville County specifically and the subjects of social history generally will always appear peripheral to the world of public matters regardless of how they are included in the analysis.[33] Chandra Mohanty offers one solution, turning conventional wisdom on its head to argue that those on the periphery actually create the center. Not only do they provide the reference point through which those in power define themselves but they also generate the political opposition that makes the distinction itself necessary.[34] From this perspective, the actions and concerns of those within Granville County can reframe events at the state and even the national level.

For those on the periphery, the stuff of private life was inherently political. Historians of Reconstruction, however, have treated such issues as if they were only tangentially related to, if not completely separate from, the era's major political debates. Even those sensitive to the concerns of common whites and African Americans often dismiss the importance of domestic matters and ignore the way they shaped other, more traditionally defined political demands. Yet, the very act of isolating certain issues in the private sphere was a political move that effectively kept certain people on the margins of power. Dragging these same issues back over the line into the public arena in the years following emancipation, African Americans and common whites claimed not just political personas for themselves but also the right to define the substance of public debate.

This book proceeds topically, beginning with marriage, one of the most critical institutions in the nineteenth century. Marriage provided the cornerstone for all other social relations, separating the private sphere from the public world, positioning people on either side of that line as either dependents or independent household heads, and then determining their public rights and social obligations. White southern lawmakers and some freedpeople promoted marriage, but for different reasons. When slaves entered freedom, conservative white legislators moved immediately to legitimize their unions. Legal marriage, as these legislators saw it, was necessary to consolidate state power over freedpeople and compel black men and women to fulfill domestic responsibilities. But if the institution of marriage imposed obligations, it also conferred a range of rights to free people. The implications were particularly dramatic for freed slaves. By institutionalizing men's and women's roles as household heads and dependents, marriage legitimized men's rights to protect their families and women's demands to that protection. African Americans seized on this aspect of marriage immediately, using it as a weapon to secure the borders of their households and fend off intrusions from unwelcome outsiders. Even as they appropriated certain tenets of legal marriage, African Americans, particularly those who were poor, insisted on defining the substance of marital relations by their own rules—rules that often overlapped with the practices of many common whites. Yet, despite the disjuncture between social practice and the letter of the law, freedpeople could still use marriage to recast their relationship to the polity and force new issues into the public arena.

Marriage provided the institutional recognition of family life and the basis for claiming civil and political rights, but African Americans also needed economic independence if they ever hoped to establish either households or public identities of their own. I turn to this issue in chapter 2, arguing that the central challenge freedpeople faced was severing the ideological tie between dependence and the need to labor for others. In the antebellum South, unskilled, propertyless laborers did not enjoy independent status. If anything, waged work implied a certain amount of dependency because laborers surrendered mastery over their lives to their employers and often lacked the means to support their own households. Freedom from slavery, then, did not imply freedom from dependence. Instead, African Americans found themselves on ambiguous middle ground, somewhere between the complete dependence of slavery and the full-blown independence of propertied men. Racial ideology then compounded freedpeople's problems, reinforcing the associations between black skin, the need to labor for others, and dependence. Acting on these assumptions, many white employers tried to define the labor relationship as one of domestic dependency, obstructing laborers' efforts to set up their own households, insisting on broad supervisory powers, and protesting any public interference as a violation of their domestic privacy. African Americans flatly refused to act as household dependents. Instead, they insisted on the legitimacy of their own households, autonomy on and off the job, wages sufficient to support their families, and public recognition of their complaints. They faced formidable opposition, composed of whites who looked back longingly to labor relations in slavery and the supporters of capitalism who also cast labor conflicts as private issues, outside the scope of public debate. Although freedpeople failed to equate waged work with independence, they did successfully resist the most extreme forms of dependency. Most important, African Americans obtained recognition of their own households from both the state and white employers through their labor struggles. This was no small victory. It simultaneously solidified their rights to control their own domestic lives and secured their place in the public arena as political actors in their own right.

In the next two chapters I turn to men's and women's roles within households. It was here that men and women in the South reconstructed their personal identities in the turbulent years following southern surrender. The implications of their efforts ultimately reached beyond the individuals themselves, guiding visions of public as well as private life. Chapter 3 focuses on elite white men and women. Shorn of land and slaves, Granville County's elite whites searched for new ways to mark their social position and political power. Their solution, which incorporated central tenets of liberal ideology and northern consumer culture, centered on the ability to construct and display a certain kind of domestic household. Women were to find meaning in their role as paragons of domestic virtue, who created a comfortable home environment and tended to the needs of their families. Their companions were industrious men of strong moral fiber, who supported their families through their own labor and provided the means to purchase items considered essential for a proper domestic setting. Although not always meeting these ideals of manhood and womanhood in their everyday lives, elite whites held them up as the theoretical standard against which to judge everyone, thereby obscuring the underlying racial and class context necessary for men and women actually to acquire the appropriate domestic retreat and fulfill their appointed roles within it. Elite whites also privatized their domestic ideology in intensely personal ways, maintaining that the ability to reach its standards was solely a matter of individual choice and moral character.

Common whites and African Americans lacked the means necessary to live up to elite white standards of manhood and womanhood, but many had no intention of trying anyway. Instead, they clung stubbornly to their own ideas about gender roles and the substance of private life. For these people, social ties and mutual responsibilities, not physical structures and material possessions, constituted households. Just as the private space of the household blended into the public world, African-American and common white men's and women's roles overlapped far more than they did among elite whites. Only too aware of the social and economic practices that constrained people of their race and class, African Americans and common whites did not judge men on their ability to support their families through their labor alone. Neither did they evaluate women solely on their ability to maintain a particular kind of domestic retreat. But if common whites' and African Americans' conceptions of manhood and womanhood resembled each other, the legacy of slavery meant that they still viewed the postwar world from very different perspectives. Similarly, the vantage point of men and women within these two groups also diverged. Although men's and women's roles overlapped, this did not imply a rough equality between the sexes or a blurring of gender difference. To the contrary, common whites and African Americans assumed a hierarchical relation between men and women based on innate gender differences. Men and women disagreed over the nature of this relationship and how much power men could exercise over women. In fact, poor women of both races saw the balance of power between husbands and wives as a serious issue of public import and regularly brought cases of domestic violence before the local courts for adjudication. Nonetheless, the basic principle of hierarchy between men and women within the household remained unquestioned.

In chapter 5 I trace the implications of these conceptions of private life in public debates over civil and political rights. African Americans and common whites publicly defended the legitimacy of their households and their roles within them as men and women. Drawing on universalistic principles and downplaying the importance of racial and class differences, they argued that basic commonalities made all men equal to each other and all women equal to each other. Of course, common whites, African Americans, and their political leaders remained divided on the question of how far to extend racial and class equality. But even more problematic was the way these people relied on gender hierarchy to erase existing racial and class barriers—from political leaders who trumpeted the cause of manhood rights to ordinary men and women at the local level who tried to realize the promise of equal rights before the law. Common white and poor African-American women were particularly vocal at this level of the struggle, filling the local courts with complaints of physical violence and demanding the protection that was supposedly the right of all dependent wives and daughters. Often, they enjoyed the support of their menfolk, who testified on behalf of and filed complaints for their female kin. Either way, these men rejected the idea that race or class positioned them as dependents and insisted on the power of household heads to represent and protect their family members. In this way, African Americans and common whites used existing legal and political discourses to wedge their way into public space, justify their presence there, and transform the content of public debate. Yet, in so doing, they also built their politics around a patriarchal structure that would later prove to be their undoing.

Whether they liked it or not, conservatives had to deal with the principle of universal rights as well as the demands of African Americans and common whites to realize this concept in practice. Yet they refused to admit defeat and searched for new ways to rebuild antebellum hierarchies in ways compatible with universalistic principles. The elite white ideals of manhood and womanhood provided a powerful tool in this political project. Common whites and African Americans who failed to live up to standards embodied in "cheerful wives" and "rich men" could be dismissed as incompetent and unworthy individuals. Ultimately, conservatives pushed the argument to its logical conclusion, insisting that all those incapable of managing their private lives should never be trusted with the responsibilities of public life. Instead, political power should lie with the "best men"—those men who lived in the right kind of homes with the right kind of wives and who, not coincidentally, were always wealthy and white.

In the final chapter I examine the process by which conservative Democrats formally excluded poor whites and African Americans from the political arena. The Republican party remained strong in Granville County throughout the 1870s, but institutional stagnation at the local level and the efforts of Democrats at the state level to dismantle its opposition had taken its toll by the mid-1880s. In 1886, the Knights of Labor stepped into the void. Although the Knights organized around labor issues in the North and in some places in the South, the organization focused on party politics in rural North Carolina, taking on the political mantle the Republicans had let slip. In Granville County, the Knights did just that, advocating the public rights of all hard-working household heads and accepting the assumptions of gender difference and hierarchy that were so central to this vision. But this time, conservative Democrats adeptly used this same scaffolding to mark differences among men and constrict public space. The interests of the "best men," Democrats maintained, were representative of everyone in their communities in the same way that a male household head's experience and interests were representative of his family. Racial and class hierarchies, from this perspective, appeared as "natural" as gender hierarchy, and the political power—and even participation—of poor white and African-American men appeared as pointless as that of women. The patriarchal power of elite white men would protect them all.

The formal end of Reconstruction came early to Granville County, but the same process repeated itself elsewhere in the state at different times in different places, culminating in the white supremacy campaign in 1898 that ultimately led to disfranchisement. Before that, many African Americans and dissenting whites retained their grip on local power, where their very presence undermined the Democrats' position that only their "best men" could represent everyone. Frustrated in their efforts to control public space, Democrats inevitably concluded that the participation of these people was unnecessary, even dangerous, because it introduced conflict into the political process. The patriarchal power that had once propelled African Americans into public space now pulled them back over the line, often violently at the hands of self-righteous common white men convinced they were defending the public interest. Harnessing images of black-male-on-white-female rape to service their disfranchisement campaign, Democrats fueled the fury. But they did not create it. Their tactics resonated among common whites in North Carolina because they were already willing to listen. Jarred by the fevered pitch of Democratic rhetoric and the ugly anger of mob violence, African Americans and white Republicans nonetheless made ready for battle. This time, however, their trusted weapons made only a little dent in the Democratic onslaught, which drew its strength from the same patriarchal presumptions but bent them back to their most undemocratic implications. In the end, Democrats successfully squelched all local power, drawing the line around public space so narrowly as to exclude virtually all African Americans and many common whites as well.[35]

Their victory left a particularly bitter political legacy for women. Elite white Democrats tied their power to the subordination of elite white women in a specific kind of gender role. When these women began trying to redefine that role, they found powerful forces arrayed against them. African-American and, to a lesser extent, common white women suffered a double defeat that placed them in a multi-sided position of vulnerability. Losing their claim to public protection through their menfolk, they labored under all the constraints of womanhood and enjoyed few of its privileges.

The end is still the same—no historian can change that. But the means of getting to the end has changed. Granville County offers up a new chronology for Reconstruction, one that extends beyond federal withdrawal from southern politics to disfranchisement, when African Americans, many common whites, and their concerns were relegated, once again, to private space. Within this chronology, the telling of the tale is also different. The assumption that the concerns of some were "private" matters with no relevance to "public" issues becomes the legacy of the Democrats' success. Many of the people in Granville County disagreed and acted on their convictions. That they ultimately lost should caution against accepting the political categories of the victors. Indeed, the "irrelevance" of some people appears as the end product of a long process, contentious and contingent, that forms the real drama of political conflict and the substance of the following analysis.

1

You Can't Go Home Again: Marriage and Households

In the fall of 1865, North Carolina lawmakers gathered to draw up a new constitution. Although the state's circumstances had changed since a legislative body had last convened in Raleigh, the faces of its representatives had not. Despite the absence of the most extreme secessionists, the state assembly was still made up of a remarkably homogenous group of planters, businessmen, and professionals. They were the same white men of the same wealthy families that had always governed the state. Because they shared so many assumptions about social relations and public power, their debates generally took place within a very narrow band of the political spectrum. But they did not agree on everything, as recent conflicts had made clear. When the war approached, old divisions between Democrats and Whigs had given way to new ones, between secessionists and unionists. During the war, unionists remained a strong force in North Carolina. They even organized a peace party, headed by William W. Holden, the man who now headed the state as provisional governor. Surrender did not extinguish these differences, which remained smoldering at the time of the constitutional convention, while new ones over the terms of peace promised to fan the fires of contention into an open blaze once again. In just a few months, legislators would find common ground so difficult to negotiate that they would retreat into two new camps—the Republicans and the conservative Democrats.[1]

For all these reasons, the politicians who sat listening to Edwin G. Reade's opening address anticipated a difficult session. Reade tried to set a positive tone, assuring the assembly that the future would be easy compared to the hardships of the past five years. The metaphor he chose was that of a homecoming. "Fellow citizens," he intoned, "*we are going home*": "Let painful reflections upon our late separation, and pleasant memories of our early union, quicken our footsteps towards the old mansion, that we may grasp hard again the hand of friendship which stands at the door, and, sheltered by the old homestead which was built upon a rock and has weathered the storm, enjoy together the long, bright future which awaits us."[2]

Just across town, African Americans called to order the first statewide freedmen's convention and issued a report that contrasted sharply with the nostalgia of Reade's speech. While elated at the outcome of the war and the possibilities of freedom, the delegates were also acutely aware of the difficulties that African Americans now faced as free people. Barred from addressing their concerns directly through the political process, they decided to submit a report to the constitutional convention. A committee, chaired by James H. Harris, a free black raised in Granville County, went to work on it immediately. In many ways, the resulting document was cautious and conciliatory, avoiding all reference to suffrage and assuring whites of a harmony of interests between the races. It nonetheless staked out new political ground by demanding recognition of freedpeople's domestic relations. Family imagery permeated the demands, which included "education for our children," protection for "our family relations," provision for "orphan children," and support for "the re-union of families which have long been broken up by war or by the operations of slavery."[3] In fact, the distance between white legislators and the delegates at the freedmen's convention could not have been wider on the subject of families and households. Unlike white lawmakers who longed to "go home" to the world they had left behind in 1860, black delegates did not consider their ex-masters' "old homesteads" to be home. "Where is the protection to shelter us from the . . . storm that now threatens us with destruction," asked Merrimon Howard in 1866. Freedpeople, continued Howard, who would soon be elected to Mississippi's House of Representatives, have "no *land,* no *house,* not so much as place to lay our head."[4] Like Howard, African Americans in North Carolina wanted households of their own.

Marriage, Households, and Power

Before the Civil War, both marriage and slavery created the boundaries that separated the household from the state and identified people as dependents or household heads.[5] Indeed, the North Carolina Supreme Court viewed family law through the prism of slavery, a perspective that linked the two firmly together. As Victoria Bynum has argued, the antebellum supreme court took a dim view of divorce. This was particularly true between 1833 and 1852, when Thomas Ruffin was chief justice. Routinely placing the sanctity of marriage above the happiness of particular individuals, Ruffin insisted that the institution grounded the entire social edifice of the slave South. His views on marriage meshed neatly with his paternalistic proslavery philosophy, which defined the household in terms of reciprocal obligations. White women, according to Ruffin, belonged within households as wives, just as African Americans belonged within households as slaves. While bound by responsibilities, wives and slaves could also demand maintenance and protection from their husbands and masters. Their claims then became the duties of their husbands and masters. The possibility that marriage could be severed at will introduced contingency into this web of relations. If husbands could easily shed their obligations and wives could easily remove themselves—or be removed—from the household, then there was nothing to keep men and women in their "natural" place. The same logic called the "natural" subordination of African Americans as slaves into question as well.[6]

Although Thomas Ruffin's paternalism was not as widely practiced as his ideology assumed, his view of the place of marriage and slavery in defining social relations was. Yet by carrying his legal principles to their logical extreme, Ruffin handed down many unpopular decisions. His position within the court itself eroded when Richmond M. Pearson joined the bench in 1848. From a family of upwardly mobile planters and merchants in the western part of the state, Pearson, like many other North Carolinians, felt little sympathy for the paternalistic ethic promoted by Ruffin. Where Ruffin emphasized the organic nature of marriage and the mutual obligations of husbands and wives, Pearson tended to take a more contractual view, focusing on wives' obligations and husbands' privileges. Consequently, he was more willing to sever the marriage tie, particularly in the interests of aggrieved husbands. Despite these differences, however, Pearson's decisions generally supported Ruffin's view that the privilege of husbands and masters and the subordination of free women and African Americans within marriage and slavery were crucial to sustaining the social order.[7]

These were not just abstract legal points. They contained assumptions about social roles that were reaffirmed daily in a variety of ways. The evangelical Protestantism embraced by a majority of white North Carolinians defined the family as the model for all social relationships. God stood at the head of the Christian household, just as men presided over earthly ones. All Christians owed allegiance to their divine master, while free women and children and slaves obeyed their earthly masters. Evangelical Protestantism did declare everyone spiritually equal in the eyes of the Lord, a message that resonated with particular force among white women and African Americans. After bearing the burden of their different forms of inequality six days a week, they flocked to their churches on Sunday to hear that their pain might subside in the afterlife. Slaves, in particular, expanded on the idea in their own ways to give their lives dignity and to sustain their hopes for a better future. The idea of spiritual equality, however, did not translate into equality in this world, particularly in the world of the slave South. With some notable exceptions, Protestant churches in North Carolina supported slavery and placed the subordination of slaves and women at the center of their social vision. Although Protestant leaders often identified southern white women as naturally more religious than men, their spirituality, like that of slaves, only underscored their weaker constitutions and their greater susceptibility to emotion. It did not give them greater authority within their churches or in other religious matters. If anything, it was men who led their families in prayer and served as moral guides. White women, like slaves, realized their spiritual mission through cheerful subordination. These roles, the South's theologians and country ministers assured their congregations, were not just natural, but divinely ordained. Any change would bring down the wrath of God.[8]

Inequalities within the household also governed the ways antebellum southerners moved through physical space. During slavery, only propertied white men could operate freely in both the private world of their households and the public world of business and politics. In contrast, all those who were supposed to be wives and slaves found their lives and work confined to the private sphere of the plantation household's buildings and fields. When acting in their masters' stead as deputy wives and trusted servants, they could take on public roles and responsibilities. But when they did so in their own names, they became vulnerable. Even for the most determined, it was never an easy undertaking. If they managed to overcome the formal barriers that obstructed their way, white women and African Americans still had to confront social conventions and public censure that could be as debilitating as any statute or legal precedent. Of course, there were exceptions. Some white women and free blacks did run successful plantations and businesses, and slaves occasionally achieved positions of prominence. But they were always the exception, not the rule. Both custom and law limited the access of white women and African Americans to public space and power.[9]

With the abolition of slavery, marriage acquired even greater importance in structuring southern society because it became the only institution that legally constituted households. As a Mississippi judge explained in 1873: "The superstructure of society rests upon marriage and the family as its foundation. The social relations and rights of property spring out of it and attach to it."[10] Far more than the rhetorical flourish of a sentimental jurist, these words provided an accurate description of the place of legal marriage in postwar southern society. Without it, there were no legally recognized fathers, and without fathers, there were no legally recognized parents, since mothers had no formal rights to their children. Without marriage the transfer of property across generations became more complex. Inheritance laws, designed to keep property in the legitimate male line of the family, supplied little guidance in a world in which there were no fathers and no sons. Marriage also framed the rules for the distribution of both property and power within households. In its absence, women no longer surrendered their property, their wages, their children, and their ability to contract in their own name to their husbands. Laws did exist to deal with children who were born out of wedlock and lived outside a legally recognized family; they became wards of the state and were apprenticed to a responsible master. But there were no comparable mechanisms to deal with unmarried women, whose number multiplied as a result of wartime casualties and emancipation. They were simply on their own, accountable for their own material needs, political interests, and moral destiny. The prospect of self-supporting women then called the allocation of public power into question as well. Household heads represented the interests of their wives and children in the public sphere because they were liable for them. Once this relationship dissolved, however, former dependents were thrust into the public world. In the existing legal and political structures, of course, those people assumed to be dependents had few rights and little power. But without marriage, the rationale for this situation also evaporated.[11]

Given marriage's importance to southern society, it is not surprising that North Carolina's supreme court buttressed the institution against change in the years directly following emancipation. The first major challenge came in 1868 with *State* v. *A. B. Rhodes.* Elizabeth Rhodes claimed that her husband had beaten her repeatedly without provocation and charged him with a criminal offense. It was a novel accusation. Having considered wife beating only in relation to civil suits, primarily divorce, the state supreme court had never determined whether it was a criminal offense. A lower court concluded that it was not, basing its ruling on generations of legal precedent that allowed a husband to whip his wife as long as the switch was no larger in diameter than his thumb.[12] The state supreme court upheld the lower court's finding, but took issue with its reasoning in a decision written by Justice Edwin G. Reade, the same man who had offered the homecoming metaphor at the opening of the constitutional convention in 1865. Appointed to a provisional position on the bench that was made permanent by the legislature in 1866, Reade wrote many of the court's decisions in family law during Reconstruction. A slaveholder, but also a unionist from a well-established family in Caswell County, Reade rallied behind the Confederate cause during the war. Afterward, he accepted emancipation and later became a Republican. But, as his decisions indicate, he believed that the hierarchies that had structured antebellum life were still essential to southern society, and he actively used the existing legal framework to support them.[13]

Reade's landmark decision in *Rhodes* set the tone. For him, the issues in the case extended well beyond those of wife beating or even the relations between husband and wife. At stake was the relationship between the household and the state, one that Reade felt the need to affirm, given the recent transformation of the southern household. The state, he flatly declared, did not "recognize the right of the husband to whip his wife." Nonetheless, the sanctity of the private sphere shielded the husband's actions from the scrutiny of the public. However loath the court was to condone violence within the domestic sphere, Reade believed that far greater evils "would result from raising the curtain and exposing to public curiosity and criticism the nursery and the bed chamber." He did not specify what, exactly, these great evils were, but it was clear that Elizabeth Rhodes was out of luck. Placing the evil from which she had sought relief in a category called "temporary pain," he advised her and others in her position to "forget and forgive." In so doing, he drew a firm line around the household, sharply separating private and public space in the process. "Family government," Justice Reade declared, "being in its nature as complete in itself as the State government is in itself, the Courts will not attempt to control, or interfere with it, in favor of either party."[14]

Reade also affirmed the lines of domestic authority. Although he maintained that the state would not take sides, the reasoning behind his words upheld the dominion of household heads over their dependents. If the state did step in, Reade explained, the courts would have to determine whether the accused had been provoked. Such questions, according to Reade, were nearly impossible for an outside authority to determine. Where it took outright violence to inflame one household head, he argued, a subtle glance would be enough to enrage another. Given these difficulties, Reade determined that the court should stay out of such matters. "Every household," he opined, "has and must have a government of its own, modelled to suit the temper, disposition and condition of its inmates." In practice, this meant that the court assumed a husband innocent until proven guilty, since it was his governance that was in question. Husbands, according to *Rhodes*, possessed individual rights the court was bound to respect. The rights of wives, by contrast, were particular and derivative. They had no independent legal personas of their own.[15]

Although Reade did not mention the abolition of slavery in his decision, the issue lurked between the lines. Focusing on "family government" and "domestic relations," he explicitly included the relationships of parent and child, master and apprentice, as well as that of husband and wife.[16] If not for emancipation, the relationship of master and slave would have been included in the list. The fact that it was not made the others unstable. After all, if one domestic relationship could be dissolved with the stroke of pen, then what was so inviolable about the rest? At the very least, they might be subject to some minor alterations. Elizabeth Rhodes thought so. But as Reade so categorically stated in his ruling on her case, this was not a possibility. The decision cast a long shadow, establishing the precedent for dealing with subsequent domestic relations cases in the remainder of the nineteenth century.[17]

Rhodes also spoke to the public dimension of the household. Despite the rhetoric of domestic privacy, marriage and the household were never wholly private matters. The firm line that separated the private world of the household from the public world outside its borders was also the device that connected the two. In fact, this link explains lawmakers' concerns about marriage. For the state's conservative leaders, marriage and the households it created were too important to their notions of social order to be left entirely to the discretion of the people, most of whom they neither respected nor trusted. Justice Reade admitted as much in *Rhodes*. Even as he drew a veil around relations within the household, defining it as a private sphere best left to the governance of the household head, he planted that private sphere squarely in the public realm. Household heads derived their power from the state, and family government, while complete in itself, was ultimately subordinate to state government. Although the state would never meddle with "trivial complaints arising out of the domestic relations," it would intervene if a husband, father, or master "grossly abuse[d] his powers."[18] The state, moreover, reserved to itself the power to decide what constituted gross abuse.

One year later, in 1869, Reade elaborated on the public aspect of marriage when he defended the state's right to prohibit interracial unions. Marriage, he contended, "is more than a civil contract; it is a *relation,* an *institution,* affecting not merely the parties, like business contracts, but offspring particularly, and society generally."[19] Because marriage contained such wide-ranging social implications, the state had a right—indeed a duty—to make sure the institution took forms that served the public interest. According to Justice Reade, interracial marriage did not. In fact, the ill effects of interracial marriage were so obvious to him that he did not even bother to explain them. What he did establish were the links that connected the private world of the household to the public order.

In these decisions, Reade confronted a world without slavery by reaffirming the household's boundaries and its connection to public power. His verdicts, however, did not resolve all the questions posed by emancipation. Carefully omitting slavery from the list of domestic relations, Reade did not explain ex-slaves' relation to legal marriage or the duties and rights that came with it. Despite their near universal rejection of racial equality, whites still disagreed about the specific rights African Americans should have and the position they should eventually occupy in southern society. Because marriage and households were so central in defining dependence and independence, the debate among white North Carolinians over the status of freedpeople inevitably turned on these issues.

Freedpeople and the Obligations of Marriage

The law had not recognized slave marriages, and emancipation did not make them legal. Northern military officials and philanthropists encountered the absence of legal marriage early in the war when escaped slaves ran to union lines and the military began to occupy southern soil. Many northerners, particularly army chaplains and missionaries, found the presence of unmarried slave couples deeply troubling. They also received numerous requests for legal marriage by African Americans themselves who, as we will see, had their own reasons for formalizing their domestic relations through the law. In response, northern officials tried to promote "the sacred nature and binding obligations of marriage" and to assist freedpeople in legalizing their unions. Even the U.S. military, which did not generally concern itself with the security or protection of black families, could not ignore the issue. In 1864, the secretary of war issued a special order providing for the legalization of slave unions.[20]

As long as slavery was in force, white southerners did not share these concerns. By law, slaves could not enter into any contracts, including the marriage contract. With emancipation, however, many southern whites began to view the absence of legal marriage among ex-slaves with the same critical eye as white northerners. North Carolina's conservative lawmakers confronted the issue even before Reade penned his decision in *Rhodes*. Marriage, for instance, figured prominently among William W. Holden's recommendations to freedpeople in his first address as provisional governor on 13 June 1865. In order "to enter upon the pursuit of prosperity and happiness," Holden advised three things: marriage, hard work, and education. Marriage topped the list, coming even before concerns with the control of labor.[21]

Other white legislators shared Holden's priorities. While squabbling continually over the terms of peace and the status of freedpeople, they could agree on this one issue: freedpeople had to be married.[22] The legal status of slave unions was among the first issues on the agenda of the 1865 constitutional convention, and the speed with which delegates dealt with it suggests how important it was. They delayed action temporarily until the 1866 legislative session, after deciding that the matter fell within the purview of the special committee charged with presenting recommendations on the status of freedpeople.[23] But when the matter did come to the floor, the brief debate revealed a general consensus on the issue. Concerns centered on how best to implement the measure and how to make it as broadly inclusive as possible. Objecting to the proposed fifty-cent fee, one legislator advised lowering it to twenty-five cents so as not to discourage freedpeople from legalizing their unions. Another took issue with the statute's wording because it "seemed to distinguish between persons formerly slaves, who had cohabited as husband and wife, under the form or color of marriage rites solemnized by clergymen or Justices of the Peace, and those who had so cohabited without such sanction." There was no difference between the two, he argued. Neither was a valid marriage and the distinction only detracted from the main point, which was to legalize all slave marriages. The other legislators apparently agreed. The final act declared the unions of all ex-slaves who "now cohabit together in the relation of husband and wife" to be lawful marriages from "the time of the commencement of such cohabitation."[24] If the date had been placed at either emancipation or the ratification of the act—both of which had been suggested— then all children born in slavery would have been illegitimate and their maintenance could have fallen to the state. Thus marriage was inextricably tied to other issues, the most prominent of which was the fear among white southerners that freedpeople would not support themselves economically.

While some ex-slaveholders continued to feel a sense of paternalism toward freedpeople, most did not. For them, the abolition of slavery meant the rejection of all responsibility for the economic welfare of African Americans. They no longer incurred any of the obligations of masters, they argued, because slaves were no longer dependents within their households. Planters across the South acted on this idea, and those in North Carolina were no exception. In Caswell County, on Granville's western border, a group of planters resolved to evict all people who were not in their employ. C. W. Raney, a planter in Granville County, reached a similar conclusion, although somewhat reluctantly. He had hired Phillis Clark, a freedwoman with three children, only to discover that, on what he paid her, she could not feed her family and pay the rent. He had tried, unsuccessfully, to find her another position that would allow her to support her family. Unwilling to supplement her salary, he wrote to the Freedmen's Bureau asking if it could do anything to help Clark. If not, he claimed he would have to force her off the plantation. The idea clearly disturbed Raney, but not enough for him to assume responsibility for her maintenance: "I dislike to turn her out to live in the woods, but will be compelled to do so unless I am assisted."[25]

Common whites were hardly willing to take up the slack. Postwar economic and social dislocations only added to existing racial biases and resentment, long directed at both slaveholders and their slaves. As one woman told a northern reporter: "We poor folks was about ekil [equal] to the niggers, about bein' hard put to it to live, I mean, and now they's free they don't do nothin' but steal, and how we'll live I don't know. . . . I wish you'd tell me how poor folk is to live among these niggers."[26] Agreeing with this woman's assessment, many common whites would have added laziness and promiscuousness to the list as well. In fact, they often complained that the federal government funneled far too many resources to freedpeople, while ignoring poverty-stricken whites, who, in their own judgment, were the truly needy people of the South.[27]

Abdication of all economic responsibility for freedpeople became the official policy of the county and state governments. The actions of individual planters like Raney and those in Caswell County combined with postwar economic hardships to create a large population of impoverished African Americans who then became dependent on counties for relief. In Granville County, the number of inmates in the poorhouse rose from somewhere between fifteen and twenty in 1867 to sixty in 1868. Most of the new inmates were black. That year, the wardens wrote to the Freedmen's Bureau, professing their inability to support the ever-growing poorhouse population and demanding financial assistance. Yet they were more concerned by the changing racial composition of the inmates than by the absolute increase in their numbers. Spouting logic similar to that of planters who ran freedpeople off their lands, the wardens absolved the county of any economic liability for freed slaves. Indigent African Americans were not the county's charge, the wardens argued. They were now wards of the national government.[28]

Without the moral influence of marriage, many white legislators and editorialists maintained, freedpeople would never take responsibility for themselves or their families. Completely ignoring the state's complicity in denying legal marriage to slaves, white commentators cited its absence as another piece of evidence proving the immorality and irresponsibility of ex-slaves. As Alfred M. Waddell, a Confederate army officer and newspaper editor, lectured an African-American audience in Wilmington: "The loose ideas which have prevailed among you on this subject must cease." "You will have to support and take care of your families," he continued, because it was no longer the duty of white masters to do so. Members of the commission that designed the state's Black Code contended that the absence of legal marriage only magnified freedpeople's other problems: "No race of mankind can be expected to become exalted in the scale of humanity, whose sexes, without any binding obligation, cohabit promiscuously together."[29] Of course, conservative white leaders disagreed over the underlying causes of freedpeople's alleged failings. Some identified the institution of slavery as the problem, arguing that freedpeople were unfamiliar with the rigorous responsibilities of family life only because they had been dependents within the households of their masters for so long. As a result, they needed the "elevating" direction of those who had more experience in the ways of freedom. Some within this camp viewed freedpeople's capacity for "elevation" with optimism and thought that ex-slaves would eventually assume greater civil, if not political rights. Others sharply criticized this position because they believed that African Americans, as members of an inferior race, could never be "elevated."[30] The underlying assumption, however, was that irresponsibility, indolence, and sexual promiscuousness characterized freedpeople's lives.[31] Even if marriage would not completely resolve these problems, it was the only way to contain them. And containment was crucial for society as a whole. Justice Reade captured the essence of this position in 1868, when he upheld the statute legalizing slave marriages. The issue, he argued, was one of "great public necessity." It affected not just "the domestic relations of one-third of our people," but "the morals of society in general."[32] From this perspective, if ex-slaves continued to cohabit out of wedlock, the resulting corruption would overwhelm society as a whole.

Despite the emphasis on morality, it was not the delicate sensibilities of white southerners that drove public policy on the legalization of slave marriages. An editorial by B. F. Moore, a strong unionist and perhaps the most instrumental figure in the creation of the state's Black Code, highlighted the practical concerns that were so often expressed in moral terms. Freedpeople had to assume responsibility for themselves and their families, Moore argued, since the responsibility for their welfare no longer fell on their masters. Yet he doubted that they would assume these obligations without coercion, and coercion was impossible without marriage. Marriage, as Moore pointed out, institutionalized family relationships in the form of the "legal responsibilities of husbands and wives" and "parents and children." Without it, the state relinquished the means to control freedpeople's marital unions and their actions within them. Where indigent women and children became wards of the state in the absence of marriage, they became the legal responsibility of individual household heads in its presence. As such, marriage compelled ex-slaves to take charge of their families' welfare by allowing the state to "enforce the performance of all these duties as it does in the case of the white race."[33]

Of course, the state could force men who fathered children out of wedlock to uphold their economic responsibilities through the bastardy laws. Unlike other domestic matters, men had little room for maneuver in bastardy cases. The law required only the word of the mother for conviction, and there was virtually no way to contest such an accusation. After the war, even white men who fathered children by African-American women were not exempt from prosecution. Upholding the charge of a black woman who named a white man as the father of her child, the state supreme court made its position on bastardy very clear: "It is not intended by nature, nor is it tolerated by the law, that men should cast their offspring upon the world, with all the disadvantages of caste and color, and leave them to perish, or else to be supported by the public."[34] The point was twofold. The economic responsibilities of fathers did not cease outside marriage. More importantly, the state would not pick up the tab.

Using the logic later employed by the state supreme court, the commission that drafted the Black Code urged the strict prosecution of bastardy laws, particularly in relation to freedpeople.[35] Nonetheless, the laws dealing with family relations assumed that most children were born in wedlock. Bastardy laws, part of the legislation dealing with the state's responsibility toward the poor, addressed a breach in the social fabric. They were never intended as a foolproof method of forcing fathers to maintain their children.[36] Mothers occasionally refused to name the fathers. Even when they did, some fathers could not adequately provide for their children, while others made every effort to evade their duties. In these circumstances, the state assumed economic responsibility for the child and, if the child was too young to be apprenticed, for the mother as well. Ultimately, fathers might have had legal obligations to the children they fathered outside of marriage, but children born outside marriage were still wards of the state. As B. F. Moore so astutely argued, only marriage could effectively "enforce the performance" of the "legal responsibilities of husbands and wives" and "parents and children."

At issue were crucial questions of governance. The extralegal status of freedpeople's unions exemplified the political problems of keeping ex-slaves outside civil society. Southern law had prohibited slaves from entering into the civil contract of marriage because they were under the direct dominion of their masters. Although emancipation released slaves from the authority of their masters, it did not fully integrate them into civil society. This was the challenge facing conservative lawmakers as they contemplated the status of freedpeople. In his call at the 1865 constitutional convention for the creation of a commission to study the status of newly freed slaves, delegate John Pool described the situation in this way: "A large class of the population, ignorant and poor, has been released from the stringent restraints of its late social and political position, and from its dependence upon the individual obligations of another class for its support, government and protection." Now free, ex-slaves were "ignorant of the operations of civil government, improvident of the future, careless of the restraints of public opinion and without any real appreciation of the duties and obligations impressed by the change in his relations to society." In other words, freedpeople were incapable of governing themselves, and the state lacked the necessary power to control them.[37]

The solution came in the form of the Black Code, in which the state assumed the authority, but not the minimum responsibilities formerly vested in masters. This relocation, however, carried its own problems because slaveholders' power could not transfer directly to the state. Masters' authority had derived from the fact that slaves were not recognized as members of civil society. In contrast, the state had to recognize freedpeople as members of civil society in order to bring them within its purview. After emancipation, measures that kept slaves outside civil society, such as the prohibition of legal marriage, became a liability because they rendered existing laws and institutional mechanisms of state governance inapplicable. In the absence of legal marriage, for instance, the state had no way of controlling freedpeople's domestic relations. Because marriage was also the foundation for so many other social and political relationships, the implications for state power went well beyond individual marital unions. To keep freedpeople from threatening civil society, they had to be brought into it. To be brought into it, they had to be married.

Marriage, however, also carried the potential to increase freedpeople's authority within the state. During slavery, North Carolina's supreme court had categorically denied slaves the right to marriage for precisely this reason. Marriage was not only a civil right but also the entering wedge into a broad range of social privileges. As such, it carried the potential to destabilize slavery. The 1858 case of *Frances Howard* v. *Sarah Howard et al.* provides the best illustration. Miles and Matilda Howard were married as slaves and were later manumitted, but did not legalize their marriage. They had several children. After Matilda died, Miles legally remarried and fathered another family by his second wife, a free black woman. When Miles died intestate in 1857, an inheritance battle ensued. The children of his first wife claimed equal shares, while the children of his second wife insisted that the property was theirs alone because the first marriage had never been legalized and, therefore, the children were illegitimate. Justice Richmond Pearson agreed with the children of the second wife, ruling that slaves who had been married according to the customs of their community did not automatically become legally married when manumitted. He first established that slaves could claim no civil rights, including the right to enter into contracts. Without the right to contract, there was no marriage and manumission did not change that fact. To conclude otherwise, Pearson argued, would be to accept the "idea of civil rights being merely *dormant* during slavery." Such a conclusion was untenable. In fact, Pearson simply dismissed it out of hand as "a fanciful conceit."[38] Slaves, according to Pearson's ruling, could never be married because that would imply that they did have other civil rights. In this sense, the opposing argument was far more than "a fanciful conceit." It could be downright subversive. When postemancipation legislators retroactively acknowledged all slave marriages to be civil contracts, they affirmed the "fanciful conceit" that the civil rights of slaves had been dormant in slavery. If slavery was what had kept slaves from claiming other civil rights, then there was nothing to keep freedpeople from them now.

It is not surprising, then, that many of North Carolina's postwar conservative leaders emphasized the obligations, not the rights, of marriage. This was the point of B. F. Moore's editorial, which actually addressed the status of freedpeople generally. An ex-Whig whose strong commitment to antebellum social hierarchies would soon propel him into the Democratic party, Moore wanted to keep African Americans on the margins of civil society. In fact, he believed that freedpeople had so little place in the institutions of the state that they should be moved to their own colony.[39] As unwilling as Moore was to integrate African Americans into public life, he was anxious to allow them the civil right of marriage. But marriage, from Moore's perspective, had little to do with individual rights, particularly as they applied to freedpeople. Instead legal marriage gave the state the right to supervise freedpeople's marital unions and their actions within them.

The marriage statute itself underscored the obligations of marriage. Once ratified, the act legalized freedpeople's marriages even if they did not formalize their vows. Yet, in a provision unusual among southern Black Codes, it also required them to record their unions with a county official and fined them if they did not. As this coercive measure suggests, North Carolina's legislators doubted the efficacy of simply legalizing existing marriages. Unless freedpeople themselves publicly affirmed their unions and accepted the attendant responsibilities, the gravity of the act might well be lost.[40]

If the statute left any doubts as to the meaning of marriage, the other provisions in the Black Code eliminated them. Severely limiting their civil rights and denying them any political rights whatsoever, the Code left African Americans with little but obligations. It recognized freedpeople's right to enter into contracts and allowed them access to the criminal and civil courts. But within the context of its other provisions and the overarching assumption that equal access did not mean equality in the eyes of the law, these rights meant little. African Americans were not allowed to testify against whites, except in cases that directly involved their own interests, and they were barred from sitting on juries. The vagrancy section required freedpeople to work and limited their freedom of movement, while other provisions denied them the right to bear arms and encumbered their ability to buy and sell property. The terms used to refer to African Americans in the Code suggest its intent. They were "negroes," "persons of color," men and women who were "lately slaves," and "inhabitants of this state." Not to be confused with citizens, African Americans acquired only the duties and obligations, not the rights, of freedom.[41]

The Code's provisions left African Americans without the means to defend the institutional integrity of their families. In fact, the status of freedpeople's families was more like that of slaves than of free whites. The apprenticeship section was the most blatant. It stated that white and black children were to be bound out in the same manner, but all pretense to equal treatment stopped there. Black children could be apprenticed "when the parents with whom such children may live do not habitually employ their time in some honest, industrious occupation."[42] White parents were not held to the same standards. With this clause, the rights of African-American parents to their children became conditional. If challenged, they had to prove themselves "industrious" and "honest," not an easy task since many white North Carolinians saw all blacks as lazy and dishonest by nature. County courts, in fact, used the clause to apprentice children at will. When the court decided to bind out African-American children, moreover, ex-masters were given preference over everyone else, including relations and friends. This provision brought the ideological legacy of slavery into sharp relief. As other historians have pointed out, ex-masters had their eyes on the labor of these "children"—some of whom were well beyond childhood.[43] Claims on the labor of black children, however, also rested on the assumption that African-American parents did not have legitimate households or legitimate rights to their children. While the abolition of slavery forced ex-masters to concede that they could no longer compel adult freedpeople to live as dependents within their households, many were still unwilling to admit that freedom made African Americans competent to form households of their own.[44] A few "industrious" and "honest" freedpeople might be able to raise their own children; but many, if not most, black children belonged within the households of white propertied men, preferably those of their ex-masters. Marriage, considered in light of the apprenticeship laws, did not make African-American men household heads with the power to protect the interests of their dependents. It simply obligated them to support their dependents because it was inconvenient and unprofitable for white planters to do so.

The notion that marriage was more about obligations than rights was not new. Justice Thomas Ruffin had defined marriage in precisely these terms before the Civil War. In practice, this emphasis had allowed the state's leaders to maintain firm control over the distribution of power among free men. For those unable to marry legally, namely slaves, other civil and political rights also remained beyond reach. Marriage alone, however, was not sufficient to claim additional rights, and it most certainly did not lead to social or political equality. Propertyless white men, whose poverty diminished their independence, never had access to the kind of public power that their wealthier neighbors did. Yet, no matter how lowly, every white man still had more rights and greater power than free black men, whose race and connection with slavery completely undermined their claims to independence. Although North Carolina was one of the few southern states to acknowledge free blacks as citizens, the status meant little because of all the qualifications to it. As an 1844 state supreme court decision unequivocally declared, the blacks cannot "be considered citizens, in the largest sense of the term." According to the logic of this decision, natural rights were only natural if a man was white. They were not the rights of free blacks and, as North Carolina's postwar legislators affirmed in the Black Code, they were not the rights of freed slaves.[45]

In fact, North Carolina's legislators created the Black Code from the laws defining the status of free blacks during slavery. After all, emancipation eliminated only slavery, not the inequalities that had always existed among free people in southern society. Thus, the state's conservative lawmakers reasoned, the position of free blacks provided the ideal model for newly freed slaves. Confident in their ability to control freed slaves as they had free blacks, they never stopped to examine the larger political consequences of granting legal marriage to freed slaves. The possibility that marriage might convey more rights to freedpeople than it had to free blacks never seemed to cross their minds.[46]

This was a major oversight. The status of antebellum free blacks depended on the assumption that all African Americans should be dependent slaves and that all slaves were denied full civil and political rights.[47] Without slavery, the status of freedpeople was not so easily contained. White lawmakers could emphasize the responsibilities incurred by African-American households in freedom, but they could not completely escape the contradictions inherent in their own legal definitions. For however much conservatives might emphasize responsibilities, they could not avoid the fact that marriage also implied rights for all free people.

The state supreme court confronted this tension almost immediately following the enactment of the Black Code. Unable to resolve it, the court gingerly avoided ruling on the rights of African-American household heads and their dependents. The first case, *P. L. Ferrell* v. *Hilliard Boykin,* a suit initiated before the war but heard by the supreme court in 1866, allowed the court to sidestep the issue completely. Unlike postemancipation cases involving African-American children taken from parents who were legally married, the young boy in this case had been born to a free black woman, whose relationship with the child's father was not recognized by law. In the antebellum period, the law was unambiguous about the fate of such children, particularly when they were born to free black women. As bastards, they were apprenticed in the county where the mother had a "settlement," defined as a residence of twelve consecutive months. Soon after the birth of her child, the mother had moved to the county where the father, a white man, lived. The court in this county then apprenticed the child to the father, while the court in the county of settlement placed the child with another man. Because the father had no rights to his illegitimate child, he could gain custody only through apprenticeship. Even if he had wanted to marry the mother, he could not have done so, since interracial marriages were prohibited. Completely unsympathetic to the situation, the other master challenged the father, maintaining that his was the rightful indenture. The supreme court agreed, ruling that the indenture held by the master in the county of the mother's settlement took precedence over the indenture of the father.[48]

As Justice Reade argued, the case hinged only on the place of the mother's settlement. There were no parental rights to consider, because this child, by law, had no parents. Aware that he could not claim parental rights, the father maintained that the state had no power in the matter because he was well-positioned to meet the child's material needs and the child was not and never would be a public burden. Reade summarily dismissed this argument, declaring the child a ward of the state: "It is the duty of the court to bind out all free base-born [illegitimate] colored children, whether they are paupers or not!" These children were the responsibility of the state, not of individual fathers, because "it was assumed by the Legislature that children in their condition would be neglected." The county of settlement, "being responsible for the proper nurture of the boy, was not to wait until he became a vagabond, and had been cast back upon it as a pauper . . . but it was its duty at once to exercise its legitimate control, and bind him as an apprentice."[49] Regardless of the intentions of those involved, the law considered all unions that produced "free base-born colored children" to be spurious. Such households were legal nonentities. Whether the fathers were white, as in this case, or enslaved, as they were in other instances, they could neither marry the women they loved nor obtain legal claims to their children. Instead, the law placed the offspring of such unions under the supervision of the courts for the same reasons that slaves were thought to require the supervision of their masters. The presumption was that biological fathers and mothers in both instances were incapable of family governance.

Emancipation complicated such cases by introducing the possibility of parental rights where there had been none before. The next apprenticeship case heard by the state supreme court, *The Matter of Harriet Ambrose and Eliza Moore,* was far more complicated because the rights of the parents could not be so easily dismissed. In fact, it unleashed a wave of controversy concerning the legal position of African-American households even before it reached the court. The case initially caused John Robinson, the assistant commissioner of the Freedmen's Bureau in North Carolina, to compare apprenticeship to slavery. As he described the events: "Mr. Russell [the white planter who apprenticed the children] seizes with violent hands children (one of these sixteen years old) living with their parents who support them, carries them off, the Court binds them, they are thrown into prison for safe keeping, and then carried off to his home, he is asked to return them, he refuses, and threatens the vengeance of the Court, the Court of which he is a member, and which Court binds to him these kidnapped children."[50] At this point, the bureau stepped in, canceling the indentures of the two children, Harriet Ambrose and Eliza Moore.

Governor Jonathan Worth, always a strong opponent of federal intervention in state affairs, then entered the fray. He was reminded by Robinson that the bureau's recently stated position on apprenticeship was quite clear: "The Civil Courts will not be allowed to make any distinction between whites and blacks in the apprenticing of children. *No child* whose parents are able and willing to support it can be bound without the consent of the parents. Children over fourteen years of age will not be bound out as apprentices under any circumstances." But where the bureau saw racial discrimination, Worth did not. He insisted that the letter of the law made no racial distinctions and that the state courts were simply exercising their discretion on a case by case basis.[51]

In Worth's eyes, however, the bureau had violated more than state sovereignty. It had jeopardized state policy toward freedpeople by enhancing the legal standing of their households. Although white children over the age of fourteen could not be apprenticed, Governor Worth thought this restriction onerous when applied to African Americans. More to the point, obtaining the consent of black parents was unnecessary. In his view, it contradicted the whole point of the apprenticeship process, which was designed to remove children from the homes of parents who were unable to raise them properly. African Americans, by definition, were deficient parents. Employing circular logic, Worth maintained that if they had the capacity to consent, then they would apprentice their children themselves. The court thus needed the power to intercede precisely because the parents stubbornly refused to accept their own incompetence. Worth suspected that the intent of the bureau's guidelines was to keep black children from being apprenticed at all, but he found it difficult to understand why the bureau would insist on such a policy. Echoing the reasoning in *Ferrell* v. *Boykin*, Worth continued to believe that the state needed broad supervisory powers over free black children. Indeed, the end of slavery only underscored the state's importance. As Worth asked the bureau, "what is to become of destitute orphans, of illegitimate children, and those abandoned by their parents, or whose parents do not habitually employ their children in some honest, industrious occupation?" In his eyes, freedpeople might be free, but they occupied the anomalous position of free dependents who could not maintain legitimate households of their own.[52]

The state supreme court agreed. Although it canceled the indentures of Harriet Ambrose and Eliza Moore, it did not recognize either the rights of African-American parents or the legitimacy of their households. Justice Reade argued that county courts have "no power to bind as apprentices persons who have no notice of the proceedings for that purpose." Furthermore, the children's presence was necessary for the court to come to a proper decision about their disposition: "A court ought not to, and will not, bind out an orphan unless it appear[s] that its condition will be improved. It is a high duty of the court, and one which they perform with pleasure, to protect these helpless children, and not only to prevent oppression and fraud, but to act as friends and guardians, and improve their condition." Reade illustrated his point with a story from his own experience with an antebellum case involving a poor, presumably white woman whose children were just old enough to work and contribute economically to the household. At this point, someone else wanted to take advantage of the children's labor and apprentice them. The court, however, was able to discern the intentions of the proposed master because the mother and children were present. As a result, it awarded custody to the mother. With emancipation and the consequent increase in the number of poor people in the state, Reade continued, there would be even more attempts to apprentice children for exploitative ends. Thus, it was even more essential that the court fulfill this supervisory role.[53]

Although his vignette suggests otherwise, Reade demanded the presence of the children only, not of the parents, at apprenticeship hearings. For all his championing of the welfare of poor children, he expressly ignored the question of parental rights. It took great effort, because the lawyers representing Harriet Ambrose and Eliza Moore built their case around this issue. They argued that the court had absolutely no right to apprentice the children because they did "not come within any of the classes which the court is empowered to bind." Only if they were bastards would the court have jurisdiction. Indeed, to apprentice these children was to treat them as illegitimate. "Great 'inconvenience' would arise," the petition continued, "from holding that the Ordinance of Emancipation," or the act that legalized slave marriages, "has the effect of turning these persons into 'free base-born children of color.'" In other words, because the parents' union had been legalized, their rights to the children were inviolable. Reade, however, avoided the issue, claiming that he did not need to address it in this case, since the children's absence from court was enough to nullify their apprentice contracts. While striking down flagrant abuses of the system and making it more difficult to apprentice children, the court thus maintained an ambiguous stance toward the rights of African-American parents. At the same time, it significantly increased the amount of power the state could exercise over their lives. After all, the idea that African-American children required "friends" and "guardians" rested on the assumption that their parents and kin were incapable of acting on their behalf.[54]

In the fall of 1865, North Carolina's lawmakers had justified their supervisory role in terms of a racially defined dependence. This position, however, became difficult to defend. As early as January 1867, the Civil Rights Act and pressure from the Freedmen's Bureau forced the legislature to repeal those parts of the constitution that established differential treatment for whites and blacks.[55] This was only the beginning. As Congress battled with President Johnson in Washington over the terms of reunion, similar struggles raged within North Carolina. Rifts soon developed within the state's ruling elite, as members parted ways over the best method of reconstructing a society without slavery. Some, including William W. Holden, onetime provisional governor and a former Democrat with strong unionist sentiments, split off with the Republican party. Justice Edwin G. Reade and

John Pool followed suit. While a few elite Republicans supported more egalitarian racial and class relationships, most still believed African Americans to be a dependent race largely incapable of self-governance. But they also questioned the wisdom of writing such beliefs into state law, convinced as they were that the future of North Carolina depended on cooperation with both the North and freed slaves. The Republican party also proved an attractive alternative to those common whites who had chafed under the political domination of slaveholders and the propertied elite. Other elite leaders, including Governor Jonathan Worth and B. F. Moore, the mastermind behind the state's Black Code, set out in another direction. Although many had been Whigs and unionists, they slowly drifted toward the Democratic party, where they were joined by other whites, rich and poor, who resisted the changes taking place around them.[56]

But problems emerged even before Congress intervened, as the supreme court's decision in the *Ambrose* case indicates. It was a highly unstable decision, for the only way the court could maintain the intent of the Black Code was by ignoring the issue of parental rights. Neither the court nor even the state's conservative legislators could continue to do so forever. Whether they liked it or not, marriage could legitimize rights as well as obligations. Indeed, emancipation, which subverted the racial and class hierarchies that had allowed elite whites to contain the rights of the state's poor and dispossessed, only increased the potential of marriage to justify rights, particularly for freedpeople. Try as they might, the state's conservative leaders could not completely control the resulting debate. African Americans, in particular, seized the opportunity immediately. In fact, they did so long before North Carolina's conservative lawmakers ever thought to consider the legal status of their marriages and households. African Americans' actions, as much as anything else, challenged and destabilized the definitions that conservative lawmakers imposed on their households.

"The Marriage Covenant Is at the Foundation of All Our Rights"

As the public celebration that formalized family ties, marriage became the first act of freedom for many black refugees during the war and, later, for many freedpeople. Yet African Americans retained their own definition of marriage. Many refused to marry legally and even those who did organized their domestic relations around far different standards from those of wealthier whites. Nonetheless, African Americans knew enough about the place of legal marriage in southern society to use it as leverage in their struggles to realize their own vision of freedom. In fact, freedpeople's struggles for fair wages, reasonable terms of employment, education, civil rights, and political power depended on their ability to establish and maintain their own households. Otherwise they would remain nominal dependents within the households of their employers, where their lives would never be certain, as the sale and separation of kin in slavery had taught them. Indeed, too much pain had already accumulated for freedpeople to wait patiently for their leaders to secure the legal status of their households for them.[57]

African Americans rejected their position as their masters' dependents long before southern surrender. During the war, many slaves undermined their masters' households from within, by slowing their work pace, sabotaging the production process, appropriating property, and, often, abandoning the plantations altogether. Entire families fled to Union lines, where they hoped to begin new lives for themselves, on their own. Emancipation then opened new opportunities to bring scattered families back together, and some ex-slaves traveled long distances, searching for family members who had been sold away during slavery. Henderson Cooper, for instance, sacrificed his freedom to be with his wife. Local authorities discovered his whereabouts after southern surrender through a letter Cooper himself had written, asking his former master to send his wife to him in Washington. Other freedpeople enjoyed far more success. But even for those families whose members had lived on neighboring plantations, the act of consolidating loved ones under one roof was highly symbolic. It meant repudiating the power masters had held over the most intimate relations in their lives and asserting the right to form households of their own.[58]

Freedpeople made a similar statement by formalizing their marriage vows. Federal army chaplains and northern missionaries had strongly encouraged slaves who escaped to union lines to marry legally, but many needed no prompting. In July 1865, nearly a year before passage of the legislative act requiring ex-slaves to register their marriages, an Episcopal minister in Warren County married 150 African-American couples in the course of just two days.[59] Over the county line in Granville, many of the 878 couples who registered their unions in compliance with the legislative act may have already formalized their vows, just as their Warren neighbors had done. The great majority recorded their unions in July and August of 1866, well before the deadline.[60] The derisive comments of skeptical white observers only underscored freedpeople's enthusiasm. According to a *New York Tribune* correspondent, white North Carolinians viewed "this eagerness among the darkeys to get married" a "good joke." A Lumberton minister concurred, noting that "whites laugh at the very idea of the thing" and "do not believe the negroes will respect those relations more than the brutes."[61]

For freedpeople, however, marriage was no joke. It provided a way to establish the integrity of their relationships, to bring a new security to their family lives, and, above all, to affirm their freedom. Even the most sympathetic whites did not fully grasp the meanings freedpeople attached to legal marriage. Many, southern as well as northern, commended the popularity of marriage among ex-slaves, interpreting it as a sign of their moral and social improvement. Some even mistakenly assumed that freedpeople were accepting the definition of marriage as a relationship primarily of "obligations" and "responsibilities." All these interpretations missed the mark, as the words of one black corporal in the U.S. Colored Troops suggest. Explaining to his troops the implications of Virginia's 1866 act legitimating slave marriages, he maintained: "The Marriage Covenant is at the foundation of all our rights. In slavery we could not have *legalised* marriage: *now* we have it . . . and we shall be established as a people." The local Freedmen's Bureau superintendent applauded the speech along with the black troops in the audience. But for these troops and for other freedpeople, marriage had become entangled with freedom in a way it had not for the Freedmen's Bureau superintendent. If the prohibition of marriage had underscored their dependent position and the precariousness of their family ties in slavery, the act of marriage now symbolized the rejection of their slave status. As the corporal's words reveal, marriage was as much about rights as obligations.[62]

Freedpeople's resistance to the apprenticeship provisions in the state's Black Code provides a particularly striking example of their position. If the apprenticeship system looked bad on paper, it was even worse in practice. Like Harriet Ambrose and Eliza Moore, children were bound without their parents' consent, often without any notification whatsoever of the proceedings, and even kidnapped from their homes. The experience of Robert Lee Pool, of Granville County, was not unusual. When Pool's mother decided to leave the Cannady plantation where they had been enslaved, their former master was not willing to let them go. Although he seized their personal possessions in an attempt to keep them on the plantation, Pool and his mother did manage to slip away. Cannady immediately began searching for them. When he found them in nearby Franklin County, he kidnapped

Pool, who was playing in the yard. Cannady could no longer force Pool's mother to remain on the plantation, but the apprenticeship laws allowed him to keep Pool. Pool's mother apparently enlisted the help of the Freedmen's Bureau, because two Union soldiers were sent to retrieve both her son and her personal belongings. The soldiers reached the Cannady plantation only to discover that Cannady was in court, apprenticing Pool. "Never the lest," as Pool remembered later in life, "those blue jacket Yankee officers went there and had my mother's belongings loaded on the wagon and ordered me to get on the wagon. And they marched with those big pistols in their belts and Mrs. Cannady did not open her mouth only to hollow and cry at the last of me." Pool was lucky. In this instance, might triumphed over the law. The "blue jacket Yankee officers" notwithstanding, the legal claim of Pool's mother to her son was tenuous, at best. Other planters, moreover, were far more persistent than Cannady, who did not bother Pool or his mother again. Not all apprenticeship incidents ended this happily.[63]

The application of the apprenticeship laws infuriated African Americans. How could they be free, if their children could still be taken from them as easily as they had been during slavery? The uproar echoed across the South, as denunciations mounted in frequency and intensity between 1865 and 1867. The delegates to a statewide freedmen's convention in 1866 described apprenticeship as the system in which "our children, the dearest ties of which bind us to domestic life, and which makes the tie of home endearing, are ruthlessly taken from us, and bound out without our consent." Singling out the practice for particular criticism among their other complaints, they resolved to "do all in our power to prevent its further continuance."[64] Ultimately, however, it was freedpeople themselves, not their leaders, who dealt the most successful blows to those laws that granted planters the power to acquire custody of freed children.

Many individual parents went to great lengths to keep their children out of the hands of former masters. Fan, a Granville County slave who had been moved to Kentucky before the war by her master, David Yarbrough, absolutely refused to apprentice her daughter Barbra to Yarbrough or any other white master. Fan clearly treasured her independence and her ability to protect the interests of her daughter. Her position, however, emerges through the words of Yarbrough, who found her actions not just puzzling, but personally insulting. Responding to relatives in Granville County who had inquired after the welfare of the family's ex-slaves, he wrote in 1867 that Fan was "doing no good on the top side of earth." He went on to explain: "Fan is the meanest negro living almost she cant get a home at all. . . . She had 4 or 5 homes last year going from pillow [pillar] to post + dragging her 4 children after her. She says white people cant whip her children I offered her $50 for Barbra last year + she would not hear to it carrin her off + got only $15 for her last year so Nick says. She lives near Nick's House. Nick told me that she was doing no good for herself nor nobody else + if he was in my place he would have Barbra bound to us." As it turns out, Yarbrough had taken Nick's advice and applied to the county court to apprentice Barbra. He expected "no difficulty as the Legislature has pass[ed] an act giving the refusal to former owners."[65]

David Yarbrough, however, may have encountered more difficulty than he expected. When evasion proved unsuccessful, African Americans began challenging the apprenticeship system directly, through the courts. They were an unlikely forum, since local court officials were the ones who apprenticed children in the first place. Indeed, before congressional Reconstruction and the subsequent redrawing of North Carolina's constitution, local courts remained as undemocratic as they had been before the war. The office of magistrate remained appointive and, with the exception of those appointed by Governor William W. Holden during his brief term as provisional governor, most magistrates were wealthy and politically conservative. Very much aware of their power, these elite men did not hesitate to use it as a political weapon. In his assessment of Reconstruction's progress in Granville County, for instance, Freedmen's Bureau agent Thomas Hay focused his concerns on the local courts: "I sincerely believe, that nearly every white man in the Counties of Warren, Franklin and Granville who was a Secessionist . . . is one at this day, and if the U.S. Troops should be withdrawn from this State at this time, leaving the great body of Magistrates unchanged and the County Courts not reconstructed, the future of the Freedmen would be *dark* indeed." This was no exaggeration. As Granville County's court records indicate, magistrates defined freedpeople's legal rights very narrowly, even within the context of the already restrictive Black Code.[66] In this context, freedpeople's suits against apprenticeship acquire that much more significance. It was against great odds that they claimed access to the judicial process on the same footing as other free people.

African Americans often enlisted the aid of the Freedmen's Bureau in their efforts to move the wheels of local justice. Indeed, the sheer number of complaints to the bureau testifies to the persistent opposition of African Americans and the role they played in making apprenticeship a political issue. Both the bureau and the local courts apprenticed children at first. The bureau officially objected to racial distinctions in the treatment of white and black children, but its otherwise ambiguous guidelines did not forcefully establish parental claims over those of white planters. Agents' interpretations of these rules varied widely. Some regularly bound out children to white planters, while others saw the potential for abuse and made every effort to place children within the black community. Local courts, however, simply ignored the bureau's sketchy guidelines and apprenticed children at will. As 1865 gave way to 1866, both local agents and officials in the bureau's state office grew increasingly concerned over the local courts' actions. In Granville County and across the state, agents shepherded cases through the local courts and sometimes canceled indentures themselves. At the state level, the bureau issued directives defending parental rights.[67] Yet even the most sympathetic bureau officers would not have been so aware of the blatant inequities of the system if not for the freedpeople themselves, who kept agents' attention riveted on the issue, whether they liked it or not. Thomas Hay, bureau superintendent for the subdistrict of Warren, which included Granville County, canceled seventy-seven indentures in the first eight months of 1867 alone. Representing only successful complaints, this figure gives just a partial accounting of freedpeople's opposition.[68]

The case of Richard Hester reveals the underlying logic to their resistance. Hester, a former slave, tried to obtain custody of his two grandsons in 1867. Unable to block their apprenticeship in court, he turned to the Freedmen's Bureau. Daniel Paschall, a sympathetic white planter and local magistrate, offered to write to the bureau on Hester's behalf. As Paschall explained in the letter: "My course on the bench of our county court has been to bind the colored children to colored friends where it was in proof that they were capable and had the means of feeding and clothing, but in many instances was overruled, if this case was before me on the bench, I should give these boys to Richard Hester." Paschall's position, however, was very different from that of Richard Hester. Paschall promoted the binding of children to family and friends when appropriate, but he did not question the right of the court to apprentice black children. Hester did. He did not want the court's permission to apprentice his grandchildren; he wanted custody of them as their grandfather. He thus challenged the court's guardianship power and its right to apprentice his grandchildren to anyone at all. Ultimately, Hester was able to proceed with the case on his own terms. With the backing of the

Freedmen's Bureau, he filed a motion in the local court, asking that the contracts "be cancelled" and that his grandsons "be placed in the custody and care of him, the said Dick Hester."[69]

Coleman Edward would have applauded the decision. The year before he had petitioned the bureau to obtain custody of his niece and nephew, who had been apprenticed to a Granville County planter. "I have bought land and have a house to bring the children to and will raise them without any expense to any one," Edward wrote. But even if he were not so well situated, Edward still would have maintained that the children had no business living with a white master. As he put it, "I have the last right to them."[70]

Such claims become more remarkable in comparison with similar cases during slavery. With no thought of the mother's or the child's desires, the courts regularly apprenticed the children of all unmarried free black women. If a white woman was poor or if her partner was black, even her race would not save her children from a court-ordered indenture. In the antebellum period, as Victoria Bynum has shown, poor white and free black women opposed the system in the best way their limited power would permit: they challenged mistreatment of their children and influenced where they would be placed. After emancipation, African Americans, in particular, questioned the system itself.[71]

In rejecting their ex-masters' claims to their children, freedpeople insisted on the sanctity of their households and their own rights as parents. Apprenticeship, they argued, was a violation of their domestic relations. In the words of a group of petitioners from Maryland: "Our homes are invaded and our little ones seized at the family fireside."[72] Legal marriage, which gave freedpeople the materials necessary to construct a wall of privacy around their households, proved particularly useful in their efforts. Positioned within these households as husbands and wives, they could now mobilize the law to support their claims to their children.

This is precisely what they did. Like Richard Hester, they asserted their rights as heads of households with legitimate claims to their own children and those of extended kin. When women filed appeals, they often did so as married women who were attached to legally recognized male household heads. Kate Durham's children, for instance, had been apprenticed before the war. Afterward, when she sued for custody, her case rested on the fact that she was now married to London Brame. Brame may have been the father of Durham's children, but the court was less interested in paternity than in Durham's marital status. It was her marriage, which positioned her as a dependent wife and assured male supervision and economic maintenance, that allowed her to claim custody of her children. Similarly, when Sallie Hicks filed a complaint charging that her child had been "badly treated," she requested cancellation of the indenture instead of reassignment to another master, as was common during the antebellum period. According to the court records, she could do so only because she was not actually Miss Sallie Hicks, but Mrs. Alfred Hartz. It was because she "now passes for a fem covert" that the court allowed her to proceed with the case.[73] Of course, this meant that women still could not claim their children in their own right. If Sallie Hicks and Kate Durham had not been married, their cases would have been treated quite differently.

The arguments of Granville County parents anticipated those that would soon be made against apprenticeship in the state supreme court. Like the lawyers in *The Matter of Harriet Ambrose and Eliza Moore*, freedpeople asserted parental rights to their children. Of course the lawyers in this case articulated the parents' claims in legal terms. But as soon as African-American parents in Granville County stepped into the local courtroom, their claims were filtered through the prism of the law. When Richard Hester demanded custody of his grandchildren, he argued that he was their grandfather and they were rightly his. In court, his arguments were translated into the legal claim that he was a household head with rights to his children—or in this instance, grandchildren. It is probably safe to assume that Hester was unaware of the body of law marshaled in his defense or its wider implications for family relations. If he had been, he probably would have disagreed with many of its provisions. Nonetheless, Hester's own claims fit neatly enough within the existing legal framework to allow him to use it for his own ends. Kate Durham and Sallie Hicks used the courts in the same way. It is unlikely that they would have agreed that mothers had no firm rights to their children, and they might well have objected to other legal restrictions placed on wives as well. Yet, when Durham and Hicks tried to get their children back, the fact that they were married to men who could help support their children made their cases that much stronger. They could use their husbands' positions as household heads and their places as dependent wives to their own benefit, and they did so with great success.[74]

During presidential Reconstruction, the state supreme court responded to freedpeople's cases by making it more difficult to apprentice children, while simultaneously ignoring freedpeople's claims to parental rights. At the same time, however, these cases also suggest the inability of conservative legislators to control the political situation around them, particularly when considered in connection with the barrage of apprenticeship cases that flooded the local courts. Denying parental privileges to freedpeople in the Black Code and reaffirming the intent of these statutes at the level of the state supreme court did not stop freedpeople from claiming what they thought to be their most basic rights. To the contrary, they did so with exhausting persistence. Successes at the local level suggest that at least a few officials found freedpeople's demands convincing. If not, they apparently found it hard to refute such claims within the existing structure of the law. Indeed, the state supreme court's maneuvering around the issue of parental rights in the *Ambrose* case suggests how increasingly difficult it was to counter freedpeople's arguments. The court's position on domestic government did not help matters. Although decided in 1868, *Rhodes* is nonetheless revealing because it affirmed the existing principle of domestic government's inviolable nature. If freedpeople were now husbands and wives, then, by implication, the concept of domestic government should extend to their households as well. After all, how could the court intervene to take children away if family government was "in its nature as complete in itself as the State government is in itself"?[75] In this context, the very law intended to coerce freedpeople into marriage so as to allow the state greater control over them also legitimized their claims to greater autonomy.

By the time Congress entered the fray, a good many freedpeople had already chipped away enough of the existing system to expose its weaknesses. Congressional Reconstruction then bolstered their position. The Fourteenth and Fifteenth Amendments prohibited racial discrimination in the construction and exercise of the law and granted full political rights to African-American men. In 1868, when a Republican-dominated convention gathered in Raleigh to draft a new constitution, it restructured the state's judicial system. Sweeping away all impediments that kept African Americans from enjoying the same rights under the law as whites, the constitution also further democratized the courts by making the key positions of magistrate and judge elective. The results were quite dramatic in Granville County, where 50 percent of the population was African American and where many whites had reluctantly supported the Confederacy. Republican magistrates and judges presided over cases; African Americans and poor whites sat on juries; and Republican sheriffs, deputies, and jailers kept the peace. Together these changes made the courts more responsive to the concerns of African Americans and marginalized whites. The term "more responsive," however, was strictly relative; the courts did not completely reverse themselves to advocate the interests of these people alone. The elite white Republicans who so often presided over the courts operated from a very different political perspective from that of rank-and-file Republicans. Furthermore, the courts by no means abandoned wealthy white Democrats. As we will see later, these two groups had a powerful common interest in the protection of property. Nonetheless, the change in the courts was perceptible, and it bolstered confidence in the system.[76] African-American households now occupied the same legal position as white households, and blacks were granted the legal power to protect their households in their own right. Not coincidentally, apprenticeship cases all but disappeared.[77] The changes did not stop there.

Marriage without Contract

Freedpeople may have willingly wielded legal marriage to defend the boundaries of their lives from the encroachments of outsiders, but they refused to surrender their own definitions of the marital relation. Most working-class freedpeople did not understand marriage primarily as a legal contract, nor did they accept the complete separation of private and public spaces sanctioned by it. Although the majority of southern African Americans forged their ideas about marriage within slave communities, class was also influential. Common whites often held similar views to those of poor blacks, while the marital concepts of propertied and professional African Americans conformed more closely to those of elite whites. Indeed, many middle-class blacks trumpeted the virtues of legal marriage as a way to elevate the race. To be sure, the poor of both races varied widely in their acceptance of the dictates of legal marriage. But, as a rule, their domestic relations looked quite different from the theoretical ones found in the law books.[78]

For slaves, marriage had been a relationship governed by custom and the community, not laws. While many freedpeople rushed to legalize their unions, others saw no advantage in changing their ways. Even Herbert Gutman's estimates suggest that a good portion of freed slaves in North Carolina, perhaps as many as 50 percent, chose not to formalize their marriages. Although saturated with racism, the comments of contemporary white observers also suggest as much. As one northerner leasing a plantation in Mississippi claimed, many freedpeople "refuse to be married, preferring the system of concubinage brought out from slavery."[79] If concubinage meant unions not sanctioned by law, the practice continued in the decades following emancipation. In Granville County, fornication and adultery cases, often involving African-American couples in long-term relationships, were common from the 1860s into the 1880s. So were bastardy cases. The *Oxford Torchlight*, the local Democratic newspaper, even launched a campaign in the 1880s to reduce the cost of marriage licenses, reasoning that lower fees would encourage African Americans to formalize their vows.[80]

With a few exceptions, whites sharply criticized the attitude of African Americans toward marriage, whether they were legally married or not. Even many white northerners believed that freedpeople were incapable of understanding or accepting the responsibilities that came with marriage. The conclusion of the white commander of a black Tennessee regiment in the Civil War was typical: "The marital relationship is but little understood by the colored race, and, if possible still less respected." A northern planter in Mississippi was somewhat more optimistic. Although characterizing marriage among freedpeople as a "loose bond," he blamed the "licentious habits" of slavery and concluded that "stringent laws, rigidly enforced" would eventually generate change.[81] Elite whites in Granville County agreed. Summarizing the news of the family's ex-slaves in a letter to his daughter, planter Henry Jones mentioned that "Shang High," an unmarried African-American woman, was "expecting another heir shortly." He continued, "I dont know who she will swear this [one] to." Bastardy, in short, was what Jones expected of this woman and perhaps most African-American women. In his mind, emancipation only heightened the problem, making bastardy so common that it was no longer "strange news."[82] One of Jones's correspondents, Lucy Edwards, maintained that unmarried mothers outnumbered married ones by three to one where she lived (apparently advancing age and declining health did not keep her from performing her own impromptu survey). In fact, the proliferation of fatherless children disturbed Lucy Edwards far more than the destruction of slavery or even a society "divided in differnt classas": "It realy makes me wish that me + mine was away from such a place."[83]

In an 1867 report, Thomas Hay, the local Freedmen's Bureau agent, described both his own concerns and those of Granville County officials with freedpeople's marital relations: "About one third of the State Docket of each County Court in this Sub. Div. is taken up with indictments against Freedmen for Larceny and Bastardy. The first of these crimes seems natural and irradicable, the second together with Fornication its necessary antecedent, is I regret to say, largely on the increase. In Oxford [the county seat] and its immediate vicinity as I am informed by the County officials, there are over fifty unmarried colored women about to become mothers. Desertion of wives by their husbands and of husbands by their wives are frequent throughout this Sub. Div."[84] White observers' complaints held a grain of truth. What Thomas Hay, Henry Jones, Lucy Edwards, and others noted were deviations from their own standards of marriage. What they did not understand was the internal logic of a culture that defined marriage and family differently than they did.

Many African-American leaders were quite aware that white northerners and southerners alike used marriage as a barometer of their people's fitness for freedom, and they urged poor blacks to adopt the domestic patterns common among elite whites. This, they argued, would help convince the nation that ex-slaves deserved the rights and privileges of freedom. The same African-American corporal who enthusiastically declared that marriage "is at the foundation of all our rights" advocated such a course: "Let us conduct ourselves worthy of such a blessing—and all the people will respect us." James H. Harris, who helped author the demands of the first statewide freedmen's convention, issued a similar warning: "Let us do nothing to re-kindle the slumbering fires of prejudice between the two races. Remember, we are on trial before the tribunal of the nation and of the world, that it may be known . . . whether we are worthy to be a free, self-governing people."[85]

If only freedpeople's problems could have been so easily resolved. Conforming to elite marital conventions would not dissolve racial stereotypes or dismantle the barriers freedpeople faced in southern society. Even when African Americans' domestic relations did meet elite expectations, many whites continued to believe that all blacks needed the guidance of their social betters before they would be good husbands, wives, and citizens. Others doggedly maintained that freedpeople would never be able to form and sustain households of their own, ignoring all evidence to the contrary.

In any case, African Americans reserved the right to establish marriages and form families as they saw fit, even when they entered into legal marriage. As Noralee Frankel has shown in her work on Mississippi freedwomen in the 1860s, poor blacks adhered to their own rules in which a legal contract was not always necessary to initiate, maintain, or end a marriage. The pension records of black Civil War veterans indicate that poor African Americans in North Carolina lived with these same marital precepts well into the twentieth century. The community recognized a couple as husband and wife when they took on certain responsibilities for each other. In these relationships, the woman washed, cleaned, cooked, and tended the house, while the man contributed to her and her children's maintenance. Although unions could be legalized, it was ultimately the substance of the relationship and the community's recognition of it, not the legal contract, that constituted the marriage. Both men and women could sever the marital bonds if their partners abandoned their responsibilities or otherwise mistreated them. Irvin Thompson, for instance, married his first wife in a legal ceremony soon after the war and lived with her about a year. "Then she associated with other men and left me," he told a pension examiner. "No I did not get any divorce. She just went off a whoring and I lost track of her." Soon afterward, he married another woman in a legal ceremony that the community also accepted as a valid marriage. Mary J. Moore ended her marriage in a similar way. Her husband beat her and ran around with other women on the sly, but when he began to live openly with another woman, she considered the marriage over and her neighbors concurred. She went on to live with several other men in a series of monogamous relationships recognized as marriages by the community, but not in law. Neighbors and family members could also step in and censure a couple, particularly if their relationship had disintegrated to the point where it jeopardized existing ties. For instance, promiscuity that destabilized family relations was different from either short-term sexual liaisons or serial monogamy that did not, although promiscuity in general was more tolerated in men than in women in either case. Most white observers, however, did not pick up on these nuances.[86]

Two Granville County divorce cases illuminate both the internal dynamics of this definition of marriage and the confusion these standards generated among white court officials. In 1876, Smith Watkins filed for divorce on the grounds that his wife, Dink, had been sleeping with other men. He gave a long list of offenses, which included his discovery of her having sex with another man in the lot of the black Baptist church. When confronted by Smith, Dink responded: "I am my own woman and will do as I please." According to E. B. Bullock, another African-American man, his wife Jane had defended her unfaithfulness in a similar manner. To Granville County's court officials, these were straightforward cases. The men's statements "proved" adultery on the part of the wife, one of the legal grounds for divorce. While not sufficient proof in and of themselves, the bold words of these two women lent credence to the charges against them by underscoring their malicious intent.[87]

In their own communities, however, the statements of Dink Watkins and Jane Bullock conveyed very different meanings. Instead of claiming their freedom to do as they pleased within marriage, it is more likely that these women were marking the end of their relationships with their husbands. As far as Dink Watkins and Jane Bullock were concerned, they had the right to select new partners because they were no longer married. Their former husbands thus had no right to interfere in their lives at all. The court records suggest that Smith Watkins and E. B. Bullock understood their wives' words in this way. Adultery, in and of itself, was not necessarily the reason the men filed for divorce even though their cases hinged on the sexual transgressions of their wives. At the time E. B. Bullock initiated his suit, for instance, he and Jane had not lived together as husband and wife for many years. In court, he used his wife's subsequent liaisons to prove that fact. Indeed, Bullock was apparently legitimizing in law what had been a reality for a long time. As he explained to the court, he had waited to file for a legal divorce because he was unaware that he needed one.[88]

The expectations expressed in these two divorce cases ran headlong into those preserved in the letter of the law. During the antebellum period in North Carolina, the marital tie could be completely severed only in a few extreme circumstances—adultery combined with abandonment on the part of either party, adultery on the part of the wife, and impotence. Abandonment and extreme cruelty were grounds for a divorce only from bed and board, a less complete separation in which the couple ceased living together, but were not allowed to remarry. Court officials did not grant divorces liberally. Women often had a difficult time proving their cases against their husbands, since the court generally granted husbands wide latitude in governing their families. Women also had the most to lose, since they could obtain no alimony and they often lost custody of their children. The guilty party, moreover, lost all rights to the family's property, a provision that also left women far more vulnerable than men.[89] Attitudes toward divorce among elite whites both reflected and reinforced legal practice. Divorce was considered scandalous in "respectable" circles, and white Granville County residents, particularly those from families of comfortable means, kept their marital conflicts from public view.[90]

To many poor African Americans, this perspective on marriage was completely foreign. The taboo against the dissolution of marital relations derived from the importance placed on the marriage contract. Although poor blacks did not take the breakup of a long-term relationship lightly, neither did they elevate the integrity of the marriage above the interests of the parties involved or the larger community. They believed that harmonious relationships, not the sanctity of the institution of marriage, promoted the public good. As a result, poor blacks were more willing to consider separation without legal sanction as an acceptable option to irreconcilable marital conflicts. When Dink Watkins told the court, "I am my own woman and I will do as I please," she asserted her right to end the marital relationship, a privilege that her husband and others in the community recognized in principle, even if they did not always agree with particular assertions of it.[91]

Within a construction of marriage that did not center on the importance of legal contract, bastardy also acquired different meanings. For children born in unions not sanctioned by law but who nonetheless lived with both biological parents all their lives, the legal classification "bastard" meant little. Even being born outside a monogamous union did not necessarily jeopardize either a child's future or a woman's ability to establish a long-term relationship. Children might eventually live in a household with their mothers and men who became their fathers even though they were not their biological parents, or they might continue to live with their mothers in households composed of related and unrelated kin. In apprenticeship cases, for instance, bureau agents were puzzled when African Americans tried to reclaim children who were either distantly related or no blood kin at all. Although federal officials often chalked such efforts up to ignorance, what they were witnessing was the operation of family ties that did not depend solely on legal marriage and that extended beyond a male-headed nuclear family.[92]

The stability of children's and mothers' lives depended as much on the amount of support they could muster from the community as on the presence of fathers. Problems often arose when women and their children strained family and community relations. Although unusually dramatic, the experience of Frances Thorp is nonetheless suggestive. When Thorp, a mother with a young son, ran out of work, her aunt and uncle, the Thompsons, took her in. As the Thompsons soon discovered, Thorp was not quite as alone as they had been led to believe. In fact, she was sleeping with their daughter's husband and continued to do so after she took up residence in their household. Furious, Peter Thompson told his wife that he would not tolerate his son-in-law "going on this way in my house." Yet his wife opposed his intention to "drive Frances Thorp off" and encouraged him to let her stay instead. Although she probably did not approve of the new sleeping arrangements either, she believed that they had a responsibility toward Thorp, who had no means of supporting herself or her child. Despite his wife's pleas, Peter Thompson prevailed. But when he ordered Thorp to leave, it was because her presence threatened existing relationships within his immediate family, not because of the stigma attached to her position as a single mother or even because of the financial demands she made on him and his wife.[93]

Common whites' views of marriage and family converged with those of African Americans to some extent. The private lives of common whites are more difficult to reconstruct because they operated from a position of greater power than African Americans and, consequently, experienced much less state intervention. Local courts, for instance, never apprenticed poor white children who lived in male-headed households. Yet fragmentary evidence suggests that many common whites lived at the periphery of legal marriage, even though they were more firmly rooted in its culture than freedpeople. While most respected the idea of the marriage contract enough to legalize their unions and separations, this was not uniformly true. Edward Isham, born in Georgia in the 1820s and executed for murder in North Carolina in 1860, provides a particularly graphic example. Shortly before his death, Isham's lawyer, David Schenck, recorded Isham's life story. A heavy drinker, irrepressible brawler, and shameless womanizer, Isham seems to have embellished an already colorful tale, which was hardly typical of the lives of antebellum poor whites or yeomen. Even so, the way he described his own marital relations and those of the other whites around him is telling. Isham lived with a series of women in the relationship of husband and wife, marrying the last in North Carolina right before his death. The other men and women in his story lived in similar relationships, "taking up" in informal unions, marrying occasionally, and "separating" without the sanction of legal contract. Isham may have legally married some of his wives. Yet he ultimately distinguished long-term relationships from short-term dalliances not through legal conventions but through informal agreements in which he assumed economic responsibilities for a woman and she began keeping house for him. John Bell, of Granville County, operated from a similar view of marriage. According to his wife, Eliza, he left her in 1862 to "take up and cohabit with one Emily Tillotson." John eventually moved on to other women and out of the state altogether. Promiscuity was not the only way he had failed as a husband. He had also made no "provision for the maintenance and support of herself or for her child." Unlike her husband, Eliza moved more clearly within the culture of legal marriage and used this evidence to establish adultery and abandonment in the formulaic language of her divorce petition. But she also understood the signs of her husband's informal separation—openly "taking up" with another woman and rejecting any responsibility for her economic support.[94]

Despite North Carolina's refusal to recognize common-law marriage in the antebellum period, the absence of other forms of state supervision, such as marriage-registration laws, allowed wide latitude in marital relations. Without public records, for instance, the courts regularly accepted the word of the parties involved as proof of their marriage. The U.S. Pension Bureau, however, preferred written documentation, and widows of white Union soldiers often had great difficulty proving the legitimacy of their marriages to examiners who tended to see them as ignorant "crackers." On closer examination, the legal grounding of some marital unions could become so ephemeral as to be almost nonexistent. Far more important was the community's recognition of the marriage. Wealthy Braddy's experience is suggestive. As a refugee in New Bern during the war, she eloped with a Union soldier. The preacher who heard their vows made no record of their marriage. Her family and neighbors, however, required no written documentation and accepted the union. The two, according to a neighbor, "were recognized by everybody to be man and wife." Soon afterward, Braddy's husband moved away from the area with his regiment and never returned. Braddy then remarried. Only when Braddy tried to claim her first husband's pension thirty years later did her marital irregularities surface. After discovering that her first husband was still alive and that the marriage was invalid since he had legally married another woman in Connecticut before the war, the Pension Bureau rejected her claim. When her second husband, also a Union soldier, died about ten years later, Braddy submitted another claim. Once again, she ran into trouble. A justice of the peace had presided at this second marriage, but he had failed to record it. As he informed the examiner, "at that time the law did not require us to record the license." Instead, Braddy turned again to her neighbors, who affirmed that the wedding had taken place and that the community recognized them as husband and wife. Although her second marriage was legal, it too existed more in the collective memory of the community than in a written record of a legal contract. Common whites' opposition to attempts at state regulation of their domestic relations before the war suggest how tightly they clung to their own ideas about marriage. The distance the state generally kept from their domestic relations also speaks volumes about the relative power of African Americans and common whites, both during and after slavery.[95]

But perhaps the strongest link between common whites and African Americans was the tendency to situate marital relations within a wider, community context. For both groups, births, deaths, and illnesses were all public events at which neighbors gathered in and around the house offering help or just observing. Even the most intimate details of domestic life were common knowledge in the community. Quarrels between husbands and wives, parents and children, sisters, brothers, cousins, and unrelated housemates all spilled out into the streets, yards, and fields, where community members and church congregations determined the guilt or innocence of those involved. Even when conflicts were contained within the four walls of individual houses, close living quarters made privacy virtually impossible.[96]

Privacy could also be problematic. Making disputes public provided a certain amount of protection for those involved, as the 1880 fight between an African-American couple, David and Dicey Burwell, suggests. During the prolonged dispute in their front yard, David knocked both Dicey and her sixteen-year-old daughter to the ground several times with a maul. Dicey, who finally wrested the weapon from David's control, dealt him a blow that left him unconscious for almost an hour. Soon after, a neighbor, Ottaway Lee, brought charges on David's behalf against Dicey for assault with a deadly weapon. The Burwells' upstairs neighbors, however, had monitored the fight with great interest from their window. These inquisitive women knew a great deal about the Burwell family. One, for instance, knew that David Burwell had been sick because she could hear his groans through the floor. Their immersion in the Burwell's lives ultimately proved fortunate for Dicey. At the trial, they gave eyewitness testimony that supported her plea of self-defense.[97]

Community involvement also figured prominently in the domestic lives of Elizabeth and Eli Jacobs, a white couple who lived just over the border in Orange County. Elizabeth died at the end of November in 1879 and was buried a few days later. In January, however, a coroner exhumed her body and called an inquest to investigate her death. He did so "from the great excitement which increased every week and at the request of very many citizens." Ever since Elizabeth's passing, the community had been awash in gossip as neighbors held forth on the incident and debated the cause of her death. A group of women who examined the body before the burial concluded that she died of natural causes. Yet many still believed that Eli was responsible. As Joseph Jacobs testified, Eli "was verry unkind to her [Elizabeth], and he had threatened to kill her." At the inquest, sixteen other witnesses lined up to tell what they knew of the incident and the events leading up to it. They knew a great deal, offering up descriptions of the most intimate domestic details as well as their own opinions and interpretations of them. The jury, also made up of area residents, determined that Elizabeth died of unknown causes, thus freeing Eli from further legal charges if not from the doubts of suspicious neighbors. If Eli Jacobs had ever thought his marital relations were his private business, he now knew otherwise.[98]

Neighbors played a similar role in the 1883 death of Frances Henderson, an African-American woman in Granville County. The night Frances died, her husband Robert, who was also black, sat visiting with friends just a few yards away from the bed where she lay, moaning in pain. When they asked what was wrong with her, he told them to ignore her, that she was sick. As news of her death spread, the entire neighborhood turned out to pay their last respects and to prepare her badly bruised body for burial. But that was not the only reason they gathered at the Henderson household. Because they knew a great deal about Robert and Frances Henderson's lives, they were suspicious about the cause of her death. Virtually everyone who testified later at the inquest knew that Robert habitually beat Frances. Based on this fact and what they also knew about the couple's activities in the days preceding her death, they called in the local authorities over Robert Henderson's protests.[99]

In so doing, the Hendersons' neighbors, like the Jacobses' neighbors, expanded the community forum to include the justice system. In this respect, the Jacobs case is somewhat unusual. After decades of experience with elite-controlled antebellum courts, common whites viewed the judicial system, whether headed by Republicans or Democrats, with a great deal of skepticism. Although African Americans were only too aware of the legal system's limitations and harbored grave misgivings about allowing wealthy white justices and judges too much power over their lives, they did see the Freedmen's Bureau and then, particularly after Republicans took control, the local courts as potential allies. When conflict erupted, particularly when it involved a person in a position of authority over them, African Americans often responded by heading for the justice of the peace. This is exactly what Leonidas Hunt did when his employer, William Rice, assaulted him in 1871. Although Hunt later described himself as being "in a helpless condition," this was not entirely accurate. "As soon as released" from Rice's grasp, Hunt "started immediately for Oxford" to make a formal complaint. As Rice yelled after Hunt's retreating figure, "go to your damned court," it was clear that Hunt was far from helpless. In 1873, Henry Wilkerson's employer, Scott Wilkerson, took even more drastic steps. As Henry Wilkerson explained: "I was going to see a magistrate and he swore I should not go, and followed me to the fence near my house, after striking me . . . with the first rock, he stoped at the fence near my house and dared me to leave the house to go to the magistrates, and kept me there a half an hour or three quarters of an hour before I could leave the house. Scott Wilkerson swore that if I got over that fence to go to the Magistrates that he would split my head open with a rail." Henry went anyway.[100]

African Americans also used the courts to arbitrate disputes within their communities, at least during the period of Republican rule. So did common whites, on occasion. Indeed, local courts often appeared as extensions of the community. Inquests and trials took place on the front yards and porches of residences and country stores. They were attended by neighbors and overseen by elected officials who were not only well known in the community but were often staunch Republicans as well. Robert Henderson's formal inquest, for instance, bore a remarkable resemblance to the earlier, informal hearing conducted by the community. Neighbors gathered once again to give their recollections of the day Frances died and their impressions of her relationship with Robert. Although the coroner, an outsider, inspected the body and presided over the hearing, the jury, composed of people in the community, rendered the decision. Indeed, the coroner derived his authority from the community, which had already concluded that Robert Henderson had a hand in his wife's death.[101] His experience was not unusual. No fewer than forty friends and relatives gave detailed testimony about the conflicted relationship between Ann Wilkins and her stepson, whom she was accused of poisoning.[102] Eli Jacobs's case proceeded in a similar fashion, with the community acting as a chorus, interpreting and judging the incident from their personal knowledge of those involved.

As Robert Henderson and Eli Jacobs discovered, the theoretical shield that removed marital relations from public view proved flimsy indeed within their own communities. Neither poor African Americans nor common whites viewed family matters as wholly private concerns. But however much their understandings of marriage differed from the legal definition, the laws governing family relations still provided a strong weapon in their struggle to acquire the power necessary to defend the borders of their households and to guard the well-being of their family members. Such a strategy also contained unforeseen consequences. The danger lay in the fact that legal marriage and family law were part of a patriarchal framework that had justified the subordination of marginalized men as well as women and could still be mobilized to serve the same ends. Even though common whites and

African Americans could use the laws governing marriage and the family for their own purposes, they had only so much room in which to maneuver. As we will see, they could not completely remake these laws nor escape their larger political implications. Beyond the basic recognition of the institutional integrity of their families, African Americans, in particular, still managed to wrest a range of concessions from the law and from their white employers. The next chapter will consider the economic component of this struggle.

2

"How Can They Do It on Three Barrels of Corn a Year?": Labor

In September 1865, just over the border in Warren County, a Freedmen's Bureau officer addressed twenty-five hundred African Americans. Among them was a *New York Tribune* correspondent with pen in hand. According to his report, the bureau officer first directed freedpeople to "rely upon their own exertions and industry," "make contracts with the planters," "abide by their bargains," and "respect the rights of property." Then, he turned to the obligations of domestic life, reminding men that "they were sacredly bound to regard the mother[s] of their children as their wives, and that the laws of God and man would require them to live with and support them." At this point, the bemused *Tribune* reporter succumbed to the temptation for editorializing in a pointed parenthetical question: "How can they do it on three barrels of corn a year?"[1] Unintentionally, he gave voice to the thoughts of many of the freedpeople standing around him. As they knew, the most diligent men found it nearly impossible to meet their families' needs by themselves. They struggled constantly to make ends meet, even when entire families hired out their labor. Once freedpeople completed work, their problems only mounted. Prying their wages loose from the grasp of planters who were reluctant to pay for labor they had so recently commanded at will could prove as demanding as the tobacco crop freedpeople tended. Indeed, African Americans' economic vulnerability jeopardized the future of their households and, in a larger sense, their ability to define freedom on their own terms. Unless they could control the fruits of their labor, they would be thrown back into positions that resembled those they had occupied during slavery.

As central as this issue was, it formed only the most visible manifestation of a much larger dilemma. For freedpeople, the challenge of establishing independent households reached beyond the question of economic compensation and into the social construction of the labor relation itself. In the antebellum South, men's claims to independence rested on the possession of sufficient land, tools, or skills to establish households and maintain control over their own and their families' labor. Although released from slavery, then, all freed-people still faced entrenched legal and customary practices that positioned propertyless laborers as nominal dependents within their employers' households. The racial legacy of slavery then compounded their problems, nourishing the belief among whites that their racial status gave them the right to control the labor and lives of all black people, regardless of skills or property. Poor, uneducated African Americans thus faced a double burden. Their position as agricultural laborers brought them into the orbit of their employers' households as nominal dependents. Once there, they found it much more difficult to escape than white workers because of the way racial ideology worked against them.

As dependents of their employers, black laborers' claims to their own households remained tenuous. If they ever hoped to disengage themselves from the ties that continued to bind them to the households of wealthy whites, they had to sever the connection between waged work and dependence. Speaking to this issue, the delegates to the 1865 freedmen's convention pointed out that structural barriers kept many African-American men from acting as the responsible husbands and fathers they wanted to be. In fact, the delegates argued, freedpeople's efforts to provide for themselves would amount to nothing unless the legislature shifted its focus away from the economic interests of planters and propertyholders. Specifically, they suggested provisions to ensure "adequate compensation," "the proper regulation of the hours of labor," and "the means of protection against rapacious and cruel employers, and for the collection of just claims."[2] The delegates' recommendations received little notice at the time. Although the Republican legislature would later pass lien laws that buttressed the position of laboring people, these measures did not address the full range of freedpeople's concerns. Black workers nonetheless pressed forward, insisting on reasonable wages, control over their working conditions, the space to conduct their own lives free from the gaze of their employers, and ultimately the right to form households of their own. In all these ways, they challenged the idea that propertylessness and the need to labor for others translated directly into dependence. In the process, poor blacks continued the move away, both materially and metaphorically, from their ex-masters' households.

Labor, Race, and Dependence

The polarization of the categories "slavery" and "freedom" in nine-teenth-century rhetoric obscured a broad continuum of labor relations. While the absolute dependence represented in slavery anchored one end, freedom covered a wide range of people who enjoyed varying degrees of dependence and independence at the other end. Freedom encompassed independent producers of the republican ideal, beholden to no one economically or politically. It also enveloped free blacks, who were denied access to economic resources, political power, and, after the *Dred Scott* decision, citizenship itself. Thus, when African Americans stepped out of slavery, they found themselves in a highly contested region, marked by varying degrees of dependence, where working people across the country had been struggling for decades to give substance to their freedom. Unfortunately for freedpeople, most of these battles had taken place in the North on terms that made it difficult for them to apply the resulting gains to their own cause. There was even less in the South's history of labor conflict for them to use.

The labor relationship had deep roots in the household. In England in the mideighteenth century, Sir William Blackstone highlighted the ties that historically bound so many workers to their masters' households, classifying all those who performed manual labor as servants and placing them squarely within the domestic realm along with wives and children. To be sure, Blackstone's codification of common law departed from tradition by lumping together a wide range of workers—apprentices, journeymen, domestics, agricultural laborers on year-long contracts, and workers who hired out by the job or week or day. Previously, different workers had occupied distinct places on a continuum between dependence and independence. Hired laborers, who moved in and out of waged labor and performed specific tasks, exercised the most independence. Although subject to their masters' rule during the period of their employment, they generally maintained their own households and relative control over their working lives. Domestics, apprentices, indentured servants, and agricultural laborers hired by the year did not. Often distinguished by their youth, these workers not only lived with their masters but also were subject to measures that compelled obedience and completion of their contracts. For all the differences, however, everyone who hired their labor entered into temporary dependence. They gave up not just property in their labor but also mastery over their lives for the term of employment. It was this aspect of the labor relationship that allowed Blackstone to subject all propertyless laborers to their masters' dominion as completely as wives were subordinate to husbands and children were to parents.[3]

The household cast a different shadow on laborers in the American colonies. As in England, common laborers exercised degrees of freedom that fell short of full independence. But Chesapeake planters began to push the outer boundaries of traditional servitude to new limits. Ultimately they created a new category of labor, distinguished by the permanent enslavement of people of African descent and the classification of them as property. The presence of slavery then recast the position of other workers. It decreased the need for white-indentured labor, the most servile form of employment for European colonists. In addition, as Edmund Morgan has argued, the oppression of African laborers also assured greater freedom for propertyless whites, particularly white men.[4]

In practice, most adult white men who sold their labor for a living exercised the kind of independence associated with hired labor long before the colonial period drew to a close. During this time, indentured servitude continued to decline in importance and, where it still remained, generally encompassed only minors. The courts dismantled laws that compelled adult white workers to stay out the length of their contracts because the practice appeared to move free whites too close to involuntary servitude. Employers and employees also shed mutual obligations that had previously defined the labor relationship. By the nineteenth century, the law no longer held masters responsible for the maintenance of laborers, even those hired for longer terms and who lived in their households. Laborers thus lost a measure of economic security, but they were also released from the most blatant demands of personal allegiance to their employers.[5]

All other laborers continued to inhabit different places on the spectrum between complete independence and the dependence of slaves, permanently subordinated to their masters as chattel. Colonial laws placing "servants" under the dominion of their masters and strictly regulating their behavior generally applied to minors. But some adults labored within their masters' households as well.- Zephaniah Swift, in his late-eighteenth-century commentary on Connecticut law, explicitly distinguished "domestics" and "menials" from all other hired laborers who "are not by our law, or in common speech considered servants." In practice many "domestics" and "menials" could move about at will, leaving their employers when they desired without bringing down the long arm of the law to force them back. Nonetheless, their employers still expected to exercise close supervision over their labor and their lives—not only at the time Swift wrote, but well into the nineteenth century and even the twentieth. The burden of these expectations fell primary on white women, African Americans, and poor non-English immigrants, all of whom clustered in employment deemed "menial" or "domestic." Their concentration there was far from accidental. Just as race, gender, and ethnicity bolstered native-born white men's claims to independence, it pushed others into positions of greater dependence. For instance, even when free black men performed the same labor as white hired men, they often found themselves treated as if they were domestics or minor servants.[6]

It was not just race, gender, ethnicity, and age that defined dependence. Waged labor did not translate into complete independence for anyone, even adult white men. If anything, it connoted dependence, particularly before the ascendancy of free labor ideology in the nineteenth century. "Wage workers," as Robert Steinfeld explains in *The Invention of Free Labor,* "were dependent in precisely the sense that they had alienated the legal right to control and dispose of their own capacities."[7] White working men might have been less dependent than women or free black men, but they were certainly not as independent as the propertied white men who employed them. Voting restrictions reveal the bonds that still shackled them to the private sphere. In contemporary logic, propertyless men had no business with the ballot. Not only did they lack a material stake in society but they were also already represented by their employers, in whom their interests were, at least in part, subsumed. By contrast, the sturdy artisans and yeomen of Jefferson's republican ideal embodied independence because they were their own masters. As Jefferson saw it, the new republic's challenge was to steer clear of the kind of industrial development taking place in Europe. A permanent working class, mired in poverty and harnessed to their employers' whims, would spell certain ruin for the nation's republican experiment.[8]

Jefferson eventually lost this battle. As the United States embraced Alexander Hamilton's vision instead, the labor relationship fundamentally changed. Waged labor became free labor, a commodity that workers could sell without surrendering mastery over their lives to the purchaser. Linked to industrialization, the concept of free labor also drew on the ideology of the Enlightenment, which undermined traditional notions of an organic, hierarchical society and emphasized the innate capacity of all men to direct their own destinies. From this perspective, individuals could not fully relinquish control over their labor or their lives to another even if they wanted to.[9]

The concept of free labor, however, did not give workers the same rights and privileges as those who owned productive property. Working people had to forge this link themselves. They were particularly vocal in the Northeast, where their ranks swelled with new recruits. Embracing the more radical implications of Revolutionary rhetoric, they maintained that all white men were masters of their own lives regardless of their current material conditions. As such, they deserved the same rights and privileges as propertied men. To claim independence, workers played on the ways free labor ideology cast waged labor as the opposite of slave labor. If slaves were defined in terms of their dependency, they argued, then wage earners should be considered independent. They also pointed to a fundamental contradiction in their position as laborers in an industrial economy. In theory, the dependence of wage workers was temporary, confined to the period of employment. In reality, it was not, since many would never acquire the means necessary to withdraw their labor from the market. If they could not move out of waged labor, then they had to change its conditions. Addressing this problem, laborers argued that their position as wage earners did not give their employers the right to control their lives, either on or off the job. Nor, in the case of white men, did it exclude them from political participation. Women workers also joined the battle. Despite the gendered meanings that kept them from claiming political rights and individual autonomy, they too demanded more freedom on the job and more power in relation to their employers.[10]

The benefits, however, accrued primarily to adult white men. Most states, for instance, eliminated property qualifications for white men in the first decades of the nineteenth century, making waged work alone the basis for their inclusion in the polity. As David Roediger and Alexander Saxton have shown, white laborers relied heavily on racial categories to further their cause. Equating whiteness with freedom and blackness with slavery, they explicitly distanced themselves from all African Americans. The experience of one European visitor in the early nineteenth century is representative. Much to his surprise, he found that "to call persons . . . *servants,* or to speak of their *master* or *mistress,* is a grievous affront." He then went on to relate the words of an unruly domestic who insisted that she had no master and that she did not live at her place of work, but only "*stay[ed]* there." Explicitly rejecting the title "servant," she identified herself as the "help": "I'd have you to know, *man,* that I am no *sarvant;* none but *negers* are *sarvants.*" By grounding her claims to independence in whiteness, this woman also relegated all African Americans to the dependence of "sarvants." Her words reflected escalating hostility toward free blacks in the years following the Revolution. In both the North and the South, African Americans faced a host of formal and informal measures that regulated their labor and limited their ability to enjoy the fruits earned thereby.[11]

The claims of this domestic notwithstanding, her racial status did not remove her from her master's household. White men would successfully use the racial distinctions she drew to bolster their own claims to independence. But domestics, like this woman, found themselves in a different category of labor than wage-earning men, as the gender ideology of the nineteenth century defined housework as part of women's natural role, not as labor. Subject to the same rules as dependent daughters or, more often, underprivileged cousins, domestic servants were denied privileges granted to other wage earners. In fact, all women labored under the weight of gender prescriptions that assigned them roles as wives and mothers within households headed by men. Because they were never expected to be the primary economic providers in their families, they endured lower wages, fewer occupational options, and far more supervision on the job than their male counterparts. These conditions then created a self-fulfilling prophesy, ensuring that few working women could be economically independent. More generally, white working men used feminine dependence to naturalize masculine independence. They also underscored their responsibility for wives and children to emphasize their commonalities with self-employed artisans and farmers as household heads who provided for dependents.[12]

In some respects, white northern working men made the road to independence more difficult for women and African Americans. While accentuating the traditional association of blackness and femininity with dependence, they also explicitly excluded women and African Americans from the category "laborer." Identified exclusively in terms of their race or gender, women and African Americans would find that dependency clung much more tenaciously to them. But even white laboring men failed to escape the household's grasp completely. As Christopher Tomlins argues, nineteenth-century courts retained traditional asymmetries of power in the labor relationship by infusing their decisions with key elements of the laws of master and servant. Legally, the workplace became the capitalist's private domain, beyond the reach of public debate and exempt from community standards. The courts then obscured these inequalities with the discourse of voluntary consent and the legal fiction that employers and employees were contractual equals. As a result, wage workers found themselves subject to employers whose command over economic resources and political power far exceeded that of their colonial counterparts and whose decisions employees could not publicly appeal. Although different in form, the association between labor and dependence remained.[13]

It was even stronger in the South. Slaveholders, of course, had a vested interest in supporting slavery and opposing free labor. However self-serving, proslavery ideologues also threw widely held assumptions about labor into sharp relief. Like many white southerners, slavery's defenders continued to think in terms of a broad middle ground between slavery and freedom. They maintained that civilization depended on the presence of a "mudsill" to perform the drudgery of life and that an unregulated laboring class posed the greatest threat to the stability of the new nation. Thus, they cast a suspicious and increasingly defensive eye northward, condemning the expansion of individual rights for working people. The social implications of "free labor," which to proslavery theorists meant little more than a license for employers to abandon all responsibility for working people, only added to their concerns. In their minds, a mass uprising would be the logical outcome of a labor system that promised freedom and delivered only grinding poverty. African slavery provided the perfect solution by reserving the most arduous and least rewarding labor for people racially unfit for anything else. As slavery's defenders argued, bound labor would eliminate the inherent instabilities of free labor by circumscribing the freedom of workers and holding their masters responsible for their welfare. Indeed, some believed that all common laborers, white and black, would eventually be placed in some form of bondage. But even when slavery's defenders did not push their ideas this far, they still assumed a continuum of subordination in which everyone who hired their labor to another was considerably less than independent.[14]

White southerners of the planter class did not place white laborers and black slaves in the same category. But they did allow for alternative possibilities somewhere between the complete dependence of slaves and the full-blown independence of freeholders, because they did not see dependence and independence in dichotomous terms. In fact, the status of free white laborers was legally ambiguous. In North Carolina, the statutes remained silent on this issue and the supreme court only rarely reviewed cases dealing with free laborers. The 1848 case of *Howell Wiswall* v. *Hiram Brinson* contained the most detailed discussion of the issue. In his dissent, Justice Ruffin distinguished free servants from hired laborers, working from the assumption that those who maintained the least control over labor were also the least free. "How do we know when two men are master and servant?" he asked. The "mode of compensation, merely, does not determine the question conclusively; for a servant may be paid by the year, month, day, or job." A servant, Ruffin determined, was a person "subject to the orders and control of the employer in the execution of the work he is to do, or not. If the employer has a right to have the work done as he pleases, can change the plans and periods of it from time to time, to suit his fancy or his other business—in fine, if the hired man works *under* the other—then one is master and the other is servant; but, otherwise not." By this definition, "officers of companies, hands on cars or ships, deputies as well as menials and domestics, are properly and truly servants." Ruffin concluded that the laborer in question, who had been hired to move a house to another location, was not a servant, but a contractor. Despite Ruffin's lengthy description, it was not so much the definition of servitude as its application in this particular case that was in question. Using virtually the identical distinctions, Justice Pearson determined the same laborer to be a servant because house-moving did not constitute a distinct trade, a decision with which the rest of the court agreed. So vague as to encompass most of those who worked for wages, the operative definition of a "servant" also gave great latitude to employers in defining the nature of the labor relation. Servants worked "under" their dominion in a private relation, the terms of which were controlled by the employers, not the state.[15]

Brantley York and his brother, both of Randolph County, learned this lesson the hard way. In the early nineteenth century when their father lost his business, the two boys hired out as farm hands. Not only did York and his brother work side by side with the slaves in the fields at one position but they also took their meals separately from their employer. While not equating white laborers with black slaves, this employer clearly saw the York boys' position as closer to that of his slaves than himself. The fact that the two brothers were minors moved them that much closer toward dependence, but youth alone did not determine their status. If they had been working on their father's farm, the York boys would have enjoyed a very different range of privileges. Among other things, they would have eaten with the white family. Many white laborers avoided the kind of treatment endured by the York brothers because they worked for relatives. As Brantley York reveals, some of his other employers took greater pains to distinguish between white laborers and black slaves. Unlike slaves and indentured servants, moreover, the two boys could exercise their freedom to quit. But they did so with great caution and apparent fear that they might be forced to complete the terms of their contracts: "We watched our opportunity, and when we thought no one saw us, we climbed over the fence and to the road for home; nor did we travel slowly, for we ran a large fraction of the way." The York boys escaped this time. But regardless of their age or the good graces of their next employer, they would continue to float somewhere between the status of slaves and freeholders as long as they worked as common laborers.[16]

Voting restrictions in North Carolina underscore the dependence attached to those who lacked the material means to control their own labor. The Democratic party persistently championed universal white manhood suffrage during the antebellum period, building its case on the idea that ownership of one's own labor was sufficient for white men to participate in the polity. Despite these efforts, the state's conservatives managed to keep propertyless white men on the periphery of the public sphere. Not until 1857 did Democrats manage to enact universal white manhood suffrage. Before that, all free white men could vote for their representatives to the state House of Commons, but to vote for state senators they had to prove ownership of fifty acres of land. Even then, the results of universal white manhood suffrage were less democratic than they might have been because so many offices were appointive, not elective. Only the offices of sheriff and county clerk appeared on local ballots. Justices of the peace, perhaps the most important local officials, were selected by the governor and served for life. Since justices filled other county positions, conducted virtually all the county business, and adjudicated most minor civil disputes, the system removed a great deal of power from the hands of ordinary people. The apportionment of the legislature only accentuated the inequality of the system, because senate districts overrepresented wealthy areas of the state and lower house districts favored slaveholding areas. North Carolina's rigidly hierarchical state and county governments were atypical, even for the South; other southern states were far more democratic, far earlier. Yet North Carolina's particular experience is telling in that it highlights the persistence of a constellation of ideas that linked material resources to personal independence and public power.[17]

In some respects, the differences between North and South on the question of labor were relative. In both regions, the majority of white men were landowners, tenants, and independent artisans, rather than permanent wage workers. Like their northern counterparts, whites in the South worked to sever the connection between propertylessness and dependence, arguing for more democratic political and economic relationships on the basis of their position as household heads and their race.

In the South, however, propertyless whites and yeomen did not launch a sustained critique of the logic that linked waged labor to dependence. In a society where the vast majority of common laborers were enslaved, they did not have to. Hired workers like Brantley York might complain about domineering employers, but waged work remained an inevitable stage in the life cycle for young people who hoped to either operate their own farms or marry someone who did. Propertyless adult men, particularly if they were married, generally made their living by renting land rather than selling their labor. Free white men might also hire out their labor or that of their children for short periods to supplement their incomes or tide them over in particularly hard times. Even then, the presence of the open range increased the ability of those on the margins to get by without resorting to waged work. Generally, those who rented land exercised considerably more control over their labor and its product than common laborers. This was true even in North Carolina, where the law distinguished between tenants and sharecroppers. Much like "servants," sharecroppers worked under the direct control of their landlords and possessed no property rights in the goods they produced. The distinction, however, was not always observed in practice. Many white sharecroppers actually enjoyed a degree of independence more in accord with tenancy. Often, the court determined the status of the party in question after the fact in order to settle a conflict between the renter and the landlord.[18]

The work patterns of common whites led them to embrace an ideology Lacy Ford has termed "country republicanism," which bestowed independent status only on those white men with sufficient means to provide for their own households and control their own labor. As Stephanie McCurry has added, economic independence rested on the ability to direct the labor of household members as well. Among the abiding fears of these men was that fortune would steal away their means of subsistence and engulf them in dependence. Even when yeomen referred to themselves as workers, they were not identifying with those who labored for someone else but were distinguishing themselves from large slaveholders who made their living by directing the labor of others. As McCurry has found, yeomen in the South Carolina low country used the term "self-working farmers" to evoke the contrast.[19]

These same assumptions still guided white southerners' conceptions of labor after emancipation. For instance, the commission that drafted the Black Code also recommended the adoption of measures designed to regulate the labor of both races. As the report explained: "While it is the duty of the lawgiver to secure to the laborer the promised rewards of his labor and toil, it is equally just to require him to comply with his deliberate and lawful contracts. . . . The inculcation of a strict observance of contracts is equally the parent and offspring of virtuous industry."[20] To be sure, the commission members carefully avoided racially specific language so as to avert the sharp criticism other southern states had received for laws that restricted only black workers. But their concerns also extended to propertyless whites. Sidney Andrews, a northern correspondent, claimed that newspapers across North Carolina continually complained of idle white men "who have no ostensible business but lounging and whiskey-drinking." Concerned with social breakdown generally, one editor openly urged the legislature "to take steps to reduce the amount of vagrancy among whites." Many other wealthy whites privately conveyed their fear of "the masses," by which they meant all propertyless people. Although privileged by race, white men could not escape the taint of dependency.[21] It was this connection between dependence and common labor that allowed the commission to limit the freedom of all wage workers, white and black.

Labor and race, however, were never entirely separable in the minds of white southerners. In fact, the dependence white southerners attached to blackness and the dependence associated with common labor reinforced each other. Conservative whites believed that race marked all African Americans as permanently dependent. Poor whites could move out of their dependent position when they accumulated the property necessary to remove themselves from the control of an employer or landlord. African Americans, however, could never alter their lot in life. Their race, according to the defenders of white superiority, destined all blacks to common labor, a position too lowly for any but the most degraded whites.

Race and labor also merged in southern workplaces. The commission members who drafted the Black Code and its corresponding labor provisions directed their comments at all wage workers. They were also well aware that most laborers were freed slaves who, they hoped, would continue to perform agricultural work. The recommendations, written into the state's statutes in 1866, resurrected traditional measures that compelled workers to stay until the end of their contracts so as to ensure a steady supply of labor. Indeed, agricultural laborers were archetypical "servants," traditionally held more closely to the households of their masters and allowed less freedom than other workers. In both England and the colonies close regulation had been considered more important for agricultural workers than for other hired hands, since their departure at crucial moments in the growing cycle could result in the loss of the entire crop. Of course, other southern states justified restrictions on African-American labor on the basis of race alone. Yet, just as the laws that spoke only to labor carried racial implications, those framed in terms of race inevitably rested on questions of labor. Affirming the dependent position of common laborers ensured the continued subordination of African Americans as a race, while emphasizing racial restrictions forced them into waged work and the dependent status that came with it. Either way, African Americans would still labor within the borders of their masters' households, this time as servants instead of slaves.[22]

Changes in the laws relating to labor after the Civil War placed more people in the category of common laborer, but did little to challenge the dependence associated with that position. After the war, other southern states adopted the distinction North Carolina already drew between sharecropping and tenancy. A response to the new working arrangements that arose after emancipation, sharecropping effectively defined most African-American agricultural workers as common laborers and denied them the relative independence associated with tenancy. With no property in the goods they produced, all laborers were vulnerable to the personal whims and economic fortunes of their employers, who might either refuse to pay them or lack the funds to do so. The economic uncertainty of the postwar period magnified the precariousness of laborers' position to the point where even conservatives could not ignore it. In 1866, the same legislature that passed the Black Code approved "An Act to Secure to Agricultural Laborers Their Pay in Kind." It declared that "whenever servants and laborers in agriculture shall, by their contracts . . . be entitled, for wages to a part of the crops cultivated by them, such part shall not be subject to sale under executions, against their employers." This measure and its companion, "An Act to Prevent Enticing Servants from Fulfilling Their Contracts or Harboring Them," defined labor relationships in terms of the mutual obligations of masters and servants: if workers were held to their employers, then employers were bound to pay them. The rough balance, however, did not last long. In 1867, the legislature extended the penalties of "enticing" to the servant as well as the new employer. It also weakened agricultural laborers' claims to the crop with new lien laws favoring suppliers.[23]

In 1868, Republicans brought the labor relationship more in line with the precepts of free labor ideology, strengthening workers' ability to collect their wages through laborers' lien laws. This new legislation, however, still restrained workers' mobility by specifying that the lien only applied if the laborer had "worked out the full term for which he shall have contracted, or shall have been discharged by the employer, without default on the part of the laborer." This act, moreover, did not change the fact that most propertyless people were hired hands with little claim to independent status in their own right. After 1877, when the Democratic legislature collapsed tenancy into the same category as sharecropping and waged labor, all propertyless people shared the burden of dependency.[24]

White planters explicitly referred to their black laborers as "servants." The term, which had become synonymous with slavery, expressed planters' desire to recreate the master-slave relationship. But it simultaneously signaled the new place they saw for African Americans as free servants somewhere between slavery and independence. One letter written to the Freedmen's Bureau by forty white "men of respectability" in Franklinton, bordering Granville County, captures the essence of this position. Complaining about the nightly meetings among freedpeople led by Reverend Crawford, they wrote: "We are not opposed to the Mental, Moral, or Religious improvement of the coloured people, but we cannot see any of the beneficial effects of Mr. Crawford's *Religious* Teachings either in the life or conduct of those who attend upon his nightly efforts." "Those in our employment," they continued, "do not work more cheerfully, neither do they demean themselves with greater circumspection than heretofore. On the contrary, if there is any change *visible,* it is for the worse, as is manifest from greater indifference to our interest, and an unwillingness to do cheerfully the most common duties of servants." The qualities these employers desired of servants were much like those they had demanded of slaves. But then servants were not so far removed from slaves on the continuum of dependence that stretched from slavery to independent freeholders. In the opinion of some white planters, slavery and servitude were so close as to be almost indistinguishable. For others, the very fact that African Americans labored for another saturated them with a dependence that freedom alone could never eliminate.[25]

The "respectable" white men of Franklinton, however, laid far too much blame at the Reverend Mr. Crawford's doorstep. "Servants" invariably fell short of the mark not because of the inflammatory teachings of outside agitators, but because they had their own ideas about the labor relationship. When freedpeople used the term "servant," they construed it narrowly to distinguish domestics from field hands without necessarily attaching more or less dependence to either category of work. If anything, black laborers aimed to show greater indifference toward the interests of their employers and give more attention to their own. Intending to control their own labor more completely, they did not wish to "demean themselves with greater circumspection." "Common duties," in their minds, were open to negotiation. The facade of cheerfulness, however, was not, since they believed employers only obtained use of their labor, not their lives. Above all, they rejected planters' efforts to confine them as dependents, insisting on recognition of their independent status and their own households. The result was conflict. In Granville County, black laborers and planters confronted each other in the tobacco fields, against the backdrop of a developing tobacco industry.[26]

Tobacco

Granville County lay at the southernmost tip of the Virginia tobacco district, renowned in the antebellum period for its fine-textured, light-colored tobacco. After southern surrender, tobacco production resumed, propelled by soaring prices. At the same time, the center of the industry shifted from Virginia to North Carolina, where scores of small factories began to open up across that state's midsection, fueling the growth of tobacco farms in the surrounding countryside. Granville County sat in the center of it all, anchoring the newly named "Bright Belt," so called for the "bright" yellow tobacco that was the area's specialty.[27] Demand for tobacco picked up even before southern surrender. Troops in both armies coveted the aromatic tobacco grown in the North Carolina–Virginia district. After they left, manufacturers arrived to refill their stocks. Some were so eager that they drove door to door and paid whatever farmers demanded.[28] The initial frenzy soon subsided, but the demand for bright tobacco remained strong for the next two decades. Between 1865 and 1870, prices in the Bright Belt rose precipitously above the national average. Despite a decline as the initial postwar shortage eased, the rapid expansion of the tobacco-manufacturing industry maintained price levels during the 1870s and into the 1880s.[29]

"Bright Tobacco Showers Gold and Silver Dollars Over Granville, the Banner County," boasted the sign over the county's booth at the 1884 North Carolina Exposition.[30] It expressed more than the wishful thinking of die-hard local boosters. Tobacco had been good to the county, raising everyone's living standards, particularly compared to those in cotton-producing areas. In fact, high prices and steady demand encouraged Granville County residents to build their postwar economy exclusively around bright tobacco. By the 1870s, virtually everyone in the county owed their livelihood to it: some tended to-bacco in the fields; some oversaw those who did; some manufactured it; some sold it; and others traded in the profits of those who worked directly with it. Few escaped its influence. The demands of the crop structured the contours of postemancipation labor arrangements, just as the market's ups and downs framed the county's social and polit-ical relations.

Bright tobacco, however, did not shower gold and silver dollars evenly among all residents. To be sure, cash and credit in Granville County were relatively accessible, even in the first few years follow-ing the war. By the 1870s, county tobacco farmers began selling their own tobacco directly through auction at local warehouses instead of through factors in Virginia cities. Farmers generally brought in a load at a time as they graded their tobacco and as they needed cash. Af-ter buyers inspected the tobacco, the bidding took place, and the farmer received payment. Cash-poor cotton farmers might have marveled at the ease with which currency changed hands at auction, but many tobacco farmers went home disappointed. Prices fluctuat-ed widely depending on the quality of the tobacco. If farmers were lucky, their crop might yield a high proportion of the quality lemon-yellow "wrappers" that drew premium prices. If they were not and produced a surfeit of worthless "scrap," they might not make enough to rub two coins together.[31]

Cultivation of the best grades was a difficult, involved process that required a substantial capital investment and years of experience to master. William W. White, a planter in northern Granville County, did not even try to grow high-grade yellow tobacco until 1875. Although he hired a knowledgeable grower to oversee the curing process, his first effort was a "partial failure." White hoped for "better success next time," and the following year he reported that his tobacco "cured up very nicely." Still, he regularly visited other bright tobacco planters to observe their growing and curing techniques, and most of the tobacco he produced in the 1870s was the lower-grade variety he had always grown. Without White's resources, more Granville County farmers found themselves below, rather than above, the average. Even wealthy farmers could not completely escape the vagaries of the to-bacco market. In 1877, White sold his fancy bright tobacco, but the prices offered for the darker variety were so low that he hauled it back home to wait for a change in the market. Those who lived closer to the edge had no alternative but to accept the prices offered.[32]

All grades of tobacco required constant, year-round attention. Unlike cotton farmers, tobacco farmers could not devote their entire acreage to their cash crop because it was so labor-intensive. In fact, they were more likely to obtain higher prices for their tobacco if they focused more effort on producing a small, quality crop. Most farmers, even renters, grew only a few acres and devoted the rest of their land to food and forage. Even then, tobacco usually outstripped a household's labor supply. Regardless of the number of slaves they owned, antebellum tobacco farmers regularly hired additional laborers during busy seasons.[33]

Emancipation did nothing to alter tobacco's voracious demand for labor, but it did dramatically change the forms labor took. Before reorganized markets stabilized credit and cash flows, Granville County planters, like their counterparts across the South, turned to share wages. In 1867, the local Freedmen's Bureau agent estimated that share-wage agreements made up about four-fifths of all the labor contracts in the area. The arrangement was well-suited to the economic uncertainty of the years immediately following surrender: planters paid laborers a portion of the harvest, in essence borrowing on the labor of share-wage workers to begin production. But the new system also presented problems for Granville County planters and laborers. Laborers did not receive payment until the end of the year when the crops were divided. Often, the wait was in vain. Planters commonly fired workers before harvest, paying them nothing at all. For those who made it to the end of the season, the process of dividing crops brought more problems. Complaints flooded the office of the local Freedmen's Bureau. Share-wage laborers claimed that planters withheld all or part of their wages, and planters argued that laborers did not deserve payment because they had not performed satisfactory work.[34]

By the 1870s, an uneven patchwork of tenancy, waged labor, and small-scale landownership emerged. Although the scarcity of cash and credit made wages difficult in the cotton South, Granville County's thriving tobacco market presented no such barriers. Planter Willis Lewis, for instance, used share wages in 1867, but three years later he had adopted cash wages, paying out $400 that year to farm laborers. Others joined Lewis, making waged labor common on Granville County farms by 1870. In two townships, Dutchville and Oxford, about half of the farms hired waged labor in 1870. In Dutchville, these farms paid out an average of $144 in wages that year; in Oxford the average was $270. Large planters who hired full-time laborers accounted for most of the money spent on wages, but a significant minority of small farmers also hired workers and paid them in cash.[35] A comparison between the number of agricultural laborers and tenants underscores the relative importance of waged labor in the county: 294 farm laborers lived in Oxford as compared to 62 tenant households; Dutchville claimed 188 farm laborers and only 35 tenant households. Of course tenant families generally contained more than one worker, but the figures are suggestive nonetheless.[36] Most agricultural wage workers were young, African-American men, under the age of thirty-one. In both 1870 and 1880, they constituted about 90 percent of those listed as agricultural wage laborers in the census. The census figures, however, also tend to obscure the actual diversity of these workers. Seasonal and occasional agricultural labor remained common in the postwar years, as men, women, and children of both races worked for wages to supplement family incomes, but did not appear in the census schedules as farm laborers.[37]

Wage rates varied. William W. White, for instance, hired between five and eight farm laborers on year-long contracts beginning in January. He and the workers negotiated terms the previous December, and wages differed from contract to contract. Some workers bargained for a yearly wage, while others obtained a monthly wage. In addition to cash, there were alternate compensations: some received room and board, others received provisions like corn and wheat, and one man's contract included a pair of new boots. Pay on the White plantation increased between 1866 and 1880—even though it was a period of general price deflation. In 1870 the highest wage paid was $50 a year and a barrel of corn. By 1875, White paid $75 and two barrels of corn. These new wages apparently remained in effect through 1880.[38]

Working conditions also varied. Because Granville County farms, large and small, grew a wide variety of crops in addition to tobacco, laborers adapted to the demands of the particular farm. In addition to full-time agricultural laborers, William W. White and William T. Patterson hired temporary labor to perform specific tasks. In 1884, Patterson hired eight laborers, paid at the rate of $.40 a day, or $5.00 a month with room and board, for various intervals over the course of the year. He also needed some day labor every month. January and February found Bob Ellington and Essex Kittrell at work for about seven days, cutting the wood required to cure the tobacco. In March, Patterson hired Willis and Eaton Burton, who apparently stayed on through the end of the year. Yet the Burtons, who seem to have focused their efforts on the labor-intensive tobacco crop, could not manage all the farm work on their own. In May, Albert and Celestia

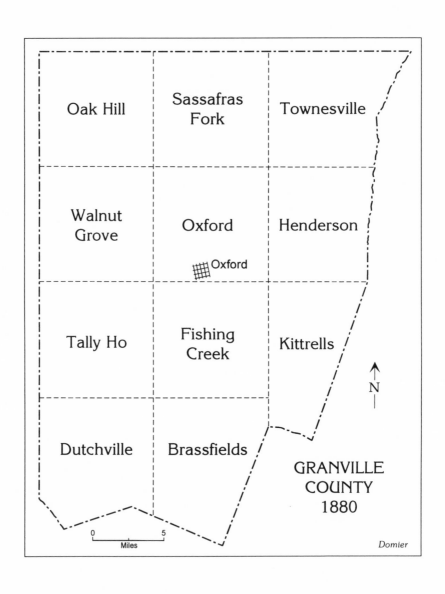

Oak Hill

Sassafras
Fork

Townesville

Walnut
Grove

Oxford

Henderson

Oxford

Tally Ho

Fishing
Creek

Kittrells

N

Dutchville

Brassfields

GRANVILLE
COUNTY
1880

0   5
Miles

Domier

planted corn and cotton, plowed, and tended the tobacco a total of four days, while Thornton spent a day weeding corn. The following month, Bob Ellington and Essex Kittrell were back for about five days each, cutting wheat and oats and clearing new fields. Patterson's diary, in which he recorded the laborers' work, then skips to the fall, when James helped with the tobacco harvest. But, according to entries elsewhere in the diary, Patterson must have hired help during the summer months to tend and then harvest tobacco, corn, wheat, and oats. In November and December, Bob Ellington and Essex Kittrell spent about ten days each working on the chimney and daubing the house. Come January, they probably hauled wood again in preparation for the next fall's curing.[39]

As Patterson's diary suggests, workers themselves used waged labor for their own ends, particularly during the flush years of the 1870s and 1880s when both work and cash were readily available. Some historians have emphasized freedpeople's distaste for waged work and their preference for sharecropping. As they argue, the supervision of white overseers made waged labor seem too much like slavery. Sharecropping, by contrast, more closely approximated independent landownership, allowing freedpeople to conduct their work and to live their lives away from an employer's watchful eyes. This analysis, however, tends to abstract the issues from their historical context, assigning fixed meanings to the terms "waged work" and "sharecropping" and ignoring the power of African Americans to shape the categories to suit their own purposes.[40] After a few bad experiences with share wages, as Gerald David Jaynes has pointed out, many freedpeople actually welcomed prompt cash payment at regular intervals. Not only did cash decrease the ability of employers to defraud freedpeople of their pay but it also gave them more freedom to determine when they would work and for whom.[41]

Given the demand for labor in a strong tobacco market, agricultural waged work gave Granville County's small farmers, tenants and owners alike, much more flexibility than they might otherwise have had. Benjamin and Mary Burwell, for instance, combined paid farm labor with small-scale agricultural production on their four and one-half acres of land. Besides the land, this African-American couple owned a horse, two cows, and four hogs—a modest accumulation that nevertheless enabled the Burwells to focus on the future of their children. Of their six children, three attended school even though they were old enough to work for pay.[42] Bob Ellington and Essex Kittrell, who performed occasional labor on William T. Patterson's farm, probably used waged work to supplement their farm incomes in a similar manner. Even young African-American men, the bulk of the county's agricultural labor force, moved in and out of such employment as their economic needs changed. Robert Lee Pool, for instance, began work in a small tobacco factory in 1871 at age twelve. Pool's father, a brick mason, taught him the trade as soon as Pool could physically manage the heavy work. When masonry work was scarce, Pool found other means of supporting himself, but he viewed these jobs as diversions from his real intent of becoming a brick mason and mechanic, an ambition he eventually realized. Like Pool, Ike Hicks worked for wages as a young, unmarried man. Soon after his marriage, however, he began farming as a tenant.[43]

Waged labor also held attractions for those who did not aspire to property accumulation. When work was plentiful during the tobacco boom, occasional labor offered a dependable source of income and minimal contact with white supervisors, both of which resulted

Tobacco factory, operated by John Watkins. Most tobacco manufactories in the antebellum period and the first few decades following the war were generally small, seasonal operations attached to farms. After curing farmers "manufactured" the tobacco for sale, relying on slaves, family, or hired hands to do the work. Many, like this one, were located in barns that were often used for other purposes. Some "factories" were no more than small sheds. (Courtesy of the Granville County Historical Society)

in a degree of autonomy not always available to a full-time wage work-er, a tenant, or even a small landowner. Unlike tenants, who were saddled with their bosses for an entire year, laborers could come and go as it suited them and still receive payment for the work they per-formed. Such arrangements were particularly attractive for married women with children. Cash wages, moreover, did not disappear dur-ing bad crop years as they did for tenants and small freeholders. For those who wanted to work just enough to earn a bare subsistence or for those who wanted to shield themselves, as much as possible, from the authority of white bosses, occasional labor was ideal. Frances Amis, for instance, scavenged (or stole, depending on the perspec-tive) and worked intermittently to purchase some necessities and to pay her rent. But her needs were few and easily satisfied. After rising late one morning in 1872, for instance, she went off to fish for her noon meal. Fish were free and finances less pressing since she had just acquired a new roommate and, presumably, a reduction in her share of the rent. It is not necessary to romanticize Amis's poverty to realize that her time was her own.[44]

Frances Amis, however, found it more difficult to earn a subsistence than her male counterparts. Although most of Granville County's agricultural wage laborers were men, many women, particularly African-American women, also worked for wages outside the home. In 1870, for instance, almost as many of Oxford Township's women (239) worked for wages as men (279). Ten years later, the number of women wage workers had fallen to 159, while the number of men held fairly steady at 242. Even then, they formed 40 percent of all wage workers in the township. Rural Dutchville contained far fewer women wage workers, who tended to congregate in towns where they obtained employment as domestic servants. But they still formed 25 percent of all of Dutchville's waged laborers by 1880. These figures, moreover, do not account for those women who worked occasional-ly for wages but were not listed as paid laborers in the census.[45]

Regardless of the work they did, women received about half as much pay as men. Those who lived outside a male-headed family made barely enough to support themselves, let alone their children. One of the most telling statistics is the distribution of wealth in the county. In Oxford Township, where the top one-fifth of household heads owned 98 percent of the personal property and 94 percent of all real estate and the bottom three-fifths owned no personal prop-erty and only 2 percent of the real estate, 73 percent of all female-headed households ranked among the poorest three-fifths of the population. In Dutchville Township, the gulf between rich and poor narrowed somewhat. Here, the top one-fifth of household heads owned 69 percent of the personal property and 66 percent of the real estate. But the more equitable distribution of wealth did not extend to women, who clustered at the very bottom on the economic scale. The bottom three-fifths of Dutchville's population, which owned only 9 percent of the personal property and 10 percent of the real estate, contained 82 percent of all female-headed households. Most working women could not even afford households of their own. Instead, they relied on the kindness of relatives, the charity of strangers, and their own ingenuity, sometimes resorting to scavenging and petty theft to get by. They might live with a series of less-than-hospitable relatives, moving on when their welcome wore thin, or depend on friends or relatives to look after their children while they worked and boarded elsewhere or band together, like Francis Amis and her roommates, pooling their resources in cooperative, if not always harmonious, households. For these women, waged labor carried more hardships than it did for single men or for families with older children who could work for wages.[46]

Agricultural waged work grew in tandem with other forms of labor. In Dutchville, which had a history of high landownership rates, farmers relied heavily on wage laborers to work their tobacco fields: between 1870 and 1880, the percentage of farms using waged labor increased from 49 to 64 percent; the amount spent on wages rose from $10,625 to $27,665; and the number of farm laborers rose from 188 to 308. Renters increased from 27 percent (35 of 131 farms) to 34 percent (94 of 279 farms). Oxford farmers blended waged labor with rental arrangements, building on their township's history of large plantations and tenant farms. Between 1870 and 1880, the percentage of farms using waged labor increased only from 44 to 48 percent; the amount spent on wages actually declined from $17,010 to $14,906; and the number of wage laborers also declined from 294 to 264. Renters increased from 45 percent (62 of 130 farms) to 63 percent (145 of 232 farms). In 1870 there were about 5 times as many wage laborers as renters in Oxford; by 1880, the proportion fell to 2 to 1. The proportion of wage laborers to renters also declined in Dutchville from about 5 to 1 to about 3 to 1. But in Dutchville this decrease probably reflects the influx of white farmers who generally could obtain better rental agreements than African Americans. Only about one-third of Dutchville's renters were black, while about three-quarters of Oxford's renters were black.[47] The differences in labor organization, however, can be overemphasized, since waged labor and rental agreements could be more alike than they were different.

Rental agreements, like wage contracts, contained multiple meanings. Renters spanned the range from abject poverty to opulent prosperity and included dirt farmers who barely eked out a subsistence
on a few acres, croppers who tended a specific piece of land but were
otherwise indistinguishable from wage laborers, and planters who
grew large quantities of tobacco in combination with other market
crops on the best farm land available.[48] While most renters clumped
at the middle and lower ends of the spectrum, generalizing about this
group remains difficult. Those who worked small farms on good tobacco-producing land could be better off economically than those
who rented large farms in another area. Other farmers worked toward different goals, avoiding tobacco altogether and counting themselves successful if they produced enough to feed themselves. It is also
problematic to evaluate renters by drawing a firm line between sharecroppers and tenants. Although the distinction was well defined in
North Carolina law, it was not always applied in practice. As late as
1875, Chief Justice Edwin G. Reade still maintained that the "dividing line between tenant and cropper is indistinct, and in many cases, hard to run." In 1877, when the legislature clarified matters by
placing tenants in the same category as sharecroppers, the distinction became immaterial.[49]

African Americans generally worked the smallest, least productive
farms.[50] Yet even this fact fails to convey a clear image of their status.
Five extra acres of prime farmland might boost output, but the only
way tenants could secure control over the operation of their farms
and their lives was through negotiation with their landlords. In addition to retaining rights over the crop, some landlords expected to
maintain tight control over both the land and the labor. For instance,
Allen Oakley, an African-American renter, did well for himself economically. In 1879, he owned his own team, other stock, and produced seven barns of tobacco worth over $1,000, three-quarters of
which he kept as his own. His material possessions, however, did not
translate directly into the freedom to run his farm or his life as he
pleased. Oakley's rental agreement with planter Fielding Knott
specified not only what he grew and where he planted it but also that
he "work by the orders of said Knott to be obedient and respectful
in his deportment . . . and that he will be governed by the rules and
regulations of the plantation."[51]

Other renters experienced only minimal control from their landlords. For these renters, the arrangement was simply a means of obtaining land to farm, with no expectation of continued supervision
on the part of the landowner. Joseph Hart, a white propertyless man,

was one such renter. In 1866, he contracted with Thomas Venable to sharecrop a large tract of his plantation. The contract specified the land and buildings Hart could use and outlined the upkeep and improvements he was to make. But unlike Allen Oakley, Hart had a great deal of freedom over the daily management of the farm. He was free to select the crop mix and to determine how best to plant, maintain, and harvest the crops. Hart even hired two laborers to work under him. There was no mention of ongoing supervisory rights on Venable's part. Another landlord's only contact with his tenant occurred when he drove out once a year to collect the rent and sign another lease.[52]

This kind of autonomous tenancy had its roots in the antebellum period, when many landless white families rented farms. Following the war, most of the renters in this category of tenancy also seem to have been white. Of course, renters who had their own resources or who came from prosperous families with established reputations in the community were always in a better position to secure more autonomous positions. Such people were not always white, but the legacy of slavery played no small part in the determination. Expectations that African Americans would continue to labor for whites made it difficult for blacks to negotiate favorable rental agreements. By contrast, propertyless whites not only had racial status on their side but they also had been working through labor issues with their landlords for generations. When white renters did have to defend their autonomy after the war, they could point to established standards, both formal and informal, to back up their demands.[53]

Some African Americans did manage to obtain favorable rental agreements. For example, Zack White retained a close relationship with his former master William W. White after the war. As a result, his tenancy agreement allowed him much more independence than other African Americans on the same plantation found in their working arrangements. While Solomon Crews may not have procured his rental agreement in the same way, he managed to rent 500 acres that produced $775 in farm products in 1880. Like Zack White, he is certainly an example of a prosperous black renter who probably enjoyed considerable independence in his working life as well. But the cost of such agreements could be quite high. As Arthur Raper notes in his landmark study of Georgia's Black Belt in the early twentieth century, African Americans had to prove themselves "acceptable" to the white person selling it and to the white community at large before they could purchase land. The white community, in other words, would tolerate economically successful blacks only if they conformed to prevailing racial conventions. Like these landowners, Granville County's black renters may have purchased their tenant contracts at the price of reinforcing racial practices that actually limited their own autonomy and that of African Americans generally.[54]

At the individual level, the lines between agricultural laborers, renters, and even landowners blurred still further. Poor households actually depended on a wide range of different kinds of productive labor to piece together a subsistence. They combined tenancy with various kinds of occasional waged work and the sale of other goods—butter and eggs, meat and vegetables, spun thread and handwoven cloth. Like Benjamin and Mary Burwell, some people were both wage laborers and landholders; others worked rented farms in addition to their own landholdings; still others were, simultaneously, wage laborers, renters, and landholders. Unlike tenants in cotton-growing areas who used all their available acreage for the staple crop, Granville County renters could reserve acreage for food crops. Even wage laborers who leased houses had space for large kitchen gardens, which combined with other forms of household production were crucial components in their families' economic calculations.[55]

These complicated strategies alter our notion of the "agricultural ladder" and its usefulness in determining the success of the poor of both races. The "ladder," on which waged labor, sharecropping, renting, and landownership formed ascending rungs, has played a central role in analyses of social and economic change not just in the postemancipation South but in U.S. history generally. A metaphor for mobility, both upward and downward, the ladder also provides an easily quantifiable measure of progress or stagnation that involves simply counting wage laborers and tenants, distinguishing between renters and sharecroppers, and then comparing the numbers with those of landowners. Yet this conceptualization of the rungs as distinct categories of labor ultimately destroys the metaphor's basic purpose by evaluating mobility in the wrong way. Whether they moved up or down, residents of Granville County generally made use of several "rungs" at once. For them, these rungs were not distinct economic positions, but inseparable components in a single economic strategy.

The ladder, moreover, took different forms depending on the race of those on it. For African Americans, no form of labor organization and no amount of property guaranteed autonomy, when measured by the distance between themselves and their former masters.[56] Even landownership did not always bring the kind of independence they desired. If landholdings were meager, African Americans still had to supplement their income with waged work or tenancy. Although free from the whims of a landlord, they were subject to the vagaries of the tobacco market. As long as the tobacco market remained strong, its presence was not nearly as noticeable as a landlord's. That too would soon change. Even with the prosperity of the tobacco boom, moreover, African Americans still struggled to secure their independence. This struggle continued over time, following them through share wages, waged labor, sharecropping, tenancy, and even landownership.

Labor Conflicts

In slavery, African Americans had constructed their own labor theory of value, based on the idea that those who labor should also reap. After emancipation, many considered the land they had worked and the moveable property acquired through their labor to be theirs. According to a North Carolina Freedmen's Bureau official, ex-slaves had the "idea that they have a certain right to the property of their former masters, that they have earned it, and that if they can lay their hands on it, it is so much that belongs to them." Possession may have been nine-tenths of the law, but neither property nor land could be attained so easily in the postemancipation South. Federal policies scuttled any hopes for the redistribution of land. Seizing their ex-masters' property only landed freedpeople in court, where, if judged guilty, they could be hired out for months to pay fines and legal fees. Frustrated in their attempts to claim the wealth they had labored to create in slavery, freedpeople were determined to take their share of whatever they produced now. They did not stop there. Forging a new path, black workers also insisted that freedom gave them control over their own labor and a measure of independence as well.[57]

Ex-slaveholders had other ideas. Like the "respectable" white men of Franklinton, they wanted "faithful servants." The term suggests the way white planters looked back to traditional laws binding servants to masters in an attempt to cope with a new labor system. Existing laws forcing menial laborers to serve out their contracts and denying them all their wages if they quit early were based on the assumption that labor contracts gave employers property in their employees' labor, thus making it impossible for workers to reclaim their labor at will. Southern planters applied these standards to their own workers when they denied wages to their "servants," who either left before the end of their contract or did not fulfill its terms "faithfully." In their minds, the labor contract created an asymmetrical relation of dependency between workers and their employers; employers might dismiss workers who failed in their obligations, but workers could not quit of their own accord. If southern planters lagged behind the North on this aspect of free labor, they did not do so by much. Northern employers did not voluntarily abandon such power over their workers. Rather, their workers forced them to do so in an onslaught of court cases. Even with the ideology of free labor behind them, northern workers made little headway before 1850.[58]

Like their counterparts across the South, Granville County planters regularly denied workers their entire wages for a single, often minor infraction. Such was the fate of Hannibal Young, who worked for Crawford Kearney. Arriving late to work one Monday morning in 1867, Young was surprised to discover how serious the consequences were. Ultimately Kearney warned him off the plantation and then refused to pay him any wages for the five months he had worked there. While Kearney's response seems extreme, it derived from the assumption that he was paying for "faithful servants" who surrendered themselves entirely to his control, not for discrete lots of labor. His obligation to pay ended at the moment a worker ceased to be a faithful servant. Hannibal Young had. Not only did he claim time for himself and privileged his own interests over those of his employer but he then had the audacity to insist that his actions were legitimate.[59]

The image of the "faithful servant" plagued African-American renters as well as wage workers. In his 1867 contract with freedman Warren Allen, Thomas Lawson promised that Allen would "have entire control" of the farm, apparently allowing him the same kind of discretionary freedom as white antebellum tenants. Halfway through the season, however, he announced that Allen was not managing the farm "as it should be done," even though the crops were in good order and yields promised to be high. As Allen told it, his landlord then "undertook to acquire authority and control." When Allen refused, Lawson became "very angry" and declared that Allen must either submit or leave without pay. Neither alternative was acceptable to Allen, who proposed instead that they settle for the labor already performed. At this point, however, Lawson was unwilling to deal with Allen at all and ordered him "peremptorily to leave," refusing any payment whatsoever. As his actions suggest, Thomas Lawson still saw himself as a master in the very essence of the antebellum legal definition of the term as discussed by Justice Thomas Ruffin. By extension, Lawson saw Warren Allen as a servant who worked "under" him. Because he, as master, retained the "right to have the work done as he pleases . . . to suit his fancy or his other business," the privileges Allen thought the contract granted him were actually contingent. When Allen balked, Lawson threw him out as he would any other unruly servant.[60]

Of course, some workers gave planters reason to complain. Problems with frequent absences and uneven work habits were like those experienced by employers elsewhere as preindustrial workers adjusted to a free labor system mediated by the market. Searching for a way to describe the efforts of his workers, one frustrated Granville County planter caustically remarked: "You might call it no work at all." But according to the local Freedmen's Bureau agent, Thomas Hay, employers regularly turned freedpeople out on "slight + frivolous pretenses." The cases in his files certainly bear out this conclusion.[61]

These attitudes lingered long after the Freedmen's Bureau left the county. In 1876, the Harris family withheld the wages of Fanny Taborn, an African-American laundress, for reasons remarkably similar to those given by Thomas Lawson and Crawford Kearney. When Taborn delivered the weekly wash to the Harris household, William Harris was not there to pay her. She decided to wait. Harris finally arrived in a foul mood. "Keep your mouth off me," he spit back at Taborn when she asked for her wages, making it clear that he had no intention of paying her at that time, if at all. Hoping to avoid a scene, Harris's mother advised Taborn to leave. But Fanny Taborn stood her ground, not wanting to go without her wages. In response, Harris knocked her down and threw her out of the house. When Taborn came back in, Harris struck her with a burning pine rail. Taborn and the Harris family actually agreed on the sequence of events up to this point. Their interpretations, however, were quite different. Taborn focused on her efforts to secure her pay, describing her work in great detail and carefully adding up the amount she would have received for it. She explained that she stayed in the house to collect her wages, not to provoke William Harris. In contrast, Conway Harris, William Harris's brother, represented her demands as insubordination. In his version, Taborn started the fight by "jawing" his brother. She then refused to leave for the sole purpose of further aggravating him. The Harris brothers assumed that they acquired broad control over Taborn's life when they hired her to perform a specific task. As such, they could determine when and if she would be paid. Fanny Taborn's persistence only reinforced the Harrises' belief that she did not deserve payment.[62]

Not all whites agreed with the Crawford Kearneys, Thomas Lawsons, and William Harrises of the county. But neither did they completely reject the image of the "faithful servant." At formal hearings, white witnesses often reached entirely different conclusions about the work of the African-American laborers in question. According to Hannibal Young, the children of his employer's wife thought he should receive his back wages. He also maintained that he could "prove by all white persons who know me that I am a good working hand and that my habits are good." Unfortunately, there is no way to evaluate Young's claims, since no recorded testimony of his case exists. Other cases, however, lend credence to them. Israel Smith flatly contradicted the testimony of a neighboring planter, George Wortham. Appearing on behalf of Aaron and Eliza Wortham, who had worked for George Wortham and were claiming withheld wages, Smith called Eliza Wortham "trustworthy" and claimed that Aaron Wortham had a reputation for being responsible. Smith also supported the character of one of Aaron and Eliza's fellow black workers, calling him "a good farmer and a good judge of work." In another case, planter and court official Daniel Paschall intervened on behalf of Frank Davis, claiming that "he thought and now thinks that there was a combination to defraud a poor negro out of his wages justly earned." Yet, the continual emphasis of white witnesses on "trustworthiness," "responsibility," and "diligence" suggests the limits of their ideas. It seems that white planters were willing to support African Americans when and if they filled the role of "faithful servant." As Daniel Paschall explained, even Davis's employer had acknowledged him to be a "most excellent and trusty servant." Thus Davis became a "poor negro" defrauded of "his wages justly earned" under very specific circumstances.[63]

Racial ideology, particularly the idea that whites commanded the labor of African Americans by right, also structured planters' expectations about labor. In practice, assumptions about race and labor fit together so neatly as to be almost indistinguishable. Vagrancy provides an excellent illustration. In the words of North Carolina's statute, "if any person who may be able to labor has no apparent means of subsistence, and neglects to apply himself to some honest occupation for the support of himself and his family, if he have one; or, if any person shall be found spending his time in dissipation, or gaming, or sauntering about without employment, or endeavoring to maintain himself or his family by any undue or unlawful means, such person shall be deemed a vagrant." The statute thus criminalized idleness for men who failed to provide a subsistence for themselves and their families. Unlike vagrancy laws in other southern states, the language of North Carolina's statute did not specifically target African Americans. Yet the emphasis on compelling men to fulfill their familial obligations betrays legislators' preoccupation with freedmen. The fact that local authorities applied the statute almost exclusively to African Americans is even more revealing. If white southerners found it difficult to think of propertyless men as their own masters, they found it virtually impossible to imagine any black man in that capacity, let alone propertyless black men. Because of the way independence and dependence were racially coded, white men's racial status mitigated doubts raised by propertylessness, allowing them much wider latitude in deciding when and in what circumstances they would labor. Black men's racial position, by contrast, raised doubts. To white southerners, blackness signified African Americans' destiny to labor for others. As other historians have pointed out, white court officials often considered any employment not supervised by whites suspiciously irregular enough to constitute vagrancy. The fact that most ex-slaves entered freedom with little or no property only added fuel to the fire. Conservative white leaders regularly held up freedpeople's poverty to confirm their racial inferiority, as if their position as an enslaved people, compelled to labor for the benefit of others, had no impact on their situation whatsoever. The result was a vicious cycle for African Americans, who were forced into the most restrictive, lowest-paying jobs, with little hope for escape.[64]

Granville County's Major Townes was only one of many North Carolina freedmen to be caught in the snares of vagrancy. In 1866, he found himself before a justice of the peace, charged with "spending his time in idleness and dissipation or having no regular employment or occupation which he is accustomed to follow." If the accusation surprised Townes, the identity of the accuser did not. Only one week before, Townes had filed charges against this same white man, Marvin Self, for assault and battery and won a small settlement at justices' court. The court records reveal no details of the fight, but apparently Major Townes was not one to quietly accept every indignity that might be heaped on him. His victory, however, was short-lived. As a vagrant, the court could bind him out for a year or for such time as it "may think fit," thus stripping Townes of the independence he clearly held so dear. It is tempting to conclude that Self filed the vagrancy complaint in retaliation. Yet, whether intentional or not, it proved far more effective than his earlier effort to beat Townes into subservience.[65]

The threat of vagrancy dissipated somewhat after Republicans gained control of state and local government, but the efforts to tie African Americans to their employers' households did not.[66] It was this tie that freedpeople sought to break. Claiming their labor as their own, African Americans maintained that it required compensation when expended for the benefit of someone else. Their views meshed with ideas of free labor held by local Freedmen's Bureau officials, who often sided with aggrieved workers and ordered planters to pay back wages. After Republicans democratized the state courts in 1868, African Americans found a sympathetic ear with local justices of the peace and the judges of the superior court.[67]

Even then, freedpeople constructed their cases carefully to play to the preconceptions of white officials. Borrowing the language of their employers, they argued that they worked faithfully and would have continued to do so if their employers had not driven them away. Hannibal Young, for instance, maintained that he was regular and prompt in his work. The only reason he had been late on that one day was that an untimely rain had delayed his return from a visit to his mother. Otherwise he had "worked faithfully for Mr. Kearney" and wanted to remain in his employ. Likewise, Warren Allen took great pains to establish his credentials as a faithful servant. Framing his complaint in deferential terms, he explained that he had protested "against the assumption of authority and reminded the said Lawson of the terms of their said contract and which he did in respectful language and took especial pains to [demonstrate?] no discourtesy towards the said Lawson other than to insist upon the observance of their said contract." Both Hannibal Young and Warren Allen contended that they had every intention of completing their contracts, while conveniently avoiding mention of the fact that they were willing to do so only on their own terms.[68]

Yet, even as freedpeople took on the mantle of the "faithful servant" to buttress their claims, they subverted the meanings their employers attached to it. Hannibal Young apologized only for returning late to the plantation, not for leaving in the first place. "Respectful language" notwithstanding, Warren Allen's insistence that he had absolute control of his rented farm utterly contradicted the definition of a faithful servant, who worked "under" and answered to a master. Indeed, the very presence of conflict exposed the chasm that separated African-American workers from their white employers on issues of labor. After all, if freedpeople had really accepted the role of the "faithful servant," they would have followed their employers' decisions without complaint. They certainly would not have initiated legal proceedings to obtain redress. Whatever the outcome of their suits, African-American workers asserted their independent identity in the act of filing charges and enlisting the power of the state. Where white planters had once acted with virtual impunity, African-American workers could now force their employers to defend themselves to an outside authority. The actions of planter Scott Wilkerson, who guarded his black employee's house to keep him from filing a complaint with the local magistrate, threatening to "split [his] head open with a rail" if he did, suggests how disturbing the experience could be. To add insult to injury, Wilkerson and others like him often had to justify themselves to a jury composed of the very people they had so recently commanded at will.[69]

The implications did not escape the notice of those who watched the proceedings. George Vann, in particular, took note. In 1867, Vann, an African American, had been hired for a day by R. D. Horner to move some wheat to a nearby storehouse. Soon after, Horner discovered thirty dollars missing from a trunk in the attic where Vann had been working. Going immediately to the tobacco factory where Vann was then employed, Horner demanded the money. When Vann insisted on his innocence, Horner took him at knife-point to the alleged crime scene to try to force a confession, threatening to "kill him if the money was not produced." Horner then searched Vann and his house for the missing cash. George Vann, however, was unwilling to let Horner define the terms of the conflict. Filing charges of assault and battery against Horner, Vann questioned both his violence and his assumption that he could discipline African-American laborers on his own terms. Horner responded by entering a complaint of larceny against Vann. But Vann, it seems, saw Horner in a very different light now that his former employer could be made to answer for his actions in a court of law. In Vann's words, "he was not afraid" of Horner. Without the fear, Horner's actions neither carried the authority nor accomplished the results they once had.[70]

African Americans not only rejected the demands placed on "faithful servants" but they also offered up a very different conception of their relationship to their employers. Hannibal Young, for instance, believed that he could be a "good working hand" while still exercising the independence to do as he pleased on his day off. Warren Allen went one step further, demanding "entire control" over his time on the job and claiming the kind of independence that white tenants had enjoyed in the antebellum period. Fanny Taborn also scored a victory against her employer. Refusing to be beaten out of her wages, she brought up William Harris on charges of assault and battery. Harris immediately paid her wages, perhaps hoping that she would drop the case. But with the memory of her bruises fresh in her mind, Taborn was not so easily satisfied. William Harris, who was indicted by the superior court, would undoubtedly think twice before he treated another black employee that way again.[71]

Where Warren Allen sought "entire control" over his working life, other laborers simply tried to exercise more control than their employers wished. In an 1866 confrontation, Leonidas Hunt, an African-American wage worker, finally nudged his employer, William Rice, to the limits of his patience. Called on to fetch horses, Hunt ignored the order. When Rice inquired as to the reason, Hunt replied simply that "he had nothing to do with the Horses." Evidently Hunt believed his job to consist of certain duties, and supervision of the horses was not among them. Rice, who clearly thought that Hunt should perform whatever duties he was directed to do, interpreted the response as insubordination and flew at Hunt in a rage. He pulled Hunt's hair so hard it later fell out and then threatened to "nock [his] brains out" with a large rock. Claiming that he "had not given any impudence," Hunt seemed genuinely puzzled by Rice's reaction: "I am forty years old [and] never saw such a fuss before."[72] Much to Rice's irritation, Leonidas Hunt did not believe himself to be at the beck and call of his employer.

Neither did William Allen, although he expressed his desires far more clearly and forcefully than Leonidas Hunt. In Allen's own words, he wanted his employer, John Stem, to treat him like a "man"—as an equal instead of a subordinate servant. The incident began in 1884 when Stem ordered Allen to stop quarreling with the white man he had brought in to oversee the tobacco-curing process. Allen responded that "he was a man, had a mouth of his own and would holler as much as he pleased." An exasperated Stem, his head pounding with a dull ache, left to rest for a few hours. During his absence, Allen stewed and finally concluded that his employer did not accord him the proper respect. When Stem returned, Allen asked him, "Mr. Stem, do you take me to be a child." His choice of words reveal precisely what irked him: John Stem dealt with him as if he were a child in need of adult supervision and answerable to parental authority. In short, Stem expected Allen to work directly under his dominion as a servant. Stem denied the accusation, probably with the conviction that he had given Allen as much consideration as a common laborer deserved. But Allen remained firm: "Mr. Stem you have not treated me right." With this ultimatum, he charged at Stem with a stick, calling him a "rascal and a liar." With this gesture, Allen tried to establish the rough equality he saw between himself and his employer.[73]

Renters had to fight the same battles. Allen Oakley, introduced in the previous section, was one who did. The *Oxford Torchlight,* Granville County's local newspaper, had featured Oakley as one of the county's most successful black farmers in 1879. Yet his landlord, Fielding

Knott, still demanded that Oakley "work by [his] orders" and "be obedient and respectful." For all the economic benefits of his position, Allen Oakley could not bring himself to keep these promises. Four years of endless orders and constant supervision finally pushed him over the edge one day in 1881. When Knott rebuked him, Oakley "seemed to fly into a passion," picked up a nearby chair, and threatened to smash Knott on the head with it. Knott, genuinely surprised, later testified that he "never had any difficulty at all except to exact obedience of those in my service"—that is, aside from the time when he had to "take up a fence rail to a fellow who refused to leave." Knott's confusion at Oakley's actions and his reference to his tenants as "those in my service" are revealing. So convinced was Fielding Knott that servants were supposed to obey their master's demands that he was at a loss to explain or understand Oakley's actions. From the text of the testimony, however, the source of Oakley's frustration seems clear enough. Like Warren Allen and Leonidas Hunt, he wished to have more control over his working life. Perhaps, like William Allen, he also longed to be treated as a "man."[74]

There are far fewer examples of conflicts between common whites and their landlords and employers. Most propertyless white men were tenants who, unlike many black tenants, were more likely to be considered closer to independent landowners than to dependent hired help. White skin, moreover, meant that they did not have to work to establish their independence in the same way as African Americans. When common whites did encounter problems, they appeared less inclined to bring their disputes to local courts for adjudication. The lack of evidence, however, does not mean that harmony always prevailed in working relations among whites. White planters often assumed a certain amount of authority over their white employees and expected some deference and obedience in return, as the comments of landowner Ed Currin indicate. Referring to both his white tenants and black wage laborers, Currin declared, "They knew from the first, I wouldn't stan' no cussin', and I was boss of my land." Currin, in short, exercised authority over all his employees. Although he boasted that he "never had no trouble with [his] tenants, nor [his] hands," he was probably exaggerating. In all likelihood, his expectations inspired resentment, if not open resistance among his workers, white and black.[75]

The 1866 dispute between two whites, Joseph Hart and Thomas Venable, who appeared in the previous section for their autonomous tenancy agreement, is suggestive. It began when Hart defied the terms of his lease by plowing up land reserved for pasturage. Venable, the

The house of Fielding Knott (*above*), probably built soon after his marriage in 1871. The tenant house (*below*) on his lands also dates from the late nineteenth century and is probably similar to the one in which Allen Oakley lived. (Courtesy of the Granville County Historical Society)

landlord, was so removed from the management of the farm that he learned of Hart's transgression secondhand, and only after Hart had already plowed under a significant portion of the forbidden pasturage. Venable stopped by the farm, but Hart refused to see him and Venable had to issue his warnings to Hart's son instead. Hart continued plowing anyway. When Venable finally confronted Hart himself, Hart, according to Venable, "became very angry and violent and refused to stop but stated that he intended to cultivate where he chose." Hart, moreover, claimed that he would continue plowing to "spite" Venable simply because he had "forbid it." As his actions suggest, Hart considered any interference on Venable's part to be unacceptable.[76] The dispute was probably not uncommon, even though there are few others like it in the court records. If Venable and Hart had been able to resolve their differences on their own, there would not be even a trace of this one. Yet the position of propertyless whites, like Joseph Hart, was very different from that of African Americans. Not as independent as freeholders, they still occupied a place far above blacks on the scale of dependency. Indeed, many African Americans worked with the hope of exercising the degree of freedom that Joseph Hart already possessed.

Demanding lost wages, control over the nature and pace of work, and some respect from their employers, freedpeople sought a measure of independence that removed them from their employers' households. But African-American men and women positioned themselves—and were positioned by others—differently in these struggles. Whether as domestics in Atlanta, rice workers in South Carolina, or cotton laborers in Mississippi, freedwomen fought to control their working conditions and as much of their own time as possible. So did women in Granville County, but even the boldest among them did not insist that they stood as equals to their male employers in the way William Allen did. To question popular views that ascribed essential differences between men and women, they would have had to marshal the language to express such sentiments. This would have been particularly difficult outside their own communities, where their voices were filtered through the preconceptions of whites and the laws of coverture. The legal and economic practices of white southerners placed black men at the heads of their families, whether they or their families liked it or not. Planters in rural areas like Granville County contracted with entire families, but dealt with men as their representatives, thus imposing a simplistic patriarchal model and ignoring women's positions of power within their families. The law further undermined women's authority by hampering their ability to contract in their own name and control their wages. As we will see in chapters 4 and 5, the majority of poor African Americans did not accept the gender roles of elite white southerners, and women were particularly vocal in claiming what they perceived to be their rights. Nevertheless, they too tended to identify men as the public representatives of their families. For all these reasons, Granville County women generally appeared as members of families with male spokesmen when they appeared in labor complaints.[77]

Black men could also use their familial responsibilities to buttress their claims in labor conflicts in ways that women could not. As Hannibal Young carefully pointed out, "I have a family to take care [of]." Warren Allen also emphasized that he was not the only person affected by his employers' actions: Allen "left his family upon the said farm, but does not know at this moment whether they have been permitted to remain. That he is now without a home and without employment, and has no means of livelihood for himself + family except his interest in said crop, and unless he can find immediate employment elsewhere, or can realize something for his labor already bestowed upon said farm in the immediate support of himself + family they will be obliged to suffer." Robert Hunt, another black tenant, explained to the Freedmen's Bureau that his employer wanted to drive him away "so that he may get all." Hunt protested not only because he had already "furnished the hardest work" but also because his employer was "trying to turn my wife + three small children out of doors." Everyone in the Hunt family worked together to meet their collective needs, but on some level, it was Robert Hunt who assumed public responsibility for their well-being. Rawlins Royster, who worked with three other black share-wage workers on William Thorp's farm, made a similar complaint to the bureau's state headquarters. Royster asked: "Please direct the Bureau office at Henderson to investigate our case and make Thorp [the employer] pay us our money which we need badly to buy provision for our family." As these men well knew, their responsibilities for their families gave added weight to their claims. The logic was hard to refute, given the legal duties of a household head to provide for the economic needs of their dependents.[78]

African-American men's insistence on filling their place as household heads limited planters' efforts to define the labor relationship on their own terms. Robert Hunt's predicament is particularly revealing. Four days before he wrote to the Freedmen's Bureau, his employer, James Edmunds, filed a complaint against Hunt with the justice of peace for "posing a threat" to his life. Two days later, Hunt filed a complaint against Edmunds for the assault and battery of his wife

Tempy. This series of events may be coincidental, but it suggests a prolonged battle between Edmunds and Hunt. A likely scenario is that Hunt resisted Edmunds's attempts to throw him out without pay. Edmunds, enraged at Hunt's assertive behavior and perhaps more than a little frightened by it, swore out a complaint against him. It seems that Edmunds then tried to evict Tempy Hunt while her husband was not around. Hunt retaliated, swearing out a complaint against Edmunds and writing to the Freedmen's Bureau for assistance. All the while, it would appear that Hunt maintained his position, refusing to bow to Edmunds's threats. As the incident escalated, Hunt's resistance took on new meanings. His attempt to collect his family's earnings turned into an open struggle against the presumed power of an elite white man to use intimidation and violence at will against an employee's family.[79]

African Americans' efforts to limit white planters' control of black women and children had similar effects. If white employers could take African Americans out of their own households and command their labor at will, then black workers would remain "servants" in the truest sense of the term. Planters could destroy a family's ability to earn a subsistence by apprenticing its children. Some even bound out children in order to coerce entire families into unfavorable labor contracts. The withdrawal of African-American women from full-time paid labor also turned on these issues. Whites angrily denounced black women who did so, revealing a strong sense of entitlement to their labor. African Americans flatly rejected such claims. Whether they stayed home to remove themselves from exploitative working conditions or to concentrate their energies on their own households, women and their families claimed the labor as their own. Even when they hired out their children's labor, African Americans refused to cede parental control to employers. Black parents closely monitored their children's working conditions and regularly intervened if they thought the employer made excessive demands or disciplined too harshly.[80]

Daniel Bullock, whose son Young worked for Robert Kirkland, was one such parent. When he learned in 1872 that Kirkland had whipped his son, Bullock immediately marched over to Kirkland's place, son in tow, and demanded to know what Young had done to deserve such treatment. Kirkland explained that Young had taken too long to complete an assigned task. Adding that he had promised to whip Young again if he ever came back, Kirkland began cutting switches. Bullock stopped him with strong words: "I said no don't do that, if you want him whiped I will do it to your satisfaction, as I have done before." Bullock's reasoning is unclear. Perhaps he was willing to admit that his son might need disciplining or perhaps he saw the futility of challenging Robert Kirkland's opinion in this matter. But whatever his reasons, Daniel Bullock believed that he, not his son's employer, should be the one to administer punishment. To do otherwise would be to undercut his own position by allowing his son's employer to assume the parental role instead. Young Bullock lost out either way. Indeed, this case provides another, more conflicted view on freedpeople's efforts to establish households that I will explore in more detail in chapter 4. African Americans did not always agree on how households should be structured from within, even if they could generally agree on the necessity of defending their borders from dangers without.[81]

African-American laborers failed to completely sever the link between waged work and dependence. In 1874, the state supreme court upheld the 1866 enticement act and affirmed that laborers fell under the private dominion of their masters. "There is a certain analogy among all the domestic relations," Justice William B. Rodman wrote in *John R. Haskins* v. *F. A. Royster,* "and it would be dangerous to the repose and happiness of families if the law permitted any man under whatever professions of philanthropy or charity, to sow discontent between the head of a family and its various members, wife, children and servants. Interference with such relations can only be justified under the most special circumstances." This decision and the assumptions that grounded it added ammunition to the arsenal of those who would later seek to exclude African-American and poor white men from public power. As dependent laborers, Democrats would argue, they had no more business participating in the affairs of state than women or children.[82]

Yet poor blacks, with the help of some propertyless whites, did manage to destabilize Rodman's view of the labor relationship. They continually brought labor disputes to local courts for adjudication, blurring the line that Rodman used to keep labor conflicts in the private realm. In the process, they also assumed public personas that no antebellum servant, white or black, ever could. This was particularly true for men, who insisted that they be recognized as heads of households with all the public privileges attached to that role. Their success was reflected in Edwin G. Reade's impassioned dissent in *Haskins* v. *Royster.* He believed the decision a grave mistake, arguing that it condoned labor practices far worse than slavery and provided no viable mechanism for employees to challenge their employers. In illustrating the implications, he used an image that echoed those of

African-American working men in Granville County. As "men with families, the year gone, and all their earnings gone," he pointed out, their only "alternative is the poor house or crime and the jail." Reade saw black tenants and laborers as household heads, and he was not the only white man in North Carolina to do so. As the 1860s gave way to the 1870s, elite whites within Granville County also reluctantly abandoned the idea that all black workers would remain as their dependents and grudgingly admitted the institutional legitimacy of African-American households. In so doing they acknowledged a degree of independence for all laborers, men and women, that they initially had been unwilling to concede.[83]

Wealthy whites in Granville County directly engaged the claims of working people who claimed independence by constructing new standards to distinguish their households from those of their poorer neighbors. It was elite white men and women, not their political leaders, who shouldered this task as part of their effort to reestablish the privilege and power they had enjoyed before the war. The implications of their daily labors carried profound political significance: if everyone now had households, not all households could be equal and, by extension, neither could their inhabitants. Therein lay a powerful new justification for racial and class inequality. Poor African Americans and common whites countered with their own social vision, which they too rooted in their own households. Thus, before turning to the subsequent political struggles, we must first spend some more time within the households of elite whites as well as those of poor African Americans and common whites. It was here that most southern men and women first confronted the frustrations and the possibilities of life without slavery and began refashioning their identities to accommodate these changes. Their responses shaped life within households and then reached out into the public world, where they grounded larger social and political goals.

3

"Rich Men" and "Cheerful Wives": Gender Roles in Elite White Households

The changes unleashed by war and emancipation shattered the center around which elite white men and women organized their identities, their roles within households, and their place in the social order. "Annie the Butterfly: A True Story" represents, in microcosm, the nature of the crisis. Appearing in an 1875 issue of the *Oxford Torchlight*, the story traces the fictitious lives of Annie and Harry Silverton from their prewar position as wealthy slaveholders to their postwar experience of poverty and personal despair. Before the war, the Silvertons took the privileges of their wealth and status for granted. Harry Silverton, a powerful patriarch, managed the business affairs of his prosperous plantation and ruled over an extended household that included numerous slaves. His success enabled Annie to become a "butterfly," a delicate creature untouched by the responsibilities and cares of life. By the time of southern surrender, however, little remained of this way of life. Despite Annie's best efforts, the family's lands lay in ruins and their money, livestock, and slaves had vanished. Harry arrives home from war wholly unprepared to rebuild what his family had lost. Hobbling on one leg and leaning on one arm, his physical injuries signal the presence of far more debilitating emotional wounds that never really heal. Unable to make the transition from slaveholder to employer, Harry rents his lands and moves to town to practice law. Unfortunately, he proves as inept at this as he was at farm management, and as his practice languishes, so does his health. Having long since ceased to resemble the man he once was, he finally surrenders when his own inability to support his family forces Annie into waged work. Unable to bear the humiliation, he dies.[1]

The loss of the family's wealth and status also destroys the core of Annie Silverton's world. But if Harry Silverton represents personal failure in the face of postwar change, Annie Silverton's example points toward successful adaptation. Curbing her lavish ways in favor of economy and sacrifice, she takes on more of the housework, works to create a pleasant home with limited resources, tries to rally the flagging spirits of her family, and even works for wages herself. During the course of the story, Annie metamorphoses from a butterfly into a "faithful and unselfish wife." In the process, she marks out a new role for herself and her class in a way that her husband does not.[2]

In its dramatic extremes, "Annie the Butterfly" misrepresents the lives of Granville County's white elites. Few slaveholding families engaged in the Silverton's self-indulgent display of material luxuries or endured their utter destitution following the war. Nonetheless, the resemblance between the name of the local author, Annabelle White, and the heroine, Annie Silverton, suggests the extent to which fiction followed fact. The similarities came not in an accurate depiction of postwar economic conditions but in a portrayal of the confusion and fear that many ex-slaveholding men and women experienced as they tried to rebuild their lives in a postemancipation world.

"Annie the Butterfly" was only one of many articles in county newspapers to offer guidance for elite white men and women by focusing on their roles within households. In a format common to local newspapers across the state, the *Oxford Torchlight, Granville Free Lance,* and *Oxford Leader* filled their pages with short stories, poems, and human-interest features that examined men's and women's proper roles and respective duties. These pieces counseled women on cooking, housekeeping, interior design, and fashion; they directed men in the details of farming and business management; and they continually lobbied both sexes on the wisdom of these ways. The *Oxford Torchlight,* the first postwar newspaper as well as the longest-running and most popular one in the county, blazed the way. Although they incorporated the same kinds of prescriptive literature, the *Granville Free Lance* and the *Oxford Leader* ran for much shorter periods and only scattered issues have survived. In this chapter, they play supporting roles to the *Torchlight*'s lead, just as they did among the county's white readership.[3]

Together, these three Granville County newspapers helped redefine elite status. But the resulting image was not simply a reflection of the editors' individual ideas. All three newspapers had local owners and editors, although they changed hands regularly and experienced a high rate of staff turnover. The content and format, however, remained remarkably stable. One reason for the continuity was the strategy used by many local newspapers at this time, mixing their own original articles with pieces gleaned from other publications—both southern and northern. As a result, these three newspapers looked strikingly similar to other small-town and rural newspapers across the state.[4]

Their editors, moreover, did not unilaterally impose their message on an unwitting audience. Granville County's local elites wrote for and commented on much of the material themselves. In fact, the *Torchlight* also served as a combined gossip column and bulletin board for them, covering the white elites' comings and goings as well as providing a public space for them to air their views. Both men and women took part. Elite white women eschewed certain public arenas, such as the courtroom, where poor white and black women appeared. But their names were highly visible and their voices were distinctly audible in the pages of the local newspapers. Like the periodicals they read and contributed to, the elite white men and women of Granville County were themselves linked to a larger social network. Writing columns of domestic advice for the *Torchlight,* Oxford's Sarah A. Elliott ultimately acquired a regional reputation with the publication of her cookbook, *Mrs. Elliott's Housewife,* and, later, a domestic novel, *Days Long Ago.*[5] Although the literary careers of other local columnists were confined to Granville County's newspapers, they too wrote from their experience within social circles that reached well beyond the county's borders. This public discussion then continued in private correspondence and diaries, in which the county's wealthier whites explored the same issues on a more personal level. What emerges from these two sources is a dialogue about personal identities with much wider implications. On one level Granville County's white elites were grappling with the changing logistics of daily life; but these practical difficulties would have been relatively easy to master if not for their connection to the larger question of power and privilege. The advice literature addressed both issues simultaneously, meshing race and class with gender to form images of ideal men and women that would ultimately provide the foundation for elite whites' status in a postemancipation world.

Granville County's white elites were not unified socially, economically, or politically: some possessed great wealth, while others made do with more modest means; some had controlled vast acreages and many slaves, while others were farmers, businesspeople, and professionals on a smaller scale; some were on their way up economically, while others were on their way down; some were from long-established families, while others were aspiring newcomers; some were Democrats, others Republican. The members of the elite actually moved in two concentric circles, encompassing a diverse group of people who nonetheless shared elements of a worldview. The first circle centered on a small core of wealthy people whose social lives and business dealings were covered by the *Torchlight* and who recognized each as part of the same "elite" group. The second circle reached wider, including people who were not wealthy, did not always meet the material standards of the new domesticity, and did not associate personally with those in the first group, but who still accepted and aspired to many of the same cultural precepts. Both groups, moreover, agreed that society should be organized hierarchically, that there should be an elite, and that they were part of it.

They also agreed that postwar change had cast society loose from its moorings, setting it adrift in dangerous waters. The collapse of slavery destabilized the racial and class distinctions on which antebellum society had rested. African Americans were not only free, they were demanding independence and, in the company of many nonelite whites, challenging the inequalities that had existed among independent citizens. To use their terminology, elite whites feared "social equality," where all distinctions among men and among women vanished and anyone could do or be anything.[6] In response, they looked to the household for ways to rebuild crumbling social hierarchies, settling finally on rigid domestic standards as well as personalized standards of manly and womanly conduct. The essential ingredient in creating proper homes and an orderly society, the domestic literature assured its readers, was neither wealth nor power, but good character. Men secured the necessities of domestic life through hard work, while women transformed the raw materials into a comforting atmosphere through creativity and love. Together, their efforts resulted in tidy, respectable households that became the building blocks of a harmonious society. As other historians have argued, the ideologies of domesticity and merit could buttress the agendas of those who sought to open up southern society in various ways: African-American leaders, both men and women, placed these ideas at the center of their efforts for racial uplift, economic progress, and political power; some common whites climbed up meritocratic ladders and others held up their good character to claim positions of social respectability previously denied to them; reform-minded elite white women later depended upon these same concepts to launch their entries into public life.[7] But in the hands of conservative white men and women, domesticity and merit could also serve very different ends. They used these interlocking ideologies to forestall their critics and to obscure and justify the glaring inequalities that actually structured postwar society. After all, the acquisition of a well-appointed house and the maintenance of the proper domestic interior required far more than good character. Such standards, moreover, universalized from the experience of the white elite, holding up their particular aspirations as the "natural" goals of all men and women and condemning those who lived otherwise as personally immoral and socially irresponsible.

Annie the Butterfly

In "Annie the Butterfly," the author defines Annie and Harry Silverton in terms of overlapping hierarchies of gender, race, and class, grounded in the institution of slavery. Harry Silverton was a slaveholder, a landowner, and the member of a prominent family, while Annie acquired her sense of self through her relationships with the men in her life. The wife of a man who owned slaves, land, and a prominent name, she was also the mother of a male heir. The same held true for Granville County's real-life slaveholders. Although no "butterfly," Sophronia Horner's view of the world closely resembled that of the Silvertons. In her mind, the lives of those in her immediate family and those of the slaves she and her husband owned were inseparable pieces of a larger whole. In fact, she so thoroughly mixed the two together in her letters that it is difficult for an outside reader to tell who is who. It was Horner's rigid sense of hierarchy that made this kind of slippage possible. She did not need to use racial markers because slavery already located everyone on the plantation in a distinct place from which, at least in her mind, they did not stray. Beyond her household's borders, the world fell out in ranked order according to class. Horner, for instance, bemoaned the hardships suffered by her husband, relatives, and family friends during their service in the Confederate army. But she accepted without question that enlisted soldiers, generally poorer white men, would have none of the conveniences she considered absolutely essential for the men in her family, who were commissioned officers. Indeed, she bristled when commissioned officers had to endure the same material deprivation as enlisted men. While genuinely fearful for her loved ones' welfare, Horner retained her sense of class position and her interest in maintaining the privileges that marked it, even during the crisis of war. Herbert Gregory, the son of a wealthy Granville County planter and elder brother of William H. Gregory, whom we will meet later in this chapter, would have agreed. In 1865 he wrote a curt letter to Governor Vance requesting either a military commission or governmental position: "I have served 15 months in the army as a private in infantry and know from actual experience that I cannot stand active service as a private." Clearly, Gregory thought this reason enough.[8]

There was little room for movement or change in Sophronia Horner's worldview, particularly for people of African descent. In 1861, as Horner awaited the arrival of her own child, a family slave named Susan delivered a very fair-skinned baby boy. Fascinated by the child's skin color, the Horner children puzzled over how to categorize the new arrival. "Ma," Horner's daughter observed, "Susan's baby's hands are just as white as *us*." Her son finally concluded that the child was not really Susan's: "Ah Suse you cant fool us, niggers dont be that white." For Sophronia Horner, who probably had her own suspicions as to how the child came by its light skin, identity and status were not so fluid. Although the child may have looked white, "it is nevertheless a negroe." Horner's statement actually revealed much more about herself than it did about the newborn slave child, because of the way she, like other elite white women and men, realized their identities and their social privilege through their relationships with those around them. Sophronia Horner could maintain her sense of self only as long as the status of Susan's child remained fixed.[9]

War and emancipation upset the relative positioning of Susan's child and Sophronia Horner within southern society, causing a personal as well as a social upheaval for both men and women in the slaveholding class. In Granville County, as elsewhere, their sense of confusion could be profound. Fearing for their property and personal safety, some barricaded themselves in their houses or stationed armed guards outside with orders to shoot to kill if they saw anything suspicious. Others frantically appealed to the court for protection from both African Americans and whites who, they alleged, had promised imminent harm. Of these, a few lived in a state of psychological siege, certain that untoward looks or muttered words cast spells that could eventually destroy them.[10] Others expressed their despair in images of decay. The despondent refrain of R. A. Jenkins, a tobacco manufacturer in Granville County, was not unusual: "With us you see on [the] wayside the blight and the mildew, every interest is ruined, morals are loose, and religion exist[s] only in name." Surveying the changes around him, planter Henry W. Jones found the scene almost unrecognizable: "It looks like the war that has past has corrupted every thing." Jones's friend, Lucy Edwards, concurred: "Our county appears to be in great confusion. . . . It appears like the whole World is turn[ed] up side down."[11] In the process, it had flung everything and everyone so far out of alignment that even men and women from the elite class could no longer fulfill accepted patterns of personal conduct.

In relation to men, the image of a world turned upside down betrayed fears that they could no longer provide for their families as they should. James H. Horner, the husband of Sophronia, entertained doubts on this score even before the war ended. A slaveholder, the head of a well-known academy for young men, and an ardent secessionist, Horner had organized one of the county's first Confederate companies, the Granville Grays. He left for battle certain that his duty to his new country and his family were one and the same. Within just a few months of his departure, however, he began questioning his earlier priorities. After separating the two as distinct responsibilities, he ultimately placed them in conflict, concluding that a married man's responsibility to the "families dependent upon them" took precedence over all other demands. This logic forced Horner to confront the possibility that he had risked everything for nothing. For him, support for the Confederacy might end only in a devastating personal failure, regardless of the outcome of the war.[12]

In fact, Confederate soldiers soon discovered that the war had beaten them at home as well. Faced with ruined fields, dilapidated buildings, confiscated stock, an emancipated labor force, and scattered fortunes, few could escape the unsettling sense that they had failed as men. The story of Harry Silverton's homecoming captures the double defeat many experienced. Walking up the path to his house after five years of war, Silverton is shocked by the sight of his son plowing the fields, work he considered appropriate only for poor white and black men: "'Plowing! my boy—my baby! It is too hard!' and he passed his thin hand across his brow. . . . And how it hurt to think his son, the heir of all these broad but worthless lands, should be compelled to toil for his scanty daily bread." Shorn of his property and slaves, Silverton can only stand by and watch as his son is reduced to manual labor. This incident is the first of many failures that impoverishes his family and emasculates Silverton to the point where he is, quite literally, no man at all. When his wife must work to put food on the table he reaches the nadir and releases his hold on life altogether.[13] Working to rebuild his academy and plantation, James H. Horner may well have sympathized with Harry Silverton's fictional frustrations. Both enterprises eventually prospered, but not before Horner experienced an emotional breakdown serious enough to warrant hospitalization at the state's insane asylum.[14]

These same feelings of guilt and inadequacy haunted Confederate men for years following the war. As other historians have shown, they exorcised the demons through "The Cult of the Lost Cause," a revision of the Civil War in which they became brave warriors in an honorable but hopeless effort to defend a noble society.[15] Like other local newspapers across the South, the *Torchlight* actively participated in this mythologizing process. Welcoming the one hundredth anniversary of the nation's founding with a large dose of Confederate pride, one writer boasted that "there is nothing in the past for which the South need be ashamed." Another article then soothed the consciences of men like James H. Horner, judging the South's defeat honorable because its soldiers' goals—the protection of their "homes and firesides"—had been so irreproachable. Although these "brave and heroic" "chieftains" went down in defeat, their personal integrity and their manhood remained intact. Behind its soothing certainty, the article's shrill insistence and defensive tone suggests that more than a few "chieftains" needed reassurance on this point.[16]

The collapse of slavery, while linked to the Confederacy's defeat, delivered its own disorienting blow. Harry Silverton might have overcome his physical injuries, his shattered confidence, and even his poverty if not for the loss of the slaves whose captive labor made his plantation profitable. Beyond the economic implications, emancipation affected Silverton in an intensely personal way, changing the reflection he saw in his mirror each morning just as surely as it changed racial and labor relations outside his front door. Without the absolute mastery he wielded as a slaveholder, Silverton slowly diminishes in stature over the course of the story until he becomes physically bedridden. His decline captured the fears, if not always the actual circumstances, of real-life slaveholders who were accustomed to occupying center stage. Slavery, which allowed African Americans only limited room to challenge their masters' assertions of authority, lulled slaveholders into thinking that the world actually did revolve around them. Emancipation shattered this illusion, providing African Americans with new opportunities to act in their own interests and leaving elite white men feeling displaced. Considering the enormous amount of power they continued to exercise over African Americans, this sense of marginalization distorted reality as much as the sense of complete mastery had. But the power they lost loomed much larger in their minds than the power they retained.[17]

The experience of Charles Harris, the adult son of a white Granville County planter, suggests why. After the war, Harris was supervising several black laborers working in his family's tobacco fields when a fight broke out between two of the men, Reuben Dodson and Dick Smith. Initiated by Dodson and Smith for reasons having nothing to do with Charles Harris, their disagreement moved quickly from verbal threats to physical violence, ending abruptly in the death of Smith. Shoved to the side, Harris was left scrambling around the edges trying to exert some control over the situation. His own words betrayed how ineffective he was: "When he [Reuben Dodson] took up the stone a second time [I] interfered and told him it was time to stop that. Dick threw down the stone but [I] cannot state [word illegible] at what particular point of time, he threw it down whether it was when [I] interfered or afterwards." Clearly, Dodson and Smith paid little attention to him. Engaged in the argument and riveted by the action, neither did the other workers. Silas Elam, for instance, focused his description of the fight on the action between Dodson and Smith, mentioning only in passing Harris's efforts to intervene. Even then, Elam's acknowledgment of Harris's presence underscored his marginality: "When Dick drew the rock upon Reuben Mr. Charles Harris interfered and told him 'to quit.' After Mr. Harris interfered Reuben said nothing but Dick kep quarrelling holding the rock in his hand." Harris faded away into the background after this brief appearance, and the fight continued with Dodson and Smith in the spotlight. If anything, Harris's unsuccessful intervention set off the self-absorbed virility of the two black men more.[18]

Harris remained peripheral even when the case came to trial. In the courtroom, his words carried much more authority because of his racial and class position. Nonetheless, his concerns did not enter into the deliberations in the same way they would have during slavery. In all likelihood, an antebellum court would not have heard a case like this one, particularly if the two men involved had been slaves. Instead, Harris would have mediated the conflict and meted out punishment, reasserting his authority over all those who worked on his plantation in the process. Emancipation foreclosed this option, at least in contrast to the antebellum period. The trial dealt solely with the events leading up to the murder, completely severing it from the workers' open defiance of Harris's authority. Perhaps Charles Harris did not notice any change in his reflection when he looked in the mirror. But it would have been difficult for him to miss his marginality during the whole ordeal or to overlook the way it undercut his authority over his work force. No doubt his workers also took note.

Elite white women viewed postwar change from a slightly different vantage point. Initially ardent supporters of the Confederacy, many lost their enthusiasm as the war dragged on, taking away their menfolk and sapping their resources. Some, like Sophronia Horner, made their reservations clear from the outset. Where her husband felt torn between his duty to the Confederacy and his duty to his family, she entertained no doubts whatsoever. "I do not think," she wrote emphatically, "it is the duty of any man to cacrifice his own life unnecesarily, and leave his own little ones to the cold charity of an unfriendly world." Other white women agreed, as a small mountain of complaints to Confederate officials suggests.[19] The cessation of hostilities brought some relief, but elite white women's lives got worse before they got better. While some of the women who lost their husbands and male relatives in battle found emotional support and material aid in their extended families, others had to piece together their lives on their own.[20] But whether their menfolk came home in one piece or not, all elite white women faced a wrenching period of transition as they came to terms with a world in which they were no longer slaveholding mistresses.

Emancipation and economic dislocation stripped them of the visible symbols of their class status, challenging their sense of womanhood just as surely as it undermined their menfolk's sense of manhood. During the war, elite women tightened their belts and continued to do so in the lean years immediately afterward. For most, however, the pain of poverty was a relative condition. A cousin of Elizabeth Hargrove, a wealthy widow in Granville County, made this point in relation to "cousin Mary" who "thinks she is very poor now, because she was once so well off." Given the precariousness of her own position, as a widow who barely eked out a living by her needle, this woman found her pampered cousin's complaints irritating. The comparison would have been lost on cousin Mary, who clearly evaluated her life in terms of what it had been. Poverty, moreover, presented a different set of problems for elite white women like Mary than it did for her poorer cousin. While poor women worried about where their next meal was coming from, wealthier white women were more concerned with the way that economic instability obliterated class distinctions. They might not be "very poor," but without the necessary material possessions, they were more easily confused with those who were. Emancipation heightened elite white women's fears by calling racial boundaries into question as well. Sophronia Horner, for instance, could identify Susan's child as black because she knew Susan to be a slave. Without slavery, racial lines became much less certain. No longer a slave, the light-skinned child of Susan might be white. Or, if the racial categories operative in slavery ceased to be meaningful, the child's race, white or black, might be of no consequence whatsoever. Armed with laws designed to prevent such racial blurring, elite white women and men diligently policed racial boundaries. Yet their preoccupation revealed more about their own sense of racial instability than anything else.[21]

Slavery had not only marked but also enabled elite white women's class position. Without it, the class distinctions that had separated elite white women from both black and poor white women blurred. In a fictional moment that mirrored the experiences of many elite white southern women, Annie Silverton watched, horrified, as all the slaves on her family's plantation left. "Poor creatures!" she observed, unable to grasp the meaning of their hasty departure, "how much better off are they now?"[22] Like so many ex-slaveholders, Silverton displayed concerns for African Americans that were more apparent than real. Projecting anxieties about her own future onto the departing slaves, her comment actually contained the question of how she would manage without slaves. On many plantations, what money there was tended to go into the farm or business. With little left to hire domestic help, elite women had no alternative but to shoulder more of the housework themselves. "There's hardly a day," wrote Doug Lacy from Raleigh to his sister in Granville County, "when some poor females who used to earn their living by sewing for the rich comes round looking for work + can't get it because those for whom they used to work now have to do all their own work." In fact, he continued, "Many of the wives and daughters of men who used to live *in style* are now taking in sewing to support their families!!" "We are right independent," wrote Jennie, a young correspondent of Elizabeth Hargrove, contrasting her current situation with her life in Granville County before the war. She, her cousin, and Mrs. Carr, the other white woman with whom she lived, "clean[ed] up the house ourselves" and even cooked, on occasion. The novelty, however, soon wore off. Exasperated by a stove that threw soot all over the house, she complained, "Nothing in the home can be kept clean. Oh! Miss Elizabeth I wash and wash, cut my nails almost to the quick and all for no purpose. I tell you it almost runs me crazy."[23] Jennie probably found a sympathetic audience in Elizabeth Hargrove. This kind of drudgery was new to most elite white women, who had always relied on slaves to perform the heaviest household chores. Indeed, the image of an elite white woman sweating over a hot stove or scrubbing on her hands and knees was comparable to that of Harry Silverton's son plowing.

Even when there was money, ex-slaveholding women still had trouble recruiting and retaining domestic laborers, particularly on the terms they favored. As we will see in the next chapter, African-American women wanted to work for their own families, not those of elite white women. When economic need compelled freedwomen to work for others, they insisted on a different set of standards, refusing to accept low wages, long and inflexible hours, and demands that they live in their employers' homes. Their defiance prompted a steady stream of complaints from their white employers about irregular work habits and presumptuous conduct. "I am so vexed + tormented by freed women I can scarcely contain myself," fumed one woman to her sister in Granville County. "The negroes," Jennie informed Elizabeth Hargrove, "are so demoralized." This included, among other things, a reluctance to perform domestic labor for elite whites. As Jennie explained, "it was a long time" before Mrs. Carr, one of the women in her household, "could get any one to cook and she can't get any one to nurse her child." As a result, Jennie found herself exploring new household frontiers, such as tending a cranky stove. Each outburst told volumes about elite white women's own difficulties adjusting to a life in which they were no longer mistresses of slaves. As free workers, African-American domestics now had the leverage to ignore their employers' whims, wishes, and orders in ways that had been impossible during slavery. Unused to having their desires pushed aside, elite white women took black women's actions as personal affronts.[24]

Not surprisingly, many elite white women floundered in their attempts to establish authority over their domestic servants. The experience of Mrs. Pines was not unusual. When her black servant, Sarah Barnett, disregarded an order, Mrs. Pines tried to coerce Barnett's obedience through physical force. Refusing to budge, Barnett struck back. More commonly, black domestic workers in similar situations would have walked out, dumping the heavy housework back into the laps of their white employers. When they did, there was little for employers to do, short of finding a more acquiescent worker. As the high rate of labor turnover in domestic service during the years following the Civil War suggests, workers of this kind were few and far between. Mrs. Pines and her husband tried another approach, charging Sarah Barnett with assault. But, however satisfying the Pineses' ultimate court victory was, it hardly resolved the couple's domestic labor problem. After watching Barnett's conviction and sentencing in court, they returned home to the task of hiring a new servant. Given recent events, it is probably safe to conclude that few lined up to apply.[25]

The fictional Annie Silverton's example set the standard for elite white women to emulate. She economized and sacrificed, while standing by her man in loyal silence, never holding him responsible for the family's hardships. Sophronia Horner also suffered in silence. Although firm in her conviction that husbands should look first to the well-being of their families, she never blamed her husband directly for his absence, conveniently overlooking that he was one of the founding members of his military company. Instead, she deflected her criticism onto the officials who, in her mind, burdened him with too many responsibilities and refused to grant him enough leave time.[26] Other elite Granville County women were not so saintly. When the *Torchlight* printed an 1874 article entitled "Hen Pecked Husbands" that portrayed women as parasitic shrews, Polly Pepper, a popular local columnist, responded indignantly. If women were grumpy, she argued, it was because of the inadequacies of their men: "Ladies, when kindly treated and properly cared, and provided for, are not the unreasonable and ungovernable creatures some surly curmudgeons would have you think them." In fact, according to Pepper, women were far more competent than their menfolk: "If some men were more under the control, and were more ruled by their prudent wives than they are, they would be much better men than they are."[27]

The hapless Harry Silverton comes to mind. Ultimately, Annie Silverton's silence on her husband's failures cut far deeper than the sharpest words of condemnation ever could. The author created a story with a heroine, but no hero, laying the blame for the family's downward slide directly at Harry's feet. Even his tragic death seems cowardly in comparison to Annie's heroic efforts to hold the family together. Yet the author was not entirely unsympathetic either. She portrayed Harry as a good person caught in bad circumstances. He never figured out how to provide for his family in a free labor society, because he failed to grasp that land and slaves were no longer the requisites of power. In this sense, the lessons of "Annie the Butterfly" were clear. Annie provided a role model for elite white women, but neither she nor her real-life counterparts could bring their families safely through the crisis on their own. For wealthier whites to avoid the Silverton family's fate, the "best wives" would have to be joined by men who could also surmount the challenges posed by emancipation, aiding their womenfolk in the reestablishment of their material fortunes as well as their power and privilege.

This was the challenge that commanded the attention of the county's newspaper editors and contributors as they retooled elite ideals of womanhood and manhood for postwar use. At first glance, the self-made men and the domestic women who populated the pages of the local newspapers and the correspondence of Granville County residents seem to be paragons of northern liberalism reincarnated on southern soil. The northern influence, however, can be vastly over-stated. With the onset of congressional Reconstruction, the North made it clear that elite white southerners could no longer flaunt a social system that denied basic rights on the basis of race and class. But soon thereafter, conservative southern elites found that they had as much to fear from their southern detractors as their northern ones. By the late 1860s, many common whites, African Americans, and all those who leaned in the direction of the Republican party actively resisted all attempts to reinstitute the antebellum social and political system. In response, conservative whites sought to explain their lives and to justify their status and power in a way that would be acceptable to both their northern victors and southern critics.

Never the exclusive property of the North, the values associated with the hardworking businessman and the domestic wife also had deep roots in the South. This was particularly true in North Carolina because of its diversified economy and the success of evangelical religion. Indeed, the gender roles promoted in the state's antebellum newspapers prefigured those that appeared after the war. Prescriptive literature and popular expressions of manhood featured self-mastery and, to a lesser extent, industriousness and attention to market incentives. Similarly, devotion to family, the importance of motherhood, household management, and the expectation that women would serve as helpmeets to their husbands regularly punctuated antebellum commentaries on womanhood. Indeed postwar invocations on all these themes resonated among elite white women and men precisely because they had already absorbed so much of the message.[28]

Yet the newspapers' contributors and readers did not simply carry the past into the present. They borrowed ideas, republishing articles and short fiction from northern newspapers, and struck out in new directions on their own, addressing specific issues they faced as a result of war and emancipation. "The change of times in the South," wrote Oxford's Sarah A. Elliott in the preface to her cookbook, *Mrs. Elliott's Housewife*, "indicates to woman there a solemn duty." Yet Elliott spoke to specific changes in the South from within the larger tradition of Victorian morality and domestic economy, spicing her recipes with a large measure of household wisdom: "Woman exerts a vast influence upon society as well as in the ordinary scenes of life, and to her is intrusted a moral power that hardly knows a limit." The best way to exercise her moral power, realize her social duty, and serve both her earthly and heavenly masters was through "a well regulated, systematic management of his household affairs." Such a house-

This photo of Sarah A. Elliott appeared as the frontispiece of the 1870 edition of *Mrs. Elliott's Housewife*. (Courtesy of the North Carolina Collection, University of North Carolina, Chapel Hill)

hold would renew the spirits of the housewife's absent companion, her economically successful husband who came home after a hard day in the world outside. Sarah A. Elliott even sent a copy of her cookbook to the paragon of domesticity, Queen Victoria, who, mindful of her manners, sent back a thank-you note. The popularity of the cookbook within North Carolina suggests the chord it struck among elite white women. According to the *Charlotte Democrat*, "Mrs. Elliott's Book ought to be in every household in the State."[29] The origins of such ideas are difficult, if not impossible, to trace. Elliott, for one, claimed them as her own and rooted them in her antebellum past. But then the origins are not as important as the way their proponents applied them within a dramatically transformed social context. The unique conditions of the postemancipation South meant that elite white ideals of manhood and womanhood performed different kinds of ideological work, even when they appeared very similar to antebellum or northern models.

"Rich Men"

The self-made men who populated the pages of the local newspapers contrasted sharply with the financially inept Harry Silverton. Where he balked at economic change, these men relished its challenges. In 1874, the *Torchlight* article "Rich Men" captured the essence of their economic outlook: "The rich men of the country are those who were trained to some business pursuit in their boyhood and have concentrated all their efforts in that direction since. Nine out of ten of the five hundred millionaires in the United States to-day began life without any capital, and have hoed their own rows to fortune and fame." For the "rich men" of this article, all work was dignified and no job was too mean: "Vanderbilt commenced his great business career by rowing people across the Hudson in a skiff at ten cents a head," A. T. Stewart began as "a bundle-carrier in a store," and the president of the Pennsylvania Central Railroad first toted "the surveyor's chain on the very road that he now has millions of interest in." The article concluded that the "roads they have traveled are open wider and smoother to the young men who follow them."[30]

Of course, few captains of industry made their homes within Granville County's borders. The *Torchlight,* which hoped that the county would one day become the "Birmingham of the South," never gave up on the prospect of changing this situation. In the meantime, however, it also addressed the needs of its largely agrarian readership. So did the *Granville Free Lance* in a weekly farm column that wove lessons on the virtues of industriousness, punctuality, and good business habits into its practical advice on tobacco, corn, chickens, mules, and manure. The same qualities outlined in "Rich Men," both newspapers assured its readers, applied equally well to farmers and aspiring businessmen who planned to stay in the county. In this view, any man, even from the lowliest background, could become rich and powerful through hard work, resourcefulness, and close attention to the latest in farming techniques. This was particularly true in Granville County, which local newspapers portrayed as a beacon of economic opportunity for all those with the spirit to heed its call.[31]

An 1879 series written by Capt. J. B. Hunter, offering agricultural hints and outlining the careers of local farmers, illustrates the kind of advice the newspapers directed at local farmers. Hunter, himself a prominent planter, described the multifaceted operations of other large-scale planters, explaining the planting and curing of high-grade tobacco, the cultivation of various other crops, the care of large herds of stock, and the supervision of paid farm laborers. But he also spent a great deal of time on small landowners and renters, emphasizing how their diligence and resourcefulness had resulted in economic success and upward mobility. Hunter and the farmers he profiled viewed their fields through a very different lens than Harry

Silverton did. Where Silverton saw only his own defeat and emascu-lation in the image of his son plowing, Hunter and his fellow farm-ers discerned new economic opportunities through which to realize their manhood. Like Vanderbilt and other "rich men," the Silverton son might well be hoeing his own row to fortune and fame.[32]

Earned wealth, in fact, came to rank higher than inherited wealth. Harry Silverton actually had many companions in the pages of the local newspaper. They, like him, served as warnings to those men who refused to adapt to postemancipation life. The romantic short stories that appeared in virtually every issue of both the *Torchlight* and the *Granville Free Lance* extolled men's diligence and hard work in vari-ous business pursuits. Those who worked hard and those who con-tinued to value hard work even after they had obtained some wealth were rewarded with lasting financial success and personal happiness, which usually took the form of a beautiful and loving wife. Those who took their riches for granted and disdained the value of labor gen-erally experienced economic collapse and personal despair.[33] "Young man go to work" was the advice in the *Torchlight*. "Maul rails, plough, cut wood, anything that is honorable, rather than loaf around on your friends and relatives." "Men everywhere," warned a writer in the *Granville Free Lance*, "want success without paying its price in thorough preparation, honest hard work, intelligent calculation and foresight, patient attention to details."[34] Wealth, in other words, was not bad, but the idle rich were.

The emphasis on labor seemed favorable to Granville County's poorer residents. Indeed, many of them approved of the lessons in these articles for precisely this reason. But the logic behind them also obscured the fact that those who held the wealth in Granville Coun-ty generally owed it to their inheritance from slavery, not their own labor or good character. Even with the setbacks caused by the war, whites in the slaveholding class entered the postwar period with far more resources than either African-American or propertyless white men. The flourishing tobacco market meant that most elite white men also avoided prolonged destitution. In this context, assertions in the *Torchlight* that every man had the power to make his own for-tune masked the economic inequalities built into the system. By in-sisting that all men "earned" success in the same way—through per-sonal sweat and blood—articles in the newspaper transformed preexisting differentials in wealth into evidence of individual merit. The valorization of labor worked on another level as well, for the fruits of propertyless men's labor, whether white or black, also went to their employers and landlords. Thus, elite whites reaped tangible benefits in the immediate present when all men were encouraged to work hard for future rewards.[35]

At the same time, wealthy whites drew the line around their private property ever more clearly. The numerous prosecutions for petty theft, by far the most common case in the court dockets between 1865 and 1870, are suggestive. Most involved white planters who accused freedpeople of stealing food, livestock, household goods, portable luxury items, tobacco, and cash. Slaves had drawn no firm line between their property and that of their masters and routinely appropriated various items for their own use. They had also claimed certain subsistence rights, such as foraging, hunting, and fishing on both public lands and unused private property. Many freedpeople probably viewed petty theft in similar terms, as a way of acquiring subsistence items that were their right. Some freedpeople may have used "theft" to regain wages they thought were unjustly withheld or to force their employers to assume some responsibility for the economic maintenance of their workers. Others were simply acting on established rights to appropriate resources that were going unused. Considering the hard times following the war, a few freedpeople may also have seen "theft" as a necessary means to redistribute wealth to those who needed it more.[36]

It was these attitudes about property that wealthy whites were prosecuting. Indeed, the effort expended on cases that involved only a few chickens, a peck of corn, or a bushel of potatoes suggests that more was involved than just the recovery of property. White planters sometimes took days to track down the culprits, measure footprints, search people's houses, and interrogate witnesses. After they identified their suspects, they spent even more time in court prosecuting the case. Conviction was almost a foregone conclusion, even when the evidence was slim, which it often was. The courts, for instance, convicted many defendants on evidence of possession. But how conclusive could possession be when all plucked chickens looked pretty much alike? Neither corn, nor potatoes, nor slabs of hog meat had any particularly distinguishing features either. In other instances, muddy shoes or footprints, which were abundant in a rural county with notoriously bad roads, constituted irrefutable "proof" of guilt. Together, these cases suggest that identifying the thief was not as important as prosecuting the theft. If successful, complainants might eventually be reimbursed for their loss after the court hired out the convicted parties to pay for their fines and court costs. But even in a depressed postwar economy, the monetary value of items like a peck of corn was small. In many cases, the amount recovered certainly would not have compensated for the time and effort spent in finding and prosecuting the culprit. The planters who prosecuted the crime, moreover, did not always obtain the direct benefit of the convicts' labor, because the court often placed them with someone else. Whether or not they ever received the equivalent value of the lost property, however, planters affirmed and enforced their vision of property rights, which they later elaborated in fence laws and hunting restrictions as well. Property, from this perspective, was a private, not a public, resource. As the *Torchlight* would add, particular individuals acquired it for their exclusive use through hard work and good character.[37]

The rhetoric of individual achievement could obscure racial inequalities as well. For instance, the praise J. B. Hunter bestowed on several successful black farmers in no way implied a positive attitude toward the race as a whole. Instead, he used their experiences to erase the racial barriers these men had worked so hard to overcome. Their example, Hunter concluded, proved that all African Americans could attain economic success as easily as whites, if they only worked hard and persevered. In one broad stroke, he made African Americans completely responsible for their own fates, while also affirming the inherent equity of existing social and economic relations: "The negro is, and will be, under our law, the architect of his own fortune, having the same rights, the same privileges and the same encouragement to stimulate him to many efforts for his own advancement and promotion as the white man enjoys."[38] Hunter's assertions, however, did not make it so. African Americans neither enjoyed the same rights as white men nor controlled the same economic resources nor wielded the same power. Low wages, inadequate acreage, poor farmland, and miserly landlords provided a far more compelling explanation for endemic poverty than did laziness. Not only did race heighten existing economic inequalities so as to place blacks at a structural disadvantage in relation to whites but whites also deployed vigilante violence to warn blacks back into their "proper" place. All this left African Americans few materials with which to build their economic fortunes.

The kind of character required for economic success was not just virtuous, but manly. Indeed, the pieces in the *Torchlight* increasingly conflated manhood with a particular kind of economic success. As one article explained, there was a good reason why some farmers had "steadily grown richer" since the war. Keeping their eyes open for new economic opportunities, these industrious farmers had shifted to tobacco production in response to market incentives. In contrast, their poor neighbors, described as starving and naked, remained hide-bound by tradition and insisted on staying with less profitable crops, such as cotton. No matter of chance, their poverty resulted from a lack of character and, more specifically, from deficiencies in their manhood: "It is all with the man whether he 'grows poorer and poor-er every day' or richer and richer every day." Just in case anyone missed the point, the author repeated it: "It is in the men."[39] Mea-suring manhood by success in profit-oriented business pursuits, the *Torchlight*'s contributors assumed that everyone found the call of the market as compelling as they did. That same year, the newspaper tried to lure "capitalists and workingmen" into Granville County's tobac-co economy with the promise of fat profits. Of course, prosperity appealed to everyone. But the article, which listed only tobacco prices and provided no other information about the area, presumed an audience that considered market incentives before all else.[40] No doubt, those who responded would have it in them as men to succeed.

While business prowess formed its core, virtuous manhood also included self-control, proper manners, and devotion to home, fam-ily, and God.[41] The temperance movement, which became popular in Granville County and elsewhere in North Carolina in the years following the Civil War, blended all of these traits together in a sin-gle cause, linking moral uplift and self-mastery with the fulfillment of men's social and economic duties. The Granville County Good Templars had both male and female members, but the organization's literature identified men as the problem drinkers. Consumption of alcohol was a sin because "God never made alcohol." This unholy product of decaying fruits and grains then destroyed the body and the mind, making men virtually unrecognizable as such: "Man, the last and noblest work of his Maker, *a slave!* Led captive through our streets, in the chains of earth's most galling slavery! A diseased and loathsome victim of the traffic in intoxicating drinks and the perni-cious customs in society!" As slaves to their appetites, unable to sup-port their families or fulfill their obligations as citizens, drinking men ultimately failed not just themselves, but all those around them. Tem-perance, then, was the only way to realize true manhood: "Stand up wherever you go, in the true nobility of your manhood, with this enemy beneath your feet . . . as you march on, MASTERS OF YOUR-SELVES."[42]

Self-mastery required years of instruction beginning at an early age. Local schools, such as James H. Horner's academy, responded to par-ents' concerns that their boys learn the qualities that would make them good men. The proud father of one student was pleased to hear that his "dear boy was living up to his promises in the discharge of his duty and the manly avoidance of every temptation." In turn, Horner expected his students to enter with a working knowledge of the rudiments of proper etiquette. His high standards startled one father, who received a written rebuke for not teaching his son to practice the proper restraint in the use of violence.[43] Horner also instructed his students to avoid indulgence in worldly pleasures and emotional excess of any kind. "By inculcating moral rectitude as the basis of character," the 1876 promotional pamphlet promised, the students would acquire "those qualities which constitute a *well regulated* mind." A strict code of discipline helped accomplish these ends. The school required students to attend church, to keep their rooms clean and orderly at all times, to extinguish their lights at night, and to arise promptly at the appointed hour. Tobacco, alcohol, swearing, visiting the nearby town without special permission, and "any other species of immorality" were all forbidden. The school's mission was to make both "good boys and good scholars."[44]

In the minds of Granville County's white elites, moral virtue complemented the acquisition of wealth as well as the acquisition of knowledge. The Horner Academy claimed that its course of instruction was "intended to furnish the student with a complete business education." M. N. Wilson would have agreed with these priorities. While in Texas in the mid-1880s, this Granville County native learned that the younger sister of a close friend had joined the church. He was very pleased, particularly since the young woman was at that impressionable period in her life, "when all the allurements and temptations of the world are so fascinating." But it seems that Wilson did not find money or the many creature comforts it could buy among the temptations he so feared. Complaining of high prices in Texas, he listed a four- or five-room house and full-time domestic help as basic necessities. Nonetheless, "if any body is willing to put up with" the "inconveniences" caused by high prices, he believed that "they will get rich after [a] while." Then, presumably, a man could provide his family with a proper lifestyle, the material standards of which seemed quite high. To William H. Gregory, who became editor of the *Torchlight* during the 1880s, wealth was so admirable a goal that he found it as natural to pray for the state of his finances as it was to pray for the state of his soul. Writing to his fiancée, Mary Davis, he urged her to include him in her evening devotional: "Please remember me, and ask softly and sweetly with gentle devotion that I may be righteous, happy, and successful in business."[45]

William Gregory's words sound self-serving. But he and other elite whites blunted the sharp edges by directing the acquisition of wealth toward particular ends. No matter how wealthy, a man remained in-

James H. Horner, from "Horner Military School, Annual Catalog, 1905."
(Courtesy of the North Carolina Collection, University of North Carolina,
Chapel Hill)

complete without a wife and home of his own. Without them, according to Gregory, "Life is a failure, our Destiny unfulfilled, and our Existence, ever, but a blank."[46] Not just any house, however, qualified as a home. As M. N. Wilson's moral priorities indicate, elite white men and women considered household goods and conveniences to be necessities, not self-indulgent luxuries or worldly temptations. A happy marriage, in fact, depended on a well-appointed home. Even romantic love could not sustain a marriage outside an appropriate domestic setting. In the *Torchlight*'s words, "But though marriage without love is terrible, love only will not do."[47] Since the trappings of a suitable household required money, men had to possess either wealth or earning potential in addition to charm and good looks to become eligible bachelors. Mary Davis, for instance, needed years of convincing before she finally married William Gregory. One of her reservations was his financial position, and Gregory gave repeated reports and assurances on this subject. He had cause for concern. Davis had already turned down at least one suitor because he did not have "the brightest prospects for success in the future."[48]

Mary Davis's and William Gregory's fascination with finances informed their courtship and even gave shape to their expressions of personal endearment. Pining over their separation, Gregory longed for the time when he could see her and "talk over business matters fully *my dear* in a pleasant familiar way." Even when Gregory daydreamed of the life they were to lead together when married, his thoughts never strayed far from business. In one such imagining, he told Davis that he saw them "sitting cosily by a cheerful sparkling fire. . . . You will be darning, while I write a few business letters."[49] To these two lovers, property was very romantic. It would allow William Gregory to purchase the material comforts that he longed to provide for his new wife, and it would enable Mary Davis to be the kind of wife she hoped to be for her husband. Here the fictional Silverton family comes to mind once again. Annie Silverton may have triumphed over poverty, but it was her devotion to home and family, not her husband's poverty, that made her a heroine.

"Cheerful Wives"

The companion of the economically successful man was the industrious, selfless housewife. As represented weekly in the pages of the *Torchlight,* the *Granville Free Lance,* and the private correspondence of Granville County residents, the ideal woman's life revolved around her home and family, both of which she tended with loving, self-sacrificing devotion. She created a comfortable, cheery home to uplift the spirits of her family, she oversaw the preparation of appetizing meals to rejuvenate their bodies, she stood by her husband's side as his most trusted companion, and she directed their children's moral, religious, and academic education. All these feminine qualities had roots in the antebellum period. Yet these values took on a new meaning and a new urgency for elite white women after emancipation, when the basis of their status had disappeared. In this new context, domesticity recentered their identity and, ultimately, renewed their sense of racial and class superiority.

Granville County's newspapers produced an endless stream of domestic advice, frequently written by local women and widely ranging in content and focus. Romantic poems and short stories, like "Annie the Butterfly," all spotlighted heroines who shunned the temptations and excesses of wealth to embrace the virtues of hard work and loyalty to their husbands and families. Although these fictional pieces might appear as a leveling rejection of wealth and privilege, they were not. The stories did reward industrious housewives with happiness and marital bliss and punished those women who wallowed in luxury and leisure with either death or spinsterhood. But when unmasking the villain, they revealed individual women who placed their own pleasure before the interests of their families, not an economic structure that supported vast inequalities in wealth.[50]

For those who were slow to glean the moral, the prescriptive literature communicated its main components more directly. Women, it maintained, achieved personal satisfaction by directing their attention away from themselves toward the needs and desires of their immediate families. "Luxurious entertainments and [a] routine of fashionable living," promised one such article, would never produce the "pleasure" that "constant attention to the physical, religious, and intellectual education" of their families would. More to the point, submerging her own identity within those of her husband and her children was the only appropriate way for a woman to realize her social role. As an article entitled "No One Lives for Herself Alone" explained, it was a woman's destiny: "There is an instinctive impression which inhabits the mind of a young girl that she is some day, to be required to live, hope and care for one other than herself, that she is to brighten the household of someone with her presence." Or, as another piece bluntly stated: "For the girl is dead that's single." This was also the moral of Sarah A. Elliott's novelette, *Days Long Ago.* After her marriage, the heroine, Aurelia, turns her back on society life in favor of domestic retirement, finding complete fulfillment in her role as a devoted wife and mother until her husband's untimely death. Overcome with grief, Aurelia faces a test of her womanhood: she can either selfishly indulge her sorrow and remain a widow or remarry and return to her proper calling as both a wife and a mother. As her favorite aunt reminds her, her sons alone cannot provide the kind of direction or purpose that marriage will. When they grow up, she will be left alone once again. Two weeks later, Aurelia arrives at the same conclusion, puts her pain aside, and takes a suitor. In Elliott's world, there is no place for a woman alone. Indeed, the women who graced the *Torchlight*'s pages took feminine self-denial to new heights, cheering along their more apathetic and self-indulgent real-life counterparts. The more extreme the sacrifices she made for her family, the better the woman. "No One Lives for Herself Alone" ends with a vignette of one mother's excruciating descent into poverty, which culminated in her refusal to eat so that her children might have more food. When questioned by a sympathetic passerby, the woman explained, "'I would be willing to die that my children might be permitted to live.'"[51] By the standards established in the prescriptive literature, there was no other response a "good" woman could give.

Fate tested the resolve of these prescriptive heroines far more often and severely than that of its female readership. Yet, if the choice faced by the starving mother was theoretical, the expectations it embodied were not. In the correspondence of Granville County's elite white men and women, the essence of a wife and mother lay in her ability to subordinate her own interests to those of her family. Congratulating his brother William on his marriage to Mary Davis, A. R. Gregory penned a rendition of womanly virtue that read as if cribbed directly from one of the *Torchlight*'s articles: "And now . . . you are blessed with . . . a good wife[,] a loving and constant companion to minister to your wants, to watch over you, to sooth and cheer you with her benign influences in all your trials, troubles and afflictions." William Gregory himself had continually referred his fiancée to similar standards on womanly conduct published in the *Torchlight*.[52] As she entered married life, Mary Davis clearly had her work cut out for her. Admittedly, her situation was unusual, since her husband-to-be was on the newspaper's staff. But then again, she strictly adhered to the same standards herself.

The events surrounding her marriage reveal the depth of her commitment. True to her role as a dutiful daughter, Mary Davis postponed her wedding to William Gregory when her father died so that she could attend to her mother. Afterward she continued to put off the marriage because her mother disapproved of the match. At this point, Davis faced an impasse. To become a good wife, she would have to assert herself and defy her mother, thus negating the very essence of the self-sacrificing role she hoped to assume. After an eight-year engagement, the couple finally arrived at a unique solution. They eloped while Davis was visiting Gregory in Richmond, where he was convalescing after a serious illness. As they explained to their friends and relatives, Davis had only agreed to marry without her mother's approval or their families' knowledge because she feared for his life. The crisis, the couple maintained, demanded that she put aside her own selfish concerns and focus on William Gregory's welfare. At least, that was their official line. At the time of the wedding, William Gregory appeared well on his way to a full recovery, not on the verge of death. Perhaps his illness and the time together away from home provided the excuse for which they had long been waiting. Or perhaps it was easier for Davis to reject her mother's wishes once she was in another state. At any rate, while nursing her new husband in St. Luke's Home for the Sick on her wedding day, Mary Davis finally managed to achieve the position of a "good wife" in the eyes of her friends and family. Her sister's reaction was typical: "I am at a loss for words to commend you enough for the grand and noble deed you have done. I am sure no man ever obtained more fully what he needed than Buck has [in] the kind sympathetic and affectionate wife you will make him." Mary's mother was considerably less enthusiastic, complaining that she had not been given the "respect due a mother." Yet, despite her grumbling, she too interpreted her daughter's decision as an admirable, selfless gesture and promised to "receive Mr. Gregory as one of my family."[53]

Other elite white women also ordered their lives around the same feminine ideal, although their expressions of it were far less dramatic. Family formed the central theme in their correspondence, providing the means through which they related events in their own lives and communicated their sense of identity. Embedding themselves so thoroughly within a dense web of family relations, they relegated their own lives to the margins, sometimes neglecting to make any direct reference to themselves at all. They noted additions to their circle of family and friends through marriage and birth and chronicled changes in the young ones as they grew, lingering with particular care on the growth and accomplishments of their children. Where some strands grew stronger, others stretched thin. Friends and family moved away and children left their parents' houses to start lives of their own, while illness and death took a staggering toll. But even

The childhood homes of William H. Gregory (*above*) and Mary Davis Gregory (*below*). While lavish by antebellum standards, both seem plain in comparison to the sprawling, highly ornamented houses built by Granville's elite after the Civil War. (Courtesy of the Granville County Historical Society)

death could not completely sever the ties that bound people to their place in this web of relations. As these women conceived it, family members simply moved from their earthly homes to their heavenly ones, where their cares would cease and they would be reunited with their families.[54]

While central to elite white constructions of womanhood, the noble subordination of self to family obscured the racial and class components of this feminine ideal by elevating the importance of individual character over all else. To a certain extent, the fictional fantasies of abject poverty expressed the hardships faced by the many elite white women widowed by the war. They also gave voice to the secret fears of many married women, who knew all too well that their economic fortunes rose and fell with those of their husbands and male relatives. An untimely death, a bad investment, or a dissolute mate might plummet even the wealthiest woman into poverty, as the story of Annie Silverton made so painfully clear. "Unforeseen circumstances," warned Sarah A. Elliott in her cookbook, "may make a change in your life": "The beautiful home of your bridal days, with all that wealth could accomplish, to beautify the grounds around your richly ornamented dwelling, surrounded by highly picturesque scenery, filled with sumptuous furniture, and with every convenience, may have to be placed under the sheriff's hammer, and exchanged for a simple cottage furnished with unpolished wood." If so, then it was a woman's responsibility to "make that home happy, by cultivating a cheerful, happy disposition." The tales of Annie Silverton and the starving mother also assured their readers that familial devotion and a little feminine ingenuity were the foundation of a wholesome home. Flowers would brighten both the inside and outside, shelves would help order the clutter, and a sunny smile would raise the spirits of everyone in the family. "A tasteful woman," the *Torchlight* informed its readers, "can make a garret beautiful and homelike, and at little cost; for the beauty of home depends more on educated and refined taste than upon mere wealth. If there is no artist in the house, it matters little that there is a large balance at the bank. There is usually no better excuse for a barren home than ignorance or carelessness."[55] From this perspective, Annie Silverton and the starving mother both followed Mrs. Elliott's advice, cleaving to the values of elite white womanhood in the most trying circumstances and thus retaining their place as true women.

The emphasis on feminine ingenuity did open up elite status to women from wealthy families impoverished by the war as well as aspiring women from modest backgrounds. But good intentions alone were not enough for all women. These same constructions of womanhood, for instance, subsumed whiteness within virtue. The racial subtext emerged not in direct references to skin color, but through an implicit contrast between the virtuous and the depraved, whose female faces were always black. The *Torchlight* scattered its references to African-American women liberally through its pages, where they appeared as the inversion of the elite ideal: promiscuous seductresses, heavy drinkers, hard fighters, ignorant housekeepers, and inattentive mothers, not to mention bad dressers. Concerned only with gratifying their own immediate desires, they always left chaos in their wake. "The usual quiet of our streets was disturbed by a rather unusual scene on last Sunday afternoon," began a typical lament:

> It seems that there had been an unpleasantness between Mr. Peter Cash, a gentleman of the African scent, and his better half, on account of his leaving her for the superior attractions of one Lina Hudson, whose blue dress and fine gingercake complexion had captured his too susceptible heart. On Sunday after noon, Mrs. C. met with her rival on the street and a pitched battle ensued, in which blood, wool, and sundry garments mixed with cuss-words, were scattered around promiscuously. Fortunately the combatants were separated before any material damage was done on either side, and they went their ways, muttering vows of vengeance on each other.[56]

While ridiculing African-American women with these negative images, the *Torchlight* set up a dynamic relationship between them and its own positive feminine role models, defining the desirability of the ideal through its opposite. This racially encoded process banished black women from the borders of elite womanhood by depicting them as the representatives of everything utterly incompatible with the most minimal standards of feminine decorum. As African-American women were forced to the margins, the whiteness of those women who defined the ideal became visible and inseparably entwined with the order and harmony they represented.

If the "best" women were not black, they also were not poor. All the newspaper's pieces linked happy domestic scenes with certain kinds of homes. Clean, neat, comfortably inviting, and tastefully decorated, these private havens separated family life from the public world. Even Annie Silverton and the starving mother were still situated in this concrete material context. They triumphed as paragons of female virtue even in the absence of a domestic setting that fostered proper family relationships. Far from negating the importance of domesticity's material trappings, the example of these women affirmed it.

The lessons to real-life women were clear. To fulfill their obligations as women, they had to maintain the proper domestic environment. Although it was possible to do so on their own, it was much easier with an economically successful husband. Indeed, elite ideals of womanhood and manhood existed in a mutually dependent relationship. Women's domestic work gave men the emotional support to go out into the world of work and politics, where men's work provided financial support and political protection for the home. It was men's responsibility, then, to supply the prerequisites of domesticity, among which was an appropriate house.[57] When Mary Davis Gregory set about homemaking, she did so in a two-story house her husband had built in anticipation of their marriage. Theirs was only one of many residences constructed in a building boom that began in the 1870s. Those with the resources to do so abandoned the relatively modest size and open floor plans of antebellum homes in favor of sprawling, elaborate layouts with a proliferation of rooms designated for specific activities and neatly divided into public and private spaces. Others updated their existing houses, fencing in their yards, modifying the interiors, and adding porches, entryways, specialized rooms, and second stories.[58]

These improvements were designed around a specific vision of family life. In *Days Long Ago*, Sarah A. Elliott has Aurelia's new husband describe his vision of their life together through the rooms of their new house: On one "side is the dining room, and contiguous, the chamber we will occupy. The upper floor has nicely furnished chambers for your guests. Under a large oak tree, in the corner of the yard, I have recently built an office, and while discharging a lawyer's onerous duties, with but little time at my disposal, I can hear your sweet voice from the sitting room, behind the parlor." Not only was her husband's workplace distinct from Aurelia's private haven but public and private spaces were clearly demarcated within it, with each room serving a particular function. Although Elliott claimed to be describing a colonial home, her description was obviously influenced by late-nineteenth-century culture and fashion. As Catherine Bishir has argued, the "Picturesque Mode"—an architectural style that "presented beguiling views of buildings as picturesque ensembles, complete with landscaping and even furnishings"—inspired many of the architectural changes in Granville County and elsewhere in the state. Picturesque house plans appeared everywhere, from popular women's magazines to the pages of local newspapers. If the images were more appealing to potential customers than traditional architectural drawings geared to the needs of builders, so was the cultural message attached to them. "Proponents of the Picturesque," writes Bishir, "asserted that its pleasing irregularity of form stirred the emotions, while the associations it stimulated in the knowledgeable viewer (or demonstrated to the less erudite) would uplift the morality of both the building's resident and society at large." In 1873, the *Warrenton Gazette* featured a picturesque gothic cottage on its front page and urged area residents to emulate its style to "raise" the standards of family and community life. Given the new Victorian structures sprouting up along Oxford's streets and the surrounding country crossroads, it would seem that such prompting was unnecessary.[59]

The contrast between Mary Davis and her mother, Ann, hints at the difference between antebellum and postbellum expectations. After Mary's marriage, Ann urged her daughter to return to her childhood home so that she could help nurse William Gregory back to health. Yet she worried that they might be reluctant to stay in her house, because both Mary and William were "much more particular" about domestic order than she.[60] Ann Davis, who was born to one of the elite slaveholding families in the county and then married into another wealthy household, could not have been referring to the lack of material comforts. Neither her letters nor those of her daughter indicate any want of money, even after Mary's father died. The allusion might have been to Ann Davis's own distaste for household management, for which, it seems, she had been criticized by her daughter before. But, if the new couple's discussions of their ideal home are any indication, Mary Davis embraced a very different set of domestic standards than those her mother had lived with for most of her life.

The real contrast, however, lay not with elite antebellum homes, but with the houses of the poor. The *Torchlight* looked down its nose at their drab one- and two-room frame dwellings with no separation of public and private spaces. Locating the immorality of the lower classes there, one article argued that "idlers, spend-thrifts, and horse-jockeys" would become "intelligent and useful farmers" if placed in the proper domestic setting. Articles in the newspaper also complained continually about irresponsible mothers who allowed their children to play on the streets instead of supervising them within the healthy confines of a properly domestic space. By the 1880s, the editors of the newspaper had identified the houses of the poor, particularly poor African Americans, as a major health risk. Instead of pressing for expanded public services to cart away trash, provide running

DESIGN FOR A COTTAGE.

FRONT ELEVATION.

We give herewith a very pretty design for a Gothic Cottage, for the engravings of which, we are indebted to Bicknell's Village Builder, the design being by Mr. A. J. Bicknell, the publisher.

The Gothic Cottage, of which, in the first plan we give a perspective view, and in figures two and three, respectively, plans of the first and second floors, can be completed at a cost of from $2,000 to $3,000, according to locality and style of finish. The plan, which is made on a scale of one-sixteenth of an inch to one foot, explains itself. The elegant exterior shown in the perspective view, will receive the approval of persons of taste. Without the commanding appearance of more ambitious edifices, such a house, surrounded by tastefully arranged shrubbery, and placed on an appropriate site, would present a very pretty appearance, as our readers will see at a glance. There is nothing, the remedy for which is always at hand, that we so much neglect, as the architectural design of our dwellings ; and we publish the plans herewith, in order that the evil may be corrected in our vicinity, at least.

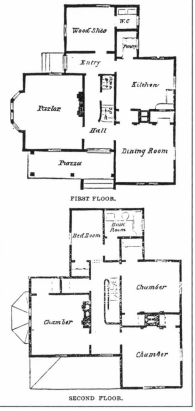

FIRST FLOOR.

SECOND FLOOR.

water, and light the streets in poor neighborhoods, the editors advocated punitive measures, blaming the poor for their failure to repair their homes and meet basic standards of cleanliness.[61]

By contrast, the editors of the *Torchlight* reserved special praise for new private residences and improvements in existing homes. More than ostentatious displays of wealth or evidence of economic progress, these domestic icons conferred respectability and imposed order on the entire county. According to articles in the *Torchlight*, the exterior facades also spoke directly to the character of those who lived within. The editors applauded men who improved their yards and residences for their prosperity and civic virtue.[62] The "best" women, of course, always accompanied such men. When editors of the newspaper boasted that Oxford's "girls" were far superior to those anywhere else because they were "the most domestic and the best wives," they were not referring to the character of all or even the majority of the town's women. Only forty-nine qualified, according to editors of the *Torchlight*. Most obviously, they were all white. It is also probably safe to conclude that they lived in the large houses over which the editors continually crooned, not in shotgun shanties or even modest cottages.[63]

Feminine resourcefulness could only go so far in transforming the house's interior into a home. Elite white brides entered married life with wedding presents, "essential" items whose value lay less in their daily usefulness than in their ability to display their owners' status. Sarah Grand, a contemporary of Mary Davis, received "numerous bridal presents, from a silver tea-set to a thimble." Fine china, table linens, and crystal often filled out the gift lists.[64] Afterward, husbands picked up the slack. William Gregory, who married after he was securely established in his career, presented Mary Davis with a rich cache of domestic paraphernalia in addition to the house: "Every day or two," he wrote, "I add [a] little something, it seems, to our household collection. It is hard for me to resist buying crockery, glassware and furniture at least occasionally."[65]

Opposite: Layouts and descriptions for cottages like this one appeared regularly in late-nineteenth-century newspapers and magazines. As the accompanying text notes, the design was not only functional and comfortable but also morally uplifting. Published house plans like this one clearly influenced Granville County residents in both Oxford and the surrounding countryside. Some built new homes and others altered, added on, or embellished their existing homes to keep up with changing fashions. (*Warrenton Gazette*, 9 Apr. 1873; courtesy of the North Carolina Collection, University of North Carolina, Chapel Hill)

Even Sarah A. Elliott betrayed the importance of the material trappings of domesticity in creating the ideal home. Explicitly addressing rural housewives, she assumed that every house had an indoor bathroom (although probably without plumbing), a formal dining room and parlor, separate bedrooms, glass windows with curtains, and finished floors with carpets. A "simple" kitchen included an array of pots, pans, dishes, and other cooking implements in addition to china, glassware, and silver, all kept in specialized storage spaces. Above all, Elliott's homes always contained domestic servants. Waxing eloquent on the importance of setting a table properly, she maintained that "the snow-white" tablecloth "speaks the character of the housewife." While allowing that a "clean white table" might do for "those unable to enjoy the luxuries of life," it soon became very clear that the labor expended on cleaning the cloth or table would never be sufficient. In the very next sentence, Elliott elaborated an extensive list of other "necessities": "With her pure white china or ware, polished from hot water and soap, her castors bright and well-filled, her knives and forks shining, the napkin folded tastily in the crystal goblet and the salt-cellar with fine sifted salt by each plate, the nicely printed butter with bright spoons lying by, her husband is not afraid to urge a friend to partake of his frugal meal." Presumably, Sarah A. Elliott was describing the ideal to which housewives should aspire, not the way farm women—even the most prosperous—actually set their tables. But the images still clash. Women who owned even a few of the items on Elliott's list would rarely be forced to preside over a frugal meal.[66]

Those women who married less propitiously than Mary Davis had to scramble to keep up. Bettie Shotwell, the wife of a comfortable but undistinguished farmer, determined to take on paid work to speed the completion of her new home and furnish it according to her tastes. Spying an advertisement that promised income for china painting, she wrote her friend in Massachusetts for advice. Although unenthusiastic about this particular scheme, Shotwell's northern friend was sympathetic with the desire for a more modern, gracious home. She also could not resist a little Yankee moralizing, pointing out that "the times are hard every where and it is only by industry and the closest economy that people with moderate means can live comfortably." Given these circumstances, she continued, northerners had to be much more industrious because living expenses were so much higher than in the South, where, presumably, people could afford to be more lazy. Bettie Shotwell, however, proved that Yankees had no monopoly on either industriousness or economic resourcefulness.

Instead of china painting, she began teaching school and was soon well on her way to achieving her goal. Even her northern friend grudgingly admitted that "few Yankee housekeepers try to do as much."[67]

Once in possession of the basic raw materials, Bettie Shotwell still had to add her own talents and expertise to transform them all into a proper domestic setting. It was no easy task. As a wide range of popular advice literature warned, there were certain ways to arrange furniture, coordinate accessories, select color schemes, display knick-knacks, lay out china and silver, discipline servants, and plan meals. Sarah A. Elliott was full of advice on these subjects. So were the *Torchlight* and the *Granville Free Lance*, which tried to keep their female readership abreast of all the latest developments. Recipes, decorating ideas, and households hints, which came from Granville County women as well as from professional domestic writers, directed women on the proper ways to feed their families, furnish their homes, and maintain appropriate levels of cleanliness and order.[68] Elite white women also exchanged decorating ideas, sewing and crochet patterns, cleaning tips, and complaints over the trials of finding "good" household servants. In addition to the local newspaper, they also drew their information from regional domestic publications and national women's magazines, both of which the local newspapers received secondhand from their female readership and quoted frequently. Elite white women then incorporated all these published precepts into a network of their own making, identifying the most useful suggestions and altering them to suit their own needs and tastes. Indeed, the seriousness with which elite white women pursued homemaking in their correspondence suggests that the newspapers echoed existing concerns as much as they created and directed them.[69]

No doubt many of these women would have agreed with the advisors who, following in the footsteps of Catharine Beecher, raised the details of domestic order to a high art. "Parents," admonished the author of one piece, "your daughter is in good society when she is with girls . . . who are useful as well as ornamental in the house; who cultivate their minds, and train their hands to skillful workmanship." Always careful to define domestic labor as a skill learned through steady practice and thorough education, Sarah A. Elliott even invested housework with a certain sexual allure. Aurelia, the heroine of her novelette *Days Long Ago,* was never more attractive than when at work. Her future husband proposed to her, flour-dusted and disheveled, while she was making bread in the kitchen: "I never saw you look so beautiful," he insisted: "Solid adornments reveal beauties that all the plastering for false show can never equal. So neat in your kitchen attire, your graceful movements placing cakes in the pans, strengthen my admiration. Parlor entertainments cannot surpass them, and I only wish I could, with the pen of an artist sketch this scene."[70]

If anything, the increasing emphasis on economic competition and political contest heightened the ideological and symbolic significance of women's role within the home. Without a wife and home, William Gregory felt that he was "without hope, without fixedness of purpose, drifting aimlessly down the stream of time in whatever direction the merciless waves may toss." With this same metaphor in mind, the author of one *Torchlight* piece described the domestic haven that a woman tended as the "pole-star" that guided men in stormy weather. J. B. Hunter, the tireless promoter of the county's self-made men, followed suit, beginning his agricultural series in the farmhouse: "Home should be made the spot where, as far as its cares are concerned, we should forget the outer world, and live in its hallowed joys." He then abruptly moved to the fields and the men who farmed them without bothering to explain the connection. But there really was no need for him to do so because it was so fully elaborated elsewhere. Cheerful wives, another insisted, were essential to good business: "If you know a man with beaming face, and kind heart, and a prosperous business, in nine cases out of ten, you will find he has a wife of this kind."[71]

Wives anchored their husband's economic exploits by tending the only remaining social space untouched by self-interest and competition. In the home, organic ties were preserved and hierarchy could still be understood as natural bonds of mutual affection and obligation. Good housekeeping may require physical effort and education, but women labored out of love, motivated by a naturally self-sacrificing maternal instinct, instead of a desire for personal gain. Of course, this image of home life downplayed the changes many elite white women actually confronted in the years following the war and emancipation. They became employers of free labor, some shouldered more of the domestic chores, and a few, following the lead of Annie Silverton and Bettie Shotwell, became wage workers themselves. Others embarked on reform work in missionary societies and the Women's Christian Temperance Union.[72] The elite domestic ideal, however, could easily accommodate hard work or even waged work and reform activity. According to its logic, women might venture—or be forced—into new areas, but they did so out of their duty to their families, not for their own fulfillment or to control economic resources in their own right. If Annie Silverton worked for wages, it was only because she was a "faithful and unselfish wife."[73] So did Bettie Shot-well, who took on paid labor because of her desire to establish a proper domestic retreat for her family. In this way, potentially progressive changes in women's roles became an example of the way they remained within the orbit of their homes and families. There, they also kept other potentially disturbing social changes at bay. "What a blessing to a household," gushed the author of one article, "is a merry, cheerful woman—one whose spirits are not affected by wet days, or little disappointments, or whose milk of human kindness does not sour in the sunshine of prosperity, such a woman in the darkest hours brightens the house like a little piece of sunshiny weather." As long as elite whites could convince themselves that the home and women's place within it retained so much that was familiar, they could better accept the changes that rocked the world outside its borders.[74]

Some elite white women ultimately used these images of womanhood as a springboard into public life. At least some Granville County women were already thinking along these lines. In an 1879 letter to the *Torchlight*, S.S. insisted that civilization and women's rights went hand in hand and advanced together. In the context of Reconstruction, however, the images of women and men that generally appeared in the newspapers' pages took on other, more pointed political meanings.[75] Actively denying the importance of racial hierarchies and a preexisting, inequitable distribution of wealth, the assumptions embedded within these ideals rendered an extremely harsh judgment on the majority of Granville County's residents.

The liberal component, with its emphasis on individual character and upward mobility instead of ascriptive inequality, could be potentially inclusive. Indeed, as Glenda Gilmore has argued, many African-American leaders in North Carolina consciously and strategically promoted the ideals of capitalist development, individual merit, and middle-class domesticity as a way to better the economic conditions of blacks, defend their civil rights, and justify their political power. This was also the case in Granville County, where the booming tobacco market made upward mobility a realistic expectation. African Americans who acquired land, businesses, homes, and public prominence had every reason to believe in the potential of these ideals. They, like other black leaders in the state, pushed for temperance, contributed to local economic development schemes, and tried to train their poorer neighbors in the work ethic and domestic respectability through mutual benefit societies, orphanages, and schools. These African-American leaders hoped to include, not exclude, blacks.[76] But they worked on treacherous ground. The rhetoric of individual merit presumed that all men and all women started out on the same footing, played by the same rules, and pursued the same goals. The playing field, however, was anything but level, and hard work did not always lead to prosperity in a capitalist economic system that required and produced economic inequalities.

Conservatives, moreover, measured success not through good intentions but through material evidence: a prosperous farm or business, well-groomed children, a neat yard, and a well-furnished, tastefully designed house. In the process, the means became the end. Good character adhered in the possession of wealth and the maintenance of a proper home, not the labor required to produce them. By these standards, only a small handful of African Americans and common whites could ever hope to measure up. Ultimately, conservatives had no intention of altering the distribution of economic resources or public power, although they were willing to add some people, even some African Americans, to the upper strata. On the contrary, they used their ideals of manhood and womanhood to legitimate the inequalities around them and beat back those who demanded change. The *Torchlight* and its conservative contributors increasingly drew the world into two camps, those with "good" and those with "bad" characters, modifiers that took the place of "white" and "black," "wealthy" and "poor." Although portrayed in terms of naturally commendable and universally accepted personality traits, the ideal men and women were, by definition, prosperous and white. These were the only men whose diligence, self-discipline, and good business sense routinely resulted in economic success and the only women whose devotion to home and family manifested itself in a particular kind of domesticity. If their lives evidenced merit, moreover, then the lives of poor whites and African Americans implied personal failings that rendered them unfit to participate in the basic rights allowed to "good" people who conformed to "normative" standards of manly and womanly conduct. This was a different explanation than the ones conservative whites had used to buttress their power and position before emancipation, but it could work just as effectively. Granville County's white elites, however, could not deploy it without consequence. They encountered fierce resistance from those who structured their relations within their houses differently and who envisioned a very different connection between individual households and the larger society.

4

"I Am My Own Woman and Will Do as I Please": Gender Roles in Poor African-American and Common White Households

William Allen chose his words carefully. When his employer, John Stem, ordered him to quit bickering with a co-worker, Allen spat back that "he was a man, had a mouth of his own and would holler as much as he pleased." With this turn of phrase he meshed his identities as a worker, an African American, and a man. Although he was not rich and white, Allen believed himself to be a man of equivalent status to his employer. As his own master, he also retained the final say in what he was going to do and when he was going to do it. Being a "free man," one Alabama freedman explained, meant that he could come "when I please, and nobody say nuffin to me, nor order me roun'." No doubt William Allen would have nodded in approval.[1]

Dink Watkins also chose her words carefully. Discovered by her former husband in liaison with another man, she dismissed him in no uncertain terms. "I am my own woman," Watkins claimed, "and will do as I please." As we saw in chapter 1, Watkins considered herself her "own woman" not because she assumed this kind of independence within marriage but because she believed the marriage had ended. Her distinctive phrasing also reveals a great deal about her own sense of womanhood. Combining race, class, and gender in her identity as a woman, Watkins drew implicit contrasts between herself and elite white women. She insisted on doing as she pleased, instead of bowing to the standards of elite white womanhood. In fact, Watkins still claimed the term "woman" for herself, although local guardians of domestic propriety would have disputed her claim. To be sure, many poor African Americans and whites would have condemned her behavior as well, if only because she chose the lot of a black Baptist church for her rendezvous. But to some extent, Watkins still worked within her community's guidelines concerning male-female relations.

She also accepted gender difference, asserting her rights as a woman and rejecting only her husband, not male authority generally. No matter how much she was her own woman, Dink Watkins could never aspire to be her own master in the same way William Allen could.[2]

Other poor blacks and common whites agreed with these basic points. They fashioned their own definitions of manhood and womanhood to fit the needs and realities of their lives. Instead of revolving around a husband and wife whose complementary roles satisfied the needs of the family, the households of the poor of both races included an array of kin who all contributed to the family's welfare. In this context, men's and women's roles overlapped considerably. The poor did not limit women's labor to domestic work within their homes, just as they did not expect men to provide for their wives and children solely through their own labor. Women led much more public lives than their elite white neighbors—although generally not quite as public as that of Dink Watkins. Poor African Americans and common whites considered women's forays into public space necessary contributions to their families' welfare and, as such, a central component of their role as women. They simply could not afford fine distinctions between public and private spaces or rigidly segregated men's and women's roles. Elite whites, however, blanched. Looking into the households and communities of the poor through the lens of their own gender conventions, they saw evidence of personal depravity and social backwardness.

These gender constructions had a public dimension as well. Poor African Americans and common whites rooted their ideas about manhood and womanhood within a social context that acknowledged the oppressive legacies of slavery and class privilege. Racial and class difference thus played a central role in defining personal and community identities, just as they did for elite whites. But the script, stage, and supporting actors were so different that the implications were worlds apart. Where conservative elite whites excluded people on the basis of race and class, common whites and poor African Americans incorporated racial and class differences into the very substance of their definitions of manhood and womanhood. By allowing for a more inclusive universal man and universal woman, these alternative constructions also opened the possibility for greater equality outside the private household. Despite racial and class differences, all women could stand together on equal footing and all men could do the same.

Yet race and gender hierarchies also lay behind the common rhetoric and the similarities in the ways common whites and poor African Americans defined men's and women's roles. Common whites did not always extend their vision of manhood and womanhood to African Americans, just as African Americans did not include those whites who were hostile to their own political goals. Both groups, moreover, relied on gender difference to describe their identity as men and women, their rights, and the social order generally. While this construction of gender difference did not match that of elite whites, it still translated into hierarchy with implications not just for men and women within individual households but for social and political relations outside those borders as well.

Although men and women accepted the presence of a certain level of inequality, they still clashed regularly over the relative distribution of power and the substance of their responsibilities as husbands and wives. Poor African-American and common white women made "private" conflicts a matter of "public" debate, bringing in the community and sometimes the state to adjudicate their disputes. Placing limits on male authority within their households and their communities, they also called into question legal precedents that subordinated wives to their husbands and left them isolated within a domestic sphere. These conflicts form yet another strand in the debate over the construction of men's and women's roles both within and outside households, one that reveals the importance of women's voices in a public discourse that so often denied their presence in its near exclusive focus on male prerogatives.

Womanhood

Emancipation presented African-American women with the opportunity to act on their ideas of womanhood in new ways. They withdrew from full-time waged labor to work in their own homes, although many subsequently went back to the fields or to other paid employment. Nonetheless, claiming the right to place their own families' interests first represented freedom for women who had been compelled to tend to their masters' families for so long. Freedwomen appropriated other privileges of elite white womanhood as well. Some donned their former mistresses' clothing, wearing veiled hats, gloves, and brightly colored stylish dresses. Others confiscated household goods. In 1866, for instance, Granville County's William Lyon accused Edith Dalby, one of his former slaves, of stealing "one water pail, one iron pot, one tea kettle, one pair pot hooks, and one yard of white cotton cloth." Clearly, all these things would be useful as Dalby set up her own kitchen in her own household. Beyond their practicality, the items spoke volumes about Dalby's sense of freedom. In liberating the kitchen utensils she had used for so long as a slave in another woman's kitchen, she became her own mistress.[3]

Poor African-American women like Edith Dalby infused these symbols of womanhood and domesticity with their own meanings. So did poor white women. They did not tie their lives to a domesticity centered on consumer items and sentimentalized ideals of motherhood. Instead, they cast their notions of womanhood more broadly to encompass whatever was required to contribute to their families' welfare.[4]

For most African Americans and many whites, economic insecurity was as much a part of life as sunshine and rain. Consequently, women expected that they would make significant economic contributions to their households. In addition to tobacco, Granville County farm families grew a range of food crops, including corn, potatoes, and other vegetables. Not everyone could afford milk cows, but chickens and pigs roamed around even the poorest yards. Women performed much, if not most, of the labor involved in food production: they tended the garden and preserved its bounty; they collected eggs, made butter, and sold them to local merchants; they butchered hogs and prepared the meat for the smokehouse; they shooed cows, chickens, pigs, and other hungry interlopers out of the fields; they hoed rows of corn; and, just as fall began to fade into winter, they dug potatoes. When they could grab a spare moment, they also wove cloth and sewed their families' clothes and linens. In all these ways, women contributed directly to their families' cash and credit reserves. Producing food and clothing at home eased dependence on the tobacco market, the instability of which could wreak havoc on a family's fortunes, particularly if its members were already living on the margin. In good years, families could then put aside the proceeds from the tobacco crop to purchase land or items not produced at home—a milk cow, mules, a sewing machine, farm implements, or a child's education. In bad years, tobacco money purchased necessities to get the family through the winter. Yet, despite the importance placed on staple-crop production by contemporaries and later historians, it formed only one piece in a successful strategy of household production. Without a full larder, a good tobacco crop was only so much smoke.[5]

In poorer families, moreover, tobacco production would have been impossible without women's labor. The demands of this crop made back-breaking field work a regular chore for poor women of both races. Certain jobs, such as hauling wood, plowing, harvesting, and curing, may have been designated as "men's work," but that did not keep women from these tasks. Women participated in virtually every stage of the production process. The tobacco-growing season began in the winter, when farm families carefully selected land for their seedbeds and sowed the tiny tobacco seeds. The men then headed to the uncleared land to cut and haul wood for curing in the fall. As spring drew near, families cleared their fields and transplanted the delicate seedlings by hand. All other household work came to an abrupt halt at planting time. As one experienced laborer described it, the process defied distinctions between housework and field work by bringing all family members and even household items into the fields: "We took biscuit pans, wash pans, and all other pans on the plantation and with a spoon we dug the plants up and placed them in pans, carrying them in small numbers to the field." After waiting a week or so for the root systems to develop, family members made their way between the rows with plows or hoes to loosen the soil, a process they repeated several times before the plants matured.[6]

Tobacco, unlike cotton, then required careful tending through the summer and well into fall. Farm families "topped" the plants to eliminate the flowery heads that stunted primary leaf growth, "primed" them to remove the useless bottom leaves, and "suckered" them to cut back secondary growth that interfered with the primary leaves. Throughout the summer, men, women, and children also picked off the tobacco hornworms by hand. The work load only increased during harvest and curing time. Men usually worked in the fields, while women readied the plants for curing in specially designed barns. After curing, as winter's chill set in, family members gathered to sort the tobacco according to grade. In poorer households, families simply piled the tobacco in the central room of the house so the work would be close at hand. Once again, field work and housework merged.[7]

The poorer the family, the more women's work expanded beyond the borders of their houses into the fields and off the farms' boundaries altogether. Before the war, many white yeoman women regularly worked in the fields and women of landless families often worked for wages outside their homes as well. After the war, African-American women took on even more economic responsibilities than common white women because of the way race increased the precariousness of their economic position. In rural areas like Granville County, field work often marked racial and class differences among women. Even though women from the wealthiest families could not escape the demands of tobacco production entirely, they generally stayed out of the fields. So did those, both white and black, who aspired to elite status. Their absence from the fields distinguished them from those women who did labor alongside their menfolk. As we learned in the previous chapter, Harry Silverton was shocked to see his son plowing. If his daughter had been the one plowing, he surely would have collapsed on the spot.[8]

Women who worked in the fields did not necessarily share this view. Far from an "unwomanly" symbol of degradation, field work formed a central component of their identity. Many women enjoyed it. Margaret Jarman Hagood's study of white tenant women in North Carolina during the 1930s is revealing, even though its subjects were sixty-five years removed from the Reconstruction period. Expecting to find "Mothers of the South," Hagood was surprised to discover that the overwhelming majority of the women she interviewed preferred field work to housework. According to one woman: "In the house you never get through." Another elaborated: "In the field there's just one thing and you can finish it up; but here in the house there's cooking, cleaning, washing, milking, churning, mending, sewing, canning, and always the children—and you don't know what to turn to next." If anything, poor black women were even more adamant on this point. A 1916 study by the U.S. Children's Bureau found that African-American women in rural North Carolina did not hesitate in selecting field work over house work. It paid better, brought more social recognition, and offered an escape from the isolation and tedium of housework by allowing for more sociability. Of course, applying the experience of women in the early twentieth century directly to that of their grandmothers is hazardous. Nonetheless, parallels between the generations do exist. Many of the women in both Hagood's and the U.S. Children's Bureau's studies lived on farms where tobacco cultivation and household economic strategies resembled those in postwar Granville County. If the actual work of women in the twentieth century bore a striking similarity to that of their grandmothers, so did their attitudes toward it. Pressed to explain the satisfaction they derived from their work in the fields, the women in Hagood's study invoked continuities with the past: "I was brought up to it."[9]

Poor African-American and common white women also took great pride in their ability to keep up with the men in the fields. One white woman in Hagood's study bragged that "my papa said he lost his best hand when I got married." Others looked back fondly at the time when they were younger, stronger, and "used to work like a man." Poor African-American women made similar claims in the Works Progress Administration's slave narratives, gathered around the same time Hagood made her study. Mattie Curtis, for instance, insisted on talking about how she had carved out a farm from the forest, despite the interviewer's attempts to guide her away from the subject. Although married, Curtis performed the bulk of the work herself: "I cut down de big trees dat wus all over dese fields an' I mauled out de wood an' sold hit, den I plowed up de fields an' planted dem." "I done a heap of work at night too," she continued, "all of my sewin' an' such an' de piece of lan' near de house over dar ain't never got no work 'cept at night." One of her proudest moments came when she sold her first bale of cotton. But most memorable of all was the day she "finally paid fer de land."[10]

Embracing a standard in which "men's work" was more valuable than "women's work," these women affirmed a gender hierarchy in which female subordination was the general rule. But they simultaneously rejected a hierarchy among women. Poor African-American and common white women may have worked like men, but they insisted that this did not exclude them from the category "woman." In fact, they boasted about their abilities and used them to measure their own womanhood. Although eighty-one at the time of her WPA interview, Mary Barbour still placed a great deal of emphasis on her capacity for hard labor, maintaining that she was still spry enough to outwork her daughter or, for that matter, any other black woman. The women's menfolk applied a similar standard. Charlie Crump, for instance, bragged about his mother's ability to plow with a particularly ornery donkey. "My mammy had more grit dan any gal I now knows of has in her craw," he noted with discernible pride. Clearly, it was his mother's "grit" that moved her near the top of Crump's scale of womanhood.[11]

Waged work was also a regular component of many women's domestic responsibilities. Some had to work to put food on the table, as the census figures suggest. In Oxford Township 40 percent of all black women age twelve and older worked for wages or headed their own households in 1870. In Dutchville Township, the figure was 14 percent for the same group. By 1880, the figures had dropped in Oxford to 27 percent, but had risen to 21 percent in Dutchville. Waged work was a necessary presence in the lives of many white women as well. Of white women age twelve and older in 1870, 12 percent worked for wages or headed households in Oxford and 7 percent in Dutchville. The percentages inched down to 10 percent in Oxford and up to 12 percent in Dutchville by 1880.[12] The census, moreover, grossly underestimates the number of wage-earning women. Most performed occasional waged work—such as ironing, washing, mending, sewing, or a few days' work in the fields—that went unrecorded in the returns. When the census takers made their rounds, they did not recognize women who engaged in work of this kind as wage workers, nor did the women themselves necessarily identify themselves as such.[13]

Elite whites expected African-American women to work as paid laborers, but they had a certain kind of female worker in mind. Their expectations found expression in the image of the self-sacrificing "Mammy," whose family was the white family of her employer. The *Oxford Torchlight*'s obituary for "Old Aunt Hannah, a colored woman, aged about seventy years, formerly the property of J.C. Cooper" could have been for Mammy herself: "She was a faithful servant and stuck by her 'master and mistress,' as she called them, after the slaves were free, evincing no change in her manners towards them." Like Mammy, "Old Aunt Hannah" came to life only through her relationship to her "master and mistress." She had no life of her own, at least not one that her white employers needed to know about.[14]

Many black women, unlike "Old Aunt Hannah," did "evince" a significant change in their manners following emancipation. Elite whites found these female laborers deeply troubling, even though they enthusiastically endorsed the abstract concept of waged work for black women. African-American women workers forced their employers to confront the unsettling possibility that they knew virtually nothing about those who cooked, cleaned, cared for their families, and worked in their fields for generations. Wages only added to the growing doubts of white employers, because money gave poor African-American women the means to pursue their own interests. Caroline Hart, for instance, found cash compelling for precisely this reason. Denying accusations that she had stolen one hundred dollars from her employer, this African-American laborer could not resist adding that if she did have the money she "would buy her a hundred dollar dress and another pair of shoes."[15] Not all female wage workers would have made the same choice, but ambitions like Caroline Hart's disturbed elite whites precisely because they were her own.

Poor black women who lived outside male-headed families upset elite white sensibilities even more. The reaction to Dicey Smith and Jennie Bass is suggestive. Smith and Bass lived together with Smith's four children in their own house, where they boarded men who worked nearby on the railroad. They also maintained a high profile in the neighborhood, hosting many popular gatherings. During one, a "quilting" party in 1890, a fight broke out. In the confusion, a shot ricocheted across the room and left one guest dead. By all accounts, Dicey Smith and Jennie Bass had nothing to do with the fight and were never considered suspects in the murder. Nonetheless, the authorities made the women's living arrangements central to their investigation, certain that the explanation for the shooting could be found there. Doubtful that Smith and Bass were operating just a boarding house, they demanded to know if the women had sexual relations with their male renters. They also asked about the paternity of Smith's children, perhaps hoping to uncover a spurned lover amidst the group of men present that night. Smith answered their questions simply: "I have four children living, one dead, I have never been married." In all likelihood, her response confirmed the suspicions of these white officials who took a dim view of her private life. All their questions pointed to an unstated assumption: if the women had lived in the appropriate domestic setting, either as subordinate servants to white families or as wives of properly deferential black men, the shooting never would have occurred.[16]

If Dicey Smith's and Jennie Bass's parties were unique, their living arrangements were not. Poor black women often pooled their resources and their labor to provide material and emotional support for each other. Of course, these women acted under the constraints of poverty, which significantly limited their choices. Yet, however poor, they still controlled their time in a way that other women did not. As Fanny Lathom described her morning schedule: "I don't know what time we ate breakfast. I don't know how high the sun was we sleep late. I know we sleep late. Sometime [the] sun is two hours high when we get up." That same day, Lathom's friend Francis Amis spent the morning fishing for her dinner. According to one of Amis's roommates, "She goes fishing often." Most African-American women chose different life paths. But even if they did not sleep late, fish for their dinners, host "quilting" parties, board strange men in their homes, and live outside male-headed households, they still had one thing in common with Francis Amis, Fannie Lathom, Jennie Bass, and Dicey Smith: a desire to remove themselves from the control of elite whites. On this scale, the flamboyant independence of this small handful of women becomes one of degree. Like them, other black women dropped the facade of servitude to go about their own business without asking permission or offering apologies. That alone was often sufficient to irritate many elite whites.[17]

Common white women did not labor under the same constraints as black women. But they were supposed to maintain a properly deferential stance toward their betters and to subordinate themselves as faithful wives, mothers, and daughters. If they asserted their own interests outside a male-headed family, they too fell under suspicion.

In June 1868, for instance, James T. Gill, a white man, went to the local magistrate with a "case of urgent emergency." The object of Gill's fear was Martha O'Mary, a propertyless, widowed white woman who had lived in a house on the lands Gill was now renting. He accused her of setting fire to "an unoccupied dwelling house" and being "engaged in an attempt to poison himself and family." But that was not all. According to the statement of Harriet Jones: "A short time before [G]ill had moved she saw Martha Omary get a bottle which was hung up in an apple tree (a snuff bottle) and put it down in the hearth and put some nails some small roots and some water (urine) in the bottle and covered it over and placed the rock over it and poured some water on the rock and made some cross marks with another root and said that Gill would go the way that water went and said that she did that to make Gill and his family sick and dissatisfied that they would leave there so she could come back next faul." In other words, James Gill believed himself to be the victim of Martha O'Mary's conjuring. Other white men filed similar charges. Like him, they complained about economically marginal women, who also may have had a history of confronting or criticizing their neighbors too often and too openly.[18]

In court, O'Mary denied the charges, insisting that she had "put the bottle under the hearth . . . to keep people from poisoning her hogs and her." In fact, her intentions were unclear. Her conjuring may have been nothing more than an effort to keep her hogs and herself from harm, but it is equally probable that she meant to scare, if not destroy, the Gill family. Gill and O'Mary had lived in the same neighborhood for years. Perhaps their conflict predated the war, when Gill tilled his own land and O'Mary lived with her husband, a landless shoemaker. If so, the Civil War could only have heated up the feud by sharpening their economic differences. A fifty-three-year-old widow with few economic options in 1868, O'Mary must have struggled to keep from sliding into the poorhouse. Although stripped of his land by war's end, Gill's economic prospects were far brighter; at least bright enough for O'Mary's landlord to evict her and give the house to Gill instead. Whether she conjured against Gill or not, O'Mary did swear to use whatever means necessary to defend her own interests and remain in her home. Indeed, O'Mary's defiant words seem to have guided the community's interpretation of the "evidence." Suddenly, the small, dirty bottle Gill found hidden in his hearth acquired ominous meanings. The local magistrate never doubted its message either. Leaping to the same conclusion as Gill, he charged O'Mary with both arson and "poisoning."[19]

Many poor African-American and common white women led very public lives, even when they lived in male-headed households. They traveled alone to visit neighbors and relatives, to market goods, to go to work, to deliver the wash and sewing they had done, and to purchase supplies. Francis Amis, last seen fishing on a weekday morning, once stopped a teamster for a ride into town. Although the teamster refused Amis a ride, he did pick up another woman that same day, ignoring his employer's orders forbidding him to carry passengers. Apparently this type of "hitchhiking" was common. From the perspective of many elite whites, unaccompanied travel opened women to the potentially dangerous world that existed outside the protected confines of their homes. Soliciting rides from complete strangers openly tempted disaster. Poorer women and their menfolk, however, viewed the situation from a very different vantage point because they did not draw such a firm line between public and private spaces. To them, such journeys formed a necessary part of life. If women could find a ride and rest their weary feet, it was a risk they were willing to take.[20]

Even if they never traveled the countryside on their own, poor women rarely confined their lives to the four walls of their houses. Both poor African Americans and common whites resolved their problems in the open air of their neighborhoods, and women were no exception to the rule. Many court cases of minor violence involved women who either initiated conflicts or aggressively defended themselves.[21] The fight between Margaret Hughie and Mary Jane Williams, two white women, was not unusual. In 1870, the two became embroiled in a verbal exchange that quickly escalated to physical threats. After Hughie repeatedly threatened to kill Williams with a large rock, Williams finally retreated and took her complaint to the local justice of the peace. In court, Hughie self-righteously defended herself on the grounds that Williams was trespassing and that she had every right to guard her family's land. Not only did she readily acknowledge her part in the dispute but she also gave no indication that she thought her behavior exceptional. Neither did Williams. Although she clearly disagreed with Hughie's position and the way she made her point, Mary Jane Williams never suggested that Margaret Hughie had violated the code of proper feminine conduct.[22]

Isabella Thorp, an African-American woman, shared this perspective. Believing that Ellick Green and Susan Mayho had cheated her out of some money, she swore vengeance. After threatening to kill the two in front of several witnesses, Thorp confronted Susan Mayho at her house. Mayho wisely kept the door closed, but to no avail.

Far too angry for a simple piece of wood to get in the way, Thorp broke in. Mayho described the ensuing struggle in her testimony: "[Thorp said] I am in the house now I will do and say what I please and I [Mayho] told her she would not do and say what you please while I am in there and . . . [Thorp said] if you fool along with me I'll cut your guts out with this knife. . . . Then she took a piece of rail and hit me with it on my head and it knocked me out of my senses." Thorp felt cheated and she acted. When she did, she displayed a distinctly "unladylike" affinity for physical violence.[23]

Within their own communities, the public stands of Isabella Thorp, Mary Jane Williams, and Margaret Hughie were extreme examples of accepted patterns of behavior. They, like other poor African-American and common white women, often had to defend themselves because there was no one else around who could. But even if there had been, poor women of both races did not always shrink from confrontations, even potentially violent ones. Isabella Thorp's words, "I will do and say what I please," suggest why. The phrase virtually duplicates the one used by Dink Watkins, whose story opened this chapter. Though the circumstances were very different, neither woman considered her behavior a compromise to her womanhood. The delicate flower of southern womanhood could not survive the harsh conditions that common white and poor African-American women endured. Even the resourceful Sarah A. Elliott would have found it difficult to adapt. Common white and poor African-American women needed a particular kind of resiliency and strength. On occasion, that might mean picking up a large rock, a pine rail, or a good sharp knife.

There was no room for such behavior in elite white standards of womanhood. Measured against them, poor women hopelessly blurred gender boundaries with their public lives and outspoken ways. But even though women's lives overlapped considerably with those of their menfolk, poor African Americans and common whites still accepted the basic notion of gender difference. They just worked from their own understanding of it, one more like colonial good wives than the "true women" of the nineteenth century. Distinctions between men's and women's roles actually centered around reproductive labor. Poor African-American and common white women assumed primary responsibility for child rearing, cooking, and housework. While they also took on "men's work," poor African-American and common white men did not expand their role to help with "women's work."[24]

Although housework devolved on women as a group, not all women approached it in the same way. The women who compared housework unfavorably to field work clearly puzzled Hagood. In fact, she skipped right over her informants' words in her analysis of their houses, attributing the spartan furnishings and general disorder to ignorance, overwork, and poverty. Hagood was only partially right. What she missed were the ways the women in her study were articulating very different standards than her own. These white tenant women extended their domestic duties beyond the four walls of their houses to emphasize their role in creating well-run farms. The interiors of their houses mattered far less. One woman, for instance, openly defied conventional associations of the home as a woman's natural sphere, claiming "no woman really likes housework."[25]

Her words punctured the myths surrounding the domestic ideal, the burdens of which were not shared equally by all women. Poor African-American and common white women could not afford to sentimentalize housework. The women in Hagood's study, for instance, not only maintained a healthy skepticism toward the alleged joys of a domesticity confined to the home but also explicitly distinguished themselves from other women who measured feminine success in such terms. Of course, most of these white tenant women would have welcomed more household conveniences and more comfortable surroundings. But they coveted the material trappings of domesticity because they could ease the burdens of daily life, not because they would enhance their own sense of themselves as women. Asked whether she preferred field work or housework, one woman gave it a great deal of thought before finally identifying washing as her favorite chore: "She always had liked it and now, since she has a gasoline engine washer, she is sure she loves washing most of all—and next to that stripping tobacco." Sometimes a washing machine is just a washing machine. It made this woman's life easier and more enjoyable, but it did not serve as a cultural expression of her feminine worth. Although separated from the women in Hagood's study by a generation or more, poor African-American and common white women in late-nineteenth-century Granville County probably would have agreed. It is unlikely that they measured their success as women in terms of the bleached damask tablecloths or rows of plates stacked neatly on decoratively papered shelves as Sarah A. Elliott and the *Oxford Torchlight* urged them to do. For them, simply putting food on the table was what mattered.[26]

In contrast to housework, motherhood occupied a far more central place in the identity of poor women, although they defined the essence of a "good mother" in their own way. The complaints in the *Oxford Torchlight* about children running unsupervised through the streets actually say a great deal about mothers. Women with husbands whose incomes supported the material needs of their families and with servants who performed the most burdensome household chores could devote a larger portion of their time to child rearing. To poorer women, motherhood meant feeding their children, putting clothes on their backs, and keeping a roof over their heads. Beyond that, they hoped to better their children's lot in life. For instance, Mary Burwell, an African-American mother with six children, worked as a farm laborer so that her children would not have to. Three of her children attended school. The younger ones stayed at home, safe from the demands of a white employer.[27] In fact, the Burwell children may well have been among those running unsupervised through Oxford's streets. If so, their mother had paid for their freedom with her own sweat.

Even if they had the resources to do so, many poor women would not have wanted to emulate the elite ideal of motherhood. Given the size of their houses, common white and poor African-American women would have been hard pressed to raise their children in domestic privacy. But the idea may never have occurred to them anyway, because they did not think of their dwellings as private retreats. Instead, domestic life occupied public space, like the laundry that hung in the yard. With open doors and windows, the houses of the poor physically mingled with the world outside. Even inside, houses were not neatly divided into private and public space. Most contained only one or two rooms, where family members slept, ate, visited, and entertained. During North Carolina's miserable summer nights, poor people abandoned their stuffy interiors altogether in favor of their front porches or yards. Just as women moved between housework and field work, the fields moved indoors during grading time, when tobacco covered virtually every inch of the house. And African-American women who worked as domestic servants turned the distinction between work and home completely on its head. In this context, where domesticity looked outward, not inward, there was no particular reason for children to remain inside. If they ran through the streets it was not because of their mothers' negligence; it was simply what children were supposed to do.[28]

A few women, like Dicey Smith and Jennie Bass, created a space for themselves outside a male-headed household. But they were the exception, not the rule. Even then, their existence was precarious. Far more typical were the poverty and insecurity of Martha O'Mary. Beyond witchcraft, women like O'Mary had very few economic options. Within their own households, common whites and African

The William Burwell house (*above*) and the Smith-Adcock house (*below*) are typical of the houses in which the poor of both races lived. With few rooms and little space, there was no room for privacy. (Courtesy of the Granville County Historical Society)

Americans held women's labor in high regard. Outside, its value fell precipitously. White employers generally paid women about half as much as men. Behind these wage rates were the assumptions that women lived in households headed by men and thus their wages constituted a secondary contribution to the household's income. These rates also reveal the relative importance most white employers placed on women's work. Women did not always perform the same labor as men, even when they worked in the tobacco fields and factories. But it was not necessarily true that women always contributed less to the final product than men. In the minds of their white employers, however, they did.[29]

As a result, wage-earning women barely made enough to support themselves. Single women with young children found it nearly impossible to support their families, especially if their children were too young to work. The experience of Philis Clark, whose story appeared in chapter 1, was not unusual. During the war, Clark's master sent her to Granville County from eastern North Carolina, so that she would not escape or fall into the hands of federal troops. Afterwards, she found herself in desperate economic straits. Clark managed to secure a house from C. W. Raney, a white planter, but "soon found that she could not maintain her children" and pay the rent. Raney then agreed to hire Clark in return for room and board. By 1868, Raney declared himself financially unable to continue the arrangement: "I make nothing by keeping her; the rent of the house and provision they consume would hire two man hands, and I have sent her out repeatedly to find a home, but no one is willing to feed her children for her services. She is a very deserving woman, works hard and should be assisted. . . . I dislike to turn her out to live in the woods, but will be compelled to do so unless I am assisted." As Raney's words reveal, neither men nor women could support their families on one wage. Women with children had even fewer options than men. Philis Clark's dwindled to two: the woods or the poorhouse. If anything, Clark thought the woods more attractive. According to Raney, she said "she will die first" before going to the poorhouse.[30]

Infanticide cases also convey women's economic marginality with vivid clarity. In 1867, for instance, Harriett Jordan, an African-American tobacco factory worker, was charged with burying her baby alive. When asked why, she responded that "she did not know what else to do with it." Her remark seems cold, but the image of a nurturing mother and her innocent children depended on a certain economic position. Lacking this kind of security, Jordan saw her own and her baby's future in very different terms. Christina Thorp also found herself torn between the love for her children and the reality of poverty. When she and her husband divorced in 1879, the court refused to give her custody of her children because the judge believed that she could not support them on her own. Three years later, after she had remarried, Thorp pulled a knife on her ex-husband, grabbed her daughter, ran off with her, and then refused to give her back. Thorp clearly cared for her children and wanted them with her. But the fact that she tried to regain custody only after she remarried suggests that economic considerations shaped her own outlook just as surely as they determined the court's custody decision.[31]

Economic insecurity ultimately propelled women into the orbit of male-headed households, if not as wives, then as daughters, aunts, sisters, and grandmothers. Of course, common white and poor African-American women strongly identified with their kin, both male and female. In these ties they found not only support and companionship but also a sense of communal solidarity. Yet the lack of economic alternatives also shaped women's vision of social change. Given their vulnerability in the world outside their families and communities, most poor African-American and common white women worked to improve their lot within male-headed households, rather than trying to dismantle the entire structure of gender hierarchy.

Manhood

Securing their place as men would prove far more difficult for African-American men than for common white men because of the way black skin had been so thoroughly conflated with dependence. The tendency of whites to identify all freedpeople through their ex-masters suggests the magnitude of the task. Because of the ways slavery routinely disrupted families and relentlessly subsumed all slaves within the identity of their masters, naming had acquired great significance to African Americans. With names, they symbolically affirmed family ties while also establishing each person's unique individuality. After emancipation, white southerners still refused to acknowledge the names African Americans chose for themselves. Such was the experience of two black men arrested for stealing some sides of bacon. The indictment referred to them as "Ned a freedman and Henry another freeman [both] formerly the property of Thomas Rogers." If they had been given a chance, Ned and Henry probably would have identified themselves quite differently. Other African Americans in their position certainly did. In these instances, the court documents sometimes alternate between two or more names, acknowledging the individual's self-designation as well as the name by which whites knew that person. One African-American man, for instance, appeared as "James Norwood," "Jim Samuel," and "Jim Samuel alias Norwood." In this case, "James Norwood" appears to have been the name he actually used.[32]

Of course, women encountered similar difficulties. But the issue carried another layer of meaning for men because of the way naming practices marked dependence and independence in nineteenth-century society. Wives, children, and slaves all carried the name of their male household head, signifying their dependence on that person. Only independent men had names that they could confer on others. The names court officials gave to Ned, Henry, and James still placed them within the reaches of their ex-masters' households. James Norwood took exception to this presumption when he shook off the name "Jim Samuel." Others followed suit. Even when they chose their masters' last names, they used these names as their own.

No one ever questioned common white men's right to their own names. Yet, like African-American men, their names carried little weight within southern society. Of course, these two groups rarely acknowledged each other with anything other than suspicion or open hostility. Still, both African-Americans and common whites incorporated many of the same elements into their notions of manhood. For common white men, no less than for William Allen, manhood meant being one's own master, not involuntarily subject to another. Personal freedom, however, formed only one component of manhood. Alongside it lay common white and African-American men's sense of responsibility toward their families. While one strand of manhood emphasized individual rights, the other bound men to the communities. Woven together, both symbolized independence from the racial and class ties that had subordinated them to other men.[33]

Both yeomen and propertyless white men articulated the components of their gender role and identity with particular clarity during the Civil War. Elite white men like James H. Horner wondered whether their responsibility to their families outweighed their duty to the Confederacy. Their poorer neighbors could not afford such self-doubt. With their families reduced to abject poverty and subject to continual violence, their priorities were clear. "It is not in the power of Yankee armies to cause us to wish ourselves at home," wrote a group of North Carolina soldiers in General Lee's army. But "we cannot hear the cries of our little ones, and stand. We must say something, must make an effort to relieve *them*." Their petition actually delivered a thinly veiled threat: they would cease fighting unless the state did something to relieve conditions on the home front. "Very many of our wives were dependent on our labor for support before the war when articles of food and clothing could be obtained easier than now. At this time they are alone, without a protector, and cannot by hard and honest labor, obtain enough money to purchase the necessaries of life." Soldiers flooded the governor's office with furlough requests, certain that the war could wait just long enough for them to put things right at home. "I want to go home," explained George Hancock, "to prepare some land for to sow some wheat for the use of my family that is my dependance." Parrott Hardee wanted to know if he could defer "until I can fatten my Poark." Fearing for their families' safety, some men felt they should be relieved of duty so that they could protect their families from harm. A company in the Home Guard, for instance, insisted that their services would be of more use in their own neighborhoods: "Having been called out, and sent into other counties to look up deserters, our families are exposed and frequent instances of depredations have occured . . . which greatly depresses the spirits of the men." Rather than waiting for permission, a growing number of soldiers registered their priorities with their feet and deserted. Of these, a few asked to be reinstated, explaining that they had only left temporarily to look after their families. Such was the request of Malcolm McRae, who "left the servis and came home" when "my famly got sick an I hear of the Death of my last child." As the war dragged on, however, far more remained unrepentant and at home, where they believed their primary responsibilities lay.[34]

Their womenfolk agreed. Left to fend for themselves, yeoman and propertyless white women complained continually of the material needs created by the absence of their menfolk. I am "a poor widow woman left with 2 little children," wrote Sue O. Coneley to Governor Zebulon Vance: "Like thousands of others I have nobody at all to do anything for me now." Nonetheless, Coneley still professed her support for the Confederacy. Tilting over the edge into hunger and homelessness, the loyalty of other women waned. "Do try and stop this cruel war," pleaded one woman, "especelly for they sake of surfering women and children": "I beg you for God sake to try and make peace on some terms and . . . let they rest of they men come home to try and take care of there poor women and children and try to make something to eat for those whose dear husbands have been killed." But both women believed that soldiering came second to men's family responsibilities. Like Sue Coneley, some women insisted that the state government step in and assume the duties of the men it had taken away, by providing supplies and military protection. Others insisted that the government return the men themselves, if not permanently, then temporarily to harvest crops or tend to other family emergencies.[35]

The women who wrote to Governor Vance also felt physically vulnerable without their menfolk. Some of their fears were only too real. Bands of deserters and gangs spread across North Carolina's countryside, capitalizing on wartime disorder. In areas torn between union and confederate loyalties, women lived in the crossfire of small-scale guerrilla wars. News of violence issued continually from war-torn Randolph County, where women as well as men were considered fair game. In Rockingham County, fifty-two women describing themselves as "Mothers, Wives and Sisters of the Members of the 45th N.C. Regiment" petitioned for the troops to be reassigned to protect them from deserters. A few weeks later, thirty-two more signed another request. Other women struggled with their racially embattled imaginations, seeing signs of slave uprisings in every black face. As one put it: "The negroes will Kile ale we women and children if they take ale the men away." Only the presence of white men stood between her and an apocalyptic race war. Even if the danger lurked only in their minds, all these women felt entitled to masculine protection. When their own husbands, fathers, and sons could not do it, white women turned immediately to a higher male authority, their Confederate leaders, to fill the void.[36]

A more palpable sense of desperation and a less conventional use of grammar distinguishes the letters of the poor from those of their wealthier neighbors. So does their perspective on the connection between class and manhood. Poor whites leveled their gazes directly at the opportunism of propertied white men and the miserliness of a government that favored the interests of the wealthy. Private O. Goddin wrote Governor Vance, "Do tell me how we poor soldiers who are fighting for the 'rich mans negro' can support our families at $11 per month? How can the poor live?" White women were also increasingly critical of both their wealthier neighbors and their government. Eliza Evans noted that the man who was evicting her had prospered during the war because his son received an exemption, even though he was "just as able bodied man as my husband." By contrast, she had suffered just because "my pore husband had the misfortun not to have land." Frustrated by those who seemed so oblivious to their plight, women like Eliza Evans began to take direct action, seizing the goods they needed, sometimes in organized bands whose actions escalated into full-blown riots. In Granville County, a group of ten women and three men stole one hundred pounds of cotton while the owner stood by, helpless to stop them. Another group of women loot-ed a local mill. The miller's son later trivialized the attack, boasting that he would have thwarted it had he been there. Apparently, he remained oblivious to the desperation engendered by the war and the fury directed at those few, like himself, who seemed immune to its hardships.[37]

Harry Silverton's homecoming paled in comparison to the scenes awaiting his poorer counterparts. Even in Granville County, where the economy rebounded fairly quickly, common whites had difficulty mak-ing up their losses. Many men lost their land, and those who managed to hang on feared that they would be next. Much more than the land itself was at stake. With it went the basis of white men's economic and political autonomy as well as their ability to perform their primary responsibilities as men—to maintain and protect their families.[38]

The troubled economy made stay laws, which shielded homesteads from seizure for debt, popular among a range of propertyholders. But those who supported such legislation did so for very different reasons. Wealthier whites tended to focus on the threat of economic leveling and the political problems created by a floating population of poor, landless whites. L. J. Horner of Granville County, for instance, consid-ered debt relief necessary to maintain racial and class distinctions: "If the sinking had been general all would have still maintained their rel-ative positions, but as it is the debtor sinks lower than those he once held in bondage." By contrast, common whites invoked the logic of a moral economy, represented in a self-sufficient household. In their minds, creditors disrupted households for no better reason than the greedy desire to benefit themselves at the expense of others. Accord-ing to Smith Powell of Caldwell County, "I think it a hard case to take all a man has who is needy + give it to speculaters who has money plen-ty." An article reprinted in the *Raleigh Gazette* extended Powell's logic, with its author arguing that a just society allowed men to meet their highest duty, "to furnish" their families "with food and raiment." "The worst feature" of the postwar years was not that many "found themselves reduced to poverty" but that men "thus reduced were surrounded by large and helpless families": "As he looked around upon his humble home . . . and thought of his relentless creditors . . . his brave heart . . . sunk down in despair, as he saw in contemplation his shivering wife and helpless little ones turned out from the old homestead by the fiat of the law, and the clang of the sheriff's malliet, under the cry of '*Going—going—gone!*' Yes, gone!"[39] This man's inability to protect his wife and children represented a perversion of the natural order that no mere human law could ever justify.

Polly Pepper, a popular *Oxford Torchlight* columnist, embraced a similar view and used virtually the same words to express it. She also pushed the argument one step further so that it was the men themselves who were being auctioned:

> "Here is a son for sale! He was a mother's fondest, strongest only hope. He is a rare piece of property. What do we hear for him?" for so runs on the auctioneer; "And here is a husband and father. He has an amiable wife and lovely children as ever bounded the fireside circle. What do you hear for him?" Tears have been shed for him, but they'll not buy him back. Prayers have been offered, but prayers are not currency. Love has been pledged for his redemption, but he must be sold. Never mind his wife's fears and tears, they are not quoted in our price current. He is "going, going."

Denied the means to support their families and reduced to the position of slaves, Pepper's men lost their identity completely. They were literally "gone." Beaten down by economic policies that supported the pursuit of profit over the integrity of the "fireside circle," they were finally sold like slaves to the highest bidder.[40]

As we have already seen in chapter 2, African-American men emphasized the themes of provision and protection in their complaints against their employers, just as common white men invoked images of "shivering wives and helpless little ones." The delegates to the first freedmen's convention provided one of the most eloquent statements of this theme with the assertion: "Our first and engrossing concern . . . is how we may provide shelter and an honorable subsistence for ourselves and families." African Americans across the South echoed the delegates' concerns. Even before the end of the war, black Union soldiers and men laboring for the Union Army often voiced their complaints about their pay and treatment in terms of their concerns for their families' well-being. Writing from Texas where they were still on duty months after southern surrender, a group of Virginia soldiers demanded to be mustered out of service to attend to their families back home: "Our wifes sends Letters stateing thir suferage saying that they are without wood without wrashions without money and no one to pertect them." In some ways, their petitions sounded much like those of enlisted white Confederates. But if the words were the same, the conditions were not. Race heightened the economic deprivations and physical dangers of African-American men and their families. The families of black soldiers faced the burning hatred of their white neighbors, while African Americans who fled to Union lines performed unpaid labor in miserable surroundings under the watchful eyes of white troops. In Beaufort, North Carolina, for instance, a group of black men protested against enforced, uncompensated labor that left them incapable of "paying Rents and Otherwise Providing for ther families." Although eager to support the Union, they wanted to do so in a way "consistant with there cause as Freemen and the Rights of their families." The Virginia troops were more blunt: "Never was wee any more treated Like slaves than wee are now." Above all, it was their inability to look to "the pertection of our wifes" that made them feel enslaved.[41]

Another illustration of poor black men's sense of their responsibilities came in the withdrawal of freedwomen from full-time paid labor for whites in the first few years immediately following emancipation. Such was the decision of Pete and his wife, who lived on the Hairston plantation just over the Virginia border from Granville County. Their employer noted her frustration at losing the labor of Pete's wife: "Pete is still in the notion of remaining but chooses to feed his wife out of his wages rather than to get her fed for her services." Her words, however, simplified a much more complicated reality. Like other black women, Pete's wife did not leave the employ of whites to enjoy a life of leisure. Their husbands' wages hardly made this a viable option. Instead, African-American women entered a life of labor in service to the needs of their own families, the demands of which eventually propelled many back into waged labor, if only for occasional stints. But black men considered paid work, whether waged labor or the cultivation of cash crops, their primary contribution to their families' economic needs. As Jacqueline Jones has pointed out, this division of labor also addressed the physical vulnerability of black women and children. When only the male household head worked for wages, the rest of the family remained beyond the reach of white employers.[42]

Black women's complaints about their husbands threw expectations about men's responsibilities into sharp relief. When Rosa Freeman filed a complaint against her husband with the Freedmen's Bureau in Georgia, her husband's physical abuse figured as only the most blatant and painful example of a general dereliction of duty: "He has abused me & refuses to pay for the rent of my room & has not furnished me with any money, food or clothing." In fact, Freeman measured her husband's manhood through his attention to these responsibilities. Refusing his offer to leave her as long as it did not cost him any money, she demanded a legal divorce, apparently because it would force him to answer for his negligence in public. "If you want to leave me," Freeman insisted, "leave me like a man!" Sarah Field, of Kentucky, would have sympathized. She swore out a complaint against her husband for desertion in 1866 because she wanted "to get her husband back to help her make a living for herself and two children." Catherine Massey, the wife of a Union soldier, held her husband to similar standards. Asking her husband's commander that some of his pay be sent to her, she explained, "I am his lawful wife and he has neglected to treat me as a husband should." More specifically, she had "not received a cent of money from him Since last March."[43]

Despite the tone of their complaints, these women did not consider provision and protection the exclusive province of men in the same way that elite whites did. According to Massey, her husband was supposed "to help me to support myself as I helped . . . support him." She also made it clear that she was asking his assistance now because ill health and hard times made it difficult for her to support herself. Like Massey, most African Americans readily acknowledged the limits of men's earning power and the importance of women's and children's economic contributions. Even the delegates to the first freedmen's convention assumed that both women and men would work for "shelter and an honorable subsistence." Indeed, African Americans measured men by their own standards of economic success. Remembering her dead husband with great fondness, one African-American washerwoman gave him the highest praise: "He was a good husband and father and provided for his family as best he could." Her choice of words is significant. Aware of the economic obstacles her husband faced, this woman emphasized her husband's intentions, not the size of his income and his ability to purchase a fine home, smartly decked out with all the trimmings. The fate of the ineffectual Harry Silverton comes immediately to mind. By contrast, this widowed washerwoman considered her husband a success because he attended to his family's needs "as best he could."[44]

She also knew how difficult it was to obtain a bare subsistence, let alone an "honorable" one. Not surprisingly, poor black men sometimes pursued alternative methods. Although hardly "honorable" in the way the delegates to the first freedmen's convention intended, many of the African-American men brought up on charges of petty theft may have actually had their own form of this ideal in mind. Corn, bacon, and chickens probably filled stomachs left empty by meager wages. A few men pursued bigger goals. Solomon Ellington allegedly lured "1 yearling, 1 heifer, 1 bull calf, [and] 1 bull yearling" away from Wesley Grissom. While Ellington may have wanted to sell the livestock for cash, keeping the animals also would have secured the foundations of his household's economy in a way that other items, even cash, would not. Oscoe Lewis's tastes ran in another direction. In 1866, he was accused of lifting "sundry articles of wearing apparel," including "three pairs of pantaloons, 6 yards of cloth suitable for pants, one silver watch, [and] several outer and under dresses." New clothes for himself and his wife symbolized not only their new position as an independent couple but also his new role as provider within that relationship.[45]

By contrast, the racial ideology of the time eased the economic trials of common white men in a variety of ways. Perhaps most significant was that their claims to economic independence and the position of household head were considered legitimate, while those of poor African-American men were not. The comparison between debt relief, which primarily affected whites, and wage rates, which primarily affected blacks, is illustrative. Stay laws and homestead exemptions suspended the rules of the market to preserve the domestic relations of propertied white families. Despite stiff opposition from conservative whites, debt relief received widespread support in North Carolina, particularly among Republicans who hoped to bring whites into the party. Yet calls to address the economic problems of agricultural workers fell on deaf ears, even though low wages and exploitative conditions produced the very same results that prompted the passage of debt relief. Most southern political leaders accepted the ideological premise that the market should determine wage rates. As a result, even the most progressive legislation sidestepped the problems faced by wage workers. Laborers' liens, for instance, enabled workers to secure compensation for the work they performed; but that right meant little as long as wages remained below subsistence.[46]

Faith in the market's ability to deliver fair wages actually masked the economy's racial underpinnings. To be sure, depressed economic conditions lowered the wages African Americans received. But a pervasive racial ideology that cast them as dependent laborers played an equally important role. Wage rates not only reflected planters' assumptions that the labor of entire black families should be available to them just as it had been in slavery but they also set up the circumstances that produced that very result. African-American men's inability to support their families ultimately forced freedwomen and children back into paid labor. Yet the economic plight of black heads of households did not elicit much response from whites, who believed that black men occupied a fundamentally different position in southern society than white men. Although all white men could rightfully claim economic independence, black men could not. In this sense, black men were not truly men. Similarly, when the "shivering wives" and "helpless children" were black instead of white, legislators felt no pressure to suspend the market's laws. If anything, they rebuked African-American women and children for failing to support themselves.[47]

Questions of material subsistence shaded imperceptibly into those of public power. In an 1869 letter to Governor Holden, a group of men in Granville County made this point quite clear. If the Republicans' hold on power slipped, they feared that Democrats would "nulify the . . . republican form of Government and place the colored Race and labering Class of white people in the same position only worse as they were before." Both white and black men signed this petition, but the issues of economic and political powerlessness fused in particularly insidious ways for African Americans. A group of black men from Gates County wrote the Freedmen's Bureau asking for assistance against "the whiteman" who threatened them with violence if they did not work "at his price." Other planters used economic coercion to keep African Americans away from the polls. Writing from Rockingham County in 1872, Edward Ancrum claimed that Democratic landowners evicted African Americans who had voted Republican: they were told "tha mus get off tha land + in this place Lavrinburg i know sum of the men that would not let them vote becouse tha liv on their land." Beyond economic threats, the Democrats "say tha intends to kill every dam neger las night tha had a [vote] + tha brought out thair 16 shooters to kill the negros." Ancrum begged Governor Caldwell to send assistance: "If you dont protect us we will protect our selves or we mus die in our blood as dogs + hogs, that cant speak."[48]

Voicing similar sentiments, other African Americans openly argued that their race neither diminished their manhood nor undercut their ability to act as masters of their own lives. Black leaders, who continually emphasized the manhood of African-American men, drove this message home with particular force. Speaking at a mass meeting in Wilmington in 1865, John P. Sampson, a native North Carolinian who was educated in the North, claimed that the denial of suffrage "affirm[s] our incapacity to form an intelligent judgment." "By this means," he continued, we "undervalue ourselves" and "feel that we have no possibilities like other men."[49] Others argued that the way freedmen had embraced hard work and self-improvement proved them the equals of other men. "Look around us!" demanded the author of one editorial in the short-lived *Raleigh Journal of Freedom,* a black-run Republican paper: "See the colored boys and girls going to school; yea the grown men and women desiring to become intel-

ligent; some striving to make money to become property holders."
"Look at this," the editor continued, "and then say they are not men
as other men, according to the circumstances under which they have
labored these hundreds of years." The author of another article made
similar observations, implying that freedmen's "strength of character" would be the key to their success, ensuring that they "will eventually take their proper place in our political arena as *men*."[50]

Taking issue with the idea that black men would "eventually" earn
their place as men, more militant blacks expressed an assertive racial
pride. The dignity of one black soldier particularly struck John Richard Dennett, a northern journalist traveling through North Carolina during the fall of 1865. Dennett met this man at the first freedmen's convention, in uniform, "neat and clean, with every button
polished," just after he had been elected to office. As he told Dennett with considerable pride: "I's black . . . jist as black as ary black
man goin', I is." The context added meaning to this soldier's words.
He had assumed a public persona that was previously denied black
men on the basis of their race. In his mind, the term "all men" now
included those with black skin, who could still retain their particular racial identity even as they stepped into the universal brotherhood
of man.[51]

Abraham H. Galloway, a black leader from eastern North Carolina, used the same sense of racial pride to flip the conventional hierarchy and place African Americans above whites. "I do not wish to
be considered as the white man's enemy," he proclaimed to a mass
meeting of freedpeople assembled at New Bern in 1865. "No, sir," he
continued, "I think the white man is as good as a negro—if he will
only behave himself." Others agreed. Not just black leaders but ordinary African-American wage earners pointed out the innumerable
ways in which white people of North Carolina regularly violated basic principles of human decency and republican government. Not
only had whites defended the immoral system of slavery but they now
burned black families out of their homes, raped freedwomen,
whipped their menfolk, gouged wage earners, and denied all blacks
the basic rights of citizenship. In their letters and petitions, black
wage laborers and tenants also articulated a deep disdain for the
character of white employers and neighbors, who did not behave as
honorable men. This was exactly how William Allen felt about his
employer, John Stem. The details of Allen's story, in which he insisted that "he was a man, had a mouth of his own and would holler as
much as he pleased," are now familiar. In the exchange with Stem,
Allen advanced his own ideas of manhood. Above all, he demanded

respect, to be treated "right." As Allen saw it, Stem's refusal to extend this courtesy reflected poorly on his character. Stem was, according to Allen, a "rascal and a liar," not a man.[52]

Manhood, in other words, inhered in the way a man conducted himself. On this score, it was only too clear that all men were not the same. Indeed, white men's less than stellar example only underscored the need for African-American men to carve out their identity as men. To these ends, many black organizations pursued racial uplift. In North Carolina, for instance, the United Brotherhood opened its membership to "all good men." As the members went on to explain, that meant "every man who has respect for himself as an individual and as a citizen, and that has the interest of our race at heart—everything that appreciates honesty, industry, sobriety and charity." Within Granville County, black men joined the Masons, temperance groups, and various charitable organizations dedicated to serving the African-American community.[53]

The poor black men who labored under the hot sun in Granville County's tobacco fields probably viewed the bourgeois emphasis on "honesty, industry, sobriety and charity" with some reservations. Yet, even as class differences increasingly separated African Americans over the course of the nineteenth century, they were not nearly as pronounced as they were among white southerners, particularly during the first few decades following Reconstruction. Still, the emerging black middle class often spoke of race in ways that tended to abstract it from the class context in which most African Americans experienced it. Poor black men, by contrast, emphasized the concrete links between race and poverty. In 1874, for instance, violence erupted when Jim Royster taunted Ed Nuttall for siding with the Democrats. Believing that the Democratic party represented those with property and white skin, Royster saw Nuttall's vote as a capitulation to those who would ultimately undermine his independence. In his words, Nuttall "was a dam conservative dog" even though he "was no white man [and] did not have a red cent." Countering Royster's image, Nuttall claimed that "he was a free man and would do as he pleased." Then he turned the tables, arguing that it was Royster who "was no man no how."[54] Nuttall insisted on his freedom to vote as he pleased, regardless of the pressure to toe the Republican line. Because he made his own decisions, he proudly described himself as a "free man." By contrast, Royster maintained that independence could only be sustained by opposing the party of their former masters. In his mind, Nuttall had surrendered his independence and, by extension, his manhood to become a "conservative dog." But even as the two men disagreed over which course to steer, they had the same destination in mind. Both emphasized their autonomy. Neither Royster nor Nuttall, moreover, believed that manhood derived from property ownership or racial position. For them, it was the ability to act as they saw fit without the interference of others that measured a man's worth.

Many common white men would have agreed with Jim Royster and Ed Nuttall. Yet race grounded their sense of manhood in ways that prevented them from identifying with African Americans. Before the war, yeomen and propertyless white men defined themselves, at least in part, in terms of what they were not: they were free men because they were not black and not slaves. African-American men, by definition, were excluded. Emancipation struck down some of the barriers that kept them out, only to erect other obstacles. Among them were the racial and class insecurities of common white men: for when black and white no longer demarcated the boundaries between slave and free, the framework that helped to establish common white men's social position and to anchor their sense of self also disappeared. In response, they often lashed out against African Americans who rejected the old rules.

Nothing demonstrates the racial component of common white men's identity better than their participation in vigilante violence against African Americans. Of course, wealthy whites also rampaged through black communities. But even when poorer white men joined with their wealthier neighbors to terrorize African Americans, the two groups acted for different reasons. The same common white men who donned white hoods and ransacked black households also condemned those who insisted on upholding class privilege. To them, a world structured by rigid class hierarchies was as objectionable as one that was color-blind.[55]

The infamous career of Thomas Bridgers provides a window on these complicated racial and class dynamics. According to a Granville County superior court judge, Bridgers was part of a "band of robbery that play between Granville and Jones County." In 1867, Bridgers and his gang stole a horse and saddle from Alexander Brazil, an African-American man in Granville County.[56] Instead of stealing away unnoticed with the horse and saddle, they purposefully revealed themselves to Brazil. The only reasons the gang members could have in taking this risk were to dramatize the theft, intimidate Brazil, and watch his reaction. While Thomas Bridgers and Charles Lyman made their way to the stable to take the horse, Medicus Bragg and John White went to Brazil's house. Meeting Brazil in the yard, Bragg and White asked

Brazil if he had a gun and "a fine horse and saddle." Brazil replied that he did. Of course, the two men already knew that Brazil owned a horse. In fact, they were well aware that Bridgers and Lyman were riding away on it at that very moment. Nonetheless, the two gang members continued their exchange with Brazil as if the horse were still in the stable. After taking the gun from his house, Bragg and White ordered Brazil to go to the stable and turn over the horse. As Brazil peered through the darkness into the empty stall, Medicus Bragg crowed with satisfaction, "All right then."[57]

The theft reveals a great deal about the conflicted identity of Thomas Bridgers, Medicus Bragg, John White, and Charles Lyman. After the war, common white men faced the prospect of large numbers of African Americans acquiring property and, more importantly, the independence that property enabled and represented. By taking Alexander Brazil's horse, Bridgers and his gang stemmed the tide, if only for a brief moment. In their minds, African Americans like Alexander Brazil should not be able to own "fine" horses. More to the point, only white males should have the wherewithal to be independent men.

Many law-abiding common whites would have agreed in principle. But while they respected property as a symbol of manly independence, they did not view it as an end in itself. As the defenders of stay laws and homestead exemptions argued, property was important because it allowed a man to provide a subsistence for his family and to direct his own labor. Additional property or luxury items did not necessarily elevate a man's position. To the contrary, they could actually lower a man's standing, at least by standards of common whites who tended to look down on those who acquired property at the expense of others or flaunted it too blatantly.[58]

Thomas Bridgers, for instance, treated wealthy whites with the same disdain as he did African-American property owners. One year after his trial for the theft of Alexander Brazil's horse, Bridgers was back in court. This time, it was a prominent planter and tobacco manufacturer, Nathaniel Whitfield, who filed the charges, claiming that his factory had been burgled and that four of the missing boxes of tobacco had been found in Bridgers's house. According to George Vann, who also participated in the theft, Bridgers had been "after him three times to get him some tobacco" from Whitfield's factory because "there was a plenty." Where Whitfield emerged from the war with land and property that enabled him to take advantage of the booming tobacco market, men like Thomas Bridgers had few options. Their poverty often forced them to surrender what was left of their independence to men like Whitfield, hiring on as either laborers or tenants. In this context, Bridgers's diminishing status seemed directly related to Whitfield's growing prosperity. No wonder Bridgers "did not like Whitfield much."[59]

Apparently, neither did Bridgers's co-conspirators. All four— George Vann, Minger Perry, James Cannady, and Banister Walters— were poor African-American men who worked in Whitfield's factory. Their opinion of Whitfield and their reasons for turning against him remain unclear. They may have thought that they should enjoy a greater share of the factory's proceeds. Perhaps they aimed to get even with a particularly tyrannical employer. Or they may have simply seen an easy opportunity to enrich themselves. Most likely, some combination of the above lured the men into Bridgers's plan. George Vann's previous brush with the law points to this same conclusion. In this earlier incident, described in chapter 2, Vann's employer accused him of stealing thirty dollars. Vann, however, fired back by charging his employer with assault. When Bridgers offered to pay ten dollars for a box of tobacco, Vann seized the initiative. With the aid of his friends, he took four boxes from Whitfield's factory, clearly expecting to quadruple his earnings.[60]

Despite commonalities between Bridgers and his four black accomplices, the relationship was fraught with racial tensions. Their concerns overlapped only enough to make cooperation possible, and even that was tenuous. Bridgers, who resented property-holding African Americans as much as the wealthy Nathaniel Whitfield, carried his racial baggage into this crime as well. Bridgers enlisted the aid of George Vann and his friends because they had access to the factory. He never promised to split the spoils evenly. For that matter, he may never have intended to pay them at all. According to Vann, "Bridgers paid them but eight dollars, giving him three, James Cannady two, and Banister Walters three dollars, and promised to give them the balance at another time." Perhaps he was serious; but George Vann thought not. Vann immediately rolled over on Bridgers, testifying against him on behalf of Nathaniel Whitfield.[61]

Thomas Bridgers may have connected George Vann and his fellow black laborers with Nathaniel Whitfield's privilege. Despite five years of war and emancipation, African Americans still worked Whitfield's tobacco fields and factory. After the war Whitfield hired wage laborers instead of purchasing slaves, but he still lived on the labor of others and still commanded great wealth. From the perspective of common white men like Thomas Bridgers, it was as if nothing had changed. Yet the war and emancipation had changed everything for them. Just as the gulf between Bridgers and other white men like Nathaniel Whitfield grew wider, the distance between Bridgers and African Americans became narrower. In this sense, a common theme unites both of Thomas Bridgers's crimes. Whether he stole "a fine horse and saddle" from an African-American man or four boxes of tobacco from a wealthy white man, Bridgers was trying to reestablish the delicate balance that had defined his social position and his sense of identity.[62]

Faced with the same confusing changes, Charles Cole, another white man of humble origins, took a different approach. After moving several times while Cole was growing up, his family finally settled down on a 222-acre farm. Both Cole and his father labored loyally for the goals of the Confederacy. Cole's father fought with the Granville Grays, one of the county's Confederate military companies. Although too young to fight in the war, Cole joined the Klan afterward. The Coles' efforts, however, carried little monetary reward, and, like other common whites in the immediate postwar years, their fortunes declined rapidly. Eighteen sixty-seven found Cole's father on the farm he had owned before the war. By 1872, he was living in another neighborhood, with no land and only one horse to his name. That same year Charles Cole was also landless.[63]

Cole ultimately became disillusioned with the "cause." He traded in his white hood for a place in the state militia, fighting in Holden's War, Governor William W. Holden's attempt to suppress the Klan. Perhaps his family's persistent poverty prompted Cole to question his politics. Democratic policies, such as the party's opposition to debt relief, did nothing to alleviate his economic problems. Within the ideology of the Democratic party, moreover, his economic marginality translated into political marginality. In Granville County and elsewhere in North Carolina, the Klan served as the paramilitary arm of the Democratic party. Despite Cole's work for the Klan, however, Democratic leaders would never allow him to participate in party politics on equal footing. Men like Charles Cole were supposed to support Democratic policies, not make them. Cole, an ambitious man, probably chafed under this kind of treatment. His subsequent career suggests as much. After his stint in the militia, Cole joined the Republican party in Granville County, rose rapidly within its ranks, and won the election for county commissioner in 1872.[64]

Cole came to the Republican party by a very different route than African Americans did. If anything, his new political loyalties grew out of his disenchantment with the Democrats, not out of his commitment to the Republicans' fundamental principles. Still, Charles Cole shared key values with the freed slaves he now represented. The parallels emerged in an 1875 exchange with Robert Blow, the editor of the virulently Democratic *Oxford Leader*. Blow publicly denounced Charles Cole as a fraud, whose political vacillations and inconsistencies proved that base self-interest alone led him to join the Republican party. Not one to avoid a fight, Cole countered with a scathing handbill, shooting down his opponent's honor and trying to win back the trust of his black constituency. To make his point, he drew on images that resonated among both common whites and African Americans. Calling Blow an "infamous and howling Ku Klux Democrat," Cole condemned the Klan for violating the sanctity of the household, stripping men of their role as household heads, and thus subverting the natural order. Given these activities, Cole claimed he had no choice but to leave the Klan. In fact, he was proud to have fought against it: "Yes I did help arrest, imprison, and have convicted these detestable monsters in human form who went about at the dead and dark hours of night, took defenceless men, women, and children from their houses, maimed, outraged and murdered them simply for their opinions sake." Cole ended by refuting Blow's accusation that he and other white Republican county commissioners did "not associate with Negroes." True, neither he nor any other white commissioners had actually stayed with African-American families while they were in town on county business. But that, Cole maintained, did not represent a slight to his black constituents who were "honest and honorable men" just like himself.[65]

It is unlikely that Charles Cole considered African-American men to be *exactly* the same as white men. Yet his understanding of "honest and honorable" manhood seems to have been closer to that of poor African-American men than that of Robert Blow. Instead of using loyalty to established authority, inherited social status, or possession of wealth, Cole conceived of his identity and his manhood in terms of the ability to act independently and to look after the interests of his household. Of course, Cole's decision to ally openly with African Americans was highly unusual. But what it reveals are the areas of overlap between common white and African-American men. Their concerns for their own independence, their families' welfare, and their fear of the power of conservative white elites enabled these two groups of men to come together occasionally, even if they did not completely identify with each other.

The Limits

Looking back, African-American Martha Allen told a WPA interviewer, "I'se wucked purty hard durin' [m]y life." She even courted her husband while working. As Allen explained, she was riding "a steer an' cart haulin' wood ter town ter sell. He wuz haulin' wood too on his wagin, an' he'd beat me ter town so's dat he could help me off'n de wagin. I reckon dat dat wuz as good a way as any." Her story illustrates the ideal balance between common whites' and African Americans' notions of manhood and womanhood. Allen's husband assumed the role of protector and provider, while still respecting his wife's strength and independence. For her part, Allen admired her husband's efforts without feeling the need to feign helplessness or dependence. In Martha Allen's words, she still "wucked purty hard" and drove her own "steer an' cart."[66]

Not all relationships, however, were this harmonious. In fact, the overlap between men's and women's roles could just as easily engender conflict, as the number of domestic disputes in the Freedmen's Bureau and county court records indicates. Many involved infidelity, pure and simple. But most also turned on questions of men's and women's respective responsibilities and the relative distribution of power within their households. Like those women who charged their husbands with abuse of privilege and neglect of duty, many women believed their menfolk could do more to fulfill their role as providers and protectors. Men claimed their wives neglected their household chores, their children, and their contributions to the family income. Some men also expected much more deference than their wives were willing to give.[67]

The law gave household heads dominion over "their" dependents. Common white men were accustomed to wide latitude in governing their households, although they did not always exercise their power without contest. After emancipation, some African-American men assumed the same authority and refused public scrutiny of their actions. Robert Henderson was one. We last saw Henderson in chapter 1, as he talked calmly with friends while his wife, Frances, lay dying only a few feet away. Later, his neighbors revealed their knowledge of his habitual abuse of Frances, mobilized against him, and facilitated his conviction. The morning after her death, Robert Henderson adamantly opposed his neighbors' call for an inquest. Considering the growing suspicions about his role, Henderson's position is not particularly surprising. Far more striking is the way he asserted a proprietary right to her body with a belligerence that probably explains Frances Henderson's bruises, if not her death: "She was mine before she died and she is mine now."[68] Only he, therefore, could determine the disposition of her body.

Samuel Lawrence, another African-American man, issued a similar ultimatum. Accused of beating his wife, he responded "that she was his wife and he would prank with her as much as he pleased." Like Robert Henderson, Samuel Lawrence drew a veil around his relationship with his wife, claiming the privilege to act "as he pleased" without interference from either the community or the court. When the justice of the peace announced his intention to protect Mrs. Lawrence "so far as the law was concerned," Samuel Lawrence flew into a rage. After showering the justice with verbal threats, he fought off the deputy charged with arresting him. Declaring that "there were not enough damned negros or poor white men on the ground to arrest him," he also denied the community's authority to act as mediator and judge.[69]

If community members ultimately censured Robert Henderson's and Samuel Lawrence's violent excesses, they did not necessarily condemn the men's assumption of authority over their wives. The domestic disputes of two white couples that ultimately wound up in the state supreme court highlight the distinction. In both, onlookers intervened when they determined the blows to be excessive. One fight, between Ridley and Mary Ann Mabry, apparently attracted a small crowd. Only after Ridley drew a knife and slashed at his wife did one of the bystanders step in and pull Mary Ann out of harm's way. Those who witnessed Cynthia Oliver's beating stopped her husband, Richard Oliver, after the first four licks. Because Richard "struck as hard as he could," the observers thought four blows enough. Richard, however, did not. If no one else had been there, he boasted in court, "he would have worn her out." Yet, in both cases, onlookers considered these men's claims to power to be legitimate, at least to a certain extent.[70]

So did the Hendersons' and Lawrences' neighbors. When Mrs. Lawrence walked into court to obtain redress, she came alone. It was the magistrate, not her neighbors, who first offered to protect her, although they did ultimately turn against her husband when his bravado got out of hand. None of the witnesses who knew that Robert Henderson regularly beat his wife approved of his behavior, but neither was anyone sufficiently outraged to interfere on her behalf. Only Frances Henderson's death shocked their sensibilities, and even that did not come as a complete surprise.[71]

If African Americans and common whites acknowledged men as masters of their households, they did not necessarily grant men full dictatorial powers. Indeed, the extent of male power remained an open question. For instance, community response to a fight between David and Dicey Burwell reveals fault lines on this issue. As discussed in chapter 1, the incident took place in the Burwells' front yard, where David kept attacking Dicey and her sixteen-year-old daughter until Dicey finally managed to knock David unconscious. Afterwards, the Burwells' neighbors took sides. Ottaway Lee, who filed charges against Dicey for assault with a deadly weapon, clearly condemned the way she had conducted herself. The upstairs neighbors, however, sympathized with Dicey and testified on her behalf at her trial.[72]

Dicey Burwell gave the most decisive testimony of all. In general, the women who made domestic violence cases public offered the clearest opposition to male assertions of power. Where Dicey Burwell fought back with a maul, Cynthia Oliver, Mary Ann Mabry, and Mrs. Lawrence brandished arrest warrants. Regardless of the weapon, however, none felt that a husband had the right "to prank" with them "as much as he pleased."

Some, like Dicey Burwell, challenged assertions of male privilege on their own. Such an approach, however, could be fraught with difficulty because the law tended to support male assertions of power and oppose challenges to it. When David Burwell hit his wife, the court could not intervene unless the incident resulted in permanent injury to Dicey. But when Dicey hit her husband with the very same maul in the very same argument, it was a different matter entirely. Either way, women had to prove themselves victims of continued or particularly brutal mistreatment in order to bring the court to their side. Common white and African-American women had much more difficulty establishing such claims, because the law presumed them to be less sensitive and more prone to violent outbursts than elite white women. Justice Reade, for instance, drew racial and class distinctions with a heavy hand in *Rhodes*. Explaining why "every household has and must have a government of its own," he wrote: "Suppose a case coming up to us from a hovel, where neither delicacy of sentiment nor refinement of manners is appreciated or known. The parties themselves would be amazed, if they were to be held responsible for rudeness or trifling violence. What do they care for insults and indignities?" Reade then contrasted the sensibilities of the poor with those of "the higher ranks, where education and culture have so refined nature, that a look cuts like a knife, and a word strikes like a hammer; where the most delicate attention gives pleasure, and the slightest neglect pain; where an indignity is disgrace and exposure is ruin."[73] If the households of the poor were "naturally" more violent than those of elite whites, then there was nothing particularly unusual about David Burwell's violent outburst.

Despite the pitfalls, many poor African-American and common white women did try to marshal the power of the state on their behalf. But even when they did not, they still drew their communities into their domestic conflicts. Although the law dismissed "trifling cases of violence in family government" and placed them beyond the concerns of the state, these women insisted on their public importance. Documentation of their cases suggests the odds against which these women struggled. Whether the complainant was white or black, court officials usually gave only minimal attention to their charges. Usually, all that remains is the formal complaint, which gives only the names of the parties involved. It provides no information on the events leading up to the charges, let alone any insight into the woman's perspective on them. Ironically, then, the court often erased women at the very moment they demanded public recognition. Mrs. Lawrence's experience is particularly telling. After she made her complaint, public attention focused on the conflict between the magistrate and her husband. In fact, the magistrate's testimony suggests that he was not really concerned with Mrs. Lawrence's well-being at all. Earlier that day, Samuel Lawrence had disrupted the courtroom during another trial and had repeatedly ignored the magistrate's orders to settle down. By the time Mrs. Lawrence appeared, the magistrate was already more than willing to make life difficult for her husband and probably agreed to arrest Samuel for this reason. Then, when Samuel threatened him and lashed out at the deputy, even better options presented themselves. Charging Samuel with resisting arrest, the magistrate dropped all reference to Mrs. Lawrence and her complaint. After all, such "trifling" cases were not really worthy of public notice anyway.[74]

When court officials did take notice, they imposed legal categories on domestic violence cases that further obscured women's voices. In order for the court to intervene, women had to cast themselves as hapless victims of men who abused their patriarchal power. Few women, however, fit comfortably in this role, as the Burwells' fight indicates. Like other cases of domestic violence, their fight was not an isolated incident, but one of many in a very turbulent relationship. Dicey Burwell testified that her husband had "been kind to me since he professed religion but was cruel before." But if David was "cruel," Dicey did not suffer in silence. This time, it was Dicey, not her husband David, who was officially charged as the assailant. Yet her position as such was purely a matter of chance. If it had been one of David's blows that had knocked Dicey unconscious, instead of the other way around, she would have become the victim. In addition to striking back, women also attempted to mobilize community support in their favor. Filing charges with the local magistrate was an extension of both strategies, but this time a woman fought back with the warrant and the power of the state.[75]

The very act of filing charges reveals that these women held a different view of their rights as wives than allowed by law. They challenged the notion that their husbands could exercise broad disciplinary rights without being subject to public scrutiny. They also flatly rejected the idea that they, as wives, were without public recourse. Ironically, the same laws that privatized domestic relations also provided common white and poor African-American women with a public forum. While the state supreme court upheld the inviolability of domestic government in *Rhodes,* it also declared that the laws of the state did "not recognize the right of the husband to whip his wife." Moreover, it reserved the right to intervene in domestic government "where permanent or malicious injury is inflicted or threatened, or the condition of the party is intolerable." Revising the older "rule of thumb," the court now judged disputes by the injuries resulting from the assault, not the size of the instrument that had been used. This opening allowed poor African-American and common white women to use the courts in disputes with their husbands and to place limits on men's power within their own households and communities. In this way, the courts became reluctant partners in the efforts of poor African-American and common white women to enforce their versions of appropriate domestic relations.[76]

Even as women questioned the distribution of power within their households and contested the structure of the law, they did not place themselves in direct opposition to their larger communities. Poor African-American and common white women made their claims to state protection on the basis of their rights as dependent wives and daughters. Within the existing legal system, there was no other way to do so. Yet the women involved were neither unfamiliar nor completely uncomfortable with this approach. To be sure, the women who brought suits against their husbands had their own ideas about the substance of those definitions and the exact location of those boundaries. Their idea of rights, moreover, was access to public institutions to mediate relations within their families. But even as they questioned how dependents should be treated, they also implicitly accepted the basic outlines of a system that located them within households headed by men. In this sense, their challenges to male privilege coincided with other efforts to acquire the power necessary to defend household borders. As we will see in the next chapter, this strategy came with a price.

Still, the alternative constructions of manhood and womanhood embraced by common whites and poor African Americans provided the basis for a political vision that softened the sharp racial and class hierarchies of southern society. The implications were not lost on conservative elite whites, as their strident complaints about the "un-manly" and "unwomanly" actions of common whites and poor African Americans suggest. More than a minor irritant, the way poor African Americans and common whites structured their private lives issued an open challenge to white conservatives by subverting the foundations that grounded their sense of public order.

5

"Privilege" and "Protection": Civil and Political Rights

As Bella Newton's daughter and son, Susan and William, were walking home one afternoon in 1869, Alexander Noblin, a white neighbor, attempted to assault Susan sexually. Although frustrated in his attempt by William, who pitched a rock at his head, Noblin fired a parting volley. In William's words, he "shook his penis at us and called me a dam little nigger." With this gesture, Noblin symbolically reasserted his power over both children. After learning of the incident, Bella Newton's first response was in keeping with community traditions. She publicized her complaint in the neighborhood and then made an informal bargain with Noblin agreeing not to prosecute in exchange for one dollar and ten pounds of bacon. Noblin delivered the goods, but Newton did not fulfill her end of the deal. Instead of remaining quiet, she filed charges with the local justice of the peace, an extremely bold move for this poor black woman. In so doing, she challenged the privilege of a white man of some prominence. She also chose a course of action that had been closed to her during slavery, when both formal and informal practices sanctioned violence against African-American and, to a lesser extent, poor white women. Much to his chagrin, Alexander Noblin learned that his recent actions carried much different consequences than they had before the war.[1]

Only a small fraction of women launched legal proceedings like this one. But Bella Newton and her daughter did resemble the vast majority of southern women in that they did not measure up to elite white standards of womanhood. And like Bella Newton, these women believed that they deserved the same social respect and legal protection as elite white women, even if they did not live in a domestic setting that would pass muster with Sarah A. Elliott. Newton also insisted on the right to air her grievances in court, demanding that state institutions recognize her legal rights as a woman. Newton challenged not only antebellum conservative political principles that positioned people in relation to public power along racial and class lines but also the postwar reincarnations that articulated the same hierarchies in the language of individual character. In the process she gave substance to the Republican party's lofty principles. Republicans stretched traditional notions of universality to argue that full citizenship rights "naturally" belonged to all men simply because they were men. Thus empowered, men could secure to their women the privileges of maintenance and protection. Of course, party leaders at the state and national levels left their words in places where historians could find them easily. People like Bella Newton did not. Yet, she and other women of both races joined the front lines of political struggle, even though they were excluded from ballot boxes, political podiums, legislative floors, and even party rhetoric.

Poor African Americans and common whites altered the content of public debate, infusing it with their own ideas about men's and women's rights and social roles. But they could not completely reframe these issues, even if they wanted to. By emphasizing gender differences deeply rooted within a patriarchal family structure, they left key components of the antebellum power structure in place. Ultimately, conservatives would use this same scaffolding to rebuild racial and class hierarchies and to constrict the public arena.

Households and Public Power

At the time of southern surrender, it was clear to North Carolina's conservative leaders that all men were not equal. In their minds, men fell out in hierarchical order based on the gradations of independence and dependence created in the private sphere. Among white men, property measured both private and public competence. Property "purchased" a stake in society, the size of which varied directly with the value of the estate. "The acquisition of property," in the words of Jonathan Worth, "proved that [men] had intelligence and interest in the well-being of society." Propertylessness, by contrast, signaled both private and public irresponsibility. "That class," planter John Stafford sniffed in 1860, "possess but little else than moral polution having no property to destroy, no conscience to overcome, no God to fear." Ruled by their passions and improvident of the future, such men were not only poor, they were poor providers. Ineptitude at family governance disqualified them from public power. Even the most honest and well-intentioned of this class would succumb to lures of wily demagogues, or so conservatives believed.[2]

When racial ideology combined with class hierarchy, the result was even more virulent. Conservative whites considered African Americans a permanently dependent race even less politically fit than propertyless whites. The inadequacies of African Americans, unlike those of poor whites, adhered in their very nature. As long as blacks remained under the supervision of their white masters, they were happy, ineffectual minors who needed the guidance of their white masters to survive. Once Sambo and Mammy ventured out on their own, however, their characters changed dramatically. They became the menacing, oversexed black male rapist and black female seductress, images that conveyed the extent to which whites believed African Americans to be incapable of self-governance.[3]

Emancipation only confirmed conservatives' suspicions that the nation was poised too precariously on the slippery slope of universal rights and strengthened their resistance to democratic change. The first state constitution bore the mark of their intransigence, not only excluding blacks from the political process but also restricting the political power of common whites. Even then, many conservatives still saw ominous signs in the few privileges allowed to common whites, particularly those without property. Fighting to keep power out of the hands of those they considered unqualified to exercise it, conservatives opposed the direct election of judges, the abolition of property requirements for office, and the repudiation of Confederate debts. They even reopened the question of free white manhood suffrage. The new apportionment system was also too democratic for the most dogmatic among them. Where the antebellum constitution had counted slaves as three-fifths of a white person, thus favoring slaveholders, the new one based legislative representation on the number of whites only. Thomas Ruffin, the eminent antebellum jurist, scoffed at the new scheme precisely because it implied that political rights were universal. Everyone, according to Ruffin, knew otherwise. Civil rights, which ensured "security in person and property by the Constitution and the laws made under it," were "natural." But political rights, which "consist, not in the rights . . . as held *under* the law, but of the powers *over* the Constitution and laws," were not. Rights to change and amend the laws, Ruffin argued, should be distributed "according to the sense of the Community of the fitness of particular classes." Political rights, then, were particular, derived from a person's position within the community. Given Ruffin's emphasis on protecting the property of the "intelligent, virtuous, and valuable portion of the population," only those men with wealth and white skin possessed the "fitness" to rule. Other conservatives shared Ruffin's fears of the democratic tendencies in the new constitution. As Jonathan Worth maintained, the "tendency" of democratic government "is to ignore virtue and property and intelligence—and to put the powers of government into the hands of mere *numbers*." When the constitution came to a vote in August 1866, conservatives were instrumental in its defeat.[4]

If rule by "mere *numbers*" rankled the sensibilities of white conservatives, then rule by African Americans was completely inconceivable. Jonathan Worth voiced widely held convictions with his assertion that "the Caucasian race always has been and always will be superior to the negro race." "I know from observation of history," he elaborated, "that the African left to its own self-control, is so indolent and improvident, that he will not—indeed I think he cannot be made a good citizen." His characterization of Henderson Cooper and William Cooper, the two black men accused of raping Susan Daniel, relied on these assumptions. To him they were brutal "monsters," incapable of either understanding or controlling their actions. In fact, it was so difficult for him to imagine African Americans as independent political actors that he remained completely blind to the black community's role in stopping Henderson Cooper's execution and removing him from local jurisdiction. Instead, he lay the blame at the feet of northern military officials, claiming that it was they who created the commotion by "allow[ing]" Henderson Cooper "to go unpunished." In his mind, only wealthy white men could initiate and sustain such weighty political conflicts. The actions of a dependent people, by contrast, carried no public import.[5]

Thomas Ruffin made the association between race and dependency explicit, likening all African Americans to other household dependents. For the same reasons it was "impolitic and unsafe" to grant white women and children political power, the state should bar black men from suffrage "for all time to come, if not forever." B. F. Moore, the principal architect of the state's Black Code, fused class and race in one image of dependency and forecasted doom if African-American men could vote: "The race, long degraded by servitude, ignorant of the politics of government, very low in its grade of morals, and wholly dependent for a living on the ability of the wealthier class of society, would, if allowed to vote, consult their material aid, and speadily engender among the whites, hosts of vile and reckless demagogues." To men of like mind, the state's Black Code granted a dependent race far too many privileges already. These conservatives absolutely refused to consider the possibility of political rights.[6]

When propertyless whites provided the reference point, however, the sharp racial contrasts softened considerably. For conservatives, race never functioned in isolation from other relations of power.

Instead, race combined with class and gender to anchor a hierarchical worldview in which the primary line of demarcation separated those who could sustain households from those who could not. Despite all their other differences, neither poor white nor black men were fit for public power. Indeed, this political categorization often caused conservatives to exaggerate the unity of interest and the potential for political cooperation between the two groups. The specter of biracial revolt haunted Jonathan Worth, who described the "majority in all times and in all countries" as "improvident and without property." Without the guidance of the "better class," they would soon degenerate into "a great mob ruled by the will of the hour."[7] He even used racial imagery to describe poor white men, referring to "the black and white negro" and "negroes and albinoes." With these labels, Worth distinguished between the races, while simultaneously destabilizing the racial identity of poor whites to highlight the similarities among all those he considered politically incompetent. "Albinoes" and "white negroes" were only nominally white. In their relation to public power, they occupied a place closer to African Americans than to propertied white men like himself. But the least reliable of all poor white men were those who refused to toe the conservative line and quietly accept their subordinate place in the political order. It was actually politically active poor whites who were the "albinoes" and "white negroes" Worth so scorned—and so feared.[8]

Whereas the likes of Thomas Ruffin and Jonathan Worth dug in their heels, moderate white North Carolinians accepted the inevitability of change and counseled prudent compromise. Some hoped to avoid more radical measures brewing in the North.[9] Others took their cue from unrest within their counties, where angry whites demonstrated their unwillingness to resurrect a social and political order that had so recently betrayed them. As propertyholders and household heads many common white men could identify with some pieces of conservative ideology, but they had never been enthusiastic about some of its more hierarchical elements. The Civil War only solidified their opposition. The burden of the Confederacy's war policies fell heavily on yeoman and poor white families, some of whom had opposed the war in the first place. As their fortunes declined, so did their enthusiasm for the war effort. Locating the problems in a political system that appeared to respond only to the interests of the wealthy, they resorted to extralegal activity. Even those from solid yeoman families often collaborated with propertyless whites, free blacks, and slaves, finding common ground in their opposition to the Confederacy's leaders and their policies.[10]

The bitterness dissipated slowly. At war's end, unionists trumpeted the dawn of a new political regime. According to the *Wilmington Herald*, a unionist newspaper that began publication during the war, the South had not gone down in defeat, only the "aristocrats who desired a government that would give them exclusive privileges and the benefits of *caste*" had. But now "their political and social influence has departed and they will be left high and dry in the future management of the state and general government, while the 'poor whites,' those whom they have looked down on and despised, will assume the reins, and henceforth led by such men as Andrew Johnson and Wm. W. Holden, moral courage and intellectual capacity and brain will govern the country, and the pure democratic principle will prevail." Agreeing with these sentiments, many moderate white leaders openly opposed conservatives' fiscal and political policies. Clearly, the same white people who suffered so much during the war now formed a formidable political force that conservatives ignored at their own peril.[11]

Yet, even as moderates sharply criticized conservatives' stubborn refusal to concede any new ground, they still accepted some of the same conservative ideas about independence and dependence. All men, they admitted, deserved full civil rights, which conferred the means to protect person and property and thus ensured "life, liberty, and the pursuit of happiness." However oppressive the state's Black Code was, it would have been that much worse if not for moderates committed to the idea that certain natural rights extended even to African Americans. While not completely victorious, they did manage to secure key concessions, most notably the right of freedpeople to testify in court, if only in cases where they were directly involved. A few moderates took the next step, including political rights under the rubric of universal rights. But many found the intellectual leap difficult. Unable to see African Americans as anything but helpless dependents requiring constant supervision, white moderates felt far more comfortable advocating the political interests of common white men. As the editor of the *Wilmington Herald* wrote in 1865: "The freed negro is not a citizen in the full sense of the term." Instead, he is "a denizen . . . having only the right to hold property, do business, and being at the same time subject to criminal taxation, and other laws, and without the privilege of voting or eligibility to office." Even William W. Holden, who would become one of the state's most fiery Republican leaders, initially opposed granting suffrage to black men.[12]

Like the *Wilmington Herald* editor, most moderates placed suffrage in a different category from civil rights, defining it as a privilege that men earned by meeting certain standards of responsible citizenship, generally property ownership and education. Although drawing heavily on the hierarchical particularism of Jonathan Worth and Thomas Ruffin, they did part ways from conservatives in the emphasis on individual merit, which implied that African-American men might eventually meet the criteria for suffrage, if they applied themselves. The same *Wilmington Herald* editorial that opposed universal suffrage, for instance, also urged the state legislators "to do every thing that they can to elevate this race, and the time *may* come, when, by giving indications of improvement and advancement, their claims for the right of suffrage will be granted by our State." Even then, those who admitted this possibility often pushed it so far in the distant future that they effectively limited the vote to white men or, as some quietly added, to propertied white men. "In our opinion" the editor of the *Herald* assured his readers, black male suffrage "cannot occur during the present, or perhaps the next generation, and consequently we need not give ourselves any uneasiness about it." Moderates, in other words, arrived at the same destination as conservatives, but by a different path. Many did not find the conservatives distasteful enough to jump ship and join the Republican party, but those who did ultimately consigned themselves to the reality of universal manhood suffrage, whether they agreed with it in principle or not.[13]

Within the North Carolina Republican party, other whites, both natives and emigrés, challenged the political significance attached to the categories of independence and dependence. Turning conservative logic on its head, they argued that the denial of full civil and political rights to freedpeople would make a mockery of the nation's founding principles. One of the most forceful proponents was Albion Tourgée, a northern abolitionist who moved to North Carolina after the war and worked actively for the Republican party there. Tourgée believed that the future of the newly reformed Union hung in the balance. But, unlike conservatives who believed that disaster could be averted only through the strict control of freedpeople, Tourgée maintained that the nation's survival depended on granting "equal civil and political rights upon all men, without regard to previous rank or station." William W. Coleman, a substantial North Carolina planter and antebellum legislator, underscored the point with a tragic allusion. "It can easily be shown," he thundered, "that if [freedpeople] are not to be allowed equality before the law, then the principles laid down in the Declaration of Independence upon which our government is based are words 'full of sound and fury signifying nothing.'"[14]

Implicitly linking the interests of African Americans to those of whites, these Republicans charted a new political course in which all men, regardless of race and class, stood as equals in the public sphere. Yet even the most idealistic among them could not completely transcend the influence of class and, more particularly, race. The dangers of which they spoke always seemed to threaten the nation in the abstract, leaving unacknowledged the hazards that freedpeople alone faced. Furthermore, the focus on the nation's well-being allowed white Republicans to avoid confronting their thoughts about freedpeople's fitness for public governance. Behind their color-blind rhetoric, many white Republicans clearly held reservations about African Americans in general. Even those whites most ardently committed to universal manhood suffrage and biracial political cooperation often depicted blacks as children in need of guidance and as passive recipients of rights they did not yet fully understand or deserve.[15]

The politics of North Carolinian Benjamin Hedrick capture the internal contradictions of Republicans who preached racial equality in theory, but found it difficult to accept in practice. Before the war, Hedrick had opposed the extension of slavery into the territories, a position so unpopular that he resigned his professorship at the University of North Carolina and left the state. With reasoning similar to that of Thomas Jefferson, whom he claimed as an intellectual mentor, Hedrick maintained that slavery corrupted the nation, jeopardizing its republican institutions and damaging the prospects of white freeholders. He did not concern himself with the plight of slaves, who, if anything, only contributed to society's degeneration through their presence. After emancipation, however, Hedrick advocated the extension of full civil and political rights to African Americans as free people. Given "'Republican Theory,'" he wrote to Jonathan Worth in 1867, "it is a political fallacy to deprive any class of full franchise." Yet he still questioned the actual practicality of granting the vote to a people he considered socially irresponsible and politically ignorant, admitting that it may well be "inexpedient and injurious." In fact, Hedrick ultimately found it impossible to reconcile his deep distrust of African Americans with his theoretical principles. Some of the time theory prevailed, for "as soon as you take the ground of political expediency almost anything may be defended, for instance monarchy, despotism, aristocracy, or any other system that has its admirers and supporters." Having taken this uncompromising stand, Hedrick then fell back on expediency himself: "If it shall be found on fair trial that universal suffrage is not conducive to the public weal, it can then be changed." With the doctrine of racial inferiority and dependency firmly ingrained in the minds of so many white Republicans, it was difficult for even the most progressive among them to include African Americans unconditionally within the rubric of universal rights, let alone accept them as equals.[16]

Most African Americans harbored no such doubts.[17] They believed freedom guaranteed their independence, the establishment and maintenance of which required full civil and political rights. As a group of black men from Goldsboro, North Carolina, wrote: "From a live-long experience as slaves of the men who now administer the laws, we cannot convince ourselves that equal justice will be meted out to us by them; but, on the contrary, we have in a year's experience of freedom, every reason to believe that without the freedmen's bureau, or some similar protection, we shall not be permitted to live even in peace, and our condition thus becomes really worse than when we were slaves and did not expect justice." Although cautiously phrased, theirs was no small claim. These freedmen challenged the idea that their interests coincided with the men who employed them. Since their employers could not represent them and the Freedmen's Bureau was a temporary measure, only one logical solution remained: they should be granted the public power necessary to defend themselves. Others were even more direct. At a mass meeting in New Bern, freedpeople denounced "the many atrocities committed upon our people in almost every section of our country" and "the enforcement of the old code of slave laws" that denied them equal protection under the law. Without public power, their lives would be impossible: Although "our condition has been changed from slavery to that of freedom, we are not insensible as to how unprotected and insecure we are left in the perpetuation of that freedom, without the elective franchise to sustain it."[18]

Black leaders and freedpeople themselves often framed such demands explicitly in the language of universal rights. In so doing, they consciously invoked a long tradition of protest that reached back to the Revolutionary period, when slaves and free blacks appropriated the rhetoric of the time to support their own struggle for freedom. Afterwards, black abolitionists continued to insist that the principles animating the nation's revolt knew no racial bounds, but justified the destruction of slavery and ultimately the extension of full civil and political rights to all free blacks as well. "We see no recognition of color or race in the organic law of the land," a black delegation headed by Frederick Douglass informed President Andrew Johnson in 1866: "It knows no privileged class, and therefore we cherish the hope that we may be fully enfranchised."[19]

In the postemancipation South, freedpeople as well as free blacks wielded these ideas in their efforts to counter efforts to limit or completely deny freedpeople's access to public power. Defining the public interest narrowly, conservatives and even some white Republicans feared that the inclusion of freedpeople within the body politic would introduce conflict into the public arena and endanger social order. For them, "universal" rights extended only to a particular group, delimited by race, gender, and often class as well. In response, African Americans used the political symbols of the nation's founding to pull at the boundaries of universality and, more boldly, to argue that attention to their well-being served the public interest. Quoting directly from the Declaration of Independence, the delegates to an 1866 North Carolina freedmen's convention rebuked the state's conservative leaders for ignoring freedpeople's rights and thus subverting the nation's founding principles. After all, they asked, was it not a white man who said that "all men are born free and equal" and "are endowed by their Creator with inalienable rights"? In the first few years of freedom, the words of the Declaration reverberated across the South, gaining authority with each repetition. Politicians, preachers, and publishers saw no need to rephrase what had already been stated so well and regularly worked pieces of the document into their speeches, sermons, and articles.[20] Like the delegates to the freedmen's convention, they held up a mirror to the nation. The reflection, they argued, told as much about the future of the country as it did about the rights of freedpeople, for the two were one and the same.

African Americans also reworked national icons. Their reading of history openly challenged conservative views by celebrating the role African Americans had played in realizing the promise of the Revolution. Where those like Jonathan Worth and Thomas Ruffin denied African Americans any place in the public arena, black speakers insisted that they had always been there. Henry McNeal Turner, a prominent leader in Georgia, included freedpeople's forefathers among the white founding fathers in a widely republished speech: "The first blood spilt in the revolution for the nation's freedom, was that of Crispus Attacks, a full blooded negro. A negro, then, was the pioneer of that liberty which the American people hold so dear." Attucks was only the first of many who had given their lives for the same principles. The delegates to an 1866 freedmen's convention in Raleigh completed the story, placing African Americans at the center of the Revolution, the War of 1812, and, finally, "in the bloody struggle through which we have just passed." If black people were now free, the delegates insisted, it was because they had fought so hard to free themselves.[21]

Within Granville County, African Americans made the Fourth of July one of their major holidays, thus connecting their own freedom to the nation's founding principles. July Fourth, the *Oxford Torchlight* moaned in 1879, "has well nigh 'played out' with the whites, and has been taken up by the colored people." According to the newspaper, the festivities lasted all day. Early in the morning, people from the surrounding countryside poured into Oxford, where they took over the downtown, decorating the streets, listening to speeches, parading, and picnicking. The Methodists served a meal in the Granville Tobacco Warehouse, while the Baptists dined in Taylor's Warehouse. According to the *Torchlight,* there was quite a "rivalry between the two factions, and each side labored hard" to attract the largest crowd. Pushed aside by African Americans who claimed this "time-honored national holiday" as their own, white Democrats stayed home.[22]

They did not do so willingly. Five years earlier, the county's black militia paraded through the streets of Oxford to celebrate emancipation day. The officers, mounted on horses and with sabers at their sides, led the rest of the uniformed company to the call of fife and drums and the admiration of an enthusiastic crowd. At the request of several white businessmen, the Democratic mayor ordered the procession to stop. The leaders of the march, however, promptly initiated a suit to test the legality of the mayor's order. They emerged victorious. One year later, the North Carolina Supreme Court upheld their right to peaceable assembly and delivered a pointed lesson in postemancipation civics to Oxford officials. "In a popular government like ours," the court declared, "the laws allow great latitude to public demonstrations, whether political, social or moral." To condemn this assembly would set a dangerous precedent that might end "all public celebrations, however innocent or commendable the purpose." It seems only fitting that a parade honoring emancipation provided the vehicle through which African Americans in Granville County demanded recognition of their rights.[23]

As this case suggests, the idea that rights adhered in the individual swept aside racial and class distinctions that were so central to the ideology of those who sought to define freedpeople as something less than full citizens. "If the abstract right to vote inheres in every citizen," asked Benjamin Wood, a prominent white abolitionist quoted in the *Wilmington Herald,* "why not in the native black man?" Echoing these sentiments, an assembly of freedpeople in Alabama announced: "We claim exactly *the same rights, privileges and immunities as are enjoyed by white men,*" for "the law no longer knows white nor black, but simply men." Or, as Henry McNeal Turner asked in the same speech that celebrated African-American contributions to the task of nation building, "Was it then because we were not really human that we have not been recognized as a member of the nation's family?" If so, then the proposition was easily refuted, since at the level of "bones, muscles, nerves, veins, organs and functions" all men were clearly the same.[24] This idea of equality actually assumed the presence of racial and class difference: all people should have the same rights even though they did not occupy the same social position or share the same cultural heritage. According to the final stanza of a poem that also appeared in the *Augusta Colored American:*

> Fair Afric's *free* and valiant sons
> Shall join with Europe's band
> To celebrate in varied tongues
> Our *free* and happy land.[25]

As the polity expanded to embrace the "varied tongues" of those from different racial and class positions, the "valiant sons" of Africa would stand shoulder to shoulder with their brothers from Europe.

The emphasis on "valiant sons," however, suggests that other differences retained their importance. If all men resembled each other and all women resembled each other, men and women still remained different at the level of "bones, muscles, nerves, veins, organs and functions." Depicting men as courageous defenders of their families' interests, Henry McNeal Turner underscored the importance of this role by portraying "our ladies" as the sexual prey of white slaveholders. The rights of freedom gave black men new power that enabled them to remove the women and children in their families from the exploitative grasp of whites. Black women, by implication, would also experience a new measure of control over their bodies and their lives, but through the protective efforts of their menfolk. Indeed, many African-American leaders referred to political rights in terms of their manhood. Demanding the vote for black men, James T. Rapier, a Republican congressman from Alabama, insisted that "nothing short of a complete acknowledgment of my manhood will satisfy me." As we have seen, African Americans and poor whites did not define the roles of men and women in the same way as more affluent whites. But even those who went so far as to advocate equal civil and political rights for women rarely challenged the basic importance attached to gender difference.[26]

In a struggle that reached back across the nineteenth century, first class and then race, although far less completely, ceased to define which men could legitimately exercise public power. In neutralizing the importance of these differences, reformers advanced a literal definition of manhood rights, emphasizing the commonalities among men. Nonetheless, assuming the mantle of manhood was no easy task, particularly for African-American men, whose proximity to slavery made them appear as perpetual minors in the eyes of many whites. To counter these perceptions, black leaders and their white supporters offered up their military service, their possession of taxable property, and their labor in building the South as proof of their masculinity. Whether in the battlefields or the tobacco fields, black men had worked as courageously and as diligently as white men to support their country.[27]

The presence of families, however, provided the most inclusive defense of manhood and the most compelling justification for full civil and political rights. Regardless of race or class, men could acquire responsibility for dependents as heads of households. All men thus shed the vestiges of dependency and assumed independent status through their essential difference from women, who relied on men for support and protection. Indeed, all men deserved access to public power simply because they were men. Summoning existing laws governing domestic relations that linked familial obligations to public rights, this logic carried great power. After all, the same body of law that required heads of households to support their families also granted them the civil rights and political power necessary to do so. Similarly, women could make claims on the state as dependent wives and daughters. African Americans thus harnessed a traditional definition of the household to serve radical ends. They placed the institution that had once buttressed slavery and defined African Americans as dependents at the center of their efforts to create a very different social order.

African-American men often began their demands for political rights with the same refrain used by the delegates to the 1865 freedmen's convention: "Our first and engrossing concern . . . is how we may provide shelter and an honorable subsistence for ourselves and families." With it, they asserted their position as independent men and affirmed their status as full citizens in a way that they had never been able to use before. "We wish to work and take care of our selfs and familys and benefit the Contary all we can and live upright just and honorable," wrote a group of men from Gates County. "How can we," they asked, when "we hav . . . no protection and no privilege?"[28] In other words, how could they without the civil rights and the political power necessary to enforce recognition of their rights?

In 1865, civil rights and the vote seemed sufficient. "What we want," demanded the editor of the *Raleigh Journal of Freedom* in the fall of that year, "is law to protect our homes, our families and all that is dear to us. When brutal ruffians stalk into our peaceful dwelling[s], insulting our wives and daughters, we want law to bring those ruffians to justice, and the right to call black men to the witness stand to testify against them. . . . When we have these rights, and not till then, will justice have been vindicated."[29]

Not coincidentally, the extension of civil and political rights prompted another round of violent actions against African Americans. The hooded vigilantes struck at the structural foundations of black power: their households. Bursting in on families in the dead of night, the Klan destroyed their belongings, burned their houses, and then beat, raped, tortured, and murdered their members. During the 1868 elections, the Klan raged with particular intensity in Granville County. "The kukulks klan," Moses M. Hester, Joseph Coley, and Jacob Winston wrote in desperation to Governor Holden, "is shooting out famlys and beeting them notoriously we do not know what to do." Elaborating on the situation, another group claimed that the violence "is geting to be a General thing": "on thursdy night last they went to a Colored mans house and Got him out and Beet him [illegible word] and beet his wife and cut her Dress open and tied her to a tree. then told Them if ever they told it or told who it was They would kill them. They then went to another ones house and comence tarring [tearing] the top of his house off . . . [they] Got hold of his wife . . . and she Got Loose and ran and they shot her In the back and by [the] side of the face and she now lies in a low state of helth and a Few nights ago they went to a nother colored Mans house and treeted him the same." In this way, vigilantes dealt a double blow. The terror might keep African-American men from voting. If not, the Klan still scored a victory, because the vote meant little as long as black men lacked power to protect their families.[30]

Some African Americans began to doubt that the vote or civil rights would ever amount to anything. A group from Halifax County, for instance, decided to throw in the towel and make a new home for themselves in Liberia. Writing Congressman Elihu Washburne for financial assistance, the men who represented the group explained that they had endured material deprivation and physical violence only to conclude that their hopes for a bare subsistence were illusory: "Some of us have not been paid for our work for two year back & they will not pay us for our work. . . . The blackman haves his family and feed himself & . . . [he] must Starve next winter he cannot live." At this point, they no longer wanted the land "because it is poluted with our blood." In a place where compensation for their labor came in the form of starving families and the likelihood of being "shot like mad dogs," they could never be men. Instead, these black men of Halifax County wished "to get home to our forefathers land." As the proliferation of emigration societies across the South suggests, many other African Americans arrived at a similar decision.[31]

The vast majority, however, determined to stay and fight. By the 1870s, the struggle had acquired a distinctly militant cast. In 1876, for instance, John W. Johnson wrote to Republican governor Curtis Brogden requesting arms for his volunteer militia of sixty African-American men. "Those that have Guns," he explained, "had to take their hard earned dimes and dollars to buy them with owing to the hardness of times there are but few that have purchased guns We are very anxious for Guns and would like to have improved guns if there is any possible chance for us to get them." African Americans in Granville County organized a similar company. The reports of brutal racial violence that filled every Reconstruction governor's correspondence leave little question as to why these men felt the need to arm themselves.[32] To the extent that justice actually was vindicated, the daily struggles of African Americans contributed as much as Johnson's guns. These people not only worked to realize the principles set down in law but also aimed to revise their content. In this arena, it was women like Bella Newton who often took the lead.

The Politics of Manhood and Womanhood

Before the war, the rights of womanhood, like those of manhood, were particular. The legal treatment of sexual assault threw the contours of this system into sharp relief. Southern law did not allow slaves the rights of men and women or even recognize them as such: slaves were slaves. Consequently, slave women could not file sexual assault charges and their menfolk could not protect them in any legally recognized way. Free women held more rights in theory, but not always in practice. If poor white or free black women summoned the courage to bring a complaint, the court often ignored them. Officials subjected the morals of those who pressed charges to intensive scrutiny, a process that generally discredited free black and poor white women, who inevitably fell short of the strict standards required to establish feminine "virtue." In this respect, Susan Daniel's case was anything but typical, revealing far more about the highly charged political climate than about the experience of white women who filed rape charges. Insulated by their racial and class position, wealthy white women were the least vulnerable of all southern women to violence by men outside their family circle. When they did cry rape, their male kin often took justice into their own hands, exacting retribution themselves rather than waiting for the slower, more impersonal court system. Flaunting legal procedure, they reinforced their place within this hierarchy, as those who embodied public power and controlled the rules to which others were subject.[33]

The Cooper-Daniel case signaled the breakdown of the antebellum order and the beginning of a new era of contest. Although sexual violence cases rarely made their way into court before the Civil War, they did so with increasing frequency afterwards. Between 1865 and 1886 the Granville County courts tried twenty-four such cases, almost evenly divided between black and common white women complainants.[34] These cases unmask the fiction of black-male-on-white-female rape perpetuated by conservative Democrats. Emancipation did not invert the social hierarchy: white men were not reduced to abject powerlessness, nor were their womenfolk exposed to sexually predatory black men. With the exception of an 1886 case that was as atypical and politically charged as the Cooper-Daniel case, no elite white woman pressed rape charges in the Granville County courts. If anything, emancipation heightened the vulnerability of African-American women to violence at the hands of white men, who used rape and other ritualized forms of sexual abuse to limit black women's freedom and to reinscribe antebellum racial hierarchies. Common white women were less vulnerable. Still, none of their cases came close to generating the public outrage that Susan Daniel's did. Even when the alleged aggressor was black, most cases went quietly through the courts, received little or no notice in the local press, and resulted in minor prison terms for the convicted men.[35]

The postwar years also opened new opportunities for African-American and common white women, particularly poor white women, to secure public recognition of their legal rights as women—rights that had previously been denied them because of their race and class. As described in the previous chapter, they asserted their own sense of womanhood through the ordinary actions of daily life—taking pride in hard physical labor, insisting on the time to tend to their own families, claiming the right to move freely in public places, and demanding a voice in shaping relations within their households. Like Bella Newton, they also refused to acquiesce to sexual violence. Of course, the race and class of the accused men played no small part

in the outcome of a case. Most of those convicted were either common white or African-American men with weak ties to or bad reputations in the community. But then race and class also determined
who could be accused in the first place. African-American women
were most successful when prosecuting assailants who were also black.
Although common white women sustained suits against white and
black men, they rarely accused white men above them on the social
ladder. The absence of cases involving wealthy white men, however,
does not exonerate them. As the Freedmen's Bureau records, Klan
testimonies, and WPA slave interviews indicate, such men regularly
assaulted African-American women and, to a lesser extent, common
white, particularly poor white, women.

Nonetheless, postwar sexual assault cases represented a significant
departure from the past, when public recourse was impossible for all
African-American women and many white women. Even more different are the verdicts, which often went in favor of the women who
brought charges. In fact, the number of sexual assault cases significantly underrepresents the extent of women's resistance. Some cases listed as assaults were actually attempted rapes. These women,
moreover, did not challenge only violence that was sexual in nature.
Between 1865 and 1886, they also initiated more than fifty-five cases
involving some kind of physical attack or personal injury. As their
harrowing descriptions reveal, violence did not have to be sexual to
be physically debilitating and emotionally devastating. All of these
cases became public precisely because notions of womanhood had
already changed enough so that African-American and common
white, particularly poor white, women could claim inclusion within
that term. In turn, these women contributed to the ongoing transformation of womanhood and its legal implications.[36]

After the war, many elite whites placed poor common and black
women on a scale somewhere between immoral and depraved, unless given strong evidence to the contrary. The term "bad character"
summed up all their prejudices. Of course, common white and African-American communities could also judge women to be "bad characters." Such women had generally violated community standards, by
introducing conflict through gossip, meddling ineffectively in other
people's lives, or making excessive demands on community resources. For elite whites, however, "bad character" encompassed different
kinds of "inappropriate" behavior—flamboyant dress, verbal or physical aggression, boisterous public display, open familiarity with men,
sloppy housekeeping, insufficient attention to the duties of motherhood, lack of deference, or simply life outside a male-headed family.

Despite the emphasis on individual character, this definition of "bad character" derived its meaning from racial and class distinctions. Women so labeled were invariably black, poor, or both.

Many common white women, according to the northern journalist Sidney Andrews, were "slatternly and utterly without any idea of decency or propriety." Lumping yeomen and propertyless whites together, northern commentators such as Andrews were fascinated with white "clay-eaters" and found in them evidence of the South's inferiority. Even so, they reserved their most biting criticism for the women. Many elite white southerners concurred, although they attributed these women's flaws to different sources. They believed that women of propertyless and even yeomen families were unable to control their passions and, as a result, succumbed regularly to sexual temptation. Such assumptions, for instance, necessitated Governor Worth's transformation of Susan Daniel into the flower of southern womanhood. For her to be a believable victim, she could not be the poor white woman that she actually was. Even Justice Edwin G. Reade, who professed Republican sympathies, used language strikingly similar to that of Andrews, drawing a sharp distinction between "the higher ranks" and those who lived in "hovels" in his decision in *Rhodes*.[37]

The experience of Temple Cass, who lived just over the border in Warren County, illustrates the operation of these class distinctions. In 1869, she charged William Somerville, a black man, with rape. After his conviction on the lesser charge of attempted rape, sixty men petitioned Governor William W. Holden for Somerville's pardon. The signers represented a cross section of the county, with Republican leaders, white and black, prominent among them. It seems likely that one of these party leaders wrote the petition, which was carefully crafted to conform to the rhetorical conventions of the time. To be sure, the politics of the county's Republican leaders disposed them toward Somerville, if only to support a cause popular among their black constituency. But whatever their thoughts about Somerville, they argued their case through Temple Cass, harnessing all the negative assumptions about poor white women to discredit her story.

According to the petition, Cass ranked high among the indecent and slatternly women Sidney Andrews described. Not only did she have an illegitimate child but she also had been recently abandoned by yet another man, who "after taking many indecent and improper liberties with her" had disappeared from the county. As the petition described the situation: "So great was the desire of the said prosecutrix [Cass] to get possession of money in order that she might have the means of pursuing and overtaking the young man Robertson who had wronged and deserted her, that she was influenced to a very great degree to submit to prostitution even at the hands of one of a different race and color." Of course, the petitioners' insistence that Cass became desperate when her lover left may have little to do with Cass's own view of the situation or her reasons for taking up with Somerville. But her sexual morality was crucial to the petitioners' argument. As a woman with no virtue to steal, she was incapable of being raped. Cass, the petition maintained, had pressed charges only to make Somerville pay up. Why else would a prostitute claim to have been raped?[38]

If the virtue of common white women was often tainted, then African-American women had none at all. They suffered in the shadow of Jezebel, an image that combined racial, class, and gender prejudices to portray black women as totally consumed with sexual desire. Two very different accounts of one black woman, a domestic servant named Sarah Barnett, suggest how strong Jezebel's influence was. The accounts grew out of a labor dispute, discussed in chapter 3, between Barnett and her white employers, Richard Pines and his wife. According to the court record, Mrs. Pines hit Barnett with a stick after she ignored an order. In retaliation, Barnett struck back with the only weapon available—her bare hands. Unfortunately for Barnett, the local court did not see her actions as self-defense and convicted her of assault. The Pines may have thought the incident settled, but news of the case made its way to Washington, D.C., through a letter to the *National Republican*. Alleging racial violence and judicial bias, this version of the incident did not end with Barnett's blows to Mrs. Pines. Instead, it was Richard Pines who delivered the final shot, quite literally with a bullet through Barnett's shoulder. Ending its account with the image of Barnett standing in court, "bathed in her own blood," the *National Republican* left no doubt as to the real victim in the incident.[39]

The editor of the *Torchlight* disagreed. Livid at the *National Republican*'s account of the case and even more incensed by its criticism of the county's judicial system, the *Torchlight*'s editor completely reversed the northern newspaper's conclusion. Sarah Barnett, he maintained, had overwhelmed Richard Pines. After mercilessly beating Mrs. Pines, she left the house "breathing vengeance" against the family. She then intercepted Richard Pines on his way to the magistrate and brutally attacked him with a "deadly weapon." Pines, the editor piously implied, had no choice but to fire on her. Besides, she received only a "slight flesh wound." Clearly, this "decrepid" man had no chance against "an athletic woman of low grade intellect and violent character, a thief and a prostitute." The editor could have been describing Jezebel herself. Indeed, it was Jezebel's offstage presence that allowed the editor of the *Torchlight* to turn Sarah Barnett into a menace who could terrorize the armed Richard Pines with virtually no effort whatsoever.[40]

As unquestioned models of feminine propriety, elite white women embodied the standard against which all other women were judged. One defense lawyer applied this measure directly to the black victim in a rape case he was trying. Speculating to himself, he mused: "Suppose it was [a] respectable white girl." By the *Torchlight's* editor's estimation, Amelia Linklaw was. After falling in love with a dashing traveling salesman, J. E. Hartman, she went against her better judgment and became sexually involved with him. The result was pregnancy. If that were not scandalous enough, Hartman then refused to fulfill his duty and marry her. Determined to exact retribution, Linklaw went to Hartman's hotel room and shot and killed him. Although the editor of the *Torchlight* admitted her guilt and conceded that the "law must take its course," he did not condemn Amelia Linklaw as he had Sarah Barnett. To the contrary, he maintained that in "a moral sense there is not the shadow of a doubt but that she was justifiable in taking the life of the man who had under false pretenses robbed her of all that was dear to her—her virtue." Unlike Sarah Barnett and Temple Cass, Amelia Linklaw had "respectable connections." In short, she was a white woman from a family of means, prerequisites that established her "virtue." Race and class thus wrapped around her like a protective cocoon, confirming her inherent innocence and excusing her from responsibility for her actions. Her story was, in the words of the *Torchlight's* editor, "the saddest affair that ever darkened the pages of North Carolina history." The same strands entangled Sarah Barnett and Temple Cass quite differently. They could not be similarly "robbed" because they had never possessed virtue in the first place. In fact, the editor of the *Torchlight* held women like these responsible for their own actions and those of everyone else around them. After all, women of "bad character" only invited abuse.[41]

The importance attached to a woman's "character" contained a legal as well as a social dimension. By law, a woman could establish rape only if she could prove that the act had been committed against her will. In cases of assault with intent to commit rape, she had to demonstrate that rape would have resulted if the attack had not been stopped. After the war, the state supreme court adopted a far more liberal stance toward rape and sexual assault, making it much easier for women to secure convictions. But sexual violence cases still hinged on evidence of resistance. Thus the law placed the woman herself on trial in the sense that her actions, as much as those of her male assailant, determined whether the act was a crime. Jane Williams learned this in 1877. She had been sleeping with her husband in their home when their hired man slipped into bed and awoke her with the feel of his hands on her body. Still groggy from sleep, she believed the advances to be those of her husband. Only too late did she discover otherwise. Sympathizing with Williams's predicament, the state supreme court used it to call for legislation protecting married women from predatory men who impersonated their husbands. Nonetheless, the court threw out the case because existing law identified the absence of resistance as evidence of consent, even if to the wrong man. A woman's reputation inevitably figured into the equation as well, because the court also considered the assailant's interpretation of the woman's actions. Resistance at the time did not necessarily cancel out any part of a woman's past that might cause a man to identify her as a consenting partner. As long as he believed her willing, he might legitimately proceed on that assumption, her protestations to the contrary notwithstanding. Needless to say, women like Sarah Barnett and Temple Cass always found it more difficult to establish their credibility than propertied white women with "respectable connections" like Amelia Linklaw.[42]

Women also found their characters on trial in other cases besides those of sexual assault, although the line between sexual assault and other forms of physical violence often blurred in practice. In 1876, for instance, Leatha Harris, a black woman, filed charges against James Stewart, also black. Although Stewart was charged with assault, the testimony suggests that Harris was also defending herself from his sexual advances. Apparently, the two were in the midst of some disagreement. On the day of the incident, Stewart sent for Harris, who went to his house, perhaps thinking that he wanted to resolve matters. What she got was a beating. Harris defended herself by striking back, first verbally and physically, and then legally. In court, Stewart maintained that Harris had started the fight by swearing at him. "Her language to me," as he put it, "were very abusive." Stewart pursued the same line of reasoning in questioning the witnesses, trying to establish that Leatha Harris had coerced him into the fight and deflecting questions about his own actions.[43]

Supposedly, women could invite physical violence through their language, dress, gestures, and other details of their daily lives. John Puryear adopted a strategy similar to James Stewart's when Bettie

Harris brought assault charges against him in 1869. Puryear maintained that she had purposefully incited him with "impertinent language." When she refused to "shut up," he defended himself from her verbal assault by beating her with a stick. William Bragg went a step further in defending himself against assault and battery charges filed by Mary Catlett in 1872. Bragg, a white man, denied committing the crime as charged in the bill of indictment. By way of explanation, he pointed his finger at Catlett, who was also white, calling her "wholly unworthy" and a woman of "general bad character." Catlett, in short, could not be trusted. More to the point, her bad reputation left Bragg no choice but to defend himself.[44]

Leatha Harris, Mary Catlett, and Bettie Harris were all assaulted by men of the same racial and class backgrounds who portrayed them as "bad characters." Yet these men did not necessarily define feminine "bad character" in the same way elite whites did. James Stewart's questioning of his key witness, the white Republican sheriff, exposed the gulf. When asked to describe Harris's character in his own words, the sheriff responded that she was "uncompromising in her temper when mad." As such, he identified Harris as an aggressive woman who fell outside elite white standards of womanly decorum. James Stewart's emphasis was slightly different. He characterized Harris as a "meddlesome person" and a known "peace breaker and disturber of her neighbors," specific traits that many African Americans and common whites deemed unacceptable for their own reasons—primarily because they disrupted established ties within their communities.[45] At the same time, Stewart, Bragg, and Puryear also seem to have believed that some women "needed" male "discipline," just like those men in the previous chapter who physically punished their wives, as the law allowed. In fact, the strategies these men pursued in court ultimately tell us as much about the legal position of women as it does about the men's attitudes. Whatever the men thought about appropriate female behavior, existing legal precedents that legitimized inquiry into women's reputations and cast a suspicious eye on those who lived in "hovels" encouraged certain lines of defense.

Many African-American and common white women disagreed. In challenging the men who assaulted them, these women pushed against the entire edifice that justified such actions. Significantly, none of these women responded to charges against their character. Instead, they confined their comments to the men they accused, thereby directing attention away from themselves and stifling speculation about their complicity in the attack. In 1881, for instance, Clarissa Wortham, a black woman, charged Jack Allen, also black, with attempted rape. Maintaining his innocence, Allen insisted that it was Wortham who acted improperly. But in Wortham's telling, the only relevant piece of information about herself was that she had rejected Allen's advances: He "came in the kitchen where I was washing. He told me to hug him. I told him I was not going to do it. He caught hold of me and threw me down and pulled up my clothes and got on me." Bettie Harris took a similar approach, stating simply that John Puryear had "violently assaulted her." "Taking hold of her," he "threw her down" and then beat "her with a stick, about the size of a common walking cane." The details she left out were as significant as those she included. By ignoring the evidence John Puryear used to establish her culpability, Bettie Harris maintained that her actions did not merit a beating.[46]

In her testimony, Leatha Harris moved the focus away from herself so effectively that she all but disappeared in the intensity of James Stewart's self-possessed aggression. As she stated in court: "He asked me what was the matter. I told him if this was what he wanted with me I was going out of his yard. He jumped up and caught me by both hands. I pulled one hand loose, he drew me up to the door, struck me in the mouth and called for a stick and said that he would beat me to death." "I got loose from him and started home," Harris continued, but "he followed and continued to knock me, after I got into my lot against Gus Bells House, he nocked me and continued to follow until he reached my House very near, when he struck me another blow which nocked me down. He then kicked me after I got up he said he intended to frail me well the next day and pay for it." Only in the last sentence does Harris come to life: "The next day I put off to Oxford to see if I could not get some friends." Harris no doubt played up her victimization to capture the court's sympathy. Yet, like Clarissa Wortham and Bettie Harris, she also rejected the idea that she was the one on trial.[47]

Sensing that others would agree with her version of the case, Leatha Harris went in search of "friends" in Oxford—Republican officials. She found them, and the grand jury indicted Stewart for assault and battery. Jack Allen, William Bragg, and John Puryear experienced a similar fate. The justice presiding over Puryear's case completely endorsed Bettie Harris's version of events. Finding her complaint "sustained in every instance," he ordered Puryear to pay a fine of $10.00 and court costs of $8.75, no small sum. Puryear appealed only to face even greater penalties.[48] Other common white and African-American women prosecuted violence, sexual and otherwise, with similar success. Each victory delivered a blow to the racial and class hierarchies that had kept these women outside the legal status of womanhood for so long.

The path African-American and common white women took to establish their rights was unconventional, to say the least. Their very presence in the courtroom as defendants in cases of violence, sexual and otherwise, confounded elite white notions of feminine propriety. Criticizing female lawyers in the North, the *Torchlight* breathed a sigh of relief that "none of our Southern ladies have deemed it consistent with womanly modesty and delicacy to enter such an arena. It is bad enough to be a witness in court, without being compelled to try cases the evidence in which are not suited to 'ears polite.'" Elite white women in Granville County rarely appeared in court even as witnesses.[49] If it was inconsistent for "ladies" to speak of or listen to indelicate matters, it was inconceivable for them to experience such things personally. When they did, as in cases of rape, they were supposed to play a retiring role, allowing their menfolk to defend them. Still, any brush with indecency, however coercive, irreparably damaged a woman's reputation. Her good name depended as much on what other people thought of her as it did on her own actions. Acknowledging this situation, the state legislature even went so far as to criminalize slander against women. "The very existence in society of innocent and protected women," the preamble to the 1879 act explained, "depends upon the unsullied purity of their characters." Consequently, they required special laws to discourage "wanton and malicious" attempts "to destroy their reputations." By this logic, women who experienced acts "not suited to 'ears polite'" and then willingly publicized their ordeals actively participated in compromising their reputations.[50]

Yet common white and African-American women did just that, upending elite white prescriptions by defending their respectability through publicity. The rhetoric of universal rights bound Republican officials to support them, whatever they might think of the individuals involved. But many of these women also acted on a less differentiated notion of private and public space, one in which women claimed access to public areas that elite whites cordoned off as male preserves. Poor African-American and common white women who brought rape cases to court, like those who prosecuted domestic violence cases, assumed that disputes between individuals would be resolved within the wider community. Regardless of the identity of their attacker, moreover, many common white and poor African-American women saw safety in publicity, which mobilized community support on their behalf. In pursuing such a course, these women stepped into an arena previously dominated by men. Bringing with them a range of new issues they thought deserving of public attention, they also rejected gender conventions that isolated women within the domestic sphere and allowed them public representation only through their male relatives.

For all their success, common white and African-American women ran up against definite limits. The one case of white-male-on-black-female rape suggests both how much and how little had changed for African-American women. In 1878, Sue Harris, a twelve-year-old black girl, accused Henry Regan, a white man, of rape. A white Republican justice referred the case immediately to the superior court and recommended that Regan remain in jail, "the offence not being in my opinion bailable." The brief comments about the case in the *Torchlight* were not only noticeably free of racial bias but also accepted the possibility of Regan's guilt. It even introduced the news of his arrest with the flashy headline "Committed Rape." Although indicted, Regan escaped conviction for lack of evidence, or so the *Torchlight* reported. Nonetheless, the court came surprisingly close to convicting a white man for raping a black female. In fact, the handling of this case suggests the extent to which African Americans successfully forced public discussion and revision of racial assumptions about black women. With its tacit recognition that white-male-on-black-female rape was a crime, the very existence of the case represented a victory of sorts for African-American women.[51]

The victory, however, was partial. If the trial measured the distance African-American women had traveled, the verdict revealed how far they still had to go. This case offended white sensibilities for particular reasons that did not apply to other cases of white-male-on-black-female rape. First there was Sue Harris's age, only two years over the limit for statutory rape, which defined any sexual act with a minor of ten years old and younger as nonconsensual. Second, the Harrises' strong community ties and Henry Regan's marginality seem to have diluted his racial privilege. Even then, the factors that brought Regan to trial were not enough to secure his conviction. No other case managed to get even this far.[52]

Common white, particularly poor white, women never muscled their way into the inner sanctums of southern womanhood either. Like Temple Cass, they usually found themselves on the outside looking in. Such was the experience of Martha Oakley, the mother of three small children and the wife of a landless man. In 1876 she and John Boothe, a relatively wealthy white landowner, pleaded guilty to adultery and were ordered to pay court costs and fines. But this was actually Martha Oakley's second punishment. Before the trial a group of black men charivaried her with drums and banjos, first circling and then marching through her house. As the testimony of one witness suggests, the group specifically targeted Oakley, waiting until she was home alone with her children to begin the ruckus. Frightened, Oakley gathered up her children and ran to her neighbor's house, claiming that "a crowd of negroes had run her off from [her] house." According to the neighbor, she had been sick ever since.[53]

The timing seems more than coincidental. Charivaris were a traditional method of social control in the South, often used to punish women and men suspected of adultery or other forms of sexual deviance. What makes this particular incident so striking is the race of those involved. The Oakley family registered its disapproval by taking the serenaders to court. The sanctity of white womanhood, however, did not extend to Martha Oakley, despite the sympathetic figure she cut as a frail invalid who had been driven out of her home by a group of unruly black men. To be sure, adultery did not do much for her image. But class and gender hindered her cause even more. Regardless of her indiscretions, class would have protected a wealthier white woman from being charivaried by a group of black men. Such an act against a wealthy white man was also unlikely, since these men usually managed to pass off their sexual transgressions as improprieties rather than serious crimes that threatened the social order. By contrast, the men who invaded Martha Oakley's house felt secure in humiliating a poor white woman, no doubt because they knew white officials would look the other way. They were right. Charged with disturbing the peace, they pleaded guilty, but received no fine.[54]

Sexual assault cases involving common white women did not elicit much more response. Even when the alleged attacker was black, the case usually made its way through the court system without much public attention. In 1885, for instance, James Huey, a white man, filed charges against Alexander Chavis, a black man, for attempting to rape his daughter. The case passed from the local justice to the superior court, where the jury declared Chavis guilty and the judge sentenced him to seven and one-half years in the state prison. That was all there was to it. Not only was there no public outcry but there was also virtually no notice of the case at all. The *Torchlight*, usually the self-appointed defender of feminine virtue, neglected it entirely. At least five other cases of black-male-on-white-female rape ended similarly.[55] That so many went through the courts so quietly highlights the relative powerlessness of common whites in a society stratified by class as well as race. Yet, if the treatment of black and common white women was sometimes similar, it was never the same. However much they suffered under the burdens of class, common white women still benefited from their racial status. Regardless of the woman's class, conviction in sexual assault cases was more likely and sentences far harsher if the victim was white and the accused man was black.

Common white and African-American women did not battle against sexual violence by themselves. They were joined by their menfolk, who supported their legal efforts and often initiated suits on their behalf. Injustice against women was injustice against them all, especially given the patriarchal values that framed social relations. Moreover, men and women shared the restrictions of race and class. If black and common white women could be abused because of their race and class, so could their menfolk. In his telling of the Cooper-Daniel case, for instance, Governor Worth did not just leave black women outside the bounds of womanhood. He depicted African-American men as unruly minors who posed a serious threat to the families of responsible white men and society generally. And he erased common white, particularly poor white, men and women from his narrative, thereby ignoring the specific class barriers they faced. African Americans and common whites in Granville County challenged these long-standing assumptions when they prosecuted violence against the women in their own families and communities. Not only did they claim their rights as men and women but they also exposed the violence regularly perpetuated against women who were not attached to wealthy white men. In this sense, the women and men who took sexual violence cases to court claimed public power just as assertively as if they had cast a ballot, giving meaning to the Republican party's rhetoric of universal manhood rights by securing "law to protect our homes" from "brutal ruffians" who "stalk into our peaceful dwelling[s], insulting our wives and daughters."[56] More than that, they bent the law to accommodate their own ideas about manhood and womanhood.

The Price of Protection

When common whites and African Americans claimed the "law" as their own, they were also compelled to work within its borders. Sexual violence cases were no exception. But the fit was close enough for them to acquire the rights and power necessary to construct and maintain households of their own. Men relied on the patriarchal rights accorded household heads in pressing charges. It was for good reason that a man's name often appeared with or instead of his wife's or daughter's on the court documents. Men's active participation benefited the women involved, given the entrenched bias against African-American and common white, particularly poor white, women and the legal presumption that defined a woman's sexuality as her husband's or father's possession. Susan Daniel's experience, for instance, suggests how difficult it was for a woman to sustain a rape charge in her own name. When she swore out her complaint, she identified herself as Susan J. Daniel. By the end of the case, however, the records referred to her as Mrs. Rufus Daniel. It is unlikely that Daniel herself had much to do with the change. The officials who produced the documentation probably just found it easier to deal with her as the married dependent of a male household head.[57]

Some women openly framed their claims to protection in terms of their rights as dependent wives and daughters. After hearing her sister-in-law's story of attempted rape, Ann Eakes went to her husband, demanding that he "kill the Black scoundrel." Apparently Eakes, a common white woman, believed that male relatives should defend "their" women. In another case, Adline Allen, a black woman, invoked the image of her husband to shield herself. Alone in the house at the time of the attack, she professed to have scared off the rapist when she "threatened him with my husband." Even those women who instigated suits without the help of male relatives did not necessarily reject the principle of male protection. Instead, they simply may have been taking on the traditional duty of deputy husband, temporarily donning the mantle of male power without changing or challenging their gender role.[58]

Ann Eakes and Adline Allen had good reason to defend their rights in the way they did. African-American and common white, particularly poor white, women hailed the promise of protection as a welcome advance from an uncertain past, marked by their vulnerability to physical attack and their inability to do anything about it. Claims to male protection, however, came with a price. To be successful, women had to play the passive victim, a role that did not always accommodate or even promote their interests. Like Susan Daniel, they tended to disappear as the law inevitably dealt with the case as a conflict among men.

The experience of Martha Overby, a young African-American woman, illustrates the dynamic that so often erased women from the proceedings. In 1883, she claimed that Major Peace, who was also black, had raped her while escorting her home from a neighborhood social gathering. Martha's father, William Overby, made out a formal complaint and righteously maintained that the "law must take its course." William apparently held a rather flexible definition of its workings, because he met with Major Peace and several other neighbors to discuss alternatives to legal action soon after filing charges. At this meeting, Peace promised to "work his hands off" for Martha's father if he dropped the charges. The prospect of free farm labor must have been attractive, but William Overby found the Peace family's mules even more enticing. William and Peace ultimately reached an agreement in which William would receive the mules if Peace did not marry his daughter. The stipulated time for compliance, one month, suggests that they were waiting to see if Martha was pregnant. As the nature of the deal suggests, however, her welfare remained peripheral to the negotiations. While William Overby clearly felt the need to protect his daughter and may have been honestly concerned for her, the fact that he also provided for himself in the process indicates the extent to which he equated his daughter's interests with his own. In fact, witnesses to the agreement later testified that William Overby was far more interested in the mules than his daughter's future.[59]

Despite the "settlement," the case went to trial. By this time community sympathy seems to have coalesced around Major Peace, who produced more than thirty character witnesses to testify for him. Martha Overby, by contrast, found herself trapped between her father's assertion of patriarchal authority and a legal process unfavorably disposed toward rape charges brought by black women. Finding no evidence that she had sexual "connections" with anyone else or that she saw other men at all, the defense attorneys could not establish Martha's bad character on these grounds. Instead, they accused her of trying to force Peace into marriage. Their notes even contain a satirical indictment that took off on official legal language and charged Martha with attempting "to violently forcibly and against the will of the said Peace make him become her lawful husband." After his acquittal, the court brought her up on charges of perjury.[60]

Martha Overby's voice was barely audible above the din. Her testimony, filling only a small scrap of paper, suggests a very different reading of events than those given by the defense lawyers or her father: "Martha Overby being sworn says she was willing for Major Peace to have some If he would marry her as Major promised to marry her she was willing for him to do it a little. Major said nothing about it and he would marry me if It happened." The story ends here; the rest of the paper was torn off and discarded. Martha's words reveal the innocence of a young woman charmed by the attentions of an older man. She also seems to have worked within conventions common to preindustrial people of both European and African descent that allowed couples wider sexual latitude when they were engaged. Setting certain limits, she consented to "a little" sex as long as Peace would marry her. As her testimony suggests, however, Major Peace made a very different promise. He agreed to marry her only if "It," presumably a pregnancy, resulted. When Martha arrived home that night, she confided in her mother, who decided to keep Martha's secret from her father for fear he would overreact. Only after it appeared that Martha might be pregnant did her mother break the news to him. The testimonies of Martha and her mother suggest that neither initially defined Martha's experience as "rape," at least not in the legal sense of the term. Instead, it was her father who labeled it as such when he filed charges against Major Peace. Once the case was in the judicial system, Martha Overby's version of events completely undermined any attempt to establish that she had been raped—perhaps that is why only a few sentences of her affidavit appear in the court record. But then, it was impossible for Martha Overby to explain her experience through existing legal categories. Obtaining redress would have been all but impossible.[61]

The laws governing rape did not accurately express William Overby's claims either. Although he was more successful than his daughter, he ultimately failed to manipulate the system for his own purposes. Indeed, the Overby case underscores the limits of this particular public arena. In cases of sexual violence, the price of success was conformity to the specific gender roles laid out in existing legal discourse. However much African Americans and common whites stretched the categories to accommodate the realities of their lives and their own ideas about appropriate conduct, there was only so much elasticity and the fit was never perfect. Try as she might, Martha Overby could not convince defense lawyers that she was the same as the "respectable white girls" around whom rape laws were designed. Nor could her father successfully carry off the part of a worthy, but aggrieved household head.

In 1883, moreover, Martha and William Overby played to a particularly unsympathetic audience. As soon as Democrats seized control of the state legislature, they moved immediately to restrict democracy at the local level, thus neutralizing Republican influence there. Their handiwork, a new state constitution ratified in 1876, made most county offices appointive instead of elective. By 1878, the Democratic state legislature had selected all the presiding justices in Granville County. Because justices exercised broad discretionary power to accept or dismiss complaints at will, the change in personnel severely limited the access of poor whites and African Americans to the justice system generally. Then, over the remainder of the century, the state legislature slowly expanded the jurisdiction of magistrates. As these Democratic appointees tried a wider range of cases without outside oversight, the legal position of African Americans and common, particularly poor, whites deteriorated still further.[62]

African Americans suffered the most. If the new justices listened half-heartedly to the complaints of poor whites, they often turned a deaf ear to those of African Americans. Although blacks in Granville County continued to use the legal system, their doubts about it grew. In 1877, for instance, John Bobbitt found himself on the losing end of a fight with his employers, Ben and Thomas Mitchell. As Bobbitt described it: "Ben Mitchell said to me, do you reckon we are going to pay you ten dollars per month to do nothing. I told him yes if I was doing nothing, I did what they told me as near as I could, he said he would burst my damn brains out with that hoe, I told him to do it then, he walked up and collared me, I shoved his hand out, Mr. Thomas Mitchell then said kill him Ben, kill him." Hoe in hand, Ben Mitchell charged at Bobbitt, who emerged with five scars on his head and one dog bite on his side (although, according to Bobbitt, the Mitchells "did not set [the] dog on me, he was there and volunteered"). As soon as Bobbitt recovered enough strength to get out of bed, he set out to file charges against the Mitchells. The justice, however, flatly refused to hear his complaint. Not so easily discouraged, Bobbitt walked to Oxford in search of the Republican sheriff. Bobbitt's perseverance testifies to his confidence in the legal system, which was no doubt bolstered by the presence of Republican officials. As they became increasingly rare, African Americans' pessimism grew. In 1880, one black Republican in Granville County labeled the inferior court the "infernal court." Warming to the subject, he joked with bitter humor that the presiding Democratic justices would lock up African Americans just for showing their faces at the courthouse.[63]

It was not just the court's personnel that changed. During the late 1860s and the early 1870s, the North Carolina Supreme Court extended new rights to African Americans and enforced those of poor whites. As Peter Bardaglio has argued, the courts were simultaneously increasing their own power to oversee and regulate the domestic sphere, transferring patriarchal power from the hands of individual men to the state. In *State* v. *Rhodes,* the North Carolina Supreme Court had refused to interfere in family relations except in the most extreme cases. But even as it upheld the sanctity of the household, the court increasingly lifted the veil surrounding it.[64]

The trend was particularly pronounced in domestic violence cases. By 1874, in *State* v. *Richard Oliver*, the court disallowed the traditional "rule of thumb," pronouncing it inconsistent "with our present civilization." In the 1879 case *State* v. *Simpson Pettie*, the court judged Pettie's abuse of his wife particularly "brutal" and gave itself the power to decide "the propriety of the punishment," "for the protection of the wife, and, through it, for the protection and good order of society." Beyond domestic violence, the court also took on new responsibilities for guarding the interests of wives and children in other domestic matters. Even so, judges carefully maintained the line that both separated and connected private households and the public order. They intervened only to promote "good order" and uphold the rules governing "our present civilization."[65]

To this end, judges delved into the characters of litigants to ferret out the "worthy" husbands, wives, and children from the "unworthy" ones. The 1877 divorce case *Sarah E. Taylor* v. *David Taylor* illuminates the court's role. Citing frequent instances of abuse, Sarah Taylor maintained that her husband had made her life intolerable. In response, Justice William P. Bynum reiterated the court's long-standing position that no universal measure of "intolerable" conditions could ever apply in all cases: "The station in life, the temperament, state of health, habits and feelings of different persons are so unlike, that treatment which would send the broken heart of one to the grave, would make no sensible impression upon another." He continued: "Among the lower clases, blows sometimes pass between married couples who in the main are very happy and have no desire to part; amidst very coarse habits such incidents occur almost as freely as rude or reproachful words." In this particular case, however, the court could not overlook such behavior because both the husband and wife belonged to "respectable walks of life." The logic of this decision would also seem to remove the "unrespectable" households from public scrutiny. In practice, however, it did not. Instead, the courts used it to label the "lower classes" as coarse, rude, violent, and uncivilized people who needed other forms of state control, while also obstructing black and common white, particularly poor white, women's claims to state protection.[66]

For a time, this legal patriarchy did work in favor of African Americans and common whites. As long as they retained their hold on public power, they could use their access to the system and their clout with Republican officials to revise the rules and include themselves among those considered "suitable" and "worthy." But, these same assumptions acquired far more ominous meanings as the tide of

Republican influence ebbed and conservatives flooded back into the judicial system in the mid-1870s. Democrats could and did use their patriarchal judicial prerogatives to act on racial and class biases. Frank Bumpass, an African American in Granville County, faced exactly this kind of scrutiny when he tried to have his three grandchildren legally apprenticed to him in 1881. "Frank Bumpass," his white employer testified, "is a colored man, well behaved and likely to treat the children in a becoming manner and I hereby recommend him as a suitable person."[67] Bumpass no doubt thought himself suitable as well. But the right to determine suitability ultimately resided with Democratic court officials. As a result, people like Frank Bumpass fought an increasingly uphill battle to prove themselves "suitable."

Nowhere were these attitudes more evident than in the 1875 attempted rape case *State v. Alexander Neely*. In July of the previous year, a young white woman got off the railroad at an isolated crossroads, said good-bye to her friend, and began the walk home alone. A short distance down the road, she heard Alexander Neely, a black man, "'holler' to her 'to stop.'" Turning around to see him running toward her, she took off. Only when she turned into the lane to her brother-in-law's house did he disappear into the woods. In court, Neely's guilt turned on his intent. His defense argued that the jury could not possibly deduce his intent from his actions, because Neely could have been pursuing the woman for any number of reasons. The superior court jury disagreed. So did Justice Richmond M. Pearson, who found absolutely no question as to Neely's intent. As he explained: "I see a chicken-cock drop his wings and take after a hen: my experience and observation assure me that his purpose is sexual intercourse; no other evidence is needed." Just for good measure, he offered another analogy: "I see a dog in hot pursuit of a rabbit; my experience and observation assure me the intent of the dog is to kill the rabbit; no doubt about it." Pearson then applied his logic to Neely, arguing that black men's instincts meant they pursued white women for only one reason—rape. No evidence was necessary because "experience" proved it.[68]

Justice William B. Rodman issued a ringing dissent. Cutting straight to the heart of the matter, he rejected Pearson's direct analogies between "brute animals" and human beings. They assume, he wrote, that Neely "is a brute, or so like a brute that it is safe to reason from the one to the other; that he is governed by brutish and, in his case, vicious passions unrestrained by reason or a moral sense. This assumption is unreasonable and unjust. [Neely] is a man, and . . . he must be presumed to have the passions of a man, and also the reason and moral sense of a man." As such, Rodman continued, "he is entitled to be tried as a man, and to have his acts and intents inquired into and decided upon by the principles which govern human conduct, and not brutish conduct." Otherwise, "what need of court and jury?" If Neely were no more than an animal, the law did not apply. Anyone could destroy him, as they did other unruly animals, "without legal ceremony." Justice Willim P. Bynum joined Rodman in arguing that Pearson had pushed the "lower classes" too far down the scale of humanity. At this time, however, they were outnumbered. Instead, Pearson's depiction of black men as brutes, completely enslaved to their passions, prevailed.[69] Unfit to govern themselves or their families, African Americans and whites of the "lower class" required direct state supervision to preserve public order.

The Democratic party drew on these same ideas in its battle to limit the political power of African Americans and common, particularly poor, whites. Only elite white men, party leaders argued, were qualified to represent everyone in the community. As soon as the Democrats regained control of the state government, they began whittling away at the political power of the Republican party and its constituents. But they faced an uphill battle against dissident whites and African Americans who refused either to subsume their interests under those of Democratic leaders or to surrender their place in the political arena. To be sure, neither full civil rights nor suffrage enabled African Americans or common whites to reshape political debate or public policy on their own terms. As we saw in chapter 2, both the legislature and the courts defined labor relationships as private matters between employers and employees. Women also ran into difficulties when they tried to bring domestic, sexual, and other kinds of violence into the public arena. Although court officials expanded public supervision in these areas, the result was to extend their own patriarchal power over all African Americans and common whites, not to elevate the women of these groups. As this trend in the courts suggests, the ability of these people to defend their interests in the "private" sphere ultimately depended on their "public" power. The patriarchal framework African Americans and common whites had so skillfully used to push their interests into public space could just as easily work against them. Once enmeshed within this patriarchal web, they found it difficult to cut themselves free.

6

The "Best Men": Party Politics and the Collapse of the Knights of Labor

In 1887, Reconstruction in Granville County ended with a bang. A suspicious fire destroyed the business district in the county seat of Oxford; a rape trial divided the African-American community; and a public scandal engulfed the Knights of Labor, which had just eclipsed the Republican party as the primary political opposition to Democratic rule within the county. The images are compelling. In 1887, Belle Booth, a white woman and the wife of a prominent doctor, accused Albert Taborn, a black man, of attempted rape. Once Taborn was ensconced in the Oxford jail, rumors began circulating that he would be lynched. That night a group of African Americans rallied to his defense, guarding the jail and marching, armed and in formation, through the streets. Taking another approach, an unidentified group informed the mayor in a threatening note that the town would burn if Taborn were lynched. The lynch mob, its passions no doubt cooled by the sight of armed men surrounding the jail, never appeared. Late that same night, however, a fire started in a downtown tobacco warehouse and destroyed half of Oxford's business district. When townspeople went to the courthouse to sound the alarm, they found the rope to the bell had been cut. Even more striking was the street scene during the fire. As white business owners dashed around, frantically trying to save their property, some African Americans celebrated in the streets, dancing, singing, and flatly refusing to help in the rescue effort.[1]

If the fire had been set deliberately, the culprits were never identified. Whatever its source, the blaze sparked off a series of events that transformed the county's political landscape. The Knights of Labor had just emerged as a serious political contender in Granville County. A biracial group with a core membership of middling artisans and shop owners, the Knights also attracted poor wage laborers, many of whom were black. Soon after its organization in 1886, the Knights turned to politics, drawing discontented voters from both the Republican and Democratic parties. That year, the Knights and independent candidates did well across the state and within Granville County. The results of Oxford's 1886 municipal elections were even more dramatic, placing Knights in the mayor's office and several town commissioners' seats.[2]

Picking up where the Republican party had left off, the Knights relied on gendered language to combat racial and class hierarchies that had relegated African Americans and, to a lesser extent, common whites to the margins of southern society. Equating manhood with political rights and womanhood with the rights to protection, the two parties invoked a "natural" gender hierarchy to legitimize all men's power to represent their families in public. These arguments resonated with African Americans and many common whites because both groups articulated their social visions in similar terms. Incorporating race and class into their identities, they insisted that neither poverty nor skin color diminished their public standing as men and women. Like the Republican party and the Knights, they too assigned men and women different rights and relied heavily on gender differences to realize their political goals. As we have seen, the focus on manhood and womanhood provided the wedge needed to open up southern society for marginalized groups. But it also allowed conservative Democrats to shift political debate toward a discussion of the relative merits of individual men and women. The effect was devastating. Democrats argued that the "best men" represented everyone's interests. By contrast, they labeled African-American and dissident white men as "unmanly" men who, like minors and women, should be excluded from politics. This brand of manhood thus used the unequal relationship between men and women in the private sphere to legitimize hierarchies among men in the public sphere. The Booth-Taborn case presented local Democrats with the ideal set of circumstances to place the "best men" at the head of their extended "family."

Party Politics

If politicians at the state and national level had declared Reconstruction over in 1876, the residents of Granville County did not. Hotly contested elections captured public attention during the 1870s and well into the 1880s. With strong opposition at the polls and defiant workers in their fields and households, Democrats had no choice but to continue their battle for power. Although their party rode easily to victory elsewhere, Granville County Democrats suffered defeat year after year. Even in 1887, they never could have mustered enough strength to gain control of local politics if not for internal divisions that fatally weakened the opposition.

Granville County Democrats employed the same techniques—violence, voting fraud, and manipulation of election rules—as other southern Democrats to subvert the electoral process. In the first few years following emancipation, violence ranked high among their favorite ploys. In 1868 Governor William W. Holden received two letters from groups of Granville County Republicans pleading for protection from Klan violence. The petitioners' accounts, which appear in more detail in the previous chapter, reported property damage and physical brutality. Given the level and scale of violence, the situation can only be described as a small-scale guerrilla war. The petitioners all linked the Klan to the Democratic party. According to one letter, a prominent Granville County Democrat had even promised that "he would stop the kukulx" if the Republicans "would stop the [Union] Leagues." Otherwise "he could not do nothing" about the Klan.[3]

When violence failed, the Democrats expanded their repertoire to include voting fraud. James Bullock, a local white Republican leader, wrote that African Americans all "appear to remain firm in their politics, although the Democrats resort to every imaginable meaness to deceive them." Republican constituents elaborated in letters of their own to Governor Holden. Charging deceit and irregularity in a recent election, a group of African-American and poor white Republicans complained that "the democrats will and do do all and every thing they can to Get in power." That same year, thirty-eight Republicans from another Granville Township informed the governor that Democratic sympathizers offered to fill out ballots for illiterate Republican voters at the polls, only to write in Democratic, not Republican, names. The cumulative results of electoral fraud could be more difficult to combat than the terror of the Klan. Frank McGhee, for instance, finally quit voting altogether. As he explained in a 1930s interview, there "really wasn't any need to, since the Democrats threw his ballots out the window with monotonous regularity." McGhee's disillusionment secured Democratic success even more effectively than stuffing the ballot box, leaving Republicans no way even to contest the vote.[4]

Granville County Republicans persevered only to face more insidious measures to destroy their party. The Democratic constitution, ratified in 1876, made key offices at the county level appointive, excluding Republicans from local government and seriously undermining the party's ability to maintain itself. Emboldened by Democratic strength in the state legislature, the local party moved to solidify its position even before voters approved the new constitution. Cleverly manipulating election rules, Granville County Democrats tried to throw out the 1876 ballots from an entire township that, not coincidentally, had voted Republican. The courts ultimately ruled against them, but that mattered little since the new constitution allowed the state legislature to fill many of Granville County's local offices with Democratic appointees without having to bother with elections at all.[5]

Of all Democratic schemes, gerrymandering proved the most effective way to gain permanent control. Democrats in the state legislature continually redrew districts during the 1870s and 1880s in an effort to gain power. Unable to eliminate black votes completely, they tried to make counties with large black populations part of the second congressional district. Sometimes called the "Black Second," it was, in the historian Eric Anderson's words, the "one 'extraordinary' district" the Democrats "could never hope to carry, but a district in which thousands of Republican votes would be neutralized." In 1881, following the Democratic defeat in 1880, the legislature severed the northeastern portion of Granville County, an area with a large black population, to form Vance County. It then made Vance part of the "Black Second," thereby diminishing the impact of Republican votes from that area and enhancing the Democratic party's chances within Granville County.[6]

Even then, Granville County Democrats barely pulled off their victory in 1882. Neutralizing black votes did nothing to unify whites. The party's leaders could cooperate in opposing the Republicans, but they regularly clashed over policy and position. Tensions, for instance, developed between Oxford and the countryside, where party members continually complained that town Democrats monopolized economic resources and political appointments. The party also failed to win the confidence of common whites, who believed that Democrats represented the interests of the wealthy and powerful. Wartime experiences had deepened their suspicions. In 1866, white voters in Brassfields Township soundly rejected Governor Worth and other conservative candidates who would emerge as leaders in the postwar Democratic party. "Brassfields," according to the *North Carolina Standard*, "was one of the firmest Union precincts during the rebellion. Rejecting the conservative slate of candidates in 1866, "it still maintains its integrity" as "a community of honest farmers, who can have no object but the good of their county." Later, some of Brassfields's unionists probably joined other disgruntled whites in voting Republican. The party's platform certainly provided good reason for them to do so. Democratization of the state and county governments meant increased power for common whites who had long resented their wealthier neighbors' domination of local affairs. Debt relief attracted those who feared losing their farms and homesteads, while laborers' liens appealed to both skilled artisans and unskilled workers. Other inviting policies included more equitable taxation, abolition of property qualifications for officeholders, penal reform, and a public school system.[7]

Rather than openly siding with the Republicans, however, most whites registered their discontent through abstention. In the 1872 election, for instance, the *Raleigh Sentinel* estimated that 56,000 registered voters across the state avoided the polls and that 41,000 men had not registered at all. It attributed such low turnout to "fearful apathy." "In Granville, Johnston, and other counties," so the complaint in the *Raleigh Sentinel* went, "we hear hundreds of white men refused to vote." Those who remained home made a political decision that seriously compromised the power of the Democratic party. In Granville County, where there were nearly equal numbers of whites and blacks, those abstaining literally meant the difference between victory and defeat for Democrats.[8]

Only too aware of the situation, local Democratic promoters pitched their rhetoric at common whites. For their part, the editors of the *Oxford Torchlight* did everything they could to support "the cause." Openly allying the newspaper with the Democratic party, the editors filled the newspaper's pages with articles instructing potential white recruits on the importance of party loyalty, predicting dire consequences for them and their families in the event of a Republican victory, and imploring them to go to the polls. "The coming campaign in Granville will be a struggle for right, justice, and common sense," announced the newspaper's editor in 1878. "The greedy grasp of imbecile Radical politicians will never relax until the people rise in their might and majesty and shake off the itching, insatiate clutches. Honest citizens of Granville your aid is needed in the coming struggle! Let us be up and doing!" Behind the bombast lay real concerns about white support for the Democratic party, as another piece from the same issue suggests. This time the editor took a more conciliatory tone, urging common whites to "be quiet" and "not let your personal feelings overcome the sense of duty you owe to your party and country."[9]

These "personal feelings" included class tensions that no amount of Democratic bravado could completely paper over. Although the booming tobacco market had raised the living standards of many common whites and African Americans, it did not eliminate class differences. Moreover, the same economic changes that brought this brief period of prosperity would soon shift power away from local tobacco producers and further divide rich and poor. One of the earliest signs of decline came in the loss of tobacco manufacturing jobs in the rural countryside, as small tobacco factories found it increasingly difficult to compete with large firms. Between 1870 and 1880, the number of factories in Granville County fell from 39 to 8, and the number of tobacco manufacturing jobs dropped from 377 to 111. Even these figures fail to communicate the full impact of the losses, as they do not include many of the small, seasonal workshops that also folded. They also do not convey the effect on factory laborers and on farmers who counted on manufacturing and peddling to supplement their agricultural incomes. As one irate farmer complained to the *Torchlight* in 1880, small-scale production provided one of the few means by which a poor man could make "a little money" and keep "his family above want."[10]

The rising popularity of smoking tobacco did not help Granville County farmers either. Smoking tobacco used lower priced grades, not the high-end tobacco for which Granville County was famous. This change in consumer tastes gave the advantage to tobacco farmers who lived in areas where conditions were not as favorable for the production of the best grades of bright tobacco. By the 1880s, Granville County farmers began to feel the effects of competition from South Carolina and eastern North Carolina.[11]

All these changes signaled a fundamental transformation in the tobacco industry, which had been expanding and centralizing over the course of the late nineteenth century. By the 1890s, manufacturing plants were large and highly mechanized; distribution, advertising, and marketing took up large portions of the industry's budget; and ownership was concentrated in the hands of a few. The peak came in 1889 when the American Tobacco Company subsumed the competition with the formation of one giant conglomerate. Afterward, complaints about low prices flew fast and furious in tobacco-growing areas. Farmers and local tobacco interests placed the blame squarely on the new monopoly, claiming that the company set prices long before the crop was even harvested. As one Granville County farmer put it: "The farmer does not have any voice in the price he receives for his produce. . . . I think the American Tobacco Company is the main cause of low prices as they have broken up nearly all competition, and we receive about one-fourth now to what we received eight or ten years ago." In 1889 the warehouse interests in Oxford took the American Tobacco Company and its local buyer to court for forming a trust. The suit generated a good deal of interest and support, but it would take much more to break up the mammoth monopoly. As centralization proceeded, the relative power of farmers and agricultural workers within the industry declined. The tide of commercial agriculture, which Granville County residents had ridden successfully for two decades, had turned.[12]

Economic conditions for both common whites and African Americans deteriorated rapidly. Faced with declining prices and less cash, farmers used less waged labor. Between 1880 and 1900, the number of farm laborers in Dutchville fell from 308 to 137. Whereas the township boasted 1.07 workers per farm in the township in 1880, the number slipped to only 0.29 by 1900. The figures for Oxford Township were no brighter. Here, the number of farm laborers dropped from 264 to 186, while the number of workers per farm declined from 1.04 to 0.53. And when laborers found work, it was for less pay than previously. The Bureau of Labor Statistics's annual reports show that wage rates in Granville County decreased between 1887 and 1900 and that wage laborers across the state faced uncertain employment conditions. But in Granville County, where laborers were accustomed to greater prosperity than those in cotton-growing areas, the downturn must have been a particularly painful development.[13]

Tenancy also increased. In both Dutchville and Oxford Townships, tenants worked about 60 percent of the farms by 1900. In Dutchville, tenancy remained relatively stable between 1870 and 1880, increasing only slightly from 27 percent to 34 percent. But the figure had skyrocketed to 61 percent by 1900. The rates rose earlier in Oxford, in part because of the long-standing practice of using both tenants and wage workers on the same property as laborers. Here tenancy rates rose from 48 percent in 1870 to 63 percent in 1880 and then to 64 percent in 1900.[14] As the number of tenants rose, their working conditions and social status began to slide downward. The comments of observers reflected this trend. Although agricultural writers had once promoted tenancy as a respectable position for hard-working young men, they increasingly described it as the exclusive reserve of lazy no-goods. Landowners who wrote into the Bureau of Labor Statistics criticized tenants for their farming practices, their work habits, and their morals. Cutting straight to the heart of the matter, one claimed that "nearly all reliable white men own their farms." At the same time, all discussion of the possibility of upward mobility through tenancy vanished.[15]

Even landownership did not convey the independence it once had. Complaints about the crop lien system began to appear just as many small landowners began to feel the squeeze of declining economic conditions. Writing to the Bureau of Labor Statistics in 1887, one tobacco farmer lamented that the "notorious mortgage system so extensively practiced in cotton sections is beginning to infest this section." The statistics bear out his observations. By 1900, 33 percent of Oxford's landowners and 24 percent of Dutchville's landowners had mortgages on their farms. Landownership could no longer protect people from the whims of an overbearing master; but this time the master was the tobacco market, not an employer or landowner.[16]

Many of these trends were already visible by the 1880s. Bright Belt farmers were notorious bellyachers, but their complaints took on a different tone in this decade, indicating changes in everyday conditions and attitudes toward future economic prospects. Farmers writing to the Bureau of Labor Statistics voiced a variety of complaints: the inability to hire "good" labor, the increase in tenancy and its declining conditions, lower tobacco prices, and, later, the pervasive influence of the American Tobacco Company. Calling these developments new, farmers contrasted them with what they saw as a brighter past. One farmer reminisced that there "was a time when it was encouraging for any young man to start to farming." He concluded with a dire prediction: "In my opinion we have lived in better times than our children and grandchildren will enjoy." The pervasiveness of such sentiments suggests that this was not the diatribe of an old man whose memories of the past grew rosier with time. Those who left the county between 1890 and 1900 concurred. In that decade, Granville County's population dropped from 24,484 to 23,263, the first decline in the postwar years solely attributable to emigration.[17]

Complaining loudly about Democratic economic policies that favored large-scale capitalist development over small-scale production, common whites across the South insisted that "redeemer" governments were soaking the poor to benefit the rich. In Granville County, the reaction to fencing legislation illuminates the economic and political differences between poorer Granville County residents and commercially successful planters and businessmen. By closing the range, stock laws abolished customary subsistence rights. Of course, few Granville County residents derived their livelihood primarily from herds of roaming hogs. But both tenants and wage laborers still relied heavily on the open range to support their livestock. In Granville County, moreover, the stock law became an issue of political as well as economic privilege because of the way local Democratic leaders guided fence legislation through the state legislature, ignoring widespread opposition at home and bypassing a local vote on the matter.[18]

Much to their dismay, Democrats discovered that passing the law and securing local compliance were two entirely different matters. The outcry was loud, angry, and sustained. Even the editor of the *Torchlight* softened his support of the legislation in an attempt to woo voters back to the Democratic fold. "The poorest possible way to get the stock law repealed," the editor advised in 1886, "is to join the radical party." Instead, he urged Democrats "to stick to your party and ask your own friends to help you." Apparently, such flimsy appeals carried little weight with the electorate, which gave the Republicans a landslide victory in that year. Reeling from the defeat, the *Torchlight's* editor grudgingly acknowledged fence laws as the party's main liability. Many whites, the newspaper reported, "refused to go to the polls, and others went over to the enemy in revenge" for the Democrats' support of the measure.[19]

Antagonism may have peaked in the 1886 election, but it did not disappear entirely. In 1887, opponents of the fence law lobbied for its repeal or, at the very least, for the chance to submit the matter to a local vote. The "little stock" of poor people, one petition explained, "is half their living." But "under the present system the renters, small farmers, [and] laboring classes are denied even the worn out fields, the scanty commons, not used by the landlords themselves." Despite opponents' efforts, the fence law survived, thanks largely to a petition drive mounted by its supporters and helped along by farmers who had complied with the new law. Yet bitterness over the measure still surfaced in party politics as late as 1890. That year, Republican James Howell opposed A. H. A. Williams, a Democratic candidate sympathetic to the Farmers' Alliance, "because he put the no fence law upon the colored people." Although Howell emphasized the law's impact on African Americans, many poor whites shared his disdain for both the law and its Democratic supporters. Indeed, the law drew the poor of both races together by emphasizing the economic and political gulf between them and their wealthier neighbors.[20]

If the Republican party provided an alternative to the Democrats, it was not a completely egalitarian one. The party did retain a loyal following among African-American and some common white men because it responded to their concerns far more than the Democrats did. But it also attracted a strong core of wealthy whites, whose economic and racial interests often clashed with those of the Republican rank and file. It was these same men who dominated leadership positions within the party. In Granville County and across the state, the divisions between the party's white leaders and its black membership found expression in factional infighting. As different groups jockeyed for position, the debate veered away from substantive issues and toward political spoils. The marginality of African Americans became increasingly clear. Although black votes made the party, few African Americans received nomination for office. Even more frustrating was the way white Republican leaders ignored the concerns of black voters. At both the state and local levels, the party not only retreated from its strong stand on civil and political rights but also adopted blatantly racist rhetoric to appeal to whites. "There are numbers of white men in the Republican party . . . who . . . have fattened from Negro votes," observed George M. Arnold, a black leader from Wilmington, after many white leaders in the Republican party refused to support the Sumner Civil Rights Act. He continued, frustration mounting with each word: "We voted for them. We stood by them. We brought down the wrath of the Ku Klux Klan, . . . but when it comes to granting us full Civil Rights with them they *flinch*."[21]

Republican economic policies only accentuated many African Americans' sense of alienation. White party leaders supported internal improvements and assiduously cultivated their image as proponents of economic growth. R. W. Lassiter, a white Republican from Granville County, announced from the senate floor, "Let a railroad be built through any country, and immediately the commercial prosperity of that region is increased an hundred fold." Meanwhile, his counterparts back home were busy collaborating with prominent Democrats to promote grand economic schemes at the local level. Railroads ranked first on their list. At the end of the Civil War, Granville County had only one line that ran through its far northeast corner, bypassing not just Oxford, but most of the county's rural residents as well. Over the next five years, Republican and Democratic business leaders spearheaded a campaign to build a more centrally located railroad that would stop in Oxford. They argued that the project would benefit everyone by contributing to the development of the entire county. "The laborer and the capitalist, the merchant, the farmer, the mechanic, the debtor, the creditor," wrote the editor of the *Torchlight*, had equal interests "in promoting this great enterprise." Of course, the railroad would boost the businesses and farming operations of "capitalists" and "creditors" far more than the economic interests of "mechanics," "debtors," and "laborers." Even before the first railroad commenced operation in 1881, these same prominent white Republicans and Democrats had launched a series of other projects, including a bank, an opera house, hotels, telephones, telegraphs, electric lights, roads, and additional rail lines.[22]

The first railroad project, however, received far less support than its promoters cared to admit. Even some of Granville County's prosperous white farmers began to criticize local development projects, echoing the complaints of whites elsewhere in the state who had turned away from the Republican party in the 1870s because of its support for internal improvements and the high taxes they entailed. Poor wage laborers and tenants, white and black, were even less willing to open up their pocketbooks for more projects that seemed to benefit only the wealthy. African Americans and poor whites resented the way both Republican and Democratic leaders blatantly promoted their own interests, while insisting that other economic issues, such as labor relations, wages, and the distribution of land and property, remained outside the scope of public debate.[23]

The tobacco market's downward spiral, which hit propertyless African Americans particularly hard, increased their doubts. Of course, not all African Americans were impoverished. Many successfully negotiated economic change in the late nineteenth century to emerge as propertied shopkeepers, professionals, skilled artisans, and farmers. In fact, the number of black landowners in Granville County continued to increase, rising from 304 to 510 between 1879 and 1898. By 1900, landowners represented 23 percent of the African-American male population aged twenty-one and older. But these figures contained a darker side as well. African Americans who became landowners in the county after 1880 acquired their property in less than auspicious circumstances. As the county's diminishing population suggests, they remained to endure the same bleak economic conditions that prompted so many others to leave. Indeed, black landowners were far poorer in 1900 than they had been just ten years earlier: the value of their farms, livestock, and moveable goods all fell.[24]

As the majority of black laborers and tenants sank deeper into the growing economic morass, the distance between them and the local Republican leadership widened. Assurances that economic development would equally benefit everyone rang hollow for poor people, particularly poor blacks. At the same time, cooperation between elite Democrats and Republicans on internal improvements tended to blur the lines separating the two parties. Even if they had wanted to, Republicans were in no position to deliver solutions to poor African Americans by the mid-1870s. Abandoned by the national party and stymied at the state level, the party had little to offer its constituents except stale debates over who would receive nomination for the few remaining elective offices. This seemed paltry indeed to many African Americans, who had risked so much and worked so courageously to secure their political rights.[25]

Apathy within both parties meant that the Knights of Labor organizer found a very receptive audience when he arrived in Oxford in

1886. By that summer the county boasted two locals, one white and one black, with a membership of artisans, shop owners, farmers, clerks, laborers, and tenants.[26] The Knights centered in Oxford, but political discontent within the town was representative of the county as a whole. In 1880, its population of 1,200 roughly equaled that of a county township. Growing rapidly after its first railroad connection opened that year, Oxford's population peaked around 1890 at 4,000, where it leveled off. The town did support a diverse occupational structure, with skilled and semiskilled artisans, clerks, merchants, and professionals in addition to all those associated with the tobacco trade. But it remained primarily a trading town throughout the late nineteenth century, not the major manufacturing center its boosters liked to think it was. Most of Granville County's few surviving tobacco factories operated in the countryside, not within Oxford's city limits. Some of the town's "factories," moreover, were actually tobacco warehouses and redrying plants that employed few workers. Oxford did have a few manufactories that made bricks, buggies, and blinds, among other things. But these businesses were really large artisanal shops, the economic importance of which paled beside the revenue produced by the tobacco trade.[27] As a trading center, though, Oxford remained firmly linked to the countryside. Skilled and unskilled laborers regularly moved back and forth between Oxford and the county's rural townships. Many planters did the same, although they were drawn by the town's social scene, not its employment opportunities. But the economic fortunes of all those in town, like those in the countryside, ultimately rose and fell with the tobacco market.[28]

Against this backdrop, the Knights organized around political discontent, not the concerns of an industrializing work force. Echoing the Republican platform of the late 1860s, the North Carolina Knights supported issues that appealed to both poor and middling Granville County residents: federal funds for public schools, more equitable bankruptcy laws and land policies, federal regulation of the currency and railways, limits on child labor and working hours, measures to encourage labor organization, and the abolition of convict labor. The Knights also preached an inclusive message of political empowerment that appealed to a range of voters, both white and black. Although the order met with immediate success, particularly within the town of Oxford, its electoral victories were precarious. Racial and class tensions lurked just beneath the surface of the organization itself. Outside were the hazardous shoals of a political discourse in which Democrats used appeals to manhood to establish and legitimize a hierarchy among men.[29]

The Best Men

Granville County Democrats were far more successful in shaping the terms of political debate than they were in eliminating the Republican party. They guided discussions away from equality among men within the public sphere and toward the quality of public leadership. Quickly adapting to Republican calls for universal rights, Democrats avoided the overt racial and class distinctions they had relied on for so long and began ranking men on the basis of individual character instead. Only the "best men," they argued, should be entrusted with public power. The comments of Frank McGhee suggest how successful Democrats were in shifting the terms of political debate. As McGhee claimed, he had been a "Republican, but not always": "I didn't mind voting for a real good man, even if he was a Democrat." Like many other African Americans and common whites, Frank McGhee probably judged the character of individual men by very different standards than those the county's Democratic leaders used. Although drawing heavily on the language of individual merit, Democrats advanced a distinctly hierarchical social vision through their "best men." Inevitably, the "best men" possessed all the same qualities as the "rich men" who industriously applied themselves to purchasing fine homes for their "cheerful wives." At times, the Democrats might admit selected Republicans within the ranks of the "best men." But even if the "best men" were not always Democrats, they were always white and wealthy. No matter how hard they tried, men like Frank McGhee would never measure up.[30]

In the *Torchlight* Republican political rallies were portrayed as ludicrous displays that mocked the entire political process: Republicans met in "pow-wows," "political hubbubs," and "rumpasses," where drunkenness and disorder reigned. Reports in the newspaper underscored the point with a heavy hand. An 1876 article was typical: "The cry of not in order is hurled through the house. The Dr. stands firm upon his feet and says I am in order. I am in order and I will contend for it. Out of order again is the cry. I am not out of order. Tell me how I am out of order. I will be heard! (much animated) Mr Chairman, listen to me a minute, I want to make one remark. I say listen. Much howling and cry out of order, intense confusion and growling." What the *Torchlight* editors and contributors saw and rejected was democracy in action. If Republican party meetings were loud and disorganized, it was because they were more open and participatory than Democratic gatherings. But the newspaper offered up its descriptions as more examples of the chaos of the party and the incompetence of its members. In the *Torchlight's* articles, the Republican rank and file surged, howling and crying, until some unscrupulous demagogue managed to capture its vote.[31]

The newspaper drove its point home with animalistic imagery. Wrinkling their noses at the barnyard "scent" of Republican meetings, the *Torchlight* editors and contributors extended the metaphor with an exotic menagerie of strange creatures. At one 1876 meeting, for instance, a Republican "leap[ed] over half a dozen benches with the yell of an untutored beast and screams from the bottom of his stomach." Trying to reach the podium, this "beast" was outflanked by a fellow party member with "the head of a screech owl and the eyes of a bat" who managed to "pounce" first. Yet another stood by, waiting patiently "like a mud turtle." A meeting that same year found the participants howling "like a lot of demons." The most degrading images were reserved for African Americans. Indeed, the images echo those used in the 1876 rape case, *State v. Alexander Neely*, in which the Supreme Court inferred the intent of the accused by comparing him to a "chicken-cock" chasing a hen and a "dog in hot pursuit of a rabbit." The *Torchlight's* editors and the local Democratic leaders they represented apparently believed African Americans to be incapable of transcending brute instincts. Like Alexander Neely, they could neither comprehend the importance of the issues at hand nor exercise political power any more responsibly than beasts or demons.[32]

Torchlight editors and contributors also racialized Republican meetings, maintaining that the "only white men who profess any allegiance to the Radical party . . . expect office at the hands of the negroes." But, while the county's voting returns indicate that the number of white Republicans paled in comparison to the mass of the party's African-American members, a significant minority of whites voted Republican and actively supported the party. For instance, one of the letters written by local Republicans to Governor Holden was signed by a group of ten white and African-American men who claimed to speak for "meny others too tedious to mention both white and Colored." Despite the insistence on the "blackness" of the Republican party, moreover, the *Torchlight* itself betrayed the presence of whites. Usually the editors and contributors did so to ridicule them, as in one 1880 piece in which they claimed the party was made up "exclusively of negroes and the most illiterate whites." If so, then the "most illiterate whites" formed a more sizeable portion of the white population than the editors and Democratic leaders admitted. According to one *Torchlight* article, one 1878 Republican gathering in rural Fishing Creek Township drew "fifty colored men and thirty whites." After giving this tally, however, the piece continued with a description of the meeting as if the candidates and the issues spoke only to African Americans. Blackening the party in this way, the *Torchlight's* editors and the local Democratic leaders they represented hoped to undercut the Republicans' attractiveness to whites generally and thus buttress the Democrats' position. The editors also singled out white Republicans for special censure. As represented in the *Torchlight*, whites who joined the Republicans forfeited their racial status and disappeared into a crowd of African Americans. "Such men," one editor wrote, "are traitors to their race and color." Another writer even jeered down one white Republican as a "nigger white man infidel."[33]

The only white Republicans regularly discussed in the newspaper were those in leadership positions. Given their high visibility, the editors would have found them difficult to ignore. But prominent white Republicans also fit neatly into the editors' view of the party generally. They agreed wholeheartedly with the delegates to an 1878 countywide Democratic convention, who described Republicans as "a mass of deluded colored men, controlled by a few cunning whites." Following the spirit of these resolutions, the *Torchlight's* editors and contributors conceded neither the legitimacy of Republican policies nor the possibility that African Americans and common whites could act on their own political interests. In the newspaper's pages, all whites were erased from the Republican party and subsumed within the Democratic fold. African Americans were cast outside the political process altogether, depicted as little more than beasts. Indeed, black Republican leaders fared no better in the *Torchlight* than the party's rank and file. Never acknowledged as leaders, they usually appeared as ignorant tools of designing whites.[34]

According to the newspaper, these white leaders used the party's constituency for personal gain. By extension, the Republican party itself was little more than a vehicle designed to profit individual white Republican officials.[35] To substantiate this claim, the newspaper's editors and contributors regularly charged party leaders with fraud and mismanagement. One incident is particularly revealing. In 1876, the Board of County Commissioners paid Martha Kinton for the care of a "lunatic" relative with a promissory note that was worth half its face value of one hundred dollars. Although the practice was common, the editor at that time maintained that the Republican commissioners had purposefully swindled Kinton. Bemoaning the fate of this "poor widow woman" he asked with dramatic flourish, "is there no redress?" Feeling pressured by the exposé, the commissioners met with Kinton to resolve the matter. Even then, the editor claimed, she did not receive the full amount due her.[36]

Considering the number of poor widows within the county's borders, the concern expressed in the newspaper for Martha Kinton was highly selective. No one connected with the *Torchlight* made any attempt to help her financially. Nor did the newspaper publicize the plight of local contractors or indigent African Americans who also received payment from the county in devalued promissory notes. But then, the editor's interest in Martha Kinton derived far more from her value as a political symbol than from a genuine concern for her welfare. As portrayed in the *Torchlight*, the victimization of this poor white widow represented the economic rape of the county at the hands of a party headed by depraved and unscrupulous opportunists. Sizing up the Republican officials involved in this scandal, the editor found them far closer to beasts than men. "This transaction," he maintained, "shows how corrupt the county officials are—how low they have descended in the scale of human degradation." The editor also blamed those who voted such men into office. He "lay the matter open before the people of Granville, especially the colored voters of Granville who are in a great measure responsible for this pestiferous board of Commissioners." Like the commissioners, the "colored voters" did not rank high enough on the scale of humanity to be entrusted with the public interest.[37]

Whereas Republicans wallowed in the mud at the very bottom of humanity's scale, Democrats soared to its highest reaches. In fact, they embodied the very essence of public leadership. They were, according to an 1878 editorial, "The Right Kind of Men for Genuine Reform": "Christian men. Men that have the welfare of their fellow men at heart. . . . Men who act from principle—not party passions and prejudices. . . . Men who are too honest to conceal jobs and jobbery, thieves and thievery, whenever and wherever found. Men who will do everything material, political, moral, social, and religious that promises good to our county." Waxing eloquent after a Democratic victory that same year, the *Torchlight*'s editor described the district's U.S. congressman as a "pure gentleman and unselfish patriot." The Democratic judges of the inferior court ranked equally high, as "gentlemen of the highest respectability," who possessed patriotism, "intelligence and firmness."[38]

Although the *Torchlight*'s editors and contributors never tired of listing the positive qualities of Democratic candidates and officials, they often referred to them simply as the "best citizens," the "best men," "gentlemen," or the "right men." More than just convention guided this gendered terminology, as the choice of modifiers suggests. The 1875 Democratic constitutional convention, for instance, "had the manliness" to deny the right of suffrage to convicted felons. Three years later, local Republicans fell "when a manful move by the Democrats wrested their power from them." Placed at the very pinnacle of manly perfection, the "best men" radiated a legitimacy denied to Republicans. For instance, the three "men of high character" who presided over the 1878 inferior court literally towered over the "Radical judges . . . we have seen presiding at our courts, bringing down into the very dust and soiling its robes most disgracefully in the eyes of the bar and the people." For those who missed the difference between the Democratic "best men" and Republican "beasts," the *Torchlight's* editors threw in an occasional cartoon depicting a Republican candidate as a woman.[39]

The concept of the "best men" actually rested on a rigid hierarchy among men based on racial and class distinctions. The few men clustered at the top end of this scale bore more than a passing resemblance to the white "rich men" of the *Torchlight's* prescriptive literature. William Gregory, one of the newspaper's editors and an enthusiastic supporter of elite postwar gender ideals, explicitly linked the political "best men" to the "rich men" in an 1880 article that appeared in the *Southern Home.* Praising the leaders of the slave South, Gregory identified them as aristocrats, a word that he translated from the Greek as "the best ruler[s]" or the "best [men] to rule." Recent changes, however, had "thoroughly republicanized" southern society so that "we are not in favor of the best man to rule." Instead, "we envy the best man, and want to pull him down. Democracy! that is the word for us; demos, the people, krates, to rule, the rule of the people; of Tom and Dick and Harry, whatever his station, whatever his morals, whatever his color." Only "half reconstructed," Gregory bristled at the mere thought of democracy. But he harbored no illusions about the possibility of recreating the old aristocracy, even as his unreconstructed half reached backward to that time for inspiration. With both feet planted squarely in the postemancipation world, Gregory's reconstructed side looked forward with the intention of creating a new kind of aristocracy. Eschewing the standards of birth and inherited wealth, he aimed for "an aristocracy of wisdom, and of worth."[40]

One implied criterion of this new aristocracy was white skin. According to one *Torchlight* article, "the Anglo Saxon race" would "ultimately return" society "to the paths of political uprightness, integrity, and honor." "All respectable voters of whatever race, color or previous condition" were encouraged to join the Democratic party and "aid us in our holy crusade." Yet the implication was never that African Americans would participate on equal footing with whites. The *Torchlight*'s editors and the local Democratic leaders they represented believed that African Americans would always follow the "Anglo Saxon race," because they thought blacks incapable of making political decisions on their own. At worst, African Americans howled like beasts, gave their votes to corrupt candidates, and played the fool in political offices beyond their meager capabilities. At best, they were "polite and accommodating" men who submitted to Democratic rule. In this sense, what was being proposed in the *Torchlight*'s pages was really a change in leadership, from white Republicans to white Democrats, the real representatives of "the Anglo Saxon race."[41]

Not just any white man, however, could assume a place at the party's helm. To rank among the best, a man had to be as economically successful as the "rich men" who appeared elsewhere in the newspaper. One article carefully detailed the business pursuits of the 1880 Democratic candidates and approvingly pointed out their prosperity. The candidate for sheriff was not just a farmer, but a "thriving and prosperous" one. Another nominee was a man of "christian virtue" and "also a very successful farmer." Although many of the candidates hailed from wealthy, established families, Democratic nominees were advertised as self-made men by emphasizing individual effort over inherited wealth and position. The 1880 candidate for state senator, for instance, had accumulated "quite a handsome competency" through "industry and attention to business." He could easily have been mistaken for one of the heroes in the newspaper's fictional pieces. In the *Torchlight,* personal economic success not only reflected well on the candidates but also benefited the community as a whole. In fact, the same article made the tobacco warehouses of two candidates in 1880 sound more like public services than private businesses. The owner of one acquitted "himself with great satisfaction to his customers, who number many of the good, honest yeomen of the county," while the other sold "tobacco for the people of Granville." According to this logic, business acumen also produced good governance. That same year, the newspaper's editor urged the election of county commissioners who "will manage the finances of the county with the same discretion that they would their individual business." Unlike the Republicans, Democrats with "good judgment" and "good business qualifications" would set the county's finances aright.[42]

Behind the best men stood their cheerful wives. One nominee's wife was high among his qualifications for office because she was, as

a *Torchlight* article noted, "a lady who by virtue of her rare accomplishments, and beautiful feminine graces, is duly beloved by all who know
her." More often, articles in the newspaper assumed or implied wom-
en's presence without referring directly to them. All the best men
lived in the kind of domestic retreats the newspaper promoted so
avidly elsewhere in its pages. There, in a world removed from public
view, wives nourished and cultivated the integrity their husbands
brought into office. As one writer observed in 1886, "Our homes
. . . are the support of the government and the church, and all the
associations and organizations that give blessings and vitality to social existence." "What are their foundation-stones, but woman's care
and devotion?" The newspaper's editors wrote this same imagery into
their campaign literature. One Democratic candidate, for instance,
"left his home" to enter "the field for the office of Sheriff." After
winning election, he served with distinction as a "good faithful officer" who "has been instrumental in redeeming the credit of our county." Presumably, the private haven created by his cheerful wife gave
him the necessary strength to weather the political storm and to serve
the public interest. Granville County's women, in turn, needed Democratic officeholders for their own domestic success. As the *Torchlight*'s
editors promised, Democrats could bring tranquility to homes now
embattled by Republican corruption and incompetence. "Only under Democratic rule," they claimed, will "the honeysuckle vines of
happiness and contentment entwine themselves around every honest man's door."[43]

With their impeccable integrity and business acumen, the "best
men" succeeded where Republicans inevitably failed—or so it appeared in the *Torchlight*'s pages. In 1874, the editor forecast doom for
the county's finances if "five honest, firm, intelligent men" did not
replace the current Republican commissioners. The newspaper underscored the wisdom of this prediction two years later in coverage
of the Kinton incident, emphasizing the absence of honesty, firmness,
and intelligence in the Republicans who still controlled the county.
Democratic talents, moreover, extended well beyond financial matters. When several Democrats won office in Oxford's 1875 municipal election, the *Torchlight*'s editor took every opportunity to publicize the accomplishments of these "men of experience, ability and
progressive ideas." He singled out the new mayor in particular, noting his attention to the town's streets, sidewalks, and cemetery as well
as his efforts "to put a stop to the use of vulgar and indecent language
on our streets" and "to preserve law and order" generally. "Under his
hand," the editor bragged, "the town has improved more than it had

in years before." In showering praise on Democratic officeholders, the *Torchlight*'s editors also heaped criticism on the Republican party, implying that it had managed the town and its unruly black population as poorly as it had handled financial matters. The following year, the editor smugly concluded that public office was best left to "gentlemen."[44]

According to the *Torchlight*, Democrats also steered clear of the pitfalls inherent in permanent political organizations. Political parties, according to an 1874 article, have frequently "engendered misfortunes and calamity" because "the private interests and passions of men will insensibly intermingle in their public transactions" thus "distracting the councils of the nation" and "diminish[ing] its power and prosperity." If so, then the newspaper's editors and contributors lay the blame on one party alone. Whereas Republicans sought office to benefit themselves, Democratic "gentlemen" looked only to serve the public interest. As one of the *Torchlight*'s editors argued, municipal elections had "been generally made use of more to try the strength of parties within the corporation, [rather] than to effect any special good to the town." But now that Democratic officials had taken over Oxford's government, "the mayor and Board have been an actual benefit to the town, and we daresay that at no period in the history of Oxford has there been such perceptible and substantial improvements made." Oxford's Democratic officials were "our best citizens," chosen "without respect to party." By contrast, legitimate Republican opposition was dismissed as the work of "negroes" determined to disrupt the "efficient" work of public-spirited officials.[45]

In fact, only the "best men" could govern effectively because they were the only ones who could represent the interests of the county as a whole. Everyone else—white Republicans, African Americans, and even "breakaway" Democrats—served their own particular interests at the public's expense. In 1878, for instance, the *Torchlight*'s editor informed African Americans that the "interest of the white man is your interest, and yours the white man's interest." It was wealthy whites who would define these interests. "Whatever tends to your interest tends to ours," the editor assured black residents again the following month, "and those things that make for our peace and happiness in like manner benefit you." The harmony in this proposed political relationship derived from its inherent inequalities. Both Democratic leaders and the *Torchlight*'s editors relied on the model of domestic relations within households to explain their leadership abilities, casting their interests as representative of everyone in their communities in the same way that a male household head's experience and interests were representative of his family. In this vision African Americans were to be "happy and contented" laborers "satisfied with low wages," and common whites were to submit to the "white man's interest" as it was defined by the wealthy and powerful of their race. Since the "best men" represented society's interests, there was no need for African Americans and common whites to have an independent political voice.[46]

The emphasis on personal character and the qualifications of individual men also deflected attention away from policy and party principles. As the *Torchlight*'s editor announced in 1880, "Candidates will hereafter be judged by their character and capacity rather than their professions of principle." Good men, in other words, would provide good government. The stance taken toward three Republican officials accused of conspiracy in 1876 is also suggestive. Even after the superior court acquitted them, the editor at that same time still adamantly demanded their resignation. Admitting their innocence in this one instance, he thought the three men should "retire" from "responsible office . . . before any more mischief is done." While he felt no "ill-will" toward them "as private citizens," this editor believed they possessed none of the qualities necessary to wield public power. As such, the three men would fall prey to their own weaknesses and produce more "mischief" than good.[47]

Already weakened institutionally, local Republicans withered under this Democratic barrage. At their most inclusive, Republican appeals to manhood posited a public sphere where there were no "best men" because all men participated on equal footing. But as the party's power slipped and it began to distance itself from its core constituency, Republican leaders channeled the language of manhood and womanhood into more conservative directions. At an 1876 party gathering in Oxford, one African-American speaker urged his fellow Republicans to "make men of yourselves." In the past, similar phrases might have rallied the party members to risk violent reprisals, act on their rights, and go to the polls. This speaker, however, hoped to impose order on the crowd, not encourage democracy within its ranks. Republicans, he argued, could "make men" of themselves only by following their leaders and toeing the party line. Responding to Democratic allegations of mismanagement and fraud, other Republican leaders also held up the mantle of manhood to defend the character of individual candidates and officials, not to open up the polity generally. Of course, the *Torchlight* regularly publicized internal dissension within the Republican party in order to divide its members and undercut its strength. The party was rarely as conflicted or as weak as articles in the newspaper made out. Yet, if not completely accurate, these reports still suggest the presence of conflict within the party as well as mounting concern over the consolidation of Democratic power. Local Republicans were in good company, for similar issues plagued the party not just in North Carolina, but across the South as a whole. In response to the Democratic onslaught and growing disaffection within their ranks, Republican leaders emphasized respectability and duty, closing off debate and turning a deaf ear to the concerns of its core membership.[48]

Republican assertions of manhood also took on an increasingly defensive tone. As party leaders responded to allegations in the *Torchlight*, they picked up the newspaper's rhetoric and duplicated the assumptions embedded in it. In 1876, for instance, H. C. Crosby called for "intelligent" and "qualified" men, white and black, to lead the party. What this outspoken African-American leader wanted were candidates who would remain true to the party's principles and not turn against blacks once in office. At the same time, however, Crosby's choice of adjectives underscored the importance of class distinctions that moved many Republicans to the margins of public power. It is unlikely that he would have included poor, uneducated laborers, whether white or black, among the "intelligent" and "qualified" party leadership. "We must pick out and trim our best men," advised another local black leader four years later, not "a jack," "a jinny," or "a woman." While his words directly countered Democratic imagery by insisting that some Republicans—even some black men—ranked among the "best men," he also affirmed the basic ideas of racial and class hierarchy by admitting that other Republicans were unsuited to exercise public power.[49]

In a letter printed in the *Torchlight* that same election year, "a Republican" urged two black candidates to drop their names from the breakaway slate of candidates. Because they were intelligent and honorable men, he argued, "the better class of colored people look to you and men like you to lead them in the right direction." By supporting a breakaway faction, these two men also provided a bad example for the rest of their race, many of whom "have not been educated either morally or mentally to correct views and high principles." "A Republican" kept his identity hidden. Yet the way he distanced himself from African Americans suggests that he, unlike H. C. Crosby, believed in the superiority of the white race. The approval he gave to the "better class of colored people" and the patronizing tone he adopted toward other blacks suggests his commitment to class privilege as well. If anything, the divide "A Republican" saw between those who were "intelligent" and "qualified" and those who were not was almost as wide as that envisioned by the leaders of the Democratic party.[50]

In 1886, the Granville Knights of Labor stepped into the space vacated by the Republican party. The national organization rooted its political vision in the same petty producer rhetoric that had been so central to the Republican party at its inception in the 1860s. Opposing the power of industrial capital, the Knights looked backward to a past in which men controlled their own labor and exercised political rights as independent household heads. As such, the guiding principles of the order tended to elevate the interests of property owners and independent artisans above propertyless wage laborers.[51]

In Granville County, the Knights organized around similar principles. As one "sympathizer" wrote in an editorial printed by the *Torchlight,* the order "gathers into its fold all branches of honorable industry" working under the assumption that "every citizen who is entitled to vote is a part of our government." The "proper scope" of the Knights, he continued, embraced "anything tending to advance the cause of humanity, lighten the burden of toil and elevate the social and moral condition of mankind." Given the political context in Granville County and the South as a whole in 1886, these words were radical indeed. By contrast, the Democrats hoped to build a society around hierarchies of race and class that would exclude the vast majority of southerners from public power. For them political harmony would result only when common whites and African Americans accepted Democratic leadership and improved themselves by concentrating on waged work and farming instead of politics. Still, the "sympathizer's" description of the order as "conservative" was also accurate.[52] The Knights' emphasis on independent producers may have captured the aspirations of many propertyless working people, but it did not directly address their current economic problems. This particular political vision posed even greater problems for African Americans because its ideological undergirding so often linked independence to whiteness. The order did organize biracially and openly discuss the possibilities for racial integration. But it remained blind to the racial dynamics that marginalized black workers and powerless to resolve the racial tensions that made biracial cooperation so tenuous.[53]

For all its emphasis on inclusion, moreover, the Knights did not invite poor whites and African Americans into the organization as equal members. White and black locals remained separate, while whites always occupied the most visible leadership roles. Prominent members, both white and black, tended to conform to the order's economic ideal, working as merchants and skilled artisans and owning significant amounts of property. As the Oxford "sympathizer" explained in his *Torchlight* editorial, the organization anointed a few leaders to "educate" the rest of the membership who needed to "free" themselves "from the corrupting influence of base politicians." Masterworkman Robert Cohen also reinforced these racial and class distinctions. In defending the integrity of the local order, he passed over the poorer members to emphasize the "property-holders, business men, mechanics and farmers" who "compare favorably with any other place." Given the growing distance between working-class and property-holding African Americans, propertied black Knights probably shared Cohen's view. In many ways, the Granville Knights' stress on self-improvement and the group's assumption that political harmony could be achieved through virtuous leadership sounded remarkably similar to Democratic propaganda. For the Knights, however, the "best men" were the artisans, tradesmen, and farmers who headed up the order, not the "rich men" of the Democratic party. Yet, from the perspective of the poor—particularly poor black wage laborers—the order probably appeared more "conservative" than the Knights "sympathizer" imagined.[54]

For all its inequalities, the Knights' political vision allowed common whites and African Americans a greater political role and spoke more directly to their economic needs than that of the Democrats or, by the mid-1880s, even that of the Republicans. For this, the order received the support of a range of Granville County residents and the enmity of many others. According to masterworkman Robert Cohen, the *Torchlight* "every week publishes . . . something tending to ridicule and slur our noble order." He was not exaggerating. With tongue in cheek, the newspaper reported in May 1886 that the "Order of Gentlemen of Elegant Leisure" was planning a strike: "They are not satisfied with the hard, uncomfortable chairs provided for them in the stores, and they want labor saving, automatic fans furnished them by the public to cool their heated brows in these warm days." The *Torchlight* continued its coverage the following week with an "interview" in which one of its editors asked a "Gentleman of Elegant Leisure" whether he would "call upon the Knights of Labor to aid you to make the strike a success." The man "desisted from whittling a piece of soft pine wood" and replied: "'Well, I don't think we will. We couldn't do it consistently. You see, we are opposed to night[s] of labor just as much as days of labor.'" These satirical portrayals betrayed growing fears of an organization that attracted so many laborers—many of whom may well have congregated at local stores in their leisure time. The vicious responses described by the Knights themselves suggest as much. "No stone," wrote Robert Cohen, "was left unturned to create ill-feeling against us": "They pointed at us with scorn, and kept crying 'Nigger! nigger!' until the two words 'nigger' and 'Knight' became almost synonymous terms."[55]

Labor unrest elsewhere in the country made the local Knights seem that much more dangerous to conservatives in Granville County. Beginning in 1886, the *Torchlight* devoted extensive space to labor movements in the United States and Europe, reporting their growth and militancy with rising concern. Like the local Democratic leaders their newspaper represented, the *Torchlight*'s editors refused to consider that the social and economic relations they supported might not work in the best interests of everyone. They did concede that distortions in the system or the excesses of individual employers might result in low wages and other occasional injustices. After describing labor violence in three major urban areas, for instance, the *Torchlight* actually supported the workers' basic claims. "It is right and just," its editor wrote, "that labor should demand proper remuneration and that unfair competition be removed." Nonetheless, he insisted that labor should work within the existing system and appeal to those in power for relief. Confident of a natural harmony between employers and employees, this *Torchlight* editor ignored the circumstances that drove workers to militant action and blamed them for irresponsibly turning to "violence, arson, and bloodshed" instead of "peaceful arbitration." But accounts that posited a natural harmony between capital and labor provided only so much reassurance as the tide of labor conflict continued to rise unabated.[56]

The *Torchlight* and Granville County's Democratic leaders viewed party politics from the same perspective as they did labor issues. To them the Oxford Knights presented the same kind of challenge as national labor organizations, but at the polls, not in the workplace. As Robert Cohen explained, those opposed to the local order linked it to the "Chicago anarchist riot," the Knights' 1886 general meeting in Richmond where several locals challenged the color line, and "the partial success of the Republican party" in North Carolina's 1886 elections. One 1887 article highlights the parallels both the *Torchlight*'s editors and local Democratic leaders saw between militancy in labor and in politics. In it, a factory owner described his confrontation with the Knights: "It was made perfectly evident that the Knights of Labor controlled our employees to a greater extent than we." "Now we are business men," he continued, "and have our capital invested.

We cannot afford to let anybody conduct our affairs but ourselves. And we propose to control." Democratic leaders in Granville County could have spoken these words just as easily about the Knights in local politics. They did not want the Knights controlling the voters or conducting the county's public affairs. Like the businessman in the article, they proposed "to control" matters themselves.[57]

Connecting the organization of the Knights within Granville County to escalating labor militancy in the nation as a whole, Democrats feared that the possibility of "control" was slipping rapidly out of their hands. The Great Southwest Railroad Strike, which began in March 1886, served as a catalyst for labor unrest all over the country. A few months later, the first Knights of Labor local appeared in Oxford. Thereafter, events underscoring the threat posed by the local order unfolded in rapid succession. Among the most spectacular were the Haymarket massacre and the Knights' challenge to segregation at their Richmond meeting. Consumed with these events and news of other strikes, the *Torchlight*'s editor even neglected the newspaper's long-favored topic, the evils of the Republican party. That November, the Democratic party lost by a wide margin in Granville County. At the state level the combined success of the Knights, Independents, and Republicans compromised the Democratic majority in the legislature. By January, Oxford's mayor, W. F. Rogers, had openly declared his loyalty to the Knights and assumed a seat on the order's state executive board. No wonder the *Torchlight*'s editor threw up his hands in despair and forecast a bleak future.[58]

The political battle between the Knights and the Democrats ultimately centered on which of the "best men" should lead. Many Knights, like their Republican predecessors, felt comfortable with a political debate focused on the character and merits of individual men. But this was an argument neither the Knights nor the Republicans could win. Although the leaders of these two parties discussed manhood as if it were an individual virtue unconnected to race and class, they tacitly accepted a standard designed around the lives and political aspirations of the Democratic elite. Only a small handful of Knights and Republicans could ever measure up. The *Torchlight*'s editors might grudgingly concede that certain white Republicans, particularly "large property holder[s]" would "try to do right" if elected to office. But they would never think of including African Americans and common whites among those fit to lead. It was these people who filled the ranks of the Knights of Labor and the Republican party. Indeed, the standards embodied by the Democratic "best men" struck at the very foundations of both organizations, affirming a hierarchy within the public sphere that marginalized virtually all of their constituents.[59]

The Knights and Knights Errant

In March 1887, Belle Booth charged Albert Taborn with burglary and attempted rape. Because there is no existing testimony, it is unclear whether a rape attempt actually occurred. But even extensive documentation might not resolve this question conclusively because Taborn's guilt depended on how broadly "attempted rape" was defined. In this instance, the criminal justice system may have construed the crime so broadly that it would have been virtually impossible for the alleged intruder not to have been guilty. For the Booths and other white sympathizers, the fact that Belle Booth had been alone in the house with an African-American man may have been enough to constitute a sexual attack. Any contact with Belle Booth, whether physical, verbal, or even just visual, increased the alleged burglar's chances of being charged with attempted rape. This is not to say that Belle Booth fabricated the charge. Given the racially charged atmosphere and the presumption among many whites that black men preyed on white women, Belle Booth may have interpreted the intruder's actions in her house that night as a sexual assault, whatever the nature of the contact or his intentions. County officials and the *Torchlight*'s editors and contributors apparently agreed, for they never questioned the validity of the charge.[60]

Taborn's arrest infuriated many African Americans, who seized the occasion to challenge the Democrats' economic and political assumptions. Despite assurances in the *Torchlight*, many African Americans did not trust Democratic officials to preserve their civil and political rights. Such doubts prompted those men who patrolled the streets to ward off any attempt to lynch Taborn. They could depend on Oxford municipal officers, many of whom were Knights and Republicans. But appointed Democrats filled most of the county offices. Moreover, the *Torchlight*, the party's official mouthpiece, had all but demanded Taborn's lynching. In this political context, some black men felt it necessary to risk their own lives and the possibility of a violent backlash to protect Taborn and ensure his right to a trial. Other African Americans expressed misgivings about Taborn's fate within the legal system. One week after the fire that swept through Oxford, a group of African Americans tried to free Taborn when the sheriff was escorting him to the Raleigh jail for safekeeping. According to the *Torchlight*, the group "attempted to create a disturbance," but were "boldly met" and "discretely quieted down." The notoriety attached to this case, the first in the postwar years to involve a prominent white woman, only underscored the continued marginality of African Americans. When black women experienced violence or when any black person suffered injustice of any kind, they and their kinfolk struggled just to make their cases public. Indeed, Albert Taborn appeared as the victim of an interlocking set of assumptions that not only predetermined his guilt but ultimately circumscribed the lives of all African Americans.[61]

Blacks' suspicions were well founded. Not only had Democratic justices and judges shown a distinct bias against African Americans generally but just six years earlier a white mob had taken two black men accused of murder out of the Oxford jail and lynched them. Recently, the *Torchlight* had devoted a great deal of space to the "problem" of black-on-white crime and its editors had endorsed vigilante violence against black suspects. While reports of such crimes were not new in Granville County, the sensational articles that began to appear in the newspaper around 1885 set a very different tone. The 1886 account of a "negro murderer . . . burned to death at the stake" was typical. According to the *Torchlight*, "his crime was a horrible one": "He attempted to outrage a young white lady." When she "prevented the accomplishment of his hellish purpose," he murdered her: He "first beat her with his fist, then shot her, and completed his fiendish work by beating her brains out with the stock of his gun." A mob then "carried him back to the scene of his crime, bound him to a stake, piled the fagots about him and applied the lighted torch, burning him to ashes." It "wreaked a most barbarous vengeance, but if any offence ever deserved so terrible a punishment in this instance it was richly merited." In this and other pieces the *Torchlight* created the impression of an embattled white citizenry facing an epidemic of violent crime committed by black men. Instead of portraying the alleged perpetrators as individuals with particular reasons for committing the crimes they did, articles in the newspaper presented them as faceless, nameless men who acted for no apparent reason whatsoever. As the articles implied, any, perhaps all black men might be rapists, murderers, and thieves.[62]

The *Torchlight* presented the Booth-Taborn case in similar terms. In a dramatic recreation of the crime, the newspaper depicted Taborn as the fiendish marauder and Belle Booth as the innocent flower of white womanhood. In one article, Taborn "entered the house at night in the absence of . . . [Belle's husband] . . . and was on the lady's bed before she discovered his presence. She had not yet recovered from a recent childbirth, and escaped to a neighbor's house with some difficulty. The excitement and exposure caused a relapse, and she is lying at the point of death." The writer concluded that lynching was "a fate he deserved."[63]

While those who protected Taborn from the rumored lynching and attempted to free him questioned the political leadership of the "best men," those who gathered to watch the fire challenged the economic leadership of the "rich men." As the fire blazed, the spectators showed little concern for the shops, offices, and warehouses that anchored the town's business district. According to the *Torchlight,* some African Americans even celebrated openly in the streets. It is possible that the revelers also included some whites, whose presence the newspaper chose to ignore just as it did when they appeared at Republican rallies. A few African-American onlookers reportedly withheld their assistance because "they were accused of stealing part of the goods they rescued" at a fire the previous year and "did not want to put themselves in a position to be insulted again." This article probably overstated the reaction to the fire. Even so, the report still suggests the distance that many African Americans saw between their own interests and those of the town's elite, be they Democratic or Republican.[64]

Aghast at the anger Taborn's arrest had exposed, the editor of the *Torchlight* denounced the black community for its lack of citizenship. "Every citizen," he lectured with palpable indignation, "is interested in the preservation of the property held in that town." It then went one step further, criminalizing those involved in the unrest on the night of the fire and disqualifying them from the rights of citizenship. They were, in the editor's opinion, "little better than the fire-bug who puts the torch to property and . . . should be regarded accordingly." Their actions placed them among "the pestilent order of anarchists and nihilists, men who desire the destruction of all that represents industry, economy and thrift in order that they may revel for a period in . . . base enjoyment." Not only did these people lack the capacity to exercise power responsibly but their unregulated presence in the public sphere also posed a real threat to the social order. "Our colored citizens," the *Torchlight's* editor warned, "should read, ponder, and inwardly digest." At least, he added, those "who are capable of comprehending."[65]

As the reference to "anarchists and nihilists" suggests, the *Torchlight's* editor ultimately blamed the Knights for the efforts to protect Taborn, the fire, and the unrest that followed. Some of those involved may have been Knights. But there is no evidence that the order formally initiated or encouraged any of these incidents. From the perspective of Democratic leaders, however, the Knights of Labor did not have to directly initiate or even condone the events surrounding Taborn's arrest to bear responsibility for them. By supporting the independent political expression of African Americans and common whites, the organization had created the conditions that encouraged social unrest.[66]

The leaders of the Knights hotly denied the charges against the order, fearing that any connection with Taborn or the unrest surrounding his arrest would undermine the order's already precarious position. "There was not a bit of evidence against us," claimed Robert Cohen, the masterworkman of the black local. "Not a Knight was directly or indirectly concerned." With this denial, Cohen actually defined the Knights in opposition to Albert Taborn and the three poor black laborers who would soon be accused of starting the fire. All Knights, he maintained, "are good citizens, and none have been in jail since the Order was started here."[67]

More than a few African Americans may have agreed with Cohen's denunciation of black militancy. The *Torchlight*'s editor used both Albert Taborn and the people who watched the fire to personify the dangers of allowing African-American men access to public power. In the newspaper's pages, Taborn appeared as an undisciplined dependent, incapable of supporting a family and potentially dangerous to existing households. The editor then used the uprising provoked by his arrest to underscore the irresponsibility of African Americans generally. The incidents on the night of the fire were reported in the *Torchlight* as if the entire black community had been involved. The allegations were so egregious that the editor felt compelled to print an apology one week after the fire. "Our account of the fire last week," he admitted, "was written in the confusion and excitement immediately subsequent to the calamity, and perhaps we did not draw as nice a distinction in referring to the colored people who assisted to extinguish the flames and save property and those who did not, as we should have done." "Oxford has a large class of negroes who compare favorably with the best of their race anywhere," he continued, and "we would not willingly do them an unjustice, or confound them with those who stood idly by and refused a helping hand." Afterward, however, the editor returned to his initial view that all African-American men were dangerous—not the hard-working household heads and public-spirited citizens that the Republicans and the Knights insisted they were.[68]

It was W. F. Rogers, the mayor and a member of the Knights of Labor, who launched the most dramatic effort to distance the order from all those the newspaper labeled bad citizens. As soon as the flames died down, Rogers began hunting the culprits. He came up empty-handed. Not so easily deterred, he then methodically manufactured evidence to frame three black laborers: John Taborn, Albert's brother; Nowell Hopkins, Albert's brother-in-law; and Aaron Lockett, a close friend of Hopkins and the Taborn brothers.[69]

Given their close relationships to Albert Taborn, these men were the most obvious suspects. Their arrest also deflected criticism away from the Knights because they were not members of the order. There was only one problem: the evidence did not substantiate the charges. In fact, Rogers constructed the entire case against the three men out of thin air. As Robert Kinton later testified: "Mr Rogers offered me 100 [dollars] to help . . . work up the case. He said he had Mike [Cook] and [William] Landing out and was going to give them 100 [dollars]." Kinton turned down the offer. Cook and Landing did not. These two black laborers claimed to have overheard a conversation in which Aaron Lockett and Nowell Hopkins admitted responsibility for the fire. They also swore that Lockett had openly bragged to them about how he had saved Albert Taborn's life by setting it, and they even produced a letter that implicated Hopkins. To corroborate the evidence, Rogers provided a white eyewitness, Calvin Harris, who had spent the night in the tobacco warehouse next to the storehouse where the fire had started. Harris swore that he saw Hopkins go into the warehouse under suspicious circumstances that night. But these memories did not come easily to Harris, who did not come forward until Rogers promised to pay him fifty dollars.[70]

Based on the letter and the testimony, the superior court indicted Aaron Lockett and Nowell Hopkins in May 1887. The evidence against Lockett, however, looked weak. Perhaps Rogers decided to include John Taborn in the case for this very reason. Sometime after the grand jury indicted Lockett and Hopkins, Rogers offered W. B. Veasey, a white farmer, one hundred dollars to "work out the burning." What Rogers meant was that he would pay Veasey to testify against Taborn. Veasey declined Rogers's offer, later testifying that Taborn was at his house on the night of the fire. Rogers then enlisted the aid of J. A. Wrenn, a white merchant whose business had been destroyed by the fire. Wrenn testified that Hopkins called for him in jail and admitted that he and John Taborn had set the fire. What Wrenn did not explain is why Hopkins suddenly chose him as a confidante. But his testimony was enough to implicate John Taborn, whose name also appeared on the indictment when the case came to trial in September. Still, W. F. Rogers's evidence seemed almost too neat to be believable. When the defense proved that the letter incriminating Nowell Hopkins was fabricated and produced witnesses whom Rogers had tried to bribe, the entire case began to crumble. In fact, the superior court eventually indicted Cook and Landing because they seemed to know so much about the fire.[71]

In September 1887, the court dropped the charges against Aaron Lockett and the jury acquitted John Taborn, Mike Cook, and William Landing. Nowell Hopkins alone shouldered the guilty verdict. The evidence, however, strongly suggests that he was paid off to take the blame. John Taborn, for instance, maintained that someone managed to obtain false testimony from Hopkins: "Nowell said he was put up to say that I [Taborn] did it." But "he knows I had nothing to do with it." That person may well have been W. F. Rogers, who regularly visited Hopkins in jail and brought him whiskey each time.[72] Later, Hopkins escaped under highly questionable circumstances. The jailer claimed that Hopkins violently attacked him, but could not produce even the smallest scratch to support his story. Nor could he explain why he failed to sound the customary alarm. The *Torchlight*'s editor was outraged: "A man that will put himself in a position to be knocked down and killed by a man sentenced to be hanged is either a fool, a lunatic, or a most consummate knave." The editor was also suspicious, insinuating that those in authority had planned the escape and were now purposefully avoiding a full-scale search. Hopkins was never found. If Rogers had struck a bargain with Hopkins, he managed to fulfill his end of the deal.[73]

Rogers's case against Aaron Lockett, Nowell Hopkins, and John Taborn, which began just as Albert Taborn's case reached trial, plunged the Knights of Labor into greater disarray than it already was in. Not only did Rogers fail to mollify the Democrats but he also alienated the vast majority of black working people on whose support the Knights depended. In this polarized political atmosphere, the Knights occupied increasingly shaky middle ground. Ultimately, they lost their footing altogether.

Democrats seized on Albert Taborn's trial to condemn all that he represented and to affirm the necessity of conservative rule. The *Torchlight*'s editor, who had never doubted Taborn's guilt, treated the trial as a formality. So did Taborn's lawyer, A. W. Graham. Although Graham did file an unsuccessful motion to move the trial to another county, he presented no evidence and called no witnesses, not even a character witness, on Taborn's behalf. As soon as the jury brought in the guilty verdict, Graham resigned as counsel, thus making it clear that he would neither appeal the case nor challenge the sentence. As the *Torchlight* reported, the judge then announced that Taborn

should "be hanged by the neck till [he] be dead, and may the Great
Giver of all life have mercy on [his] soul." Silence settled over the
crowded courtroom. The sentence was the most extreme the judge
could issue. In all previous postwar cases, men convicted of attempted rape, even black men convicted of assaulting white women, had
received only a prison term.[74]

Just in case the sentence did not convey its intended message, the
Democratic county commissioners decided to emphasize it by making the execution public. This too was a first for the postwar years.
The last public execution had taken place in 1864, when William
Cooper had been hanged for the attempted rape of Susan Daniel.
Henderson Cooper, who was supposed to have joined William on the
gallows, escaped to Washington, D.C., and later foiled the efforts of
local officials to carry out his sentence. Perhaps it was this experience
that led some to oppose the commissioners' decision. Although
agreeing with the extreme punishment, they were concerned that a
public execution would not fulfill its intended purpose: "It is often
the case that a red-handed villain is carried in triumph to the gallows
and is regarded as a positive hero, if not a martyr, by the gaping and
admiring crowd." More to the point, Oxford would "be filled to over
flowing with negroes from every point of the compass, which to say
the least of it, will not be of any peculiar advantage to the place." As
conservative whites had learned when they captured Henderson
Cooper and carried him back to Granville County, the "gaping and
admiring crowd" might well turn the tables and seize control themselves.[75]

But this time was different. Flanked by the Granville Grays, the local military company that took its name and uniforms from one of the
county's Confederate companies, Taborn walked to the gallows and
ascended the scaffold. As five thousand people watched, he declared
his innocence and was hanged. The lesson was clear: only valiant elite
white men could protect the social order (embodied by Belle Booth)
from impending chaos (represented by Albert Taborn and, by extension, all African Americans and many poor whites as well). With
Taborn's execution, Belle Booth and society at large were safe: the
patriarchal power of elite white men would protect them all.[76]

Through all this the Knights and the Republicans stood by silent-
ly, apparently unable to respond. Threats of violence, while intimi-
dating, had never stopped political opposition in the county before
now.[77] Far more immobilizing was the way Democrats so effectively
built their own power on the same ideological scaffolding the opposition had relied on for so long. The awkward position of the jury at

Taborn's trial captures, in microcosm, the problems facing the Knights and Republicans more generally. The jury's foreman was none other than Robert Cohen, masterworkman of the black Knights of Labor local. Without membership lists for the Knights of Labor, it is impossible to tell whether any of the other jurors were also Knights. But the group did include two leading black Republicans as well as six African-American artisans and property owners who were prominent within the black community. At the very least, the fact that these jurors chose Cohen as their foreman indicates their respect for him. Indeed, the composition of Taborn's jury seems more than a little coincidental. If Democratic court officials had stacked the jury to force the Knights and African-American leaders to take a position on Taborn's alleged crime they could not have picked a better group of people. If the jury convicted Taborn, they would alienate many poor African Americans. If they acquitted him, they would bring down the wrath of the Democratic party.[78]

The jury voted unanimously to convict Taborn. Given the overwhelming evidence presented by the prosecution and the virtual silence of Taborn's attorney, jury members would have been hard pressed to reach any other conclusion. But they may well have had their own reservations about Taborn, who was not a sympathetic figure to everyone in the black community. Indeed, Taborn defied the essential elements of manhood as many African Americans and common whites had constructed it. An unattached man charged with attempted rape, Taborn hardly fit the model of a responsible household head who sought public power only to protect the interests of his family. Both the Republican party and the Knights clung to the rhetoric that all men stood as equals in public and ignored the growing sense among some of their constituents that these words diverted attention away from the vast inequalities of wealth and privilege in the "private" sphere. Those who came to Taborn's defense seemed only too aware of the disparities among supposedly "equal" household heads that could never be resolved within the terms of a debate that tended to suppress racial and class differences as private matters of no public consequence. But for those who still believed in the power of a gendered discourse that centered on men's rights as household heads, Taborn posed a real threat to their public standing. Acquitting him would mean sanctioning attempted rape, condoning the violation of household borders, and undermining their political arguments. If Republicans and Knights wanted to maintain their image as respectable men who acted with the good of the community in mind, they had no choice but to declare Taborn guilty.[79]

Nonetheless, the jury convicted Taborn of robbery and attempted rape only. It was the Democratic judge who sentenced him to death and the Democratic county commissioners who made his hanging a public event. But the distinction between the jury's decision and the Democratic handling of it were soon lost. Similarly, the Democratic drama of Taborn's trial swallowed up the particular reasons the Knights distanced themselves from Taborn and the unrest on the night of the fire. To many of the African Americans who watched, it looked as if both the Knights and the Republicans had collaborated with the Democrats in a cruel charade that affirmed conservative rule and their own political marginality. The silence of Taborn's lawyer, which was noticeable enough for the *Torchlight* to comment on, probably did not pass unnoticed in the county's black community. Those who missed the significance of the trial's dynamics could not ignore the extreme sentence and public execution, both of which were intended to attract their attention. To them, it seemed that Taborn had escaped a lynch mob only to face a legal system that routinely subverted the interests of poor African Americans.[80]

The racial and class tensions exposed by the events surrounding Taborn's trial slowly ravaged both the Knights of Labor and the Republican party. A few months after the May 1887 election, the Knights disintegrated and then disappeared entirely from view. It is unclear what happened to Robert Cohen, but soon after the election, W. F. Rogers abruptly left town. When called as a witness in Mike Cook's and William Landing's trial, he refused to return to Oxford to testify. The Republican party survived, but only as a shell of its former self.[81]

One year after Albert Taborn's execution, Democratic city fathers would seal their victory by gerrymandering Oxford Township to eliminate the power that black voters once wielded. Common whites would drift back to the Democrats or, more often, simply stay home on election day. Even the Populist party would not attract propertyless people, black or white, as the Republicans and Knights had.[82] Thus Democratic party leaders accomplished what they had been trying to do since the end of the Civil War. They had reestablished their prewar position by reclaiming the institutions of public power and reshaping the terrain of political conflict. In this context, even the question of participation in the political system was not as important as it had been earlier. Democrats had excluded not only African Americans and common, particularly poor, whites from the public arena but also the issues of most interest to them. Even if they still participated, their voices fell like so many silent drops in a roaring Democratic current.

As if to explain the recent political upheaval, the *Torchlight* printed the article "A Lesson in Morals" in December 1887. The author began with the proposition that "the state" is "the organization necessary to protect and preserve society." But, the author continued, there were different kinds of governments:

> Government will be good or bad, as the people are good or bad—more or less free, as they are more virtuous or vicious, and people in a body will generally command as good a government as they merit. If, as a body, they are truthful, intelligent, honest, industrious and virtuous, they will need fewer restraints, and will be entitled to, and will have, a comparatively free government. If, on the other hand, [they are] ignorant, selfish, dishonest, idle and vicious the greater will be the restraints necessary to protect society and the stronger the force of government. From this difference in the characters of people arises the different forms of government. . . . The better the people, the better the government—the more wicked the people, the stronger and more despotic must the government be; it must be strong enough to preserve society—to restrain the wicked and vicious, and punish them for criminal acts. If it does no more than this, then as much freedom is left to the people as a body, as their condition will admit of.[83]

Those "bad" people in Granville County deserved less freedom and fewer rights than those who were "good." Moreover, it was the responsibility of the "good" people to make sure the "bad" ones did not destroy society. Of course, the characters of these "good" and "bad" people were judged according to standards set by white elites, who also defined the substance of a "good" society.

Eleven years later, Democrats made black-male-on-white-female rape the centerpiece of their strategy in the statewide 1898 white supremacy campaign that resulted in disfranchisement. Under Republican rule, Democratic governor Charles Brantley Aycock explained, "lawlessness stalked the State like a pestilence. . . . The screams of women fleeing from pursuing brutes closed the gates of our hearts with a shock." Fortunately, "good men" and the proponents of "good government" had finally won: "We did not dislike the negro, but we did love good government. We knew that he was incapable of giving us that, and we resolved, not in anger, but for the safety of the State, to curtail his power." The disfranchisement amendment actually excluded all men who could not read or write, although it temporarily grandfathered in those descended from someone who could vote in January 1867. The provision protected the vote of many common white men, but not for long. The literacy test, moreover, was merely a means by which to push African Americans and common, particularly poor, whites out of public space. These people were not yet ready to participate in public life, Aycock insisted. To prepare them, he instituted an ambitious plan of universal education. Thus, disfranchisement "takes no step backward, it distinctly looks to the future; it sees the day of universal suffrage, but sees that day not in the obscurity of ignorance, but in the light of universal education." Until then, Aycock and his fellow Democratic leaders would uphold "good" government by keeping "bad" people out of power.[84]

Notes

Introduction

1. The court of inquiry did not name the crime it suspected Henderson Cooper had committed, although it tried him on two counts, assault and battery with intent to commit rape and aiding and abetting the commission of rape. Documentation of the case comes from two main sources, the Freedmen's Bureau and the correspondence of Governor Jonathan Worth. Besides some of the orders and reports of the Freedmen's Bureau, the local court records contain documentation of only the formal proceedings of the case—the complaint, indictment, order of execution, etc. See Robert Avery to James V. Bomford, 27 Mar. 1867, and William W. Jones to M. Cogswell, 16 Mar. 1867, both in Letters Received, Second Military District, Records of the U.S. Army Continental Commands, RG 393, National Archives, Washington, D.C.; William W. Jones to the Assistant Commissioner, 28 Mar. 1867, Letters Received, Records of the Assistant Commissioner for the State of North Carolina, Records of the U.S. Bureau of Refugees, Freedmen, and Abandoned Lands, RG 105, National Archives Microfilm Publication M843; *State v. William and Henderson Cooper,* 1864–67, Criminal Actions Concerning Slaves and Free Persons of Color, Granville County, North Carolina Division of Archives and History, Raleigh (hereafter NCDAH); Worth to William A. Philpott, 16 Oct. 1866, 231, Worth to the Governor of Virginia, 16 Oct. 1866, 234, James V. Bomford to J. M. Clous (a copy was forwarded to Worth), 22 Apr. 1867, 471–72, Worth to Maj. Gen. Sickles, 21 May 1867, 472–73, William A. Philpott to Worth, 8 Oct. 1867, 608, and Worth to Robert Avery, 10 Oct. 1867, 607, all in Jonathan Worth, Governor's Letter Book, 1865–67, NCDAH; Worth to Pres. Andrew Johnson, 31 Dec. 1867, 5–9, and E. W. Dennis to Louis V. Cazario (a copy was forwarded to Worth), 26 Mar. 1868, 111–15, both in Worth, Governor's Letter Book, 1867–68; Robert Gilliam to Worth, 22 Nov. 1866, 2:844–45, Worth to Thomas Settle, 20 May 1867, 2:959–60, Worth to William A. Philpott, 18 Dec. 1867, 2:1089, Worth to W. A. Graham, 10 Jan. 1868, 2:1128–31, and Worth to Lewis Hanes, 17 Jan. 1869, 2:1265–67, all in Hamilton, *The Correspondence of Jonathan Worth.* See Hamilton, *Reconstruction in North Carolina,* 229–30, for a summary.

2. Perhaps local authorities simply felt it was their duty to close the case and bring Henderson Cooper to justice. Yet, judging from the crowded court docket, they clearly had enough to occupy their attention at home without

embarking on a long and costly interstate manhunt. The attention lavished on this particular case suggests that it was important in ways that the others were not. Robert Avery to James V. Bomford, 27 Mar. 1867, Letters Received, Second Military District, Records of the U.S. Army Continental Commands; Worth to William A. Philpott, 16 Oct. 1866, 231, Worth, Governor's Letter Book, 1865–67. There were hundreds of cases before the local courts at this same time; see Criminal Action Papers, 1865–67, Granville County, NCDAH.

3. Worth signed the papers necessary to secure Henderson Cooper's capture in 1866, but he did not become actively involved in the case until 1867. Worth to William A. Philpott, 16 Oct. 1866, 231, and Worth to the Governor of Virginia, 16 Oct. 1866, 234, both in Worth, Governor's Letter Book, 1865–67. For the correspondence about his series of articles, see Worth to W. A. Graham, 10 Jan. 1868, 2:1128–31, and Worth to Lewis Hanes, 17 Jan. 1869, 2:1265–67, both in Hamilton, *The Correspondence of Jonathan Worth*.

4. Worth to Pres. Andrew Johnson, 31 Dec. 1867, 8–9, Worth, Governor's Letter Book, 1867–68.

5. For parallels with the political rhetoric in South Carolina during the nullification crisis, see McCurry, *Masters of Small Worlds*, 260–61.

6. Even a brief look at the literature reveals the separation of political history and social history. Perhaps the most notable exceptions are Du Bois, *Black Reconstruction*, and Rose, *Rehearsal for Reconstruction*. For more recent work that builds on these insights, setting social and political history in a more dynamic relationship, see Bercaw, "The Politics of Household"; Berlin, Reidy, and Rowland, *The Black Military Experience;* Berlin, Fields, Glymph, Reidy, and Rowland, *The Destruction of Slavery;* Berlin, Glymph, Miller, Reidy, Rowland, and Saville, *The Wartime Genesis of Free Labor: The Lower South;* Berlin, Miller, Reidy, and Rowland, *The Wartime Genesis of Free Labor: The Upper South;* E. Brown, "To Catch a Vision of Freedom" and "Uncle Ned's Children"; Fields, *Slavery and Freedom on the Middle Ground;* Foner, *Reconstruction;* Frankel, "Freedom's Women"; T. Holt, "'An Empire over the Mind'" and *The Problem of Freedom;* Rosen, "Race, Gender, and the Politics of Rape"; Saville, *The Work of Reconstruction;* and Schwalm, "The Meaning of Freedom."

In general, political historians have focused on federal and state policies and party politics, although some have taken a wider view of politics, incorporating both race and class into their analyses. See Anderson, *Race and Politics in North Carolina;* Billings, *Planters and the Making of a "New South";* Escott, *Many Excellent People;* Evans, *Ballots and Fence Rails;* Fitzgerald, *The Union League Movement in the Deep South;* Goodwyn, *The Democratic Promise* and "Populist Dreams and Negro Rights"; T. Holt, *Black over White;* Kousser, *The Shaping of Southern Politics;* O'Brien, *The Legal Fraternity and the Making of a New South Community;* Perman, *The Road to Redemption;* Robinson, "Beyond the Realm of Social Consensus"; Thornton, "Fiscal Policy and the Failure of Radical Reconstruction"; and Woodward, *The Strange Career of Jim Crow* and *Tom Watson.*

Much has been written on the struggles involved in establishing new economic and social relationships between planters and freed slaves. Planters sought to reestablish the power they wielded as slaveowners, while African Americans resisted these efforts in an attempt to establish their independence. Widening the traditional focus on party politics, some scholars have emphasized the role played by African Americans and common whites during Reconstruction as they worked to take control of their own lives; see Cohen, *At Freedom's Edge;* Foner, *Nothing but Freedom;* Glymph and Kushma, *Essays on the Postbellum Southern Economy;* Hahn, *The Roots of Southern Populism;* Jaynes, *Branches without Roots;* Jones, *Labor of Love, Labor of Sorrow;* Litwack, *Been in the Storm So Long;* Rachleff, *Black Labor in the South;* Reidy, *From Slavery to Agrarian Capitalism;* Strickland, "Traditional Culture and Moral Economy"; Wayne, *The Reshaping of Plantation Society;* and Weiner, *Social Origins of the New South.*

7. Work focusing on gender has generated challenging critiques of public and private as well as innovative analyses that connect the two spheres; see Boydston, *Home and Work;* Davidoff and Hall, *Family Fortunes;* Faue, *Community of Suffering and Struggle;* Fraser, *Unruly Practices;* Gordon, *Heroes of Their Own Lives;* J. Hall, "Private Eyes, Public Women"; Landes, *Women and the Public Sphere;* Nicholson, *Gender and History;* MacLean, *Behind the Mask of Chivalry;* McCurry, *Masters of Small Worlds;* Pateman, *The Sexual Contract;* Riley, *Am I That Name?;* Ryan, *The Cradle of the Middle Class;* and J. Scott, *Gender and the Politics of History.* The debate over the separate spheres paradigm centers on many of the same issues; see, for instance, Kerber, "Separate Spheres, Female Worlds, Woman's Place"; and Hewitt, "Beyond the Search for Sisterhood." For the critique of public and private from the perspective of race, see Bercaw, "The Politics of Household"; E. Brown, "To Catch a Vision of Freedom" and "Uncle Ned's Children"; Fields, *Slavery and Freedom on the Middle Ground;* Frankel, "Freedom's Women"; Gordon, "Black and White Visions of Welfare Reform"; T. Holt, "'An Empire over the Mind'" and *The Problem of Freedom;* Glymph, "Freedpeople and Ex-Masters"; Higginbotham, *Righteous Discontent;* and Schwalm, "The Meaning of Freedom."

8. For discussions of the social and political importance of southern households, see Bercaw, "The Politics of Household"; Bardaglio, *Reconstructing the Household;* Bynum, *Unruly Women;* Fox-Genovese, *Within the Plantation Household,* esp. 37–99; McCurry, *Masters of Small Worlds,* "The Two Faces of Republicanism," and "The Politics of Yeoman Households in South Carolina"; Oakes, *Slavery and Freedom;* and Whites, *The Civil War as a Crisis in Gender.*

9. For the difficulties experienced by free women, white and black, in assuming the position of household head, see Bardaglio, *Reconstructing the Household;* Bellows, "'My Children, Gentlemen, Are My Own'"; Bercaw, "The Politics of Household," esp. chap. 3; Bynum, *Unruly Women;* Clinton, *The Plantation Mistress;* Faust, "'Trying to Do a Man's Business'"; Fox-Genovese, *Within the Plantation Household;* Lebsock, *Free Women of Petersburg;* and Wyatt-

Brown, *Southern Honor*. For those encountered by free blacks, see Berlin, *Slaves without Masters;* Franklin, *The Free Negro in North Carolina;* Genovese, *Roll, Jordan, Roll*, 398–413; and Johnson, *Ante-Bellum North Carolina*, 582–612. Southern courts continued to define parental rights primarily as paternal rights, but they began to view the claims of mothers to their children more favorably toward the end of the antebellum period, a change that brought the courts more in line with courts in the North. But custody was given at the discretion of the court. Even widows did not have absolute claims to their children until postwar statutes gave them parental rights. See Bardaglio, *Reconstructing the Household;* and Grossberg, *Governing the Hearth*, 234–53.

10. Bynum, *Unruly Women*, 118; J. Hall, "'The Mind That Burns in Each Body'"; Hodes, "The Sexualization of Reconstruction Politics"; Wyatt-Brown, *Southern Honor*, 50–55.

11. Bardaglio, "Rape and the Law in the Old South"; Bynum, *Unruly Women*, 109–10; Clinton, "Caught in the Web of the Big House"; Davis, "Reflections on the Black Woman's Role"; Higginbotham, "African-American Women's History and the Metalanguage of Race"; J. Hall, "'The Mind That Burns in Each Body'"; Hine, "Rape and the Inner Lives of Black Women"; McLaurin, *Celia, a Slave;* Rosen, "Rape as Reality, Rape as Fiction"; D. White, *Ar'n't I a Woman?* 152–53; Wriggins, "Rape, Racism, and the Law."

12. Bardaglio, "Rape and the Law in the Old South"; Bynum, *Unruly Women*, 109–10, 117–18; Edwards, "Sexual Violence, Gender, Reconstruction, and the Extension of Patriarchy." For the ways that the treatment of rape revealed class divisions in the North, see Stansell, *City of Women*, 23–28.

13. Some historians have argued that white southerners began to construe black-male-on-white-female rape as problematic only after the Civil War. See Hodes, "The Sexualization of Reconstruction Politics" and "Wartime Dialogues on Illicit Sex"; and Sommerville, "The Rape Myth in the Old South Reconsidered." Other work, however, has shown that white southerners had always tied racial power to sexualized images, including black-male-on-white-female rape. The classic statement is Jordan, *White over Black*. Indeed, as Bardaglio has argued in "Rape and the Law in the Old South," judicial decisions in antebellum rape cases reveal both the complex play of race, class, and gender as well as the firm connection of rape to larger structures of power. It was this connection that made rape such a potent symbol in the social and political upheavals of the postwar years.

14. In the following chapters I will elaborate on the ideology of Governor Worth and his fellow white conservatives more fully. For the link between sexuality and racial ideology, see J. Hall, *Revolt against Chivalry*, 129–57, and "'The Mind That Burns in Each Body'"; Hodes, "The Sexualization of Reconstruction Politics" and "Wartime Dialogues on Illicit Sex"; and Painter, "'Social Equality,' Miscegenation, and the Maintenance of Power." See also Jordan, *White over Black;* Williamson, *The Crucible of Race;* and Wyatt-Brown, *Southern Honor*.

15. Worth's obsession with the Freedmen's Bureau and its interference with the governance of the state pervades his correspondence. For racialized references to whites, see Hamilton, *The Correspondence of Jonathan Worth,* 2:1004, 1048, 1215. For the blame Granville officials placed on the Freedmen's Bureau, see E. W. Dennis to Louis Cazario (a copy was forwarded to Worth), 26 Mar. 1868, 111–15, Worth, Governor's Letter Book, 1867–68.

16. Quotes from Robert Avery to James V. Bomford, 27 Mar. 1867, Letters Received, Second Military District, Records of the U.S. Army Continental Commands. See also James V. Bomford to J. M. Clous (a copy was forwarded to Jonathan Worth), 22 Apr. 1867, 471–72, Worth, Governor's Letter Book, 1865–67.

17. William W. Jones, the local Freedmen's Bureau agent in Granville County, worked from similar assumptions. An abolitionist and a strong defender of equal civil and political rights for freedpeople, Jones had initially asked the bureau to investigate the case because he suspected that the ruling of the Confederate court that had sentenced Henderson Cooper might not be valid in the eyes of the U.S. government. But when local white residents—the "most respectable citizens"—approached him to request federal troops to keep order at Henderson Cooper's execution, he was inclined to support their request. Apparently, he too saw the actions of the "Freedmen and others" as an inappropriate circumvention of the rule of law. William W. Jones to M. Cogswell, 16 Mar. 1867, Letters Received, Second Military District, Records of the U.S. Army Continental Commands; William W. Jones to Assistant Commissioner, 28 Mar. 1867, Letters Received, Records of the Assistant Commissioner. For Jones's abolitionism, see William W. Jones to Jordan Chambers, 20 Apr. 1869, William W. Holden, Governor's Papers, NCDAH. For the ways northern racial ideology developed within the context of emancipation in the South, see Fields, "Ideology and Race in American History"; and T. Holt, "'An Empire over the Mind.'" See also C. Hall, "Missionary Stories" and "Competing Masculinities" in *White, Male, and Middle Class;* and T. Holt, *The Problem of Freedom.*

18. For Worth's view of Susan Daniel, see Worth to Pres. Andrew Johnson, 31 Dec. 1867, 5–9, Worth, Governor's Letter Book, 1867–68; Worth to W. A. Graham, 10 Jan. 1868, in Hamilton, *The Correspondence of Jonathan Worth,* 2:1128–31. For the bureau's view, see Robert Avery to James V. Bomford, 27 Mar. 1867, Letters Received, Second Military District, Records of the U.S. Army Continental Commands; and James V. Bomford to J. M. Clous (a copy was forwarded to Worth), 22 Apr. 1867, 471–72, Worth, Governor's Letter Book, 1865–67. Many women's historians have discussed the racial and class dimensions of this bifurcated view of women; see, for instance, Bynum, *Unruly Women;* Karlsen, *Devil in the Shape of a Woman;* Stansell, *City of Women;* Smith-Rosenberg, *Disorderly Conduct;* and D. White, *Ar'n't I a Woman?* 27–61.

19. J. Hall makes this point in *Revolt against Chivalry,* xv–xxxviii. I am also indebted to conversations with Hannah Rosen on this topic. There are many similar cases of black-male-on-white-female sexual violence that did not re-

ceive the attention that the Cooper-Daniel case did; see, for instance, *State v. Elias,* 1865, Criminal Action Papers, Orange County, NCDAH; *State v. McMinn* (documents of the case forwarded to Worth in relation to a request for a pardon), 9 June 1866, Jonathan Worth, Governor's Papers, NCDAH. Black-male-on-black-female and white-male-on-black-female rapes are referred to frequently in the records of the Freedmen's Bureau and in local court cases, but they rarely elicited much response from white officials or the press.

20. See Escott, *Many Excellent People,* 103–4, 136–70; Hodes, "The Sexualization of Reconstruction Politics"; Olsen, *A Carpetbagger's Crusade;* and Trelease, *White Terror.* See also Tourgée, *A Fool's Errand* and *The Invisible Empire.* Political conflict in Granville County remained heated throughout the 1870s, but was particularly intense in the late 1860s. I will discuss this issue in more detail in chapters 5 and 6.

21. William W. Jones to the Assistant Commissioner, 28 Mar. 1867, Letters Received, Records of the Assistant Commissioner.

22. It was the local Freedmen's Bureau agent, William W. Jones, who brought the Cooper-Daniel case to the attention of his superiors when he wrote to the headquarters of the Second Military District asking whether "this sentence should be executed without approval of the President of the United States" since Cooper had been tried in a Confederate Court. William W. Jones to M. Cogswell, 16 Mar. 1867, Letters Received, Second Military District, Records of the U.S. Army Continental Commands. Nonetheless, it would be a mistake to divorce Jones's interest in the case from the turmoil and conflict surrounding it. For instance, although local white residents requested his aid in getting federal troops sent to the area, it was Jones's own sense of the potential for violence and disorder that prompted him to forward the request to his superiors. Similarly, Jones probably would never have written his first letter, inquiring about the legal status of Henderson Cooper's imminent execution, if he had not known about the conflicts surrounding the case and the position of those who doubted Henderson Cooper's guilt.

23. E. W. Dennis to Louis V. Cazario (a copy was forwarded to Worth), 26 Mar. 1868, 111–15, Worth, Governor's Letter Book, 1867–68.

24. Ibid.

25. Governor Worth gave lengthy descriptions of the case without naming Susan Daniel; see, for instance, Worth to Maj. Gen. Sickles, 21 May 1867, 472–73, Worth, Governor's Letter Book, 1867–68.

26. James V. Bomford to J. M. Clous (a copy was forwarded to Worth), 22 Apr. 1867, 471–72, Worth, Governor's Letter Book, 1865–67. For sexual relationships among whites, slaves, and free blacks, see Bynum, *Unruly Women,* 88–110, 122–25, 152–53; and Hodes, "Sex across the Color Line." For the problems of white women during the Civil War, see Bynum, *Unruly Women,* 111–50; and Escott, "Poverty and Governmental Aid for the Poor in Confederate North Carolina."

27. See Edwards, "Sexual Violence, Gender, Reconstruction, and the Extension of Patriarchy"; and Hodes, "Sex across the Color Line."

28. Women's historians have long noted the vast gulf that can exist between representations of women and women's lives. Moreover, as some scholars have shown, images do more than misrepresent women's lives; they also reaffirm particular perspectives of historical events by hiding conflict and contradiction. See, in particular, J. Hall, "Private Eyes, Public Women"; and Faue, *Community of Suffering and Struggle*. See also Gordon, "Social Insurance and Public Assistance"; and J. Scott, "American Women Historians" in *Gender and the Politics of History*.

29. Some scholars have emphasized the importance of the diversity of women's experiences; see, for instance, E. Brown, "Womanist Consciousness," "African-American Women's Quilting," "Polyrhythms and Improvisation," and "'What Has Happened Here'"; Carby, *Reconstructing Womanhood;* Collins, *Black Feminist Thought;* Davis, *Women, Race, and Class;* Giddings, *When and Where I Enter;* J. Hall, "'The Mind That Burns in Each Body,'" "O. Delight Smith's Progressive Era," and the introduction to *Revolt against Chivalry*, xv–xxxviii; Hewitt, "Beyond the Search for Sisterhood," "Reflections from a Departing Editor," "The Right Chemistry," "Compounding Differences," and "In Pursuit of Power"; Higginbotham, "African-American Women's History and the Metalanguage of Race"; hooks, *Ain't I a Woman;* Hull, Scott, and Smith, *All the Women Are White;* Mohanty, "Cartographies of Struggle" and "Under Western Eyes"; Moraga and Anzaldúa, *This Bridge Called My Back;* and Smith, *Home Girls.*

30. In subsequent chapters I will analyze the role of women in greater detail. With notable exceptions, including A. Scott, *The Southern Lady*, women have been conspicuously absent from analyses of Reconstruction. When women did surface in accounts of the period, historians generally subsumed their experiences within those of their communities, the contours of which were defined through the interests and actions of men. Some scholars, however, have begun to emphasize the differences between men and women, while still remaining attentive to the ways race and class separated women as a group and bound them to the men in their communities. See Bercaw, "The Politics of Household"; Bynum, *Unruly Women;* E. Brown, "Uncle Ned's Children" and "To Catch a Vision of Freedom"; Clinton, "Bloody Terrain"; Faust, "Altars of Sacrifice and "'Trying to Do a Man's Business'"; Frankel, "Freedom's Women"; Rosen, "Race, Gender, and the Politics of Rape"; Schwalm, "The Meaning of Freedom"; and Whites, *The Civil War as a Crisis in Gender* and "The Civil War as a Crisis in Gender."

31. Bailyn, "The Challenge of Modern Historiography"; Bender, "Wholes and Parts." For an opposing view, see Monkkonen, "The Dangers of Synthesis." Similar calls for synthesis have also issued from within fields, such as women's history and labor history to name just two. For instance, John Higham, in "Multiculturalism and Universalism," criticized the proliferation of work on gender and race, arguing for class as the preeminent category around which to center a new synthesis.

32. These issues have generated debate within women's history that centers on the move toward work on the gendered nature of power relations and differences among women. Although criticism comes from various perspectives, it tends to focus on the ways synthesis is achieved by ignoring the particulars of women's lives. Some women's historians have criticized "gender history" because it ignores women as subjects and casts them as victims whose lives are wholly constructed by outside forces. Other feminist scholars are wary of uncritically embracing the postmodern and poststructuralist theories that inform work on gender because of the ways in which they implicitly validate current power relations and the privilege of elite white men. They are also troubled by the political implications of a socially constructed subject, a concept that has emerged at just the point when women as well as other marginalized peoples are claiming subject status. For a discussion of these issues, see Auslander, "Feminist Theory and Social History"; Bennett, "Feminism and History"; Hawkesworth, "Knowers, Knowing, Known"; Mascia-Lees, Sharpe, and Cohen, "The Postmodernist Turn in Anthropology"; Modleski, *Feminism without Women;* Newman, Williams, Vogel, and Newton, "Theoretical and Methodological Dialogue on the Writing of Women's History"; Nicholson, *Feminism/Postmodernism;* and J. Wilson, *Law, Gender, and Injustice,* 9–20.

Working from another direction, scholars of African-American, working-class, and other minority women have questioned the utility of previous paradigms that tended to emphasize a common women's experience, defined by separate spheres and manifested in a sense of sisterhood. That approach, they maintain, tended to subordinate differences and conflicts among women within a given society, across cultures, and over time to a transcendent female experience that was actually exclusive to middle-class white women in the industrial West. When the historical specificity of this experience of womanhood and its racial and class components are left unexamined, women's lives are homogenized and a whole host of women are marginalized. Understandably, many of those who emphasize the limits of previous paradigms remain suspicious of calls for a new synthesis within women's history. See note 29 for scholarship dealing with this issue.

33. Those who reproach social history from the left draw the line differently, defining class issues as a matter of public interest but often questioning the inclusion of other concerns as "private." "Race, ethnicity, gender or physical condition," as John Higham argued in his critique of multiculturalism, are "the inescapably given traits," "personal," "internal," and "part of the very substance of who we are" (195–96). As private matters, in other words, they are neither publicly created nor the proper focus of political inquiry. Other critiques also rely on this same public/private split to legitimize discussion of some issues and not others. See also Bailyn, "The Challenge of Modern Historiography"; Bender, "Wholes and Parts"; Genovese and Fox-Genovese, "The Political Crisis of Social History"; and Judt, "A Clown in Regal Purple." My analysis here draws on the comments made in the forum on multiculturalism in *American Quarterly* 45 (June 1993).

34. Mohanty, "Cartographies of Struggle" and "Under Western Eyes." See also Fraser, *Unruly Practices;* and Hewitt, "Reflections from a Departing Editor."

35. Anderson, *Race and Politics in North Carolina;* Escott, *Many Excellent People,* 241–62; Gilmore, *Gender and Jim Crow;* Greenwood, *Bittersweet Legacy,* 185–213; J. Hall, *Revolt against Chivalry,* xv–xxxviii; Williamson, *The Crucible of Race.*

Chapter 1: You Can't Go Home Again

1. Escott, *Many Excellent People;* Olsen, "An Incongruous Presence"; H. Raper, *William W. Holden.*

2. *Journal of the Convention of North Carolina,* 7. The speech was not only well received but also widely complimented; see, for instance, *Raleigh Journal of Freedom,* 21 Oct. 1865, reprinted from the *Baltimore American.*

3. Quotes from *Raleigh Journal of Freedom,* 7 Oct. 1865. R. Alexander, *North Carolina Faces the Freedmen,* 24–27; Escott, *Many Excellent People,* 124–25; Foner, *Reconstruction,* 112–19. For eyewitness descriptions of the convention, see Andrews, *The South since the War,* 119–31; and Dennett, *The South as It Is,* 148–54.

4. Quoted in Foner, *Freedom's Lawmakers,* 110.

5. Although the results of apprenticeship and parenthood were similar to those of marriage and slavery, neither institution was as central as marriage and slavery. Parenthood was actually dependent on marriage; in its absence, the law treated illegitimate children as orphans. Apprenticeship involved fewer people and was less important to the southern economy than slavery or, after emancipation, hired labor.

6. Bynum, "Reshaping the Bonds of Womanhood," 322–23. For the connection between the subordination of women in marriage and that of African Americans in slavery, see also Bynum, *Unruly Women;* Bardaglio, *Reconstructing the Household;* McCurry, *Masters of Small Worlds,* esp. 85–91, and "The Two Faces of Republicanism"; and Fox-Genovese, *Within the Plantation Household,* 334–71. See also Genovese, *Roll, Jordan, Roll,* 3–112.

7. Bynum, "Reshaping the Bonds of Womanhood," 323–24. For an example of Pearson's position on the subordination of all African Americans, see *State* v. *Jowers,* 33 N.C. 555 (1850).

8. As McCurry has argued in *Masters of Small Worlds,* 130–207, domestic dependencies were at the center of southern evangelical religious doctrine. Whatever radical edge evangelicalism had was given by slaves. For discussions of southern religion from various perspectives, see Ford, *Origins of Southern Radicalism,* 19–37; Friedman, *The Enclosed Garden;* Genovese, *Roll, Jordan, Roll,* 159–284; Genovese and Fox-Genovese, "The Social Thought of the Antebellum Southern Divines" and "The Divine Sanction of Social Order"; L. Levine, *Black Culture and Black Consciousness,* 3–80; Maddex, "Proslavery Millennialism" and "'The Southern Apostasy' Revisited"; Mathews, *Religion in the Old South;* Raboteau, *Slave Religion;* Snay, "American Thought and Southern

Distinctiveness"; and Tise, *Proslavery*. By contrast, evangelical Protestantism buttressed northern white women's power as moral guardians; see Cott, *The Bonds of Womanhood;* and Ryan, *The Cradle of the Middle Class.*

9. Bardaglio, *Reconstructing the Household;* Bynum, *Unruly Women,* esp. 59–110; Faust, "'Trying to Do a Man's Business'"; Fox-Genovese, *Within the Plantation Household,* 192–241; Lebsock, *Free Women of Petersburg;* McCurry, *Masters of Small Worlds.*

10. Quoted in Grossberg, *Governing the Hearth,* 99. The attitude was common; see Keller, *Affairs of State,* 470–72.

11. For the importance of marriage to a wide range of social relations, see Cott, "Giving Character to Our Whole Civil Polity"; Grossberg, *Governing the Hearth;* Kerber, "The Paradox of Women's Citizenship in the Early Republic"; J. Wilson, *Law, Gender, and Injustice;* and Pateman, *The Sexual Contract.*

12. *State* v. *Rhodes,* 61 N.C. 453 (1868).

13. For biographical background on Edwin G. Reade, see Powell, *Dictionary of North Carolina Biography,* 5:183–84.

14. *State* v. *Rhodes,* 61 N.C. 453 (1868). For the position of the antebellum North Carolina Supreme Court on wife beating, see Bynum, *Unruly Women,* 70–72. I will discuss this issue at greater length in chapter 4.

15. *State* v. *Rhodes,* 61 N.C. 453 (1868). See also *Joyner* v. *Joyner,* 59 N.C. 331 (1862); and *White* v. *White,* 84 N.C. 340 (1881). There are parallels to the state's reluctance to intervene in slavery; see Tushnet, *The American Law of Slavery.*

16. *State* v. *Rhodes,* 61 N.C. 453 (1868).

17. Although the court later repudiated a husband's right to physically chastise his wife and increased its own powers to intervene in the domestic sphere, it still upheld the separation of private from public established in *Rhodes.* See *State* v. *Mabrey,* 64 N.C. 592 (1870); *State* v. *Oliver,* 70 N.C. 60 (1874); *State* v. *Davidson,* 77 N.C. 522 (1877); *State* v. *Pettie,* 80 N.C. 367 (1879); and *State* v. *Jones,* 95 N.C. 588 (1886). Although they did not directly cite *Rhodes,* other cases supported it in principle; see *Horne* v. *Horne,* 72 N.C. 530 (1875); *Miller* v. *Miller,* 78 N.C. 102 (1878); *Syme* v. *Riddle,* 88 N.C. 463 (1883); *State* v. *Huntley,* 91 N.C. 617 (1884); and *State* v. *Edens,* 95 N.C. 693 (1886).

18. *State* v. *Rhodes,* 61 N.C. 453 (1868). Hartog, in "Marital Exits and Marital Expectations," also emphasizes the courts' conception of marriage as a public relationship. Nonetheless, the courts were reluctant to interfere in the dynamics of that relationship. See Keller, *Affairs of State,* 467–68.

19. *State* v. *Hairston and Williams,* 63 N.C. 451 (1869). For a discussion of the court's regulation of "fit" marital unions, see Grossberg, *Governing the Hearth,* 103–52.

20. Chaplain of a Louisiana Black Regiment to the Regimental Adjutant, quoted in Berlin, Reidy, and Rowland, *The Black Military Experience,* 624. See 623 for a reference to Special Order 15, which provided for the legalization of slave marriages; for a discussion of marriage, see 660–61. See also Foner, *Reconstruction,* 84.

21. *Raleigh Daily Record,* 13 June 1865. Holden reiterated the point in his address to an 1866 statewide freedmen's convention: "The first thing" freedpeople should do "was to *get homes*" (emphasis in original). *North Carolina Standard,* 17 Oct. 1866. A few white southerners who believed that some changes would have to be made to the slave system if it were to survive began thinking about the issue of slave marriages even before southern surrender. Governor Vance received a pamphlet entitled *Thoughts on Government, the Marriage of Negroes* from one of his correspondents; see A. McDaniel to Zebulon B. Vance, 10 Jan. 1865, Zebulon B. Vance, Governor's Papers, NCDAH. The pamphlet echoed arguments from the antebellum period, when the instability of family life under slavery had come under sharp criticism by some leading lights of the planter class. In 1855 a group of North Carolinians even attempted to change the slave code to recognize slave marriages, but these efforts went nowhere; see Genovese, *Roll, Jordan, Roll,* 52–53.

22. For the eagerness of conservative legislators to legalize slave unions, see R. Alexander, *North Carolina Faces the Freedmen,* 47–48; Grossberg, *Governing the Hearth,* 133.

23. *Journal of the Convention of North Carolina,* 41–47; Dennett, *The South as It Is,* 163–65. After the abolition of slavery, marriage was the first issue involving freedpeople to be discussed by the legislature. Alfred O. Dockery expressed opposition to the marriage statute on the basis that freedpeople would not respect the marital relation anyway. But the primary reason the delegates delayed action was that they believed they should consider marriage as part of an entire code of laws dealing with the status of freedpeople. The question, moreover, was not quite so pressing since General Schofield, the state's military commander, had issued a temporary order establishing the provisional status of freedpeople. In addition to sketching out basic rights and labor guidelines, Schofield also allowed for the marriages of freedpeople who requested the ceremony and declared the freed children to be the legal wards and economic responsibilities of their parents, whether or not they were married legally. Schofield's guidelines meshed with those in General Order 8, issued the previous month by General Halleck, which laid out the means by which freedpeople in Virginia and North Carolina could legally marry and encouraged local authorities to marry them. Significantly, his concerns paralleled those of the delegates to the state constitutional convention. The issue demanded immediate attention, according to Schofield, so that freedpeople would not become a "huge white elephant," dependent on the state and their former masters for support. See Hamilton, *Reconstruction in North Carolina,* 148–49 (quote from 149). Both Schofield's and Halleck's orders were widely reproduced in many of North Carolina's papers. See, for instance, the *Raleigh Daily Record,* which reprinted both for several weeks running in June and July, 1865. The legislature, however, had to write these provisions into the civil code in order to clarify the legal position of freedpeople and to provide for those who refused to marry according to law.

24. Quotes from *Raleigh Sentinel,* 1 Feb. 1866, and *Public Laws of North Carolina* (1866), chap. 40, sec. 5. For the debate, see also *Raleigh Sentinel,* 10 Feb. 1866, 12 Feb. 1866, and 22 Feb. 1866; and *North Carolina Standard,* 7 Feb. 1866. At a time when the state's readmission to the union and the status of freedpeople were topics of continual and heated debate, there was virtual silence on the subject of freedpeople's marriages both in the press and in the legislature. While the absence of debate could indicate the relative insignificance of the issue, the statements that made it to print indicate otherwise. All characterized legal marriage among freedpeople as a matter of utmost importance. See, for instance, *Raleigh Daily Record,* 4 July 1865; and *Raleigh Sentinel,* 8 Aug. 1865, 29 Aug. 1865, 31 Jan. 1866. The silence, then, is better explained in terms of a general consensus about the issue. There is a marked contrast, for instance, in the debate over freedpeople's right to testify in court, which all but eclipsed discussions of the Black Code's other provisions. In a *Raleigh Sentinel* editorial the testimony issue was identified as "the great question of the session." See 2 Feb. 1866. The evidence supports this conclusion. After days of acrimonious debate, the provision was still contested at the bill's final reading in the House. For a summary of the session, see *Raleigh Sentinel,* 1 Feb. 1866, 2 Feb. 1866, 9 Feb. 1866, 22 Feb. 1866, and 27 Feb. 1866. Governor Jonathan Worth also spoke frequently of the subject in his correspondence; see, for instance, Hamilton, *The Correspondence of Jonathan Worth,* 1:467, 509, 571–72, and *Reconstruction in North Carolina,* 154–55. So did common whites; see Dennett, *The South as It Is,* 132–34, 168–69, 181. Not all southern states legalized slave marriages from the time of cohabitation or required the registration of marriage, as North Carolina did. Although they legitimated the children of slave unions, most states legalized marriages from the date their ordinances went into effect, leaving the courts to resolve details concerning the legal status of unions in slavery. See Burnham, "An Impossible Marriage"; and Grossberg, *Governing the Hearth,* 133–36, 221–22.

25. C. W. Raney to N. A. Miles, 19 Apr. 1868, Kittrell's Springs, Letters Received, Records of the Assistant Commissioner. For the Caswell County Country Line Agricultural Society, see Powell, *When the Past Refused to Die,* 479. The "Report of the Commission . . . to Prepare a Code for the Freedmen of this State" emphasized that freedpeople needed to rely on themselves, not their masters, for their subsistence; see *Raleigh Sentinel,* 31 Jan. and 1 Feb. 1866. See also *Wilmington Herald,* 24 July 1865. For similar actions by planters across the South, see Fields, *Slavery and Freedom on the Middle Ground,* 151–52. Two editorials in the *Raleigh Semi-Weekly Record,* 12 and 23 Aug. 1865, advocated a more paternalistic view toward the poor, particularly indigent freedpeople. So did James A. Bullock of Granville County, who sharply criticized local doctors who refused to treat indigent freedpeople. He requested money for medical supplies so that he could provide medical care for them just as he had always done for his "*numerous family*" in times past." See James A. Bullock to Dr. H. C. Vogell, Superintendent of Public Instruction, 1869, Holden Papers.

26. Dennett, *The South as It Is,* 146.

27. For the general tenor of common whites' opinions of freedpeople, see Escott, *Many Excellent People,* 116–19. See Cecil-Fronsman, *Common Whites,* 67–96, for their racial stance before the war. The "Report of the Commission . . . to Prepare a Code for the Freedmen of this State" argued that the depressed conditions of common North Carolinians made it that much more imperative for freedpeople to become economically self-sufficient; in these conditions, presumably, white taxpayers would be even less willing to contribute to their welfare. See *Raleigh Sentinel,* 31 Jan. 1866 and 1 Feb. 1866.

28. Board of Wardens of the Granville County Poorhouse to the Freedmen's Bureau, 6 May 1868, Letters Received, Records of the Assistant Commissioner. See also Foner, *Reconstruction,* 207–8; and Reidy, *From Slavery to Agrarian Capitalism,* 144–45.

29. Quotes from *Raleigh Sentinel,* 8 Aug. 1865, and 31 Jan. 1866. See also Dennett, *The South as It Is,* 164–65; and R. Alexander, *North Carolina Faces the Freedmen,* 47–48.

30. These positions emerged in sharpest relief in the debate over the right of freedpeople to testify in court; see *Raleigh Sentinel,* 1 Feb. 1866, 2 Feb. 1866, 9 Feb. 1866, 22 Feb. 1866, and 27 Feb. 1866. For further elaboration of the conciliatory view, see, for instance, Alfred M. Waddell's speech, *Raleigh Sentinel,* 8 Aug. 1865; untitled editorial on the status of freedpeople, *Raleigh Sentinel,* 21 Aug. 1865; and report of the committee, headed by John Pool, on the status of freedpeople, in *Raleigh Sentinel,* 12 Oct. 1865. For the opposing position, see, for instance, "Views of the Late Senator Douglas on the Negro as a Voter," *Raleigh Sentinel,* 15 Aug. 1865. See also R. Alexander, *North Carolina Faces the Freedmen,* 40–41; and Dennett, *The South as It Is,* 162–65.

31. Slaveholders made the same claims about slaves; see Genovese, *Roll, Jordan, Roll,* 482–83.

32. *State* v. *Harris,* 63 N.C. 1 (1868).

33. *Raleigh Sentinel,* 29 Aug. 1865. This position was also written into the recommendations of the commission, headed by Moore, that drew up the draft of the state's Black Code; see *Raleigh Sentinel,* 31 Jan. 1866.

34. *State* v. *Henderson,* 61 N.C. 229 (1867). Before the repeal of the Black Code, African Americans were not allowed to testify against whites unless they were able to prove a compelling personal interest in the case; see *Public Laws of North Carolina* (1866), chap. 40, sec. 9. Bastardy was one such instance. See also Grossberg, *Governing the Hearth,* 215–18.

35. As the commission noted, "It is naturally just that the father should support his offspring, whether born in or out of wedlock." "Report of the Commission . . . to Prepare a Code for the Freedmen of this State," in *Raleigh Sentinel,* 31 Jan. 1866.

36. Justice Pearson reaffirmed the construction and application of the laws as part of the "Poor Act," in *State* v. *Elam,* 61 N.C. 460 (1868).

37. Quotes from report of the committee, headed by John Pool, on the status of freedpeople, in *Raleigh Sentinel,* 12 Oct. 1865.

38. *Howard* v. *Howard*, 51 N.C. 235 (1858). For discussions on the ideological importance of the denial of legal marriage to slaves for southern society as a whole, see Genovese, *Roll, Jordan, Roll*, 32, 52–53; Grossberg, *Governing the Hearth*, 129–32; and Oakes, *Slavery and Freedom*, xvi–xvii, 3–39.

39. *Raleigh Sentinel*, 29 Aug. 1865. See also Ashe, Weeks, and Van Noppen, *Biographical History of North Carolina*, 4:294–95; Escott, *Many Excellent People*, 126–27; Hamilton, *North Carolina since 1860*, 66, 75, 110–11; and Hamilton, *North Carolina Biography*, 13.

40. *Public Laws of North Carolina* (1866), chap. 40, secs. 5, 6. See also R. Alexander, *North Carolina Faces the Freedmen*, 47–48; and Gutman, *The Black Family in Slavery and Freedom*, 417–18.

41. *Public Laws of North Carolina* (1866), chap. 40. See also R. Alexander, *North Carolina Faces the Freedmen*, 39–51; Foner, *Reconstruction*, 198–216; Litwack, *Been in the Storm So Long*, 364–71; and T. B. Wilson, *The Black Codes of the South*.

42. Quoted in R. Alexander, *North Carolina Faces the Freedmen*, 45.

43. R. Alexander, *North Carolina Faces the Freedmen*, 112–19; Fields, *Slavery and Freedom on the Middle Ground*, 139–42; Foner, *Reconstruction*, 201–2; and R. Scott, "The Battle over the Child."

44. White resistance to African-Americans attempting to reunite their families is also suggestive; see Gutman, *The Black Family in Slavery and Freedom*, 383–85.

45. Quote from *State* v. *Newsom*, 27 N.C. 250 (1844). In *State* v. *Manuel*, 20 N.C. 144 (1838), Judge Gaston had divided the inhabitants of North Carolina into two categories, citizens (free people of both races) and aliens (slaves). Over the course of the nineteenth century, however, free blacks were increasingly denied full rights of citizenship on the basis of race. See Berlin, *Slaves without Masters;* Franklin, *The Free Negro in North Carolina;* Genovese, *Roll, Jordan, Roll*, 398–413; and Johnson, *Ante-Bellum North Carolina*, 597–606. As Grossberg describes the situation in *Governing the Hearth*, free blacks could marry, "but this right was couched in terms that ensured that their marriages posed no threat to the slave system" (350n69).

46. As the commission that drafted the Black Code explained: "Upon the emancipation of the slaves, the laws especially respecting them, ceased to have any force, and that class fell under the laws respecting free negroes: the political and civil condition of all the colored population became that which had already been established for the free negro." Its duty was to clarify and codify this legislation. "Report of the Commission . . . to Prepare a Code for the Freedmen of This State," in *Raleigh Sentinel*, 31 Jan. 1866 and 1 Feb. 1866. As Theodore Brantner Wilson argues in *The Black Codes of the South*, 13–41, southern lawmakers based their states' Black Codes on the laws relating to free blacks before the war with the express purpose of making the position of ex-slaves like that of free blacks.

47. Berlin, *Slaves without Masters*, 79–107; Franklin, *The Free Negro in North Carolina*, 58–120.

48. *Ferrell* v. *Boykin*, 61 N.C. 9 (1866).

49. Ibid.

50. John C. Robinson to Jonathan Worth, 30 Oct. 1866, 239, Worth, Governor's Letter Book, 1865–67.

51. Quote from ibid., 238–39. For Worth's letter, see Jonathan Worth to John C. Robinson, 29 Oct. 1866, 234, Worth, Governor's Letter Book, 1865–67. See also Hamilton, *The Correspondence of Jonathan Worth*, 2:827, 832–33, 890. Interference of the military in the jurisdiction of the state courts was a continual complaint of Worth; see Hamilton, *The Correspondence of Jonathan Worth*, 2:862, 963, 974, 983–84, 1056–57, 1062–64, 1097, 1107–10, 1128–31, 1201–3. See also Hamilton, *Reconstruction in North Carolina*, 161–70.

52. Jonathan Worth to John C. Robinson, 29 Oct. 1866, 237.

53. *In the Matter of Ambrose and Moore*, 61 N.C. 91 (1867).

54. Ibid.

55. *Public Laws of North Carolina* (1866–67), chap. 6; R. Alexander, *North Carolina Faces the Freedmen*, 50–51.

56. Escott, *Many Excellent People;* Perman, *The Road to Redemption;* H. Raper, *William W. Holden.* For a blow-by-blow account of the factionalism that developed among North Carolina's white leaders during 1866 and 1867, see Hamilton, *Reconstruction in North Carolina*, 176–92. For a revealing portrait of an elite white Republican in Alabama, see Rogers, *Black Belt Scalawag.*

57. Grossberg, in *Governing the Hearth*, makes a similar point about freedpeople using legal marriage "to fortify their domestic relationships with as many legal protections as possible" (133). See also Bardaglio, *Reconstructing the Household*, 131–34. The literature on the importance of family ties to slaves and freedpeople is vast. For example, see Berlin, Reidy, and Rowland, *The Black Military Experience*, 656–61; Gutman, *The Black Family in Slavery and Freedom;* and Malone, *Sweet Chariot.*

58. For Henderson Cooper, see Robert Avery to James V. Bomford, 27 Mar. 1867, Letters Received, Second Military District, Records of the U.S. Army Continental Commands. See also Foner, *Reconstruction*, 82–84; Gutman, *The Black Family in Slavery and Freedom*, 204–7; Hunter, "Household Workers in the Making," 6–58; and Litwack, *Been in the Storm So Long*, 3–63, 229–47. Questioning the conventional assumption that the North freed the slaves, historians have emphasized the active participation of African Americans and the various ways in which they worked to secure their own emancipation; see Berlin, Reidy, and Rowland, *The Black Military Experience;* Berlin, Fields, Glymph, Reidy, and Rowland, *The Destruction of Slavery;* Fields, *Slavery and Freedom on the Middle Ground*, 100–130; Hunter, "Household Workers in the Making," 21–23; Oakes, "The Political Significance of Slave Resistance"; Reidy, *From Slavery to Agrarian Capitalism*, 108–35; and Schwalm, "The Meaning of Freedom," 123–81.

59. *New York Tribune*, 8 Sept. 1865.

60. Register of the Marriages of Free People, vols. 1–2, Granville County, NCDAH. In *The Black Family in Slavery and Freedom*, 415–16, Gutman esti-

mated the percentage of couples who registered their unions by comparing registered marriages with the register of slaves aged twenty and over in 1860. Using records from fourteen counties in North Carolina, he concluded that the number of recorded marriages represents about 47 percent of all possible marriages. For further explanation of Gutman's estimates, see note 79. The number in Granville County comes to 41 percent of the marriageable African-American population, a figure far less than the 70 percent for nearby Warren County, but one that still nears Gutman's average. For the symbolic importance of marriage and its popularity among freedpeople, see Berlin, Reidy, and Rowland, *The Black Military Experience*, 660–61, and the documents on 604–5, 623–24, 709–12; Gutman, *The Black Family in Slavery and Freedom*, 412–18; Hunter, "Household Workers in the Making," 39–40; and Litwack, *Been in the Storm So Long*, 240–41. See also Reid, *After the War,* 126–27.

61. *New York Tribune*, 8 Sept. 1865; Lumberton minister quoted in Gutman, *The Black Family in Slavery and Freedom*, 620n35. For similar comments among whites, see Andrews, *The South since the War,* 178–79; and Dennett, *The South as It Is,* 164–65.

62. Quoted in Berlin, Reidy, and Rowland, *The Black Military Experience,* 672. Cullen, "'I's a Man Now,'" is also suggestive.

63. Journal of Robert Lee Pool quoted in B. White, *In Search of Kith and Kin,* 53. Pool later went to live with his birth father and his new wife, whom he accepted as his mother, and in his journal he never refers to his birth mother by name. See also R. Alexander, *North Carolina Faces the Freedmen,* 112–19; Fields, *Slavery and Freedom on the Middle Ground,* 139–42; Foner, *Reconstruction,* 201; Gutman, *The Black Family in Slavery and Freedom,* 402–12; Reidy, *From Slavery to Agrarian Capitalism,* 153–55; and R. Scott, "The Battle over the Child."

64. *North Carolina Standard*, 10 Oct. 1866. See also R. Alexander, *North Carolina Faces the Freedmen,* 117.

65. D. A. Yarbrough to Henry W. Jones, 3 Apr. 1867, Henry W. Jones Papers, Special Collections Library, Duke University, Durham.

66. Thomas W. Hay to Jacob F. Chur, Annual Reports of Operations Received from Staff and Subordinate Officers, Records of the U.S. Bureau of Refugees, Freedmen, and Abandoned Lands (hereafter RBRFAL). William W. Holden, the provisional governor in North Carolina appointed by Andrew Johnson, was a unionist with strong anti-elitist sentiments. During his brief term in office in 1865, he appointed many unionist justices of the peace. While the political sensibilities of these men were different from those who preceded them, they were still propertied men from the middle and upper classes. While limited, these changes were, nonetheless, harbingers of more substantial change. Jonathan Worth was elected to the governorship that same year and immediately replaced all Holden's appointees with those who had controlled local political offices before the war. See Escott, *Many Excellent People,* 92–94, 101–2.

67. R. Alexander, *North Carolina Faces the Freedmen*, 112–19. For the bureau's increasing opposition to the apprenticeship system, see, for instance, Circular issued by Clinton A. Cilley, 27 Feb. 1866, J. R. Mason to E. Whittlesey, 12 Mar. 1866, L. R. Jernigan to E. Whittlesey, 14 Mar. 1866, Report of George S. Hawley, 9 Apr. 1866, Nat Parker and twenty other freedmen to the Assistant Commissioner, 4 Apr. 1866, Report of George S. Hawley, 18 May 1866, Clinton A. Cilley to the Assistant Commissioner, 27 Apr. 1866, Clinton A. Cilley to the Assistant Commissioner, 10 May 1866, James Littleton to O. O. Howard, 3 Sept. 1866, George Tipton to Allen Rutherford, 28 Aug. 1866, James Littleton to O. O. Howard, 3 Dec. 1866, Allen Rutherford to Jacob F. Chur, 18 Oct. 1866, and Robert Avery to Jacob F. Chur, Raleigh, 6 July 1867, all in Letters Received, Records of the Assistant Commissioner. See also *The Freedmen's Bureau v. B. M. Richardson*, in Report of Courts, Allen Rutherford, Wilmington, Mar. 1867, Records Relating to Court Cases, Records of the Assistant Commissioner; and Report, Allen Rutherford, 29 Oct. 1866, Report of Operations, Records of the Assistant Commissioner. For the development of the bureau's position on apprenticeship in North Carolina, see R. Alexander, *North Carolina Faces the Freedmen*, 112–19; and R. Scott, "The Battle over the Child." The bureau's policies elsewhere in the South were similar; see Nieman, *To Set the Law in Motion*, 78–82, 137–38; and Reidy, *From Slavery to Agrarian Capitalism*, 154.

68. Thomas W. Hay to Jacob F. Chur, 25 Sept. 1867, Annual Reports of Operations Received from Staff and Subordinate Officers, RBRFAL; the subdistrict of Warren included Warren, Franklin, and Granville Counties. For examples of complaints within Granville County, see Coleman Edward to the Freedmen's Bureau, 31 July 1866, William Jones to A. G. Brady (regarding the complaint of James Malone), 5 July 1866, and Wesley Mayfield to William Jones, 11 May 1866, all in Letters Received, Assistant Superintendent's Office, Oxford, RBRFAL. See also John Washington to James V. Bomford, 11 Sept. 1867, Letters Received, Records of the Assistant Commissioner. For apprenticeship cases in the county court, see *Brame and Wife v. Brame*, Aug. 1866, *Durham v. Rowland*, Aug. and Sept. 1866, *Unnamed v. Hester*, Jan. 1867, *Hobgood v. Lyon*, Feb. 1867, *The Court v. Williams*, Feb. 1867 (the case was instigated by John Marrow and Fred Malone), *The Court v. Harris*, Jan. 1867, *Bullock, Bullock, and Bullock v. Sneed*, Feb. 1867, *The Court v. Moore*, Aug. 1867, *Hester v. Hester*, Nov. 1867, *Hicks v. Hunt and Hunt*, Feb. 1868, and *The Court v. Hunt* (a separate charge), Feb. 1868, all in Apprentice Bonds, Granville County, NCDAH. Across the state, freedpeople deluged the bureau with complaints; see R. Alexander, *North Carolina Faces the Freedmen*, 117. Freedpeople also sent in petitions to the bureau; see, for instance, J. R. Mason to E. Whittlesey, 12 Mar. 1866, Nat Parker and twenty other freedmen to Assistant Commissioner, 4 Apr. 1866, James Littleton to O. O. Howard, 3 Sept. 1866, and James Littleton to O. O. Howard, 3 Dec. 1866, all in Letters Received, Records of the Assistant Commissioner. The reaction of African Americans elsewhere in the South was similar; see Berlin, Miller, and Row-

land, "Afro-American Families," 107–11; Fields, *Slavery and Freedom on the Middle Ground*, 148–49; Foner, *Reconstruction*, 201; Gutman, *The Black Family in Slavery and Freedom*, 402–12; and Hunter, "Household Workers in the Making," 34–35.

69. Daniel A. Paschall to N. A. Miles, 17 Sept. 1867, Letters Received, Records of the Assistant Commissioner; *Hester* v. *Hester*, Nov. 1867, Apprentice Bonds, Granville County.

70. Coleman Edward to the Freedmen's Bureau, 31 July 1866, Letters Received, Assistant Superintendent's Office, Oxford, RBRFAL.

71. Bynum, "On the Lowest Rung," and *Unruly Women*, 103–9. See also Bellows, "'My Children, Gentlemen, Are My Own.'"

72. Quoted in Gutman, *The Black Family in Slavery and Freedom*, 411.

73. *Durham* v. *Rowland*, Aug. 1866 and Sept. 1866, and *Hicks* v. *Hunt and Hunt*, Feb. 1868, both in Apprentice Bonds, Granville County. For similar evidence, see Berlin, Miller, and Rowland, "Afro-American Families," 116–18; Gutman, *The Black Family in Slavery and Freedom*, 409–10; and Reidy, *From Slavery to Agrarian Capitalism*, 154–55.

74. Kate Durham received custody of her children; the records do not reveal whether Sallie Hicks did. See *Durham* v. *Rowland*, Aug. 1866 and Sept. 1866, and *Hicks* v. *Hunt and Hunt*, Feb. 1868, both in Apprentice Bonds, Granville County.

75. *State* v. *Rhodes*, 61 N.C. 453 (1868).

76. For changes in local political and judicial institutions during Reconstruction in North Carolina, see Evans, *Ballots and Fence Rails;* Escott, *Many Excellent People;* and Foner, *Reconstruction*, 354–57. Other historians have also noted that black and white Republicans had access to and power within the legal system during Reconstruction; see Bryant, "'We Have No Chance of Justice before the Courts'"; Bynum, "On the Lowest Rung"; Foner, *Nothing but Freedom;* and Nieman, "Black Political Power and Criminal Justice." See also Ayers, *Vengeance and Justice*. See Escott, *Many Excellent People*, for the common class interests of elite Republicans and Democrats. In Granville County, where the Democratic party did not consolidate its hold on local politics until 1887, the elected Republican officials in the local justice system certainly encouraged African Americans to identify with their party.

77. The changes are illustrated well in *Mitchell* v. *Mitchell*, 67 N.C. 307 (1872). The reports of the local agents show that the bureau and the local courts were apprenticing very few black children after 1867. The low number is particularly striking when compared with the hundreds of indentures made out in 1865–66. See Records Relating to Indentures, Records of the Assistant Commissioner. The system, however, lingered in North Carolina and in other parts of the South. See, in particular, Fields, *Slavery and Freedom on the Middle Ground*, 153–56; Fields, however, maintains that the system continued in a truncated form. In the 1890s, it resurfaced again in North Carolina with the "discovery" of the widespread abuse of apprentices by their masters, who worked their charges for their own profit with no thought to

the children's well-being. The situation, however, was different from that during the years following emancipation. Although the apprentices were black and badly treated, they were no longer taken from parents to be apprenticed to more "suitable" guardians. See Bureau of Labor Statistics, *Second Annual Report* (1888), 211–35.

78. Hartog, in "Marital Exits and Expectations," makes a similar point for the nineteenth century as a whole, noting the disjuncture between individuals' conceptions of marriage and legal definitions of it. There was, as he argues, a widespread understanding of marriage as an unequal relationship between a husband and wife in which both parties assumed certain obligations. But the actual operation of that relationship varied widely among individuals and, as I suggest here, across race and class as well.

79. Quoted in Berlin, Reidy, and Rowland, *The Wartime Genesis of Free Labor: The Lower South,* 859. In *The Black Family in Slavery and Freedom,* 415–16, Gutman estimated the percentage of couples who registered their unions by comparing the number of registered marriages with the slave population aged twenty and over in 1860. Surveying fourteen counties in North Carolina, he concluded that the number of recorded marriages represented about 47 percent of all possible marriages. Of course, the figure is really a "guesstimate." Comparing registered unions to the entire slave population twenty and older presumes that all these people would be married and thus grossly underestimates the percentage of heterosexual couples who formalized their vows. Moreover, there is no way of knowing whether or not existing records are complete. Still, the estimate suggests that many freedpeople did not rush to legalize their marriages, as Gutman himself argues. For the reluctance of freedpeople to marry legally, see Frankel, "Freedom's Women"; and Schwalm, "The Meaning of Freedom," 340–44. Lebsock, in *The Free Women of Petersburg,* 103–11, also notes similar reservations among free black women in the antebellum period.

80. Bastardy Bonds, Granville County, NCDAH. *Oxford Torchlight,* 20 Jan. 1885, 2 Feb. 1886, 11 Jan. 1887, and 15 Feb. 1887. According to the *Oxford Torchlight,* 2 Feb. 1886, marriage license fees were being discussed in many southern state legislatures at this time. In Georgia, one legislator even proposed a bachelor tax. The court records are filled with fornication and adultery cases involving both whites and African Americans; the sheer number as well as the repeat offenders suggests that many of these people were involved in long-term relationships. There were fifty-three such cases from 1870 to 1886; see Criminal Action Papers, Granville County. The Criminal Action Papers in Orange and Edgecombe Counties yielded similar patterns.

81. Quotes from Berlin, Reidy, and Rowland, *The Black Military Experience,* 714; and Berlin, Fields, Glymph, Reidy, and Rowland, *The Wartime Genesis of Free Labor: The Lower South,* 859. See also Berlin, Miller, Reidy, and Rowland, *The Wartime Genesis of Free Labor: The Upper South,* 181, 223; Reid, *After the War,* 126; and Schwalm, "The Meaning of Freedom," 330–35.

82. Henry W. Jones to Susan Currin, 27 May 1867, Jones Papers.

83. Lucy N. Edward to Henry W. Jones, 21 May 1867, Jones Papers.

84. Thomas W. Hay to Jacob F. Chur, 25 Sept. 1867, Annual Reports of Operations Received from Staff and Subordinate Officers, RBRFAL.

85. Quotes from Berlin, Reidy, and Rowland, *The Black Military Experience,* 672; and R. Alexander, *North Carolina Faces the Freedmen,* 94. See also Foner, *Reconstruction,* 87; Gilmore, *Gender and Jim Crow;* and Higginbotham, *Righteous Discontent.*

86. Quote from Irvin Thompson alias Cherry Thompson, 37th Reg., Co. K, U.S. Colored Troops, Infantry, Records of the Pension Bureau, RG 15, National Archives, Washington, D.C. Jacob Moore, 14th Reg., Co. A, U.S. Colored Troops, Heavy Artillery, Records of the Pension Bureau. My analysis is based on hundreds of Civil War pension files, which provide an excellent source for the construction of marriage within black communities because widows had to establish the legitimacy of their relationships to claim pensions. In North Carolina, most of the testimony comes from the eastern counties, which were occupied early by Union troops and where many black Union veterans continued to live after the war. But pension records from other parts of the South are similar, suggesting that these basic attitudes were widespread, although the nuances of the community's recognition of various relationships did take different forms. Divorce cases and other local court records dealing with marital relations elsewhere in North Carolina confirm that this view of marriage was not confined to the state's eastern shore or even just to African Americans. My reading of these records relies heavily on Frankel's conceptualization of African-American marital relations in "Freedom's Women." Although she does not draw the same conclusions as Frankel, Schwalm discusses African-American families in "The Meaning of Freedom," see esp. 87–90, 335–49. See also Litwack, *Been in the Storm So Long,* 243–44.

87. Quote from *Watkins* v. *Watkins,* 1876, Divorce Records, Granville County, NCDAH. See also *Bullock* v. *Bullock,* 1876, Divorce Records, Granville County.

88. *Watkins* v. *Watkins,* 1876, and *Bullock* v. *Bullock,* 1876, both in Divorce Records, Granville County. Bigamy cases are also suggestive on this point; see *State* v. *Williams,* 1875, *State* v. *Jordan,* 1877, *State* v. *Speed,* 1878, *State* v. *Thorp,* 1878, *State* v. *Newman,* 1878, *State* v. *Harris,* 1879, and *State* v. *Blain,* 1882, all in Criminal Action Papers, Granville County.

89. For the legal changes in divorce before and after the Civil War in North Carolina, see Bynum, "Reshaping the Bonds of Womanhood" and *Unruly Women,* 68–77. According to Bynum, decisions in superior courts often ran counter to the state's strict statutes and the edicts issued by the state supreme court. With greater personal knowledge of the couples, judges and juries at the local level were also far more sympathetic to their difficulties and thus more willing to bend the abstractions of the law to fit the complex realities of individual cases. After the Civil War, the courts and the legislature liberalized divorce even more, although they did so gradually and the changes made wives vulnerable by making it easier for husbands to sue

for divorce. See also Bardaglio, *Reconstructing the Household*, 32–34, 134; Censer, "'Smiling through Her Tears'"; Clinton, *The Plantation Mistress*, 79–85; and Wyatt-Brown, *Southern Honor*, 242–47, 283–91, 300–307.

90. For a particularly dramatic example, see Child Custody Case of Alphonso Royster Jr., 1894, Miscellaneous Records, Granville County, NCDAH. See also *Satterwhite* v. *Satterwhite*, 1871, and *Satterwhite* v. *Satterwhite*, 1859, both in Divorce Records, Granville County. Censer, "'Smiling through Her Tears'"; and Wyatt-Brown, *Southern Honor*, 244–47, 283–91.

91. Frankel, "Freedom's Women"; see also D. White, *Ar'n't I a Woman?* 156–57.

92. Frankel, in "Freedom's Women," points out that federal pension examiners had an equally difficult time comprehending the structure of black families in Mississippi. For the importance of extended family ties, see Berlin, Miller, and Rowland, "Afro-American Families," 114–66; Burton, *In My Father's House Are Many Mansions*, 237–38, 263–64, 274–79; Fields, *Slavery and Freedom on the Middle Ground*, 156; Hunter, "Household Workers in the Making," 34–38; Jones, *Labor of Love, Labor of Sorrow;* Joyner, *Down by the Riverside;* and Schwalm, "The Meaning of Freedom," 87–90, 335–49. Although emphasizing the importance of male-headed, nuclear families, Gutman in *The Black Family in Slavery and Freedom* also gives evidence for the importance of extended families. See also Coleman Edward to the Freedmen's Bureau, 31 July 1866, A. G. Brady to William Jones (regarding the complaint of James Malone), 5 July 1866, and Wesley Mayfield to William Jones, 11 May 1866, all in Letters Received, Assistant Superintendent's Office, Oxford, RBRFAL. See also John Washington to James V. Bomford, 11 Sept. 1867, Letters Received, Records of the Assistant Commissioner.

93. *State* v. *Thorp*, 1875, Criminal Action Papers, Granville County. It is unclear whether Peter Thompson and his wife were related to Frances Thorp or whether she just referred to them as aunt and uncle. Either alternative, however, supports the importance of an extended family not based on marriage contracts.

94. Quotes from Biography of Edward Isham alias Hardaway Bone in the Notebook of David Schenck, David Schenck Papers, NCDAH; and *Bell* v. *Bell*, 1871, Divorce Records, Granville County. Eliza Bell filed her first complaint in 1866, but had to wait several years to legally prove abandonment. See also *Lancaster* v. *Unnamed*, 1866, Divorce Records, Granville County. In 1835, William Hines also emphasized his wife's fulfillment of her domestic obligations as the underpinning of the marriage when he filed for divorce on the tenuous legal grounds that his wife "utterly neglected to attend to the well management of the kitchen & household affairs and other duties incident to a married woman." Quoted in Cecil-Fronsman, *Common Whites*, 144. For the presence of both legal and customary forms of marriage and separation, see McCurry, *Masters of Small Worlds*, 89–90, 183; and Flynt, "Folks like Us." For Edward Isham, see also Bolton, *Poor Whites of the Antebellum South*, 1–10; and Culclasure, "'I Have Killed a Damned Dog.'"

95. Quotes from Benjamin Braddy, Regiment 1, Co. F, North Carolina Infantry, Records of the Pension Bureau. Grossberg, *Governing the Hearth*, 75–81. The court recognized common law marriages after the war; see *Jones* v. *Reddick*, 79 N.C. 290 (1878).

96. In addition to informal mediation by family and neighbors (who were often kin as well), local church congregations also adjudicated family conflicts. See Cecil-Fronsman, *Common Whites*, 156–64; Kenzer, *Kinship and Neighborhood in a Southern Community*, 20–22; and McCurry, *Masters of Small Worlds*, 171–207. See also Stansell, *City of Women;* and Ulrich, *Good Wives*.

97. *State* v. *Burwell*, 1880, Criminal Action Papers, Granville County.

98. *State* v. *Jacobs*, 1880, Criminal Action Papers, Orange County. For similar cases, see Cecil-Fronsman, *Common Whites*, 133; and McCurry, *Masters of Small Worlds*, 130–35.

99. *State* v. *Henderson*, 1883, Criminal Action Papers, Granville County.

100. *State* v. *Rice*, 1871, and *State* v. *Wilkerson*, 1873, both in Criminal Action Papers, Granville County. See also Foner, *Reconstruction*, 362–64, and *Nothing but Freedom*.

101. *State* v. *Henderson*, 1883, Criminal Action Papers, Granville County.

102. *State v. Wilkins*, 1880, Criminal Action Papers, Granville County.

Chapter 2: "How Can They Do It on Three Barrels of Corn a Year?"

1. *New York Tribune*, 8 Sept. 1865; see also 5 Sept. 1865.

2. *Raleigh Journal of Freedom*, 7 Oct. 1865.

3. Tomlins, *Law, Labor, and Ideology*, 232–39; Steinfeld, *The Invention of Free Labor*, 15–54.

4. Morgan, *American Slavery, American Freedom*.

5. Tomlins, *Law, Labor, and Ideology*, 239–58. By contrast, Steinfeld, in *The Invention of Free Labor*, 15–121, argues that the customary restrictions that defined common laborers as dependents within their masters' households remained in force longer. The difference, in part, results from Tomlin's emphasis on practice and Steinfeld's emphasis on the law itself. But, like Tomlins, Steinfeld concludes that laws regulating the labor of adult white men began to disappear before the Revolution.

6. Swift, *A System of Laws of the State of Connecticut*, 1:218. According to Swift, servants included "menial servants or domestics, who are not however particularly recognized by law, and are so denominated from the nature of their employment." He did allow for the fact that some might not be treated as servants in practice, writing that "the right of the master to their services in every respect, is grounded on the contract between them." Nonetheless, all "menials" and "domestics" were different from "labourers, or persons hired by days work, or any longer time" (218). For a discussion of the continuation of various forms of bound labor into the late eighteenth century, see Montgomery, *Citizen Worker*, 25–31; and Salinger, *"To Serve Well*

and Faithfully. " For the application of servant laws to minors in the colonial period, see Tomlins, *Law, Labor, and Ideology,* 241–58. According to Shane White, one in three free blacks in New York City lived in the households of whites, where they worked as domestic servants; see *Somewhat More Independent,* 156–57. Between 1790 and 1810, the terms of gradual emancipation in many northern states, moreover, meant that free blacks still labored under indentures, even though they were nominally free. See Horton and Horton, *Black Bostonians;* Litwack, *North of Slavery;* Nash, *Forging Freedom;* and Nash and Soderlund, *Freedom by Degrees.* In the South, the position of free blacks deteriorated rapidly in the antebellum years, as they were increasingly seen as threats to the institution of slavery; see Berlin, *Slaves without Masters;* and Franklin, *The Free Negro in North Carolina.* For the ambiguous position of free domestic servants in the South, see Cole, "Servants and Slaves."

7. Steinfeld, *The Invention of Free Labor,* 79.

8. For overviews of the extensive literature on republicanism, see Rodgers, "Republicanism"; and Shalhope, "Toward a Republican Synthesis" and "Republicanism and Early American Historiography." See also McCoy, *The Elusive Republic,* 13–75.

9. Foner, *Free Soil, Free Labor, Free Men* and *Politics and Ideology in the Age of the Civil War.* The apprenticeship, another traditional form of encumbered labor, was also transformed during this period from a form of labor contract to a substitute for parental guidance; see Steinfeld, *The Invention of Free Labor,* 131–38, 174–75; and Grossberg, *Governing the Hearth,* 259–68.

10. For the ways that working men in the antebellum North tested and expanded the boundaries of free labor, see, for instance, Montgomery, *Beyond Equality;* and Wilentz, *Chants Democratic.* For women, see, for instance, Dublin, *Women at Work;* and Stansell, *City of Women.* See also Steinfeld, *The Invention of Free Labor,* 147–72; and Tomlins, *Law, Labor, and Ideology.* For the connection between free labor ideology and the expansion of suffrage to propertyless white men, see Montgomery, *Citizen Worker,* 13–25; and Steinfeld, *The Invention of Free Labor,* 185–87.

11. Quoted in Steinfeld, *The Invention of Free Labor,* 126–27, emphasis in the original. For a general discussion of the demands of white northern workers to distance themselves from the term "servant," see 126–28. For the racial component of white working men's labor struggles, see Saxton, *The White Republic;* and Roediger, *The Wages of Whiteness.* For the way race became embedded in notions of citizenship in the early nineteenth century, see Montgomery, *Citizen Worker,* 19–21, 131, 139–40; and Smith-Rosenberg, "Discovering the Subject of the 'Great Constitutional Discussion.'" For provocative analyses of the ways that the racial identity of whites informs class in the United States, see Frankenburg, *White Women, Race Matters;* Roediger, *Towards the Abolition of Whiteness;* and P. Williams, *The Alchemy of Race and Rights.* In *Somewhat More Independent,* Shane White argues that the emphasis on racial restrictions in the historical literature tends to cast free blacks as victims, obscuring the sense of promise that existed among free blacks in

the North as well as their efforts to build new lives as free people. Nonetheless, as even the title of his book implies, free blacks in the North faced an array of racial restrictions. Not only did many remain under indenture well into the nineteenth century, but free blacks generally were segregated into low-paying, highly supervised occupations.

12. As Boydston argues in *Home and Work,* domestic labor was so thoroughly shaped by the gender ideology of the nineteenth century that it was eventually excluded altogether from the category of labor; see also Poovey, *Uneven Developments;* and Stansell, *City of Women,* 155–68. For the naturalization of housework, see Boydston, *Home and Work.* For antebellum women domestics, see Stansell, *City of Women,* 155–68. For women's legal position in the early republic, see Grossberg, *Governing the Hearth;* Kerber, *Women of the Republic;* and Salmon, *Women and the Law of Property in Early America.* For working-class conceptions of gender and the gendered distinctions that grounded white working men's struggles for greater independence, see essays on the nineteenth century in Baron, *Work Engendered;* Blewett, *Men, Women, and Work;* and Stansell, *City of Women.* See also Kerber, "The Paradox of Women's Citizenship in the Early Republic"; Kessler-Harris, *A Woman's Wage;* Pitkin, *Fortune Is a Woman;* Ryan, *Women in Public;* and Smith-Rosenberg, "Dis-Covering the Subject of the 'Great Constitutional Discussion.'"

13. Tomlins, *Law, Labor, and Ideology.*

14. Faust, *Sacred Circle;* see also G. Frederickson, *The Black Image in the White Mind;* Genovese, *The Slaveholders' Dilemma;* and Tise, *Proslavery.* In 1860, when the U.S. House of Representatives repealed an act by the territorial legislature of New Mexico that allowed both slavery and involuntary servitude, several southern congressmen issued a dissenting, minority report. Operating from an older view in which laborers were not their own masters and transferred control over their lives with their labor, these congressmen considered indentured servitude voluntary because laborers had entered "voluntarily" into long-term agreements. "It is laid down as elementary under the 'common law,'" they wrote, "that 'a servant may hire himself for what time he pleases,' and that the relationship which grows out of the contact between the servant and master, gives to the master on the one hand 'superiority and power,' and imposes on the servant 'duty, subjection, and, as it were, allegiance on the other.'" What had been labeled involuntary servitude was, in fact, voluntary, just as the extensive power granted employers over their workers in indentured servitude was acceptable. As the final house vote indicates, northern congressmen found it much more difficult to think in these terms. Quoted in Steinfeld, *The Invention of Free Labor,* 180–81.

15. Quotes from *Wiswall* v. *Brinson,* 32 N.C. 554 (1849). See also Hamilton, *The Papers of Thomas Ruffin,* 4:313–23. There were very few antebellum cases that dealt with "servants," and the courts did not attempt to define the term or categorize their rights; see *Lane* v. *Dudley,* 6 N.C. 119 (1812); *Harris* v. *Mabry,* 23 N.C. 240 (1840); *Coxe* v. *Skeen,* 25 N.C. 443 (1843); and *Dover* v. *Plemmons,* 32 N.C. 23 (1848). When the state supreme court did deal comprehensively with the status of servants after emancipation, it did so with the

self-consciousness that this was a new issue as yet unconsidered. As Edwin G. Reade noted in his dissent to *Haskins* v. *Royster,* 70 N.C. 601 (1874): "Under the new *regime,* much of the labor of the country is performed under contract. This is the first case which has been before us in which the incidents of the relation of employer and laborer have been under discussion, and will probably be looked to as a precedent." According to Cole in "Servants and Slaves," the status of domestic servants also exposes this middle ground between slaves and free workers.

16. York, *The Autobiography of Brantley York,* 12–14 (quote on 14). York does state that the planter's children were fed no better than he and his brother.

17. For North Carolina, see Cecil-Fronsman, *Common Whites,* 55–66; Escott, *Many Excellent People,* 3–31; and Johnson, *Ante-Bellum North Carolina,* 73–77. The situation was similar in South Carolina; see McCurry, *Masters of Small Worlds,* 240–51. But whites in other states enjoyed a much more democratic system; see Thornton, *Politics and Power in a Slave Society.* Although conservatives in Georgia eventually acceded to universal white manhood suffrage, as Reidy notes in *From Slavery to Agrarian Capitalism,* 177, many still remained unconvinced that hirelings—propertyless wage laborers—could ever exercise suffrage independently.

18. The goal of economic independence through landownership or artisanal work described the reality of most southern whites, who either headed or lived within such households; see Ford, *Origins of Southern Radicalism,* 44–95; Hahn, *The Roots of Southern Populism,* 21–24; and McCurry, *Masters of Small Worlds,* 37–91. McCurry also notes that tenancy and waged labor were stages in the life cycle for white men. For the legal status of antebellum renters in North Carolina, see Applewhite, "Sharecropper and Tenant in the Courts of North Carolina." Research indicates that few adult white men in the South permanently hired out their labor for a living, although the number seems to have been increasing over time; see Bolton, *Poor Whites of the Antebellum South;* Ford, *Origins of Southern Radicalism,* 47–48, 50; Cecil-Fronsman, *Common Whites,* 14–16; Hahn, *The Roots of Southern Populism,* 21–24; and Reidy, *From Slavery to Agrarian Capitalism,* 91–101. Occasional waged labor was more common than permanent waged labor; see Durrill, *War of Another Kind,* 13–14; and McCurry, *Masters of Small Worlds,* 58, 187. For the importance of the range to southern white households, see R. Brown, "The Southern Range," 47–163; Hahn, "Common Right and Commonwealth"; J. King, "The Closing of the Southern Range"; and McDonald and McWhiney, "The Antebellum Southern Herdsman." See also the exchange between Kantor, Kousser, and Hahn in the *Journal of Southern History* (May 1993). On his tour through North Carolina in 1865–66, Dennett noted the pervasive presence of roaming pigs; see *The South as It Is,* 130. In addition to using the open range, some propertyless whites simply squatted on unused land; see Johnson, *Ante-Bellum North Carolina,* 69.

19. McCurry, *Masters of Small Worlds,* 47–48. For the ideal importance of independence to common white southerners and the ways they linked independence to control over productive property, see Ford, *Origins of South-*

ern Radicalism; Hahn, *The Roots of Southern Populism;* McCurry, *Masters of Small Worlds;* Thornton, *Politics and Power in a Slave Society;* and Watson, "Conflict and Collaboration."

20. Quote from "Report of the Commission . . . to Prepare a Code for the Freedmen of this State," in *Raleigh Sentinel,* 31 Jan. 1866.

21. Quoted in Andrews, *The South since the War,* 183. For a discussion of idle whites, see 183–84. See also Johnson, *Ante-Bellum North Carolina,* 67–73. Reidy, in *From Slavery to Agrarian Capitalism,* 148, notes that freedpeople had reservations about waged labor because they equated it with the position of hireling; the observation suggests that they recognized the connection white southerners drew between dependence and the need to labor for others.

22. For legal restrictions on the mobility of agricultural laborers generally, see Steinfeld, *The Invention of Free Labor,* 27–34.

23. Quoted material from *Public Laws of North Carolina* (1866), chaps. 58 and 59. The rough balance of obligations did not last long; see *Public Laws of North Carolina* (1866–67), chap. 124; for lien laws, see chap. 1.

24. Quoted material from *Public Laws of North Carolina* (1868–69), chap. 117; for the companion statue on tenancy, see chap. 156. The laborers' lien laws include *Laws and Resolutions of North Carolina* (special session, 1868), chap. 41; and *Public Laws of North Carolina* (1869–70), chap. 206. For the 1877 tenant act, see *Public Laws of North Carolina* (1876–77), chap. 283. But as Applewhite points out in "Sharecropper and Tenant in the Courts of North Carolina," the lien laws had been slowly chipping away at the legal position of tenants even before the passage of these acts. After they overthrew the Republicans, Democratic legislators across the South passed a series of measures designed to keep laborers and tenants in a dependent position; see Cohen, *At Freedom's Edge;* Perman, *The Road to Redemption,* 237–63; Reidy, *From Slavery to Agrarian Capitalism,* 221–27, 232–33; and Woodman, "Post–Civil War Southern Agriculture and the Law" and *New South, New Law.*

25. L. W. Martin to T. H. Hay, 5 Oct. 1866, Letters Received, Assistant Superintendent's Office, Oxford, RBRFAL. See also F. A. Fisk to Jacob F. Chur, 22 Oct. 1866, Letters Received, Raleigh Headquarters, RBRFAL. For other references among white Granville planters to servants, see William Jones to A. G. Brady, 6 Sept. 1866, Letters Received, Assistant Superintendent's Office, Oxford, RBRFAL; and Daniel Paschall to Gen. Miles, 17 Sept. 1867, Records of the Assistant Commissioner. See also Litwack, *Been in the Storm So Long,* 358–63. The image of the unreconstructed slaveowner who insisted on playing the master when it came to demanding obedience from his black workers and rejecting other aspects of this role, namely responsibility for his workers' material well-being, is commonplace in the literature. Employing a framework that polarizes slavery and free labor, historians have often identified such behavior as yet another example of slaveholders' unwillingness to abandon slavery and adopt the practice of free labor. Of course, many slaveholders did try to hold onto slavery. But such a view miss-

es the nuances of the slaveholders' view, in which independent free holders, not free common laborers, represented the opposite of slavery. From
their perspective, African Americans may have stepped out of slavery, but
their position as common laborers still gave their employers broad power
over their lives and placed them in a position of dependence within their
masters' households.

26. The specific meaning freedpeople attached to the term "servant" is
clear in their testimony in labor-related court cases. See Affidavit of Thomas Brodie, 21 June 1866, and Affidavit of Leonidas Hawkins, 21 June 1866,
both in Miscellaneous Records, Assistant Superintendent's Office, Oxford,
RBRFAL. *Bullock* v. *Bullock,* 6 July 1866, *Johnson* v. *Reavis,* 3 Aug. 1866, *Lynn*
v. *Williams,* 29 May 1866, *Marrow* v. *Marrow,* 12 May 1865, *Nicholson* v. *Russell,*
2 May 1866, and *Wortham* v. *Wortham,* 27 May 1866, all in Records Relating
to Court Cases and Complaints, Assistant Superintendent's Office, Oxford,
RBRFAL.

27. Tobacco is so susceptible to external environmental conditions, namely soil and the curing process, that different types are defined by these external factors. Before the war, this combination of factors in the Virginia–
North Carolina district produced tobacco lighter in texture and color than
that elsewhere in the United States. Afterward, farmers improved on these
same conditions to create "bright" tobacco, starving the plant even more to
accentuate the leaves' bright yellow color and perfecting the curing process
to "set" it reliably. For the categorization of tobacco types, see Jahn, *Tobacco
Dictionary,* 35. For developments in the growing and curing process, see
Tilley, *The Bright Tobacco Industry,* 3–88. Tilley, 22–25, notes that the first
official crop of bright tobacco was cured in 1839. Others set the date in the
1850s. See, for instance, Robert, *The Tobacco Kingdom,* 49; and Emory, "Bright
Tobacco in the Agriculture, Industry, and Foreign Trade of North Carolina,"
7–12. Both Tilley and Robert, however, agree that bright tobacco culture did
not really spread until the postwar period.

28. Tilley, *The Bright Tobacco Industry,* 124–25, 201–2. For the tenor of the
market in the first few years following the war, see, for instance, Dorman and
Johnston (Petersburg, Virginia, tobacco factors) to John Bullock, 24 Aug.
1865, John Bullock Papers, Special Collections Library, Duke University,
Durham.

29. For a discussion of postwar tobacco prices, see Tilley, *The Bright Tobacco Industry,* 346–73. Prices quoted by Tilley, 353–54, and those in U.S.
Bureau of the Census, *Historical Statistics,* 1:517–18, indicate that Granville
prices remained consistently above the national average from 1865 through
1900. Tobacco prices did fall during this period, even in the Bright Belt, but
this downward trend should be measured against the general decline in
prices for all products.

30. Quoted in Tilley, *The Bright Tobacco Industry,* 135.

31. Most antebellum Granville tobacco farmers either sold their tobacco through factors in Virginia or peddled their tobacco by wagon through

the southern countryside; see Robert, *Tobacco Kingdom*, 53–75, 178; and Tilley, *The Bright Tobacco Industry*, 529–38. Peddling continued and may have even expanded after the war, but most farmers sold unprocessed tobacco in warehouses. Makeshift warehouses conveniently located along railroad lines sprang up immediately after surrender, as North Carolina tobacco factories tried to gather enough tobacco to meet the rising demand; see Tilley, *The Bright Tobacco Industry*, 206–14. By 1873, Granville residents had access to warehouses in Durham, Henderson, and Oxford. In *History of the Town of Durham*, 93–94, Paul argues that the postbellum marketing system was developed to address the need for cash following the Civil War. Once-a-year marketing did not emerge until later in the nineteenth century; see Tilley, *The Bright Tobacco Industry*, 234–36. For tobacco auctions, see Tilley, 205–6. Apparently, tobacco warehouses generally made payments in hard currency. For instance, Cooper's Warehouse in Granville County suspended specie payment in 1876, but it was only a brief lapse; see *Oxford Torchlight*, 23 May 1876. For further evidence of payment in gold as well as silver, see *Oxford Torchlight*, 31 Oct. 1876, 4 Dec. 1877, and 3 Feb. 1880.

32. Quotes from W. White, *Diary*, 94, 104; see also 89, 90, 92, 104, 113, 115, 117. Other farmers also switched slowly to bright tobacco cultivation; see, for instance, the description of Dennis Tilley, whose skill in cultivating the crop ultimately earned him the title "Yellow Tobacco King," in Hunter, "Useful Information Concerning Yellow Tobacco and Other Crops," 44. The published weekly reports of the Oxford tobacco market in the *Oxford Torchlight*, 1874–80, suggest the continued presence of the heavier, lower-quality tobacco. The testimony in one case of tobacco theft outlines the state of tobacco culture in a section of Oxford Township, revealing that the techniques used to produce high-quality grades were not widely used, particularly by smaller farmers; see *State* v. *Jenkins, Jenkins, and Jenkins*, 1874, Criminal Action Papers, Granville County. See also Tilley, *The Bright Tobacco Industry*, 125.

33. For acreage, see U.S. Bureau of the Census, Manuscript Records, Agricultural Schedules, 1870, 1880. For the widespread use of temporary wage laborers before the Civil War, see Robert, *The Tobacco Kingdom*, 20–21.

34. For the estimate of the number of share-wage contracts in Granville, see Thomas W. Hay to Jacob F. Chur, 25 Sept. 1867, Annual Reports of Operations Received from Staff and Subordinate Officers, RBRFAL. For discussions of the share-wage system, see Glymph, "Freedpeople and Ex-Masters"; Jaynes, *Branches without Roots;* and Woodman, "Sequel to Slavery."

35. Lewis is mentioned by Jaynes in *Branches without Roots*, 175–76. Other planters in Granville seem to have been using cash wages as early as 1866; see *Gregory* v. *Stark*, 25 May 1866, Records Relating to Court Cases and Complaints, Assistant Superintendent, Oxford, RBRFAL. In 1870, of those farmers in Dutchville Township farming over 124 acres (the top 50 percent of the farmers ranked by farm size) 68 percent hired wage laborers, at an average of $155 per farm. In Oxford Township 67 percent of the same group

hired laborers, paying an average of $323 per farm. In Dutchville Township 29 percent (22 of 75) of those who farmed less than 125 acres (those in the bottom 50 percent of farmers when ranked by total acres) hired waged labor, spending an average of $117 per farm. The figures were similar for Oxford; 22 percent, spending an average of $113 per farm. See U.S. Bureau of the Census, Agricultural Schedule, 1870. For a discussion of the barriers to waged labor elsewhere in the South, see Jaynes, *Branches without Roots.*

36. The figures on tenants and wage laborers were compiled from U.S. Bureau of the Census, Agricultural Schedule, 1870; U.S. Bureau of the Census, Manuscript Records, Population Schedule, 1870. The number of farm laborers does not include those people listed as farm laborers who worked on farms owned or operated by family members. The tenure figures used for 1870 are close, but not exact, since they were obtained by matching information on the agricultural and population schedules. The 1870 agricultural schedule does not indicate tenure. The population schedule, however, indicates the value of real estate owned by each individual; in addition, the census taker distinguished between farm owners and tenants in the occupation category. This information on real estate and tenure was matched with those farmers listed in the agricultural census. The match was quite successful; for Dutchville 87 percent of the names matched, and for Oxford, 91 percent matched.

37. In 1870, 91 percent of farm laborers were black and 90 percent were men; in 1880, 85 percent were black and 88 percent were men. In 1870, 69 percent of these laborers were under thirty-one, and in 1880, 74 percent of them were. Figures compiled from U.S. Bureau of the Census, Population Schedules, 1870, 1880. Many sources mention seasonal agricultural laborers, including women, children, and whites, who worked during particularly busy times—of which there were many in tobacco culture. See, for instance, W. White, *Diary;* W. T. Patterson's Farm Journal, 1884–85 (appended to the Roll Book of the Good Templars), Independent Order of Good Templars, Grand Lodge of North Carolina, Health Seat Lodge, No. 40, Papers, Special Collections Library, Duke University, Durham; Bureau of Labor Statistics, *First Annual Report* (1887), 125; and Bureau of Labor Statistics, *Ninth Annual Report* (1895), 77–78.

38. W. White, *Diary,* 36, 44, 70, 88, 97.

39. Patterson's Farm Journal, 1884–85. See also W. White, *Diary.* The wide variety of chores done by laborers on the Patterson and White plantations is probably representative of the work patterns on many Granville County farms.

40. Historians of the postemancipation South have rightly identified landownership as a primary goal among freedpeople. Yet landownership provides only a partial indication of their economic success because it fails to register the efforts of African Americans who were unable to purchase land but who nonetheless worked to achieve autonomy within the constraints of their working lives. Du Bois, in *Black Reconstruction,* provides the most compelling

example of an approach sensitive to the myriad ways freedpeople struggled to shape the postwar labor system to their own needs. See also Fields, *Slavery and Freedom on the Middle Ground;* T. Holt, *The Problem of Freedom;* Jaynes, *Branches without Roots;* Reidy, *From Slavery to Agrarian Capitalism,* 136–60, 215–24; Schwalm, "The Meaning of Freedom," esp. 302–7; and Woodman, "Sequel to Slavery."

41. Jaynes, *Branches without Roots,* 141–57, 215–23. For an example in Granville County, see Affidavit of Lucy A. Russell, 28 July 1866, and Affidavit of Sprigg Russell, 27 June 1866, both in Miscellaneous Records, Assistant Superintendent's Office, Oxford, RBRFAL.

42. Tax List, 1879, Granville County, NCDAH; U.S. Bureau of the Census, Agricultural Schedule, 1880.

43. B. White, *In Search of Kith and Kin,* 52–55, 111.

44. *State* v. *Amis,* two different counts of larceny, 1872, and *State* v. *Amis,* 1876, both in Criminal Action Papers, Granville County. Reidy makes a similar point in *From Slavery to Agrarian Capitalism,* 239–40. The notion of working to satisfy ever-growing material desires was new not only to freedpeople in postemancipation societies but also to the nineteenth-century United States and Britain generally; for a discussion of the connection between liberal capitalism and racial ideology, see T. Holt, *The Problem of Freedom.* See also Fields, *Slavery and Freedom on the Middle Ground;* Holt, "'An Empire over the Mind'"; and Woodman, "The Reconstruction of the Cotton Plantation in the New South."

45. U.S. Bureau of the Census, Population Schedules, 1870, 1880.

46. For pay rates, see Thomas W. Hay to Jacob F. Chur, 25 Sept. 1867, Annual Reports of Operations Received from Staff and Subordinate Officers, RBRFAL. See also wage statistics for Granville County, which appear in the annual reports of the Bureau of Labor Statistics (1887–1900). Figures on the distribution of wealth are compiled from U.S. Bureau of the Census, Population Schedule, 1870. Testimony in the local court records reveal a glimpse of the daily difficulties of wage-earning women who lived outside male-headed households. Housing posed a particular problem; many could not afford rent and those who could ran up against landlords who were unwilling to rent to women who lived outside a male-headed household. Even with a house, there was food, fuel, and clothing to think about. Faced with expenses they could not hope to meet on their wages, women pieced together precarious living arrangements. Some shared households; see *State* v. *Amis,* 1872, and *State* v. *Pritchett,* 1890, both in Criminal Action Papers, Granville County. Frances Thorp stayed with relatives while leaving her child elsewhere; see *State* v. *Thorp,* 1875, Criminal Action Papers, Granville County. Dora Grissom, a single mother with two small children, lived with at least two sets of relatives and stayed temporarily with many more. She was barely tolerated wherever she went. In fact, her father kicked her out so often that she accepted temporary homelessness as natural and simply found shelter with aunts and uncles when necessary. *State* v. *Grissom,* 1890, and *State* v. *Tanner, Tanner, and Grissom,* 1888, both in Criminal Action Papers, Granville County.

47. In Oxford the ratio of wage laborers to tenants in 1870 was 4.74 to 1; in 1880 it was 1.82 to 1. In Dutchville the ratio was 5.37 to 1 in 1870; in 1880 it was 3.28 to 1. All figures from U.S. Bureau of the Census, Agricultural Schedules, 1870, 1880, Population Schedules, 1870, 1880. The race of tenants in 1880 was determined by matching the names on the agricultural and population schedules and then combining the information on the two schedules. The match was quite successful: for Dutchville in 1880, 97 percent of the names matched, and for Oxford in 1880, 91 percent matched. A similar method was employed for 1870. For consistency, I have used figures from these matches throughout the analysis.

Large plantations and tenancy had been common in Oxford during the antebellum period; in one section of Oxford Township, for instance, 36 percent (45 of 124) of the farmers were tenants in 1860. In contrast, most antebellum Dutchville farmers were poor, but they owned their own farms. After the war, when it was discovered that bright tobacco flourished particularly well in Dutchville's thin soil, the fortunes of the township's farmers changed, but their labor patterns remained rooted in the past. For antebellum Granville County, see Carlson, "Homeplace and Tobaccoland," 27–49. For antebellum tenancy see U.S. Bureau of the Census, Agricultural Schedule, 1860. In 1860 the county was not divided by townships in the same way it was in 1870 and 1880, but this one section lay entirely in what later became Oxford Township. Tenants were indicated by the census taker by writing "tenant" beside the farmer's name. In the sections that lay in the Dutchville Township area there were no tenants indicated on the census returns. For a more detailed discussion of antebellum tenancy see Bode and Ginter, *Farm Tenancy and the Census in Antebellum Georgia;* and Winters, "The Agricultural Ladder in Southern Agriculture."

48. Reuben Boyd, for instance, was an average tenant. In 1880, on a 46-acre sharecropped farm valued at $460, he planted 5 acres of tobacco, 20 acres of corn, 19 acres of oats, and 1 acre of potatoes, for a total product value of $312; he also owned a mule and $35 worth of farm implements. James P. Mize and M. A. Gregory, in contrast, are representative of wealthier tenants. Mize sharecropped a 110-acre farm worth $1,000; on it he grew 8 acres of tobacco, 15 acres of corn, 17 acres of oats, 4 acres of wheat, and 2 acres of potatoes; he also owned 2 mules, 2 milk cows, 3 head of cattle, 38 chickens, 14 pigs, and $65 worth of farm implements. In 1880, the total value of all the products from Mize's farm was $2,145. M. A. Gregory sharecropped 525 acres of land worth $2,500. He grew 4 acres of tobacco, 25 acres of corn, 45 acres of wheat, 20 acres of oats, and 1 acre of potatoes. In addition, he owned 4 horses, 2 oxen, 8 milk cows, 14 head of cattle, 37 sheep, 38 chickens, 33 pigs, and $50 worth of farm implements. The total value of Gregory's farm products in 1880 was $890. Both Mize and Gregory spent significant sums on hired labor: Mize paid $160 to hired laborers and Gregory paid $300. All three farmers lived in Oxford Township. See U.S. Bureau of the Census, Agricultural Schedule, 1880. See also U.S. Bureau of the Census, Agricultural Schedule, 1870.

49. Quote from Applewhite, "Sharecropper and Tenant in the Courts of North Carolina," 142. Laws in other southern states had the same effect; see Woodman, "Post–Civil War Southern Agriculture and the Law" and *New South, New Law*. The array and complexities of labor practices in Granville County illuminate the difficulties the law was attempting to address. In the decades following the Civil War, sharecroppers rented some of the largest, most prosperous tenant farms and often owned their own tools and livestock; see note 48 for examples. In *State v. Burwell*, 1869, Supreme Court Justice Thomas Settle upheld a Granville County landlord's right to go into the tenants' fields and collect crops for payment on advances of seed and fertilizer, basing his decision on the 1866–67 legislative act that affirmed the antebellum distinction between croppers and lessees. Settle determined the tenant to be a cropper, and therefore the crop remained the landlord's until he collected rents and reimbursements from it. Yet, the fact that the superior court had decided against Burwell indicates that Settle's interpretation was not universally accepted. See Criminal Action Papers, Granville County. Reidy, in *From Slavery to Agrarian Capitalism*, 235–41, also emphasizes the flexibility and fluidity of tenure arrangements in Georgia.

50. A comparison between white and black renters within townships is most revealing, because land values were higher and farm sizes smaller in Dutchville than they were in Oxford. In 1880, the average black renter in Dutchville worked 20 improved acres on farms worth $758, owned $27 in farm implements, owned $91 in livestock, and produced goods worth $308. The average white renter in the same township worked 25 improved acres on farms worth $900, owned $32 in farm implements, owned $123 in livestock, and produced goods worth $413. White renters in Oxford worked 38 improved acres on farms worth $636, owned $20 in implements, owned $101 in livestock, and produced goods worth $377. By contrast, the average black tenant in Oxford worked 26 improved acres on farms worth only $333, owned $14 in implements, owned $59 in livestock, and produced goods worth $249.

51. Quote from *Oxford Torchlight*, 18 Nov. 1879. For the terms of Oakley's contract, see *State v. Oakley*, 1881, Criminal Action Papers, Granville County. These expectations were common in labor contracts; see R. Alexander, *North Carolina Faces the Freedmen*, 105–6; Foner, *Reconstruction*, 135; Ransom and Sutch, *One Kind of Freedom*, 91; and Schwalm, "The Meaning of Freedom," 250–51.

52. U.S. Bureau of the Census, Agricultural Schedules, 1870, 1880, Population Schedules, 1870, 1880. Planter William Wallace White, who kept detailed accounts of all work done on his farm, mentions a tenant working his sister's farm only in passing; see W. White, *Diary*, 84. See also *Venable v. Hart*, 1866, Civil Action Papers, Granville County.

53. White antebellum tenants did not assume the independent status of freeholders, but they were allowed wide latitude in farm operations; see Ford, *Origins of Southern Radicalism*, 84–88; and Hahn, *The Roots of Southern Populism*, 64–69. Fields, in "Slavery, Race, and Ideology in the United States of America," makes a similar point about the importance of precedent and the

history of struggle in enabling English workers to defend their rights in the colonial period.

54. For Zack White, see W. White, *Diary*. For Solomon Crews, see U.S. Bureau of the Census, Agricultural Schedule, 1880, Population Schedule, 1880. Similar economically successful black tenants appear in Hunter, "Useful Information Concerning Yellow Tobacco and Other Crops." See A. Raper, *Preface to Peasantry*, 110–11, 121–25. See also Shifflett, *Patronage and Poverty in the Tobacco South*. Landownership could reduce the circumstances of poor Granville residents in other ways as well; in "A Time to Plant," 241, Sharon Ann Holt argues that many African-American landowners may have actually owned less personal property than African Americans who owned no land, for landowners often had to sell farm animals and other moveable goods to hold onto their farms.

55. In "Making Freedom Pay," Sharon Ann Holt claims that the focus on market-oriented tenant farming is misleading. Instead, she argues that household production—which she defines as all productive labor not controlled by a yearly agricultural contract—was the linchpin in most freedpeople's economic lives. Holt's emphasis on nonmarket production, however, discounts the potential importance of tenancy and waged labor to African-American households, particularly in tobacco-growing areas, where the staple crop was more profitable than in cotton-growing areas. See also Holt, "A Time to Plant," 19–63; a discussion of dual tenure arrangements appears on 256–82; Reidy, in *From Slavery to Agrarian Capitalism*, 235, makes a similar point about the wide-ranging economic strategies of black renters in Georgia. For such efforts among poor southerners generally, see Hall, et al., *Like a Family*; Shifflett, *Coal Towns*.

Generally only a small fraction of a farm's acreage was planted in tobacco. In 1880, Dutchville tenant farms had, on average, 23.0 improved acres, of which 13.0 percent (3.0 acres) was planted in tobacco; owned farms had, on average, 36.0 improved acres, of which 11.9 percent (4.3 acres) was planted in tobacco. In 1880, Oxford tenant farms had, on average, 32.0 improved acres, of which 19.0 percent (6.0 acres) was planted in tobacco; owned farms had, on average, 105.0 improved acres, of which 4.8 percent (5.0 acres) was planted in tobacco. The other acreage went to corn, wheat, oats, potatoes, and probably large kitchen gardens. In Dutchville, tenant farms averaged 10 acres in corn, 3 acres in wheat, and 2 acres in oats. In Oxford, tenant farms averaged 11 acres in corn, 3 acres in wheat, 4 acres in oats, and 1 acre in potatoes. Figures are compiled from the match between U.S. Bureau of the Census, Agricultural Schedule, 1880, and Population Schedule, 1880.

56. Reidy, in *From Slavery to Agrarian Capitalism*, 237–38, makes a similar point.

57. Quoted in T. B. Wilson, *The Black Codes of the South*, 49. For discussions of African Americans' views of the property and land they had worked in slavery, see Bercaw, "The Politics of Household," chap. 3; Foner, *Reconstruction*, 104–6; Reidy, *From Slavery to Agrarian Capitalism*, 61; and Schwalm, "The Meaning of Freedom," 293–317.

58. Steinfeld, *The Invention of Free Labor,* 149–52. During the antebellum period, the state supreme court granted wages to employees who left before completion of their terms only if their contracts stipulated that either party could terminate the agreement at will; see *Steed* v. *McRae,* 18 N.C. 435 (1836); and *Coxe* v. *Skeen,* 25 N.C. 443 (1843). In *Dover* v. *Plemmons,* 32 N.C. 23 (1848), the court took a more liberal tact, granting back wages to a laborer who completed only four months of a six-month contract, but the specifics of the case limited its applicability. The laborer had agreed to clear three acres of new ground in exchange for the two months remaining on his contract. Although he had completed the task, his employer refused to pay him because he considered the quality of the job inadequate. Thus, the case actually hinged on whether or not the employer had the right to refuse payment on this particular job and not whether all workers who left before completing the terms of their contracts should be paid for the work they had done.

59. Hannibal Young to Freedmen's Bureau, 4 Sept. 1867, Letters Received, Raleigh Headquarters, RBRFAL. Litwack, in *Been in the Storm So Long,* 135–36, describes one white plantation manager who became obsessed with freedpeople's level of "faithfulness," by which he meant devotion to himself personally as well as attention to work. The great majority of complaints and cases that came through the local bureau office dealt with withheld wages. See also Dennett, *The South as It Is,* 124–25; and Fields, *Slavery and Freedom on the Middle Ground,* 161. Some white employers simply did not have the money to pay workers. But the brutal actions that were often combined with the refusal to pay wages also suggest the anger and frustration of planters who were accustomed to commanding the labor of African Americans at will. At the same time, withholding wages and other punitive measures were tied up with the larger transition from slavery to free labor and reflected assumptions, common in the Western world, that the "lower orders" would not work without compulsion. See, in particular, Foner, *Nothing but Freedom;* and T. Holt, "'An Empire over the Mind'" and *The Problem of Freedom.*

60. Quotes from the Lawson and Allen case from Warren Allen to N. A. Miles, 10 July 1867, Letters Received, Records of the Assistant Commissioner; quotes from Ruffin's definition of the rights of employers from *Wiswall* v. *Brinson,* 32 N.C. 554 (1849).

61. Quotes from *Johnson* v. *Reavis,* 3 Aug. 1866, Records Relating to Court Cases and Complaints, Assistant Superintendent's Office, Oxford, RBRFAL; and Thomas Hay to Jacob F. Chur, 25 July 1867, Letters Received, Records of the Assistant Commissioner. Not every complainant was an innocent victim in the proceedings. For some freedpeople, controlling their own labor meant working when they pleased, which might not be very often at all. Even freedpeople themselves disagreed over the quality and appropriate pace of work, as the testimony of Dudley Shanks against William Hicks suggests: "With the exception of about one hours work in pulling some flax," according to Shanks, "the said Wm. Hicks performed no work at all." Moreover, "after the Federal army passed him the boys of the said Wm. Hicks shirked their work all they could and that with all of his scolding they would not work

like they should have done." William Jones to A. G. Brady, 6 Sept. 1866, Letters Received, Assistant Superintendent's Office, Oxford, RBRFAL. For discussions of freedpeople adapting to work under free labor, see Fields, *Slavery and Freedom on the Middle Ground*, 156–66; T. Holt, "'An Empire over the Mind'"; Jaynes, *Branches without Roots;* and Reidy, *From Slavery to Agrarian Capitalism*, 136–60, 215–41. For the process of laboring people adapting to industrialization and its peculiar work patterns generally, see Gutman, "Work, Culture, and Society in Industrializing America"; and Thompson, "Time, Work-Discipline, and Industrial Capitalism."

62. *State* v. *Harris*, 1877, Criminal Action Papers, Granville County.

63. Hannibal Young to Freedmen's Bureau, 4 Sept. 1867, Letters Received, Raleigh Headquarters, RBRFAL; *Wortham* v. *Wortham*, 27 May 1866, Records Relating to Court Cases and Complaints, Assistant Superintendent's Office, Oxford, RBRFAL; *Davis* v. *Davis*, 8 May 1867, Letters Received, Records of the Assistant Commissioner.

64. *Public Laws of North Carolina* (1866), chap. 42.

65. *State* v. *Townes*, 1866, and *State* v. *Self*, 1866, both in Criminal Action Papers, Granville County.

66. The vagrancy statute remained on the books, only to be strengthened in 1879 by "An Act to Prevent Tramps Infesting or Depredating on Citizens of this State," which targeted all homeless people; see *Laws and Resolutions of the State of North Carolina* (1879), chap. 198. For continuing efforts to restrict the mobility of black workers, see Cohen, *At Freedom's Edge*. For similar efforts elsewhere in the United States, see Stanley, "Beggars Can't Be Choosers."

67. Out of thirty-two separate cases and complaints in Granville County filed with the Freedmen's Bureau, eighteen were decided in favor of freedpeople, three were decided in favor of planters, and the outcomes of eleven are unknown.

68. Hannibal Young to Freedmen's Bureau, 4 Sept. 1867, Letters Received, Raleigh Headquarters, RBRFAL; Warren Allen to N. A. Miles, 10 July 1867, Letters Received, Records of the Assistant Commissioner. In virtually every case involving withheld wages freedpeople maintained that they had worked "faithfully."

69. *State* v. *Wilkerson*, 1873, Criminal Action Papers, Granville County. See also *State* v. *Rice*, 1871, Criminal Action Papers, Granville County.

70. *State* v. *Horner*, 1867, and *State* v. *Vann*, 1867, both in Criminal Action Papers, Granville County.

71. Hannibal Young to Freedmen's Bureau, 4 Sept. 1867, Letters Received, Raleigh Headquarters, RBRFAL; Warren Allen to N. A. Miles, 10 July 1867, Letters Received, Records of the Assistant Commissioner; *State* v. *Harris*, 1877, Criminal Action Papers, Granville County. Other historians have also pointed out that control over the work process was a crucial point of contention between planters and freedpeople; see, for instance, Jaynes, *Branches without Roots;* and Reidy, *From Slavery to Agrarian Capitalism*, 156–60.

72. *State* v. *Rice*, 1871, Criminal Action Papers, Granville County. Dick Gregory refused to abide by the terms of his contract, to "do anything" that

his employer "told him to do"; *Gregory* v. *Stark*, 25 May 1866, Records Relating to Court Cases and Complaints, Assistant Superintendent's Office, Oxford, RBRFAL. See also William Jones to A. G. Brady, 6 Sept. 1866, Letters Received, Assistant Superintendent's Office, Oxford, RBRFAL.

73. *State* v. *Allen*, 1884, Criminal Action Papers, Granville County.

74. *Oxford Torchlight*, 18 Nov. 1879. For the terms of Oakley's contract, see *State* v. *Oakley*, 1881, Criminal Action Papers, Granville County. For a description of a very similar case, see *Granville Free Lance*, 21 Mar. 1879.

75. Interview with Ed Currin, 14 Jan. 1939, Oxford, N.C., Federal Writers' Project, Southern Historical Collection, University of North Carolina at Chapel Hill.

76. *Venable* v. *Hart*, 1866, Civil Action Papers, Granville County.

77. Bercaw, "The Politics of Household"; Frankel, "Freedom's Women"; Hunter, "Household Workers in the Making" and "Domination and Resistance"; and Schwalm, "The Meaning of Freedom." Some women in Granville County filed their own complaints; see Affidavit of Ann Elizabeth Hicks, 10 July 1866, Miscellaneous Records, Assistant Superintendent's Office, Oxford, RBRFAL; and *Moss* v. *Moss*, 8 May 1866, Records Relating to Court Cases and Complaints, Assistant Superintendent's Office, Oxford, RBRFAL. In other cases, male kin acted on behalf of women; see Affidavit of Thomas Brodie, 21 June 1866, and Affidavit of Leonidas Hawkins, 21 June 1866, both in Miscellaneous Records, Assistant Superintendent's Office, Oxford, RBRFAL; *Lynn* v. *Williams*, 29 May 1866, Records Relating to Court Cases and Complaints, Assistant Superintendent's Office, Oxford, RBRFAL. But most often, women appeared as members of families who had been hired as a unit and were represented by a male household head. See also Berlin, Miller, and Rowland, "Afro-American Families," 113–14; and Mann, "Slavery, Sharecropping, and Sexual Inequality."

78. Quotes from Hannibal Young to Freedmen's Bureau, 4 Sept. 1867, Letters Received, Raleigh Headquarters, RBRFAL; Warren Allen to N. A. Miles, 10 July 1867, Robert Hunt to Jacob F. Chur, 27 July 1867, and Rawlins Royster to N. A. Miles, 19 Sept. 1867, all in Letters Received, Records of the Assistant Commissioner. See also Jordan Overby to N. A. Miles, 30 Aug. 1867, and Mark Overby to Freedmen's Bureau, 30 Aug. 1867 (letter filed with a letter written by Jordan Overby on the same date), both in Letters Received, Records of the Assistant Commissioner.

79. *State* v. *Hunt*, 1867, Criminal Action Papers, Granville County; Robert Hunt to Jacob F. Chur, 27 July 1867, Letters Received, Records of the Assistant Commissioner; *State* v. *Edmunds*, 1867, Criminal Action Papers, Granville County.

80. Berlin, Miller, and Rowland, "Afro-American Families," 107–11; Fields, *Slavery and Freedom on the Middle Ground*, 141–42; Frankel, "Freedom's Women"; Jaynes, *Branches without Roots*, 229–32; Jones, *Labor of Love, Labor of Sorrow*, 44–109; Reidy, *From Slavery to Agrarian Capitalism*, 155–56; and Schwalm, "The Meaning of Freedom," 295–96, 318–24. For further discussion of

African-American women's attempts to withdraw their labor from white planters, see chapter 4.

81. *State* v. *Kirkland*, 1872, Criminal Action Papers, Granville County. For a similar case, see *State* v. *Wilkerson*, 1873, Criminal Action Papers, Granville County.

82. *Haskins* v. *Royster*, 70 N.C. 601 (1874). The decision was upheld in *Morgan* v. *Smith*, 77 N.C. 37 (1877).

83. *Haskins* v. *Royster*, 70 N.C. 601 (1874).

Chapter 3: "Rich Men" and "Cheerful Wives"

1. *Oxford Torchlight*, 16 Nov. 1875.

2. Ibid. The story line of "Annie the Butterfly" was quite common in southern publications in the late nineteenth century. As the work of other scholars suggests, it bore more than a passing resemblance to the lives of many planter-class men and women in the years during and after the Civil War; see Bleser and Heath, "The Clays of Alabama"; Burr, "A Woman Made to Suffer and Be Strong"; Muhlenfield, *Mary Boykin Chesnut;* Painter, "The Journal of Gertrude Clanton Thomas"; A. Scott, *The Southern Lady;* and Whites, "The Civil War as a Crisis in Gender" and *The Civil War as a Crisis in Gender,* 132–59.

3. The *Oxford Torchlight* runs from 1874 to the present; the *Granville Free Lance,* from 1877 until the mid-1880s; the *Oxford Leader's* run is unclear, but only a few years or less, with only one extant issue remaining.

4. Not all local newspapers in the state followed the same format as the *Oxford Torchlight,* the *Granville Free Lance,* and the *Oxford Leader,* with their heavy use of short stories, poems, and prescriptive literature, as well as household and farm advice. But many of those with the same general mission, combining national, state, and local news and targeting a local audience, did; see, for instance, the *Newbernian,* the *Warrenton Gazette,* and the *Tarboro Southerner.* Newspapers that focused primarily on state and national issues, such as the *Charlotte Democrat,* the *Raleigh Sentinel,* and the *North Carolina Standard,* devoted far less space to advice literature. So did newspapers whose mission centered exclusively on promoting the interests of a particular party or political purpose, such as the *Wilmington Herald* (which supported unionism and the Republican party afterward), the *New Bern Daily Times* (Republican), the *Raleigh Weekly Republican,* and the *Raleigh Journal of Freedom* (both supported black rights and the Republican party). But even these newspapers published the occasional short story, poem, and advice column.

5. Sarah A. Elliott's cookbook went through two printings; see Elliott, *Mrs. Elliott's Housewife.* See also Elliott, *Days Long Ago.* The cookbook was similar in format and content to others of the time; see Grubb, "House and Home in the Victorian South."

6. Many of the newspapers' short stories centered around false identity or confused identification, a theme that suggests elite white fears of level-

ing in a world where distinctions that once ordered society no longer mattered; see Halttunen, *Confidence Men and Painted Women*. The stories, however, were not uniformly critical; some expressed a sense of possibility in these same changes. See *Oxford Leader,* 28 Sept. 1875; *Granville Free Lance,* 11 Jan. 1878, 1 Feb. 1878, 22 Feb. 1878, 8 Mar. 1878, 15 Mar. 1878, 29 Mar. 1878, 3 May 1878, 24 Oct. 1879, 30 July 1880, 27 Aug. 1880, 22 Oct. 1880, 5 Nov. 1880, 12 Nov. 1880, 10 Dec. 1880, 14 Jan. 1881, 11 Feb. 1881, 22 Apr. 1881, 6 May 1881, 28 Oct. 1881, and 18 Nov. 1881; and *Oxford Torchlight,* 15 Sept. 1874, 29 Sept. 1874, 25 May 1875, 14 Nov. 1876, 5 Dec. 1876, 2 Jan. 1877, 6 Nov. 1877, 5 Feb. 1878, 17 Sept. 1878, 1 Oct. 1878, 24 Dec. 1878, 14 Jan. 1879, 8 July 1879, and 22 July 1879.

7. For African-American men and women, see Gilmore, *Gender and Jim Crow;* Greenwood, *Bittersweet Legacy;* and Higginbotham, *Righteous Discontent.* For white women, see A. Scott, *The Southern Lady;* Sims, "'The Sword of the Spirit'"; Thomas, *The New Woman in Alabama;* Wedell, *Elite Women and the Reform Impulse in Memphis;* Wheeler, *New Women of the New South;* and Whites, *The Civil War as a Crisis in Gender.*

8. Quote from Herbert Gregory to Zebulon B. Vance, 20 Oct. 1864, Vance Papers. Sophronia Horner to James H. Horner, 12 July 1861, 14 July 1861, 11 Aug. 1861, 18 Aug. 1861, 29 Oct. 1861, 18 Apr. 1862, James H. Horner Papers, Special Collections Library, Duke University, Durham; see also Sophronia Horner to Col. Hoke, 17 Apr. 1862, Horner Papers.

9. Sophronia Horner to James H. Horner, 18 Aug. 1861, Horner Papers. See also Fox-Genovese, *Within the Plantation Household,* esp. 334–71; and Painter, "The Journal of Gertrude Clanton Thomas."

10. *State* v. *Smith,* 1866, *State* v. *Merriman,* 1866, *State* v. *Hunt,* 1867, *State* v. *O'Mary,* 1868, and *State* v. *Alston,* 1869, all in Criminal Action Papers, Granville County. See also Litwack, *Been in the Storm So Long,* 425–30. For the disorienting impact of the Confederacy's collapse on the identities of elite white women, see Bercaw, "Defeat from Within" and "The Politics of Household," chap. 2; Faust, "'Trying to Do a Man's Business'"; Rable, *Civil Wars,* 221–39; and Whites, *The Civil War as a Crisis in Gender,* 96–131.

11. Quotes from R. A. Jenkins to Pres. Andrew Johnson, 26 May 1865, Miscellaneous Letters Received, Records of the Adjutant General's Office, RG 94, National Archives, Washington, D.C.; Henry W. Jones to Susan Currin, 27 May 1867, and Lucy N. Edwards to Henry W. Jones, 21 May 1867, both in Jones Papers.

12. Quotes from James H. Horner to Sophronia Horner, 27 Dec. 1861, Horner Papers. See also James H. Horner to Sophronia Horner, 19 Aug. 1861, 8 Nov. 1861, 10 Nov. 1861, 9 Dec. 1861, 27 Dec. 1861, and 18 Feb. 1862, all in Horner Papers. For discussions of this issue, see Rable, *Civil Wars,* 50–90; and Whites, *The Civil War as a Crisis in Gender,* 15–95.

13. *Oxford Torchlight,* 16 Nov. 1875. Gertrude Thomas, an elite white diarist, reacted similarly when her son took to plowing instead of attending college in the lean years following the war; see Painter, "The Journal of

Gertrude Clanton Thomas," 49–50; Burr, *The Secret Eye*, 320–22; and Whites, *The Civil War as a Crisis in Gender*, 154–55.

14. On Horner's hospitalization, see Eugene Grissom, Superintendent of the North Carolina Insane Asylum, to Sophronia Horner, 23 Nov. 1876, Rome Horner to Sophronia Horner, 20 Nov. 1876, and Eugene Grissom to Rev. T. J. Horner, 22 Nov. 1876, all in Horner Papers. For the trajectory of the Horner Military Academy, see Carlson, "Homeplace and Tobaccoland," 86. Ironically, Horner received his own education from the Reverend John Chavis, a free black man educated at Washington Academy (now Washington and Lee University) and Princeton, who taught many young men from the planter class at his schools in Raleigh as well as in Granville, Orange, and Chatham Counties. See Carlson, 48–49; and *Oxford Torchlight*, 28 Sept. 1880. For the way military defeat challenged the manhood of white southern men, see Foster, *Ghosts of the Confederacy*, 24–29; and Whites, "The Civil War as a Crisis in Gender" and *The Civil War as a Crisis in Gender*, 132–59. See also Silber, *The Romance of Reunion*, 13–38.

15. Foster, *Ghosts of the Confederacy;* Whites, *The Civil War as a Crisis in Gender*, 160–224. While other scholars have not emphasized gender, it is often implicit in their analyses; see Osterweis, *The Myth of the Lost Cause;* and C. R. Wilson, *Baptized in Blood.*

16. *Oxford Torchlight*, 4 July 1876. Elite whites in Granville County participated in the mythologizing of the war in a number of ways. Women organized Memorial Day to decorate the graves of Confederate soldiers; see *Oxford Torchlight*, 5 May 1874 and 28 Apr. 1885. Young men organized feudal tournaments, in which they rode as knights in armor on horseback, to commemorate their chivalrous past. See *Oxford Torchlight*, 29 May 1877; W. White, *Diary*, 81; and W. W. Jones, G. B. Harris, V. E. Turner, and E. G. Cheatham to William H. Gregory, 20 Oct. 1865, William H. Gregory Papers, Special Collections Library, Duke University, Durham. Oxford businessmen contributed to the Confederate Soldiers' Home in Virginia; see *Oxford Torchlight*, 27 July 1886. Elite white men also reorganized the Granville Grays, the first and one of the most famous of the county's Confederate companies, as a social club and, at times, paramilitary arm of the Democratic party. Elite white women enthusiastically supported the Grays. See *Oxford Torchlight*, 29 May 1877, 21 May 1878, 3 Feb. 1885, 17 Feb. 1885, and 3 Mar. 1885.

17. Elite whites' reminiscences of devoted black slaves were a projection of their current desires for mastery backward in time, fundamentally reworking the past in the process; see, for instance, *Oxford Torchlight*, 10 Aug. 1886. See also Oakes, "The Present Becomes the Past."

18. *State* v. *Dodson*, 1867, Criminal Action Papers, Granville County. Painter describes a similar scene in "The Journal of Gertrude Clanton Thomas," 54–55.

19. Sophronia Horner to James H. Horner, 1 Nov. 1861, Horner Papers. See also Bercaw, "The Politics of Household," chap. 2; Faust, "Altars of Sacrifice"; Rable, *Civil Wars*, 73–90; and Whites, *The Civil War as a Crisis in Gen-*

der, 64–95. The papers of Governor Zebulon B. Vance are filled with letters from white women, rich and poor, who framed their requests with the same logic used by Sophronia Horner. Whether they asked for exemptions or leave time for husbands and sons, troops to protect them from marauders, food to get them through the winter, or an end to the war that was making their lives miserable these people maintained that the demands of war did not override their menfolks' responsibilities for their families. The letters are too numerous to list here; for representative documents see Petition of the Mothers, Wives, and Sisters of the Members of the 45th N.C. Regiment, 24 Oct. 1864; and Petition of Wives of Soldiers and Widows of Sampson County, 12 Nov. 1864.

20. Historians have long argued that the Civil War was a watershed for white women, weakening patriarchy and opening the way for an expanded women's sphere, at least for elite women; see A. Scott, *The Southern Lady;* and Wiley, *Confederate Women.* Other historians have challenged this thesis. In *The Free Women of Petersburg,* Lebsock argues that free black and white women were able to carve out a significant amount of autonomy in the antebellum period. It was after the war, when male authority was wounded, that men felt the need to publicly assert their dominance over women. See also Lebsock, "Radical Reconstruction and the Property Rights of Southern Women." Friedman, in *The Enclosed Garden,* argues that southern women's lives, both black and white, were shaped by the concerns of family, community, and the church both before and after the Civil War. She contends that the war was not a watershed for women because it did not fundamentally alter these institutions. Rable, in *Civil Wars,* also emphasizes continuity. Because white southerners went to war to preserve their social order and saw wartime changes in women's roles as temporary aberrations, he maintains that the war produced no radical break with antebellum gender roles. In *Ghosts of the Confederacy,* 26–33, Foster also argues that elite white women readily embraced prewar gender relations and gender roles after the southern surrender. By contrast, historians focusing on race and black women have highlighted the importance of emancipation, but have characterized the nature of postwar change differently than Anne Scott. Bercaw, in "The Politics of Household," E. Brown, in "To Catch a Vision of Freedom," Frankel, in "Freedom's Women," Hunter, in "Household Workers in the Making," Jones, in *Labor of Love, Labor of Sorrow,* Rosen, in "Race, Gender, and the Politics of Rape," and Schwalm, in "The Meaning of Freedom," all highlight the numerous ways in which black women worked to make freedom a reality in their daily lives. Using a similar analytical framework, others have emphasized the importance of war and emancipation for altering the lives of elite white women; see Bercaw, "The Politics of Household"; Painter, "The Journal of Gertrude Clanton Thomas"; and Whites, *The Civil War as a Crisis in Gender.* As I argue, the Civil War was a watershed for elite white women because it forced them to redefine womanhood. In so doing, wealthy white southerners drew on their antebellum background, but in the new context of the postwar years,

various parts of these older definitions took on new meanings. The implications of the new definitions of womanhood, however, tended to reinforce antebellum gender hierarchies, even as they pointed in new directions for elite white men and women.

21. M. I. Sturdivant-Ringgold to Elizabeth Hargrove, 5 Dec. 1867, Elizabeth R. Hargrove Papers, Special Collections Library, Duke University, Durham. See also Painter, "The Journal of Ella Gertrude Clanton Thomas," 34–42.

22. Quotes from *Oxford Torchlight*, 16 Nov. 1875. The scene with Annie Silverton looking on as her slaves left was common in real life; see Litwack, *Been in the Storm So Long*, 149–63; and Rable, *Civil Wars*, 253–54.

23. Quotes from Doug Lacy to Susan Bullock, 9 Mar. 1866, Bullock Papers; and Jennie [last name illegible] to Elizabeth Hargrove, 25 Nov. 1866, Hargrove Papers. See also Rable, *Civil Wars*, 241–49; Whites, *The Civil War as a Crisis in Gender*, 132–59.

24. Quotes from Lucy [last name unknown] to Susan Bullock, 11 June 1867, Bullock Papers; and Jennie [last name illegible] to Elizabeth Hargrove, 25 Nov. 1866, Hargrove Papers. White southerners discussed their postwar problems with domestic servants as a labor issue; see, for instance, *Wilmington Herald*, 16 Jan. 1866. For discussions of the relations between white women and their black servants, see Hunter, "Domination and Resistance" and "Household Workers in the Making"; Painter, "The Journal of Ella Gertrude Clanton Thomas," 51–55; Rable, *Civil Wars*, 250–64; and Whites, *The Civil War as a Crisis in Gender*, 128–31.

25. *Oxford Torchlight*, 23 Sept. 1879; *State* v. *Barnett*, 1879, Criminal Action Papers, Granville County; Fields, *Slavery and Freedom on the Middle Ground*, 162–63; Hunter, "Household Workers in the Making," 52–53, 81–82.

26. See, in particular, Sophronia Horner to Col. Hoke, 17 Apr. 1862, Horner Papers; see also Sophronia Horner to James H. Horner, 29 Oct. 1861 and 18 Apr. 1862, both in Horner Papers.

27. For "Hen-Pecked Husbands," see *Oxford Torchlight*, 3 Mar. 1874; for Polly Pepper's response, see *Oxford Torchlight*, 24 Mar. 1874.

28. Bynum, in *Unruly Women*, 47–52, 55–56, argues that between 1830 and 1850 a new version of white womanhood arose in the piedmont of North Carolina that reflected the political sentiments of the area's economically and socially diverse population. While proslavery, this brand of womanhood was also anti-aristocratic and, on this score, it bore a remarkable resemblance to northern ideals. The work of other southern historians, even those who emphasize southern exceptionalism, reveals striking parallels between the gender ideals of elite white northerners and southerners. White southern women centered their lives around home and family, while men sought to establish mastery over their own lives and those of their dependents; see Censer, *North Carolina Planters and Their Children;* Friedman, *The Enclosed Garden;* Lebsock, *The Free Women of Petersburg;* McMillen, *Motherhood in the Old South;* Rable, *Civil Wars;* A. Scott, *The Southern Lady*, 3–21; and Whites, *The Civil War as a Crisis in Gender.*

Yet the flourishing debate over southern exceptionalism has obscured the parallels between North and South by polarizing the terms of the analysis. As the debate escalated, scholars tended to focus either on the South's essential difference from the North or its essential similarity. A middle ground, however, has begun to emerge. In *Slavery and Freedom,* James Oakes links the unique conditions of the slave South to liberal capitalism, arguing that slavery existed as the inversion of freedom. Ultimately, he argues, slaveholders were unable to sustain the delicate balancing act required to preserve slavery within the context of liberal capitalism, elements of which they also embraced. Elizabeth Fox-Genovese and Eugene Genovese have also addressed the ways that liberal capitalism shaped the slave South and the inability of slaveholders to completely escape its social, economic, and ideological implications; see Fox-Genovese, *Within the Plantation Household;* Genovese and Fox-Genovese, *Fruits of Merchant Capital;* and Genovese, *The Slaveholders' Dilemma.* Yet sharp differences remain. Oakes ties together the North and South by emphasizing the common bond of liberal ideology. Genovese and Fox-Genovese focus on the structural differences between one society built on free labor and another on slave labor. In Fox-Genovese's words, "The South was in but not of the bourgeois world." *Within the Plantation Household,* 55. No matter how much the discourse of the South drew on the language of liberalism, it could never signify the same things because the context that gave the words their meaning was essentially different. For a summary of the debate's trajectory, see Ayers, "The World the Liberal Capitalists Made."

David Roediger has questioned this dichotomy in "Precapitalism in One Confederacy," in *Towards the Abolition of Whiteness,* suggesting that the cold war tendency to view the world in terms of polarized economic systems informed Genovese's analysis and explains much of its popularity. Following Roediger's lead, my analysis assumes a less totalizing idea of southern difference that allows for regional variations and internal contradictions within the South. Instead of existing as neat theoretical dichotomies, differences between the two regions actually existed along a continuum. Individuals fell out in various places along it, with southerners clustered at one end, northerners at the other, and people from both regions spread along a broad midsection. This perspective's emphasis on context allows us to see nuances in the ways southerners and northerners applied liberal ideology and the ways that liberal ideology shaped political discourse and social relations. The fact that antebellum prescriptive literature in both the South and the North stressed elite white women's domestic duties highlights the importance of social context. Given the differences between the two regions, the same ideal role resulted in very different practices in these two areas. In the North, domesticity elaborated a new role for women in a developing market economy, expanding their influence over the home and family. In the South, however, domesticity and motherhood affirmed the existing position of elite white women in the patriarchal order of a slave society, where they were both mistresses and subordinates within a male-headed household. The emphasis on housekeeping reaffirmed slaveholding women's position as overseer and manager of the household, since they did not actually perform all or, in some instances, any of the duties for which they were held responsible. Yet, for all their differences, elite white women in the North and South were not totally unrecognizable to each other. To the contrary, they shared a great deal, as their mutual engagement in domestic literature would suggest. Such an approach allows a way to reconcile the strong parallels that many scholars have shown between northern and southern ideals of womanhood and manhood without concluding that the South was just like the North.

29. Quotes from Elliott, *Mrs. Elliott's Housewife*, v, vi. *Charlotte Democrat*, 23 Jan. 1872. See Whites, *The Civil War as a Crisis in Gender*, 132–59, for the development of similar gender ideals in Georgia at the same time.

30. "Rich Men," *Oxford Torchlight*, 10 Mar. 1874. Throughout the 1870s and 1880s both the *Oxford Torchlight* and the *Granville Free Lance* promoted economic change of some sort—from railroads to better roads to more scientific farming methods to electric lighting—in virtually every issue. Sometimes explicit, as in the article "Rich Men," sometimes implicit, the message was the same: capitalism was the path of economic development that would benefit all. Escott, in *Many Excellent People*, 172–74, notes that such articles were common in North Carolina newspapers at this time. See also Gilmore, *Gender and Jim Crow*, chap. 3. In *Bittersweet Legacy*, Greenwood argues that Charlotte's white community went through two stages of class development, the first in the immediate postwar years when a business and professional class came to define its interests differently from farmers in the countryside and the second later in the nineteenth century as the "town" group split again as a strong core of industrialists formed; see 56–69, 114–46. These divisions were far less pronounced in Granville County, where tobacco production tied Oxford to the surrounding countryside and where industry never developed as it did in Charlotte. Instead, market-oriented farmers aligned with the town's business and professional class to promote a wide range of economic development schemes.

31. The farm section was a regular weekly feature in the *Granville Free Lance*. See also *Oxford Torchlight*, 15 Feb. 1876, 23 May 1876, 22 Aug. 1876, 21 Oct. 1879, 30 Nov. 1880, 8 Feb. 1881, 17 May 1881, 7 June 1881, 21 June 1881, 5 July 1881, 12 July 1881, 19 July 1881, 26 July 1881, 31 Mar. 1885, and 16 Mar. 1886.

32. For Hunter's columns, see *Oxford Torchlight*, 18 Nov. 1879, 2 Dec. 1879, 9 Dec. 1879, and 23 Dec. 1879. Hunter published his series as a promotional pamphlet; see Hunter, "Useful Information Concerning Yellow Tobacco and Other Crops." For similar profiles of local businessmen and farmers by other authors, see 3 Feb. 1880, 17 Feb. 1880, 9 Mar. 1880, 16 Mar. 1880, 20 July 1880, 27 July 1880, 17 May 1881, and 28 Feb. 1882. The *Oxford Torchlight* represented Granville County and Oxford as economic meccas; see 10 Feb. 1886, 9 Mar. 1886, 6 Apr. 1886, 29 June 1886, 12 Oct. 1886, 14 Dec. 1886,

20 July 1887, 2 Nov. 1887, 9 Nov. 1887, and 8 Feb. 1888. See also *Granville Free Lance,* 2 Jan. 1880. The *Oxford Torchlight* also proudly printed articles that touted the region's economic potential; see 12 Oct. 1886 and 5 July 1887.

33. Although it would be overly simplistic to reduce the newspapers' short stories to one theme alone, they usually emphasized the virtues of temperate, economically successful men and properly domestic women, while condemning lazy men who wanted money without working for it and self-obsessed, profligate women. For the *Oxford Torchlight,* which concentrated on short fiction in the 1870s but later abandoned it in the 1880s, see 10 Mar. 1874, 17 Mar. 1874, 26 May 1874, 15 Sept. 1874, 29 Sept. 1874, 23 Feb. 1875, 9 Mar. 1875, 25 May 1875, 14 Nov. 1876, 5 Dec. 1876, 2 Jan. 1877, 6 Mar. 1877, 6 Nov. 1877, 5 Feb. 1878, 20 Aug. 1878, 17 Sept. 1878, 1 Oct. 1878, 24 Dec. 1878, 14 Jan. 1879, 25 Feb. 1879, 18 Mar. 1879, 8 July 1879, and 22 July 1879. For the *Granville Free Lance,* see 11 Jan. 1878, 1 Feb. 1878, 22 Feb. 1878, 8 Mar. 1878, 15 Mar. 1878, 22 Mar. 1878, 29 Mar. 1878, 3 May 1878, 10 May 1878, 17 May 1878, 28 Feb. 1879, 21 Mar. 1879, 28 Mar. 1879, 24 Oct. 1879, 16 Jan. 1880, 25 June 1880, 27 Aug. 1880, 15 Oct. 1880, 22 Oct. 1880, 5 Nov. 1880, 12 Nov. 1880, 10 Dec. 1880, 14 Jan. 1881, 21 Jan. 1881, 4 Feb. 1881, 11 Feb. 1881, 1 Apr. 1881, 8 Apr. 1881, 22 Apr. 1881, 6 May 1881, 4 Nov. 1881, 18 Nov. 1881, 23 Dec. 1881, 20 Jan. 1882, 7 July 1882, and 10 Nov. 1882.

34. Quotes from *Oxford Torchlight,* 5 Dec. 1876; and *Granville Free Lance,* 28 Feb. 1879. For similar advice, see *Oxford Torchlight,* 5 May 1874, 6 Nov. 1877, 4 Mar. 1879, 5 Aug. 1879, 8 Mar. 1887, and 7 Sept. 1887; and *Granville Free Lance,* 1 Feb. 1878, 28 Mar. 1879, and 18 Nov. 1881. Similar articles appeared in other newspapers; see *Wilmington Herald,* 2 June 1865; and *North Carolina Standard,* 2 May 1866.

35. Granville's elite were particularly well placed to build on their resources given the booming tobacco market. The prospects of other North Carolinians were less bright, but the Civil War and emancipation did not result in a massive redistribution of wealth anywhere in the state. Despite the loss of their slaves, elite whites retained control of the vast majority of the state's property. See Billings, *Planters and the Making of a "New South."* See also O'Brien, *The Legal Fraternity and the Making of a New South Community.* Furthermore, few of the very wealthy in North Carolina could boast a rags-to-riches rise in their families' antebellum past; see Censer, *North Carolina Planters and Their Children,* 10–11.

36. Foner, *Reconstruction,* 106–7; Fields, *Slavery and Freedom on the Middle Ground,* 182–86; Hunter, "Household Workers in the Making," 21–22; Litwack, *Been in the Storm So Long,* 139–44; Perman, *The Road to Redemption,* 242–43; Reidy, *From Slavery to Agrarian Capitalism,* 67–71, 150–52; Schwalm, "The Meaning of Freedom," 206–8. Petty theft cases were concentrated in the late 1860s before congressional Reconstruction. But the decline thereafter probably does not reflect a change in the attitudes of white elites. Instead, it is probably due to a combination of factors: record keeping, growing prosperity even among African Americans, the greater influence of African Americans

and poor whites in the court system, and perhaps the sheer number of prosecutions in the 1860s ultimately discouraged thieves.

37. Criminal Action Papers, 1865–80, Granville County. Planter William Wallace White regularly interrupted his work schedule, taking laborers off farm work to help him track down "rogues" who made off with corn, potatoes, bacon, or pigs; see W. White, *Diary*, 42, 57, 115; see also *State* v. *Bullock and Bullock*, 1869, Criminal Action Papers, Granville County. I will discuss fence laws in chapter 6.

38. Quotes from *Oxford Torchlight*, 18 Nov. 1879; for a similar success story, see 3 Feb. 1880. See also *Oxford Torchlight*, 11 Sept. 1877, 29 Apr. 1879, 7 June 1881, and 5 Oct. 1886.

39. *Oxford Torchlight*, 15 Jan. 1878. See also *Granville Free Lance*, 18 Nov. 1881.

40. *Oxford Torchlight*, 16 July 1878. In the newspaper's call for immigration in 30 Nov. 1880 other attractions, including "health, and church privileges, pure air, pure water, intelligence and virtue," were mentioned but the discussion of business prospects came first and received the most space.

41. Writers of other *Oxford Torchlight* articles placed economic success within this context, at times implying, at times explicitly arguing that wealth alone meant nothing without attention to these other virtues; see, for instance, *Oxford Torchlight*, 17 Mar. 1874, 23 Jan. 1877, 16 Mar. 1886, and 26 Oct. 1887; the writer of one piece, on 1 Feb. 1888, advised women not to marry men for financial considerations alone. See also *Granville Free Lance*, 22 Oct. 1880.

42. Quotes from Past Degree Templar's Card, Good Templars Papers. Notices in the *Oxford Torchlight* indicate that the temperance movement flourished in Oxford throughout the 1870s and 1880s and finally succeeded in making Oxford dry in June 1886.

43. Quote from P. C. Cameron to James H. Horner, no date, Horner Papers. R. H. Kingsbury to James H. Horner, no date, Horner Papers.

44. Announcement of the reopening of the Classical and Mathematical School, 1876, Henderson, N.C., Jones Papers. See also "Horner School, Oxford, North Carolina" and "Catalog of Horner School, Oxford, N.C., A Classical, Mathematical, Scientific and Military Academy, 1882–1883." For a reminiscence of a student at Horner's school, see Horner's entry in Ashe, Weeks, and Van Noppen, *Biographical History of North Carolina*, 8:253–61. Elite white families from across the state sent their boys to the Horner School, which continued in reputation and in the same course of instruction under Jerome Horner after his father's death; see "Horner Military School, Annual Catalog, 1906"; and "Horner Military School, Annual Catalog, 1905." In addition to Horner's Academy, there were several other schools in the vicinity of Oxford that catered to the boys and girls of elite white parents.

45. Quotes from "Catalog of Horner School, 1882–1883," 14; M. N. Wilson to Mary J. Davis, 9 June 1885, and William H. Gregory to Mary Davis, 2 Jan. 1886, both in Gregory Papers. In addition to his duties as a schoolmas-

ter, James H. Horner apparently kept a hand in farming. In 1885, he patented a new device for bright tobacco cultivation and marketed it through a descriptive pamphlet; see Horner, "Patent Plant-Bed Burner, and Its Application to Curing Tobacco in Barns."

46. William H. Gregory to Mary J. Davis, 1 Mar. 1879, Gregory Papers. Mrs. Elliott put virtually the same words into the mouth of one of the male characters in her novelette, *Days Long Ago*. "With you," he says to his intended, "life will be profitably spent, without you it will be a blank, and I a nonentity" (50). See also *Oxford Torchlight*, 19 Apr. 1887. Gregory was the one who spearheaded a local effort to obtain legislation to lower the cost of marriage licenses; see chapter 1, note 80.

47. *Oxford Torchlight*, 12 Mar. 1878; see also 14 Jan. 1879.

48. For Davis's rejection of a suitor because of his shaky financial position, see Mary J. Davis to William H. Gregory, 27 Oct. 1881, Gregory Papers. For Gregory's reports on his economic status, see William H. Gregory to Mary J. Davis, 12 Apr. 1882, and William H. Gregory to Mary J. Davis, 1 Jan. 1886, both in Gregory Papers.

49. William H. Gregory to Mary J. Davis, 1 Jan. 1886, and William H. Gregory to Mary J. Davis, 1 Jan. 1882, both in Gregory Papers.

50. See note 33 for a list of romantic fiction in the *Oxford Torchlight* and the *Granville Free Lance*.

51. Quotes from *Oxford Torchlight*, 9 June 1874, 1 Sept. 1874, and 4 Feb. 1879. Elliott, *Days Long Ago*. See also Grubb, "House and Home in the Victorian South." For similar prescriptive articles, see *Oxford Torchlight*, 4 July 1876, 30 Oct. 1877, 4 Dec. 1877, 18 Dec. 1877, 8 Jan. 1878, 29 Jan. 1878, 5 Feb. 1878, 5 Mar. 1878, 28 May 1878, 27 Aug. 1878, 8 Oct. 1878, 3 Dec. 1878, 7 Jan. 1879, 4 Feb. 1879, 15 Apr. 1879, 14 Oct. 1879, 23 Mar. 1886, 11 May 1886, 3 Aug. 1886, 15 Feb. 1887, 21 June 1887, and 26 Oct. 1887; *Granville Free Lance*, 11 Jan. 1878, 8 Mar. 1878, 17 May 1878, and 1 Apr. 1881; and *Oxford Leader*, 28 Sept. 1875. Obituaries also depicted women in the same way, as self-sacrificing servants to the needs of their families; see, for instance, *Oxford Torchlight*, 2 Nov. 1887.

52. Quote from A. R. Gregory to William H. Gregory, 15 June 1888, Gregory Papers. William H. Gregory to Mary Davis, 8 Apr. 1881, 10 Jan. 1883, 16 Jan. 1886, and Mary J. Davis to William H. Gregory, 6 Oct. 1883, all in Gregory Papers.

53. Quotes from Nannie Davis to Mary Davis Gregory, 12 June 1888, and Ann K. Davis to Mary Davis Gregory, 15 June 1888, both in Gregory Papers. See also William H. Gregory to Mrs. Ann K. Davis, 10 June 1888, Mollie L. to Mary Davis Gregory, 11 June 1888, B. R. S. Amis to Mary Davis Gregory, 15 June 1888, and Pattie to Mary Davis Gregory, 15 June 1888, all in Gregory Papers.

54. For examples, see women's letters in Gregory Papers, Bullock Papers, Hargrove Papers, and Bettie Shotwell Papers, Special Collections Library, Duke University, Durham. See also Censer, *North Carolina Planters and Their*

Children; Fox-Genovese, *Within the Plantation Household;* Friedman, *The Enclosed Garden,* esp. 5–6, 39–53, 111–12; McMillen, *Motherhood in the Old South;* Rable, *Civil Wars;* and Whites, *The Civil War as a Crisis in Gender.*

55. Quotes from Elliott, *Mrs. Elliott's Housewife,* 162; and *Oxford Torchlight,* 20 Feb. 1877. See also *Granville Free Lance,* 10 May 1878, 28 Mar. 1879, 4 Feb. 1881, and 11 Mar. 1882. One *Oxford Torchlight* article, 18 Jan. 1888, even urged women to learn a marketable skill so that if need be, they could support themselves.

56. *Oxford Torchlight,* 23 May 1876. For similar comments, see 17 Nov. 1874, 23 Feb. 1875, 18 May 1875, 23 Nov. 1875, 29 May 1877, 15 Jan. 1878, 4 May 1880, and 1 Feb. 1887. See also the *Oxford Torchlight's* coverage of the infanticide case against Frances Thorp, an African-American woman. The newspaper determined her guilt long before her trial, apparently finding it difficult to apply the "natural" characteristics of self-sacrifice and familial devotion to black women. The language used to describe Thorp set her in opposition to elite white feminine ideals: the newspaper described her as "indifferent to her fate," while the judge claimed that she was either "too obstinate in villainy to care" or that it was her "stupidity" or that she had a "heart of stone." Quotes from *Oxford Torchlight,* 3 Nov. 1874. See also *Oxford Torchlight,* 26 May 1874 and 27 Oct. 1874; and *State* v. *Goodwin,* 1874, and *State* v. *Thorp,* 1875, both in Criminal Action Papers, Granville County. An article reprinted by the *Oxford Torchlight* from the *Chicago Inter-Ocean* reinforced these images by applauding the wives of two black congressmen and then attributing their charm to the fact that it "would be difficult for a stranger to detect their relation to the African race"; see 16 Feb. 1886. For the ways virtuous white womanhood was constructed against black womanhood, see Carby, *Reconstructing Womanhood;* Higginbotham, "African-American Women's History and the Metalanguage of Race"; D. White, *Ar'n't I a Woman?*

57. The *Oxford Torchlight* insisted that men should provide for their families through their labor alone, see 3 Aug. 1886 and 7 June 1887.

58. For the building boom, see *Oxford Torchlight,* 18 Jan. 1876, 2 Apr. 1878, 24 Feb. 1880, and 12 Oct. 1880. See also *Granville Free Lance,* 6 May 1881. Although much of the new construction took place within Oxford, it was not specific to the town. Many of the new Oxford houses were actually built by rural planters, who either made their homes there or had dual residences in town and on their farms. Rural residents also patterned their homes along similar lines, although the changes were not as noticeable since the population was less concentrated. See Carlson, "Homeplace and Tobaccoland," 70; and M. Brown, "The Architecture of Granville County," 199–207. See also Bishir, *North Carolina Architecture,* 273–343; and M. Williams, *Homeplace.* Both Williams and Bishir, 287–95, point out that rural elites often adopted new styles and floorplans to signal their prosperity and differentiate themselves from their neighbors, but adapted the new designs to their own needs. As Williams argues, just because people lived in a house with specialized rooms that rigidly distinguished between private and public space did not neces-

sarily meant that they completely organized their lives around the same rigid separation; see esp. 93–114. See also Glassie, *Folk Housing in Middle Virginia*.

59. Quotes from Elliott, *Days Long Ago*, 26; Bishir, *North Carolina Architecture*, 223; and *Warrenton Gazette*, 19 Apr. 1873. See also Bishir, *North Carolina Architecture*, 245–57, 281–87, 342–54. The "Picturesque" was introduced to North Carolina in the antebellum period, but did not became popular until the postwar years. The houses built during the 1870s and 1880s in Granville County generally followed this design; for examples, see M. Brown, "The Architecture of Granville County," 199–207, 217–19.

60. Ann Davis to Mary Davis Gregory, 15 June 1888, Gregory Papers.

61. *Oxford Torchlight*, 28 May 1878. For children running in the streets see 9 June 1874, 22 June 1875, and 4 Mar. 1879; these complaints contrast sharply with the *Granville Free Lance* piece, 28 Mar. 1879, which advises that children must have a separate, quiet space within homes just for reading. For the connection between race, class, and elite whites' health concerns with poor black people's houses, see Hunter, "Household Workers in the Making." For these attitudes in Granville County, see *Oxford Torchlight*, 23 Nov. 1880, 22 Feb. 1881, 26 Apr. 1881, 14 June 1881, and 31 Aug. 1887. For the lack of definition between private and public in the houses of the poor, see Bishir, *North Carolina Architecture*, 281–95; M. Brown, "The Architecture of Granville County," 214–19; Hunter, "Household Workers in the Making," 59–111; Vlach, *Back of the Big House*, 18–32, 153–82; and M. Williams, *Homeplace*.

62. See, for instance, *Oxford Torchlight*, 31 Mar. 1874, 17 July 1874, 27 Oct. 1874, 29 June 1875, 5 Apr. 1881, 12 Apr. 1881, 26 Apr. 1881, 17 May 1881, 7 June 1881, 14 June 1881, 21 June 1881, 5 July 1881, 26 July 1881, 29 June 1886, 5 Oct. 1886, and 19 Oct. 1886.

63. *Oxford Torchlight*, 27 Aug. 1878.

64. *Oxford Torchlight*, 27 Oct. 1874.

65. William H. Gregory to Mary Davis, 2 Feb. 1888, Gregory Papers.

66. Quoted in Elliott, *Mrs. Elliott's Housewife*, 4; see also 1–21, 334–36.

67. S. A. Skinner to Bettie Shotwell, 31 Jan. 1887, and S. A. Skinner to Bettie Shotwell, 7 May 1888, both in Shotwell Papers. Bettie Shotwell's solution, however, was not the approved method of attaining the accoutrements of domesticity. The *Oxford Torchlight*, 7 June 1887, condemned women who worked to supplement their husbands' earnings, whose efforts were not only unnecessary, but harmful to their families. Such women "ruined" their husbands, who "were not compelled to support their wives"; they indulged in "extravagant" habits and squandered their paychecks on "personal adornment"; and, finally, they only needed extra money because of "their own deficient knowledge of housekeeping."

68. See *Oxford Torchlight*, 27 Oct. 1874, 22 Feb. 1876, 20 Feb. 1877, 18 Dec. 1877, 22 Jan. 1878, 5 Feb. 1878, 12 Feb. 1878, and 19 Feb. 1878. The home section, which always included household tips, was a regular feature in the *Granville Free Lance;* see also 27 Sept. 1878, 28 Feb. 1879, 11 Mar. 1881, and 10 Nov. 1882.

69. Julie Frayser to Mary J. Davis, 26 Sept. 1879, and Julie Frayser to Mary J. Davis, Aug. 1880, both in Gregory Papers. See also Shotwell Papers and Hargrove Papers.

70. *Oxford Torchlight*, 5 Aug. 1879; Elliott, *Days Long Ago*, 19, 20. See also *Oxford Torchlight*, 5 May 1874 and 31 May 1887; *Granville Free Lance*, 10 May 1878; and Elliott, *Mrs. Elliott's Housewife*. See also Grubb, "House and Home in the Victorian South."

71. Quotes from William H. Gregory to Mary J. Davis, 16 Jan. 1884, Gregory Papers; and *Oxford Torchlight*, 17 Feb. 1874, 2 Dec. 1879, and 8 Jan. 1878. See also *Oxford Torchlight*, 28 May 1878, 4 Feb. 1879, 28 Feb. 1882, 14 Mar. 1882, 23 Mar. 1886, 11 May 1886, 15 Feb. 1887, 21 June 1887, and 26 Oct. 1887; and *Granville Free Lance*, 3 Dec. 1880. The ideal of the home as a haven was central to the newspapers' short fiction and to Elliott, *Days Long Ago* and *Mrs. Elliott's Housewife*, esp. 63, 287–88.

72. For the importance of this transition, see Fields, *Slavery and Freedom on the Middle Ground*, 162–63; Painter, "The Journal of Ella Gertrude Clanton Thomas"; A. Scott, *The Southern Lady;* and Whites, *The Civil War as a Crisis in Gender*, 151–57.

73. *Oxford Torchlight*, 16 Nov. 1875.

74. *Oxford Torchlight*, 8 Jan. 1878. For similar analyses, see Bloch, "The Gendered Meanings of Virtue in Revolutionary America"; Hall and Davidoff, *Family Fortunes;* and Poovey, *Uneven Developments*.

75. *Oxford Torchlight*, 27 May 1879. The *Granville Free Lance* printed an article that, while applauding the domestic values of Middle Eastern culture, found it lacking because women were so restricted to that space that they could not improve themselves with education and other activities in the public sphere. For studies of the ways white middle-class southern women used domesticity to move into the public space, see note 7. Scholars have also emphasized that white women not only retained but often reinforced the racial and class hierarchies implicit in their particular view of domesticity and women's nature; see Hewitt, "In Pursuit of Power"; Painter, "The Journal of Ella Gertrude Clanton Thomas"; Rable, *Civil Wars*, 265–88; Wheeler, *New Women of the New South;* and Whites, "Rebecca Latimer Felton and the Problem of 'Protection' in the New South" and *The Civil War as a Crisis in Gender*, 132–98. This did not preclude the possibility for biracial cooperation among southern women, as other work reminds us; see J. Hall, *Revolt against Chivalry;* Lebsock, "Woman Suffrage and White Supremacy"; M. Frederickson, "'Each One Is Dependent on the Other'"; and Roydhouse, "Bridging Chasms." But it did make such work much more difficult.

76. Gilmore, *Gender and Jim Crow*. See also Higginbotham, *Righteous Discontent*.

Chapter 4: "I Am My Own Woman and Will Do as I Please"

1. *State* v. *Allen*, 1884, Criminal Action Papers, Granville County; Reid, *After the War*, 389.

2. *Watkins* v. *Watkins*, 1876, Divorce Records, Granville County.

3. *State* v. *Dalby*, 1866, Criminal Action Papers, Granville County. For complaints among whites in North Carolina about black women dressing out of their station, see Andrews, *The South since the War*, 186–87. See also Foner, *Reconstruction*, 85–87; Jones, *Labor of Love, Labor of Sorrow*, 69–70; and Litwack, *Been in the Storm So Long*, 244–47. For the confiscation of household property, see Hunter, "Household Workers in the Making," 6–7, 21–22; and Schwalm, "The Meaning of Freedom," 206–8.

4. Scholars have emphasized the ways African-American women in the late-nineteenth-century South carved out their own notions of womanhood and domesticity; see Bercaw, "The Politics of Household"; E. Brown, "Womanist Consciousness"; Bynum, *Unruly Women;* Frankel, "Freedom's Women"; Gilmore, *Gender and Jim Crow;* Hunter, "Household Workers in the Making"; Jones, *Labor of Love, Labor of Sorrow;* Rosen, "Race, Gender, and the Politics of Rape"; and Schwalm, "The Meaning of Freedom." See also Carby, *Reconstructing Womanhood;* Giddings, *When and Where I Enter;* Higginbotham, *Righteous Discontent;* and Tate, *Domestic Allegories of Political Desire*. Although far less work has been done on poor white women, it suggests that these women also defined their role as women very differently from their elite neighbors; see, for instance, Bynum, *Unruly Women;* and McCurry, *Masters of Small Worlds*. Hagood, in *Mothers of the South*, 75–76, makes this point in relation to white tenant farm women in North Carolina in the 1930s.

5. For the importance of women's labor to rural households in the South, see S. Holt, "Making Freedom Pay"; McCurry, *Masters of Small Worlds*, 56–61, 75–84; and Schwalm, "The Meaning of Freedom." For the importance to nineteenth-century households generally, see Boydston, *Home and Work;* and Jensen, *Loosening the Bonds*.

6. Quoted in Daniel, *Breaking the Land*, 26. On tobacco production, see Daniel, *Breaking the Land*, 25–26; and Tilley, *The Bright Tobacco Industry*, 37–49.

7. Daniel, *Breaking the Land*, 26–31; Tilley, *The Bright Tobacco Industry*, 49–88. See also Hagood, *Mothers of the South*, 87–88, 94–95; and McCurry, *Masters of Small Worlds*, 73–75.

8. For the way field work served to distinguish poor women from elite women, see Hagood, *Mothers of the South*, 75–91; and McCurry, *Masters of Small Worlds*, 78–84. Common white women regularly performed field work and, often, waged work. In addition to the above, see Bolton, *Poor Whites of the Antebellum South*, 38–39; Bradley and Williamson, *Rural Children in Selected Counties of North Carolina*, 72–73; and Friedman, *The Enclosed Garden*, 23. For African-American women, see Bercaw, "The Politics of Household," chap. 5; Bradley and Williamson, *Rural Children in Selected Counties of North Carolina*, 34–35; Frankel, "Freedom's Women"; Hunter, "Household Workers in the Making"; Jones, *Labor of Love, Labor of Sorrow*, 58–66, 74–75, 81–99; Schwalm, "The Meaning of Freedom"; and D. White, *Ar'n't I a Woman?* 119–41. See Janiewski, *Sisterhood Denied*, 28–38, for both poor white and African-American women in North Carolina.

9. Quotes from Hagood, *Mothers of the South*, 90, 89. For the discussion of women's preference for field work, see 77–91. See also Bradley and Williamson, *Rural Children in Selected Counties of North Carolina*, 35; Janiewski, *Sisterhood Denied*, 32; and Schwalm, "The Meaning of Freedom," 48, 50–51, 287–310, 316–24.

10. Quotes from Hagood, *Mothers of the South*, 89, 91; and Rawick, *The American Slave*, 14:220, 221. See also Rawick, *The American Slave*, 14:15, 81, 214, 217–22; Janiewski, *Sisterhood Denied*, 30–31; and Jellison, *Entitled to Power*.

11. Rawick, *The American Slave*, 14:81, 214.

12. U.S. Bureau of the Census, Population Schedules, 1870, 1880. In "Household Workers in the Making," Hunter makes a similar point on 139. See also E. Brown, "Womanist Consciousness"; Frankel, "Freedom's Women"; Gilmore, *Gender and Jim Crow;* Higginbotham, *Righteous Discontent;* and Schwalm, "The Meaning of Freedom," 316–24.

13. Hunter, in "Household Workers in the Making," 82, argues that in Atlanta, most, if not all black women worked for wages at least intermittently in the late nineteenth century. This strikingly high labor participation among women was largely attributable to the urban setting, which offered few economic alternatives other than waged work. But Hunter's research also suggests the monetary importance of women's waged labor to all African-American families in the postwar years. For the underrepresentation of black and white women's waged work in the census, see Bolton, *Poor Whites of the Antebellum South*, 38–39; Janiewski, *Sisterhood Denied*, 28; and Jones, *Labor of Love, Labor of Sorrow*, 74.

14. *Oxford Torchlight*, 1 Dec. 1874. J. C. Cooper was probably the son of the planter who owned William and Henderson Cooper, the two men accused of raping Susan Daniel; the son was instrumental in prosecuting Henderson Cooper after the war. For discussions of white images of the ideal black female servant, symbolized in the image of Mammy, see D. White, *Ar'n't I a Woman?* 46–61. White southerners generally frowned on even the small degree of independence waged labor allowed black women; see chapter 3. See also Hunter, "Household Workers in the Making" and "Domination and Resistance"; Painter, "The Journal of Ella Gertrude Clanton Thomas," 51–55; Rable, *Civil Wars*, 250–64; and Whites, *The Civil War as a Crisis in Gender*, 128–31.

15. Quote from *State* v. *Hart*, 1868, Criminal Action Papers, Granville County. See also Frankel, "Freedom's Women"; Hunter, "Household Workers in the Making" and "Domination and Resistance"; Jones, *Labor of Love, Labor of Sorrow*, 68–72; and Schwalm, "The Meaning of Freedom," 252–60, 293–324.

16. *State* v. *Pritchett*, 1890, Criminal Action Papers, Granville County. See Bynum, *Unruly Women*, 88–110, for elite distrust of poor single women, white and black.

17. *State* v. *Amis*, 1872, Criminal Action Papers, Granville County. For collective households, see Hunter, "Household Workers in the Making,"

75. Such collective strategies were important given the lack of economic options for black women in rural areas; see Janiewski, *Sisterhood Denied*, 42–43; and Jones, *Labor of Love, Labor of Sorrow*, 73–74.

18. *State* v. *O'Mary*, 1868, Criminal Action Papers, Granville County. For similar cases involving both poor white and African-American women, see *State* v. *Williams, Williams, and Humphries*, 1866, *State* v. *Merrimon*, 1866, *State* v. *Hicks*, 1868, and *State* v. *Bullock*, 1868, all in Criminal Action Papers, Granville County.

19. *State* v. *O'Mary*, 1868, Criminal Action Papers, Granville County. For O'Mary's and Gill's economic status, see U.S. Bureau of the Census, Population Schedule, 1850, 154, 155; and Tax List, 1872, Granville County. For the vulnerability of poor white women who lived outside a male-headed family, see Bolton, *Poor Whites of the Antebellum South*, 62–63; and Bynum, *Unruly Women*, 88–110. The dynamics of this case bears a close resemblance to those underlying witchcraft accusations in colonial America, described by Karlsen in *Devil in the Shape of a Woman*.

20. *State* v. *Amis*, 1872, Criminal Action Papers, Granville County. For poor white women's movement in public, see Friedman, *The Enclosed Garden*, 24–25. Some historians have noted that elite white women's roles were changing after the war in such a way as to allow them greater freedom of movement in the public sphere; see, for instance, Painter, "The Journal of Gertrude Clanton Thomas"; and A. Scott, *The Southern Lady*. Friedman, however, maintains that these changes did not really begin until the end of the nineteenth century; see *The Enclosed Garden*, 128–30. See Whites, *The Civil War as a Crisis in Gender*, 132–224, for a slightly different interpretation of this theme. The truth probably lies somewhere in between: some elite white women took on a more public role, while most did not until the end of the century. At any rate, elite white women's public lives were still circumscribed in comparison with those of poorer women.

21. There are at least twenty-one such cases between 1865 and 1888; see Criminal Action Papers, Granville County.

22. *State* v. *Hughie*, 1870, Criminal Action Papers, Granville County. For the assertive acts of poor white women in the North and South, see Bynum, *Unruly Women;* and Stansell, *City of Women*.

23. *State* v. *Thorp*, 1881, Criminal Action Papers, Granville County. See also Bynum, *Unruly Women*, 80–82; Hunter, "Household Workers in the Making," 80–81, and "Domination and Resistance"; Jones, *Labor of Love, Labor of Sorrow*, 70–71; Schwalm, "The Meaning of Freedom," 252; and D. White, *Ar'n't I a Woman?* 133–39, 151–52.

24. For the expectation that black women would assume primary responsibility for housework and childcare, see Frankel, "Freedom's Women"; Jones, *Labor of Love, Labor of Sorrow*, 63, 85–86; Schwalm, "The Meaning of Freedom," 84, 90–97; and D. White, *Ar'n't I a Woman?* 121–32. Hagood, in *Mothers of the South*, 92, makes a similar observation about poor white women. See also Ulrich, *Goodwives*, and *A Midwife's Tale*.

25. Quoted in Hagood, *Mothers of the South*, 100. See 92–107 for a discussion of housework. Janiewski, in *Sisterhood Denied*, 31–33, notes that few poor rural women, white or black, displayed much interest in housework despite promotional literature in farm journals.

26. Quote from Hagood, *Mothers of the South*, 90. Hunter, in "Household Workers in the Making," argues that black domestics, who performed the heaviest household labor, viewed elite white domestic standards from a very different perspective than their employers did. See also Bradley and Williamson, *Rural Children in Selected Counties of North Carolina*, 35–36, 72–73. Ransom and Sutch, in *One Kind of Freedom*, 99–103, point out that share-cropping provided no incentive to either employer or employee to improve the land or physical structures on it. But even if it had, poor southerners did not necessarily aspire to the creation of a bourgeois domestic home; see McCurry, *Masters of Small Worlds*, 73–75. Jones, in *Labor of Love, Labor of Sorrow*, and Hagood, in *Mothers of the South*, emphasize the practicality of black and poor white women's senses of domesticity. Yet, like twentieth-century rural women, they probably desired more domestic comforts and labor-saving household appliances; see Jellison, *Entitled to Power*.

27. For the Burwell family see Tax List, 1879, Granville County; and U.S. Bureau of the Census, Population Schedule, 1880. For the importance of motherhood to black women's lives, see Jones, *Labor of Love, Labor of Sorrow;* Schwalm, "The Meaning of Freedom," 84, 91, 104–9; and D. White, *Ar'n't I a Woman?* 105–18, 159–60. For poor white women, see Hagood, *Mothers of the South*.

28. In contrast to the housing of the elite, most North Carolina houses contained only a few rooms, where the residents lived without making elaborate distinctions between public and private spaces; see Bishir, *North Carolina Architecture*, 287–99; M. Brown, "The Architecture of Granville County," 214–19; Vlach, *Back of the Big House*, 153–82; and M. Williams, *Homeplace*. Hunter, in "Household Workers in the Making," 78–81, notes a lack of distinction between both "home" and "work" and "family" and "community" in the lives of Atlanta's black washerwomen. Hagood, in *Mothers of the South*, 92–107, makes a similar observation about white tenant women. See also Cecil-Fronsman, *Common Whites*, 150–68; Kenzer, *Kinship and Neighborhood in a Southern Community;* and McCurry, *Masters of Small Worlds*, 73–84.

29. For women's wage rates, see Thomas W. Hay to Jacob F. Chur, 25 Sept. 1867, Annual Reports of Operations Received from Staff and Subordinate Officers, RBRFAL; wage statistics for Granville County in the annual reports of the Bureau of Labor Statistics (1887–1900). See also Frankel, "Freedom's Women"; Hunter, "Household Workers in the Making," 130–31; and Janiewski, *Sisterhood Denied*, 38.

30. C. W. Raney to N. A. Miles, 19 Apr. 1868, Kittrell's Springs, Letters Received, Records of the Assistant Commissioner. Other planters were also reluctant to hire women with children for the same reasons; see, for instance, Henry W. Jones to Susan Currin and Family, 27 May 1867, Jones Papers. One

of the complaints of the first freedmen's convention was that women and children were being turned out by planters; see *Raleigh Journal of Freedom,* 7 Oct. 1865.

31. Quote from *State* v. *Jordan,* 1867, Criminal Action Papers, Granville County. See also *State* v. *Thorp,* 1882, Criminal Action Papers, Granville County. Frances Thorp's infanticide case highlights these same themes. The testimony revealed that Thorp found it difficult to secure housing as a single mother and that her lover had pressured her to get rid of her child; see *State* v. *Goodwin,* 1874, and *State* v. *Thorp,* 1875, both in Criminal Action Papers, Granville County.

32. *State* v. *Rogers,* 1866, and *State* v. *Norwood,* 1866, both in Criminal Action Papers, Granville County. The court records contain many other examples. In *State* v. *Smith,* 1866, Criminal Action Papers, Granville County, the indictments identified the prisoner as Caswell Smith, while the complaint named him as Caswell Davis. In *State* v. *Norman,* 1867, Criminal Actions Concerning Slaves and Free Persons of Color, Granville County, the complaint identified him only as "William a Freedman," the summons gave him the last name of his former master, "Burwell," and the indictment named him "William Norman"; even then, the court mistakenly identified him as "Bill," which had to be crossed out and replaced with "William." In *State* v. *"Cato" a Freedman,* 1868, Criminal Action Papers, Granville County, "Cato" never acquired a last name or lost the quotes surrounding his name because he extracted himself from the case by jumping bail. For discussions of the importance of names and naming practices among African Americans, see Gutman, *The Black Family in Slavery and Freedom,* 230–56; and Hunter, "Household Workers in the Making," 1–2.

33. For scholars emphasizing the individualistic aspect of antebellum common white men's identity, see Cecil-Fronsman, *Common Whites,* 62–66, 137–38, 170–78; Gorn, "'Gouge and Bite, Pull Hair and Scratch'"; and Wyatt-Brown, *Southern Honor.* In *Subduing Satan,* Ownby also argues that the fighting, drinking, and carousing existed in a tense, but symbiotic relationship with a strong religious tradition and idealization of the home. The relationship between the two aspects of white male culture is probably best understood in terms of the way men's individualism outside their homes rested on their particular position as men who could claim independent status as heads of households or potential heads of households, which thus linked them back to their places within their families and communities.

34. Quotes from North Carolina Soldiers of Lee's Army to Zebulon B. Vance, 24 Jan. 1865, George L. Hancock to Zebulon B. Vance, 25 Sept. 1864, Parrott Hardee to Zebulon B. Vance, 16 Oct. 1864, Petition of the Senior Reserves of the Home Guard to Zebulon B. Vance, 14 Sept. 1864, and Malcom B. McRae to Zebulon B. Vance, 29 Jan. 1865, all in Vance Papers. Governor Vance's papers are filled with similar requests. For desertion, see Bardolph, "Inconstant Rebels"; and Escott, *Many Excellent People,* 64–65. In "A Test Case of the 'Crying Evil,'" Reid emphasizes that disorder and poverty

back home led many to leave the army, although he maintains that desertion among North Carolina troops was less than previously assumed. As some scholars have emphasized, common white men supported the Confederacy because of the importance they placed on their own independence, which they defined as a combination of property ownership, control over their own labor, and the ability to support and protect their families; see Hahn, *The Roots of Southern Populism*, 86–133; McCurry, *Masters of Small Worlds* and "Two Faces of Republicanism"; Ford, *Origins of Southern Radicalism*, 338–73; and Whites, *The Civil War as a Crisis in Gender*, 15–40.

35. Quotes from Mrs. Sue O. Coneley to Zebulon B. Vance, 5 Jan. 1865, and [illegible] to Zebulon B. Vance, 10 Jan. 1865, both in Vance Papers. Governor Vance's papers are filled with similar requests. See also Bynum, *Unruly Women*, 112–29, and "War within a War"; and Janiewski, *Sisterhood Denied*, 33–34.

36. Quotes from Petition of the Mothers, Wives, and Sisters of the Members of the 45th N.C. Regiment to Zebulon B. Vance, 24 Oct. 1864, Vance Papers; and Bynum, *Unruly Women*, 117. See also these letters to Vance: Petition of the Mothers, Wives, and Sisters of the 45th N.C. Regiment, Sept. 1864, Sue O. Coneley, 5 Jan. 1865, and no name [a woman], 13 Dec. 1864, all in Vance Papers; Bercaw, "Defeat from Within"; Bynum, *Unruly Women*, 130–50; Faust, "Altars of Sacrifice"; and Hunter, "Household Workers in the Making," 26.

37. Goddin quoted in Yearns and Barrett, *North Carolina Civil War Documentary*, 98; Eliza Evans to Zebulon B. Vance, 18 Oct. 1864, Vance Papers. See also these letters to Vance: Nancy Jordan, 12 June 1864, J. C. Hackney, 13 Oct. 1864, Eliza Evans, 10 Nov. 1864, and Maria L. Samkin, 15 Nov. 1864, all in Vance Papers. For the cotton raid, see *State v. Henley and Others*, 1865, Criminal Action Papers, Granville County. For the reference to the women plundering the mill, see Bynum, *Unruly Women*, 128–29. Some propertied people hid goods or hired guards to protect them; see unnamed case (testimony of Moses Bullock) 1866, and *Hardy et al. v. Clark*, 1868, both in Civil Action Papers, Granville County. For other examples of wartime resistance to Confederate policies, see Auman, "Neighbor against Neighbor"; Bynum, *Unruly Women*, 111–50, and "War within a War"; Durrill, *War of Another Kind;* Escott, *Many Excellent People*, 32–84, and "The Moral Economy of the Crowd in Confederate North Carolina"; and Foner, *Reconstruction*, 11–18.

38. Escott, *Many Excellent People*, 52–58; Foner, *Reconstruction*, 17; Hahn, *The Roots of Southern Populism*, 137–69.

39. Quotes from L. J. Horner to William H. Holden, 15 Jan. 1869, Holden Papers; Smith H. Powell to Tod R. Caldwell, 27 Jan. 1873, Tod R. Caldwell, Governor's Papers, NCDAH; and *Raleigh Gazette*, 4 Feb. 1871. For a petition similar to Horner's, see James A. Bullock to R. W. Lassiter, 22 Mar. 1869, Holden Papers. See also *Raleigh Blasting-Powder,* 19 June 1872; and *North Carolina Standard*, 6 June 1866, 18 July 1866. For discussions of debt relief generally, see Escott, *Many Excellent People*, 40, 96–97, 100, 140–42; Foner,

Reconstruction, 212, 326–27; Hahn, *The Roots of Southern Populism*, 193–203; and Reidy, *From Slavery to Agrarian Capitalism*, 164–65.

40. *Oxford Torchlight*, 13 Oct. 1874.

41. Quotes from *Raleigh Journal of Freedom*, 7 Oct. 1865; Berlin, Reidy, and Rowland, *The Black Military Experience*, 725, 726; Berlin, Miller, Reidy, and Rowland, *The Wartime Genesis of Free Labor: The Upper South*, 166. See also documents in Berlin, Miller, Reidy, and Rowland, *The Wartime Genesis of Free Labor: The Upper South*, 202–3, 238, 239–40; and in Berlin, Reidy, and Rowland, *The Black Military Experience*, 389–90, 680–88, 694–702, 713–30. See also Fields, *Slavery and Freedom on the Middle Ground*, 143–44; and Frankel, "Freedom's Women."

42. Quote from T. B. Wilson, *The Black Codes of the South*, 52. Jones, *Labor of Love, Labor of Sorrow*, esp. 44–109. See also Bercaw, "The Politics of Household," chap. 5; Foner, *Reconstruction*, 85–87; Frankel, "Freedom's Women"; Jaynes, *Branches without Roots*, 229–32; and Schwalm, "The Meaning of Freedom," 295–96, 318–24.

43. Rosa Freeman's petition from Berlin, Miller, and Rowland, "Afro-American Families in the Transition from Slavery to Freedom," 99–100 (quote from 100); Sarah Fields and Catherine Massey quoted in Berlin, Reidy, and Rowland, *The Black Military Experience*, 675, 667. The expectations that men should support their families economically figured prominently in the letters and petitions of other African-American women as well. See Berlin, Reidy, and Rowland, *The Black Military Experience*, 402–3, 664–65, 678–80, 682, 686–87, 698–700.

44. Berlin, Reidy, and Rowland, *The Black Military Experience*, 667; *Raleigh Journal of Freedom*, 7 Oct. 1865; Hunter, "Household Workers in the Making," 74.

45. *State* v. *Ellington*, 1866, and *State* v. *Lewis*, 1866, both in Criminal Action Papers, Granville County. For illuminating discussions of bandits and tricksters as heroes in African-American culture, see Joyner, *Down by the Riverside*, 172–95; L. Levine, *Black Culture and Black Consciousness*, 81–135, 367–440; and Roberts, *From Trickster to Badman*.

46. Some black leaders opposed debt relief measures because it would keep land in the hands of its present owners and out of the reach of African Americans; see Foner, *Reconstruction*, 326. Some of the most common and persistent complaints among black soldiers and other black men working for the Union army were insufficient and irregular wages that were also far less than those received by whites; see Berlin, Reidy, and Rowland, *The Black Military Experience*, 20–21, 362–405. This is not to say that African Americans operated as "rational," profit-maximizers of classical liberal ideology, but that they considered reasonable, steady wages essential to their independence. For discussions of African Americans' views of their labor and the value that should be placed on it, see Foner, *Reconstruction*, 102–10, 377–79, and *Nothing but Freedom;* T. Holt, *The Problem of Freedom;* and Jaynes, *Branches without Roots*. Although Republican officials and black leaders sponsored

legislation designed to help black workers, they rarely questioned free labor precepts and the market economy that resulted in low wages and landlessness; see Foner, *Reconstruction*, 346–411; and T. Holt, *Black over White* and *The Problem of Freedom*. There were, however, some notable exceptions, particularly among black leaders; see Reidy, "Aaron A. Bradley"; see also Foner, *Black Lawmakers*, 38, 48, 52, 72, 80–81, 110, 135, 136, 227.

47. It never occurred to most white employers that black men should receive a wage that enabled them to support their families; see Bercaw, "The Politics of Household," chap. 5; Frankel, "Freedom's Women"; and Hunter, "Household Workers in the Making," 114. See Foner, *Reconstruction*, 86–87, for black women's return to paid employment for whites.

48. Silas Curtis et al. to William W. Holden, 11 Aug. 1869, Holden Papers; Gates County petition quoted in R. Alexander, *North Carolina Faces the Freedmen*, 102; Edward Ancrum to Tod R. Caldwell, 15 Sept. 1872, Caldwell Papers. For the economic and political aspects of terrorism against African Americans, see Escott, *Many Excellent People*, 113–35; Fields, *Slavery and Freedom on the Middle Ground*, 143–47; and Foner, *Reconstruction*, 425–44.

49. Quoted in R. Alexander, *North Carolina Faces the Freedman*, 19.

50. Quotes from *Raleigh Journal of Freedom*, 21 Oct. 1866 and 30 Sept. 1865. See also Foner, *Freedom's Lawmakers*, 212.

51. Dennett, *The South as It Is*, 150. See also Dittmer, "The Education of Henry McNeal Turner"; Moss, "Alexander Crummell"; Painter, "Martin R. Delany"; and Stuckey, "A Last Stern Struggle."

52. For Galloway's speech, see *Raleigh Semi-Weekly Record*, 2 Sept. 1865; and *State* v. *Allen*, 1884, Criminal Action Papers, Granville County.

53. The United Brotherhood quoted in R. Alexander, *North Carolina Faces the Freedmen*, 79. See also *Augusta Colored American*, 13 Jan. 1866.

54. *State* v. *Nuttall et al.*, 1874, Criminal Action Papers, Granville County.

55. For discussions of this point, see Fields, *Slavery and Freedom on the Middle Ground*, 146–47, and "Slavery, Race, and Ideology"; and Senechal, *The Sociogenesis of a Race Riot*.

56. Samuel W. Watts to William W. Holden, 14 Aug. 1869, Holden Papers. Postwar thieves showed a particular fancy for horses. Livestock of all kinds was scarce at the time, and horses were particularly dear. That horses also functioned as status symbols only heightened their value. In fact, Democratic lawmakers were so concerned with horse theft in the years immediately following southern surrender that they made the crime a capital offense. The preamble explains the legislators' concerns: "Whereas the crime of stealing horses and mules hath, of late, notwithstanding the punishment provided by law, become much more common than formerly, to the great loss of many persons, and the injury of public morals." See *Public Laws of North Carolina* (1866–67), chap. 62. A Union plantation superintendent on St. Helena's Island, South Carolina, described the status associated with horses with particular clarity in requesting a horse from his superiors: African Americans "have always seen a white man on a horse, and have got to think it so far a

badge of power & caste, that they will hardly lift their hats to a white man on foot." See Berlin, Glymph, Miller, Reidy, Rowland, and Saville, *The Wartime Genesis of Free Labor: The Lower South,* 174. See also Isaac, *The Transformation of Virginia,* 53–57, 98–101.

57. *State* v. *Bragg et al.,* 1867, Criminal Action Papers, Granville County.

58. Cecil-Fronsman, *Common Whites,* 40–55, 98–111, 154–56. See also Bolton, *Poor Whites of the Antebellum South;* Ford, *The Origins of Southern Radicalism;* Hahn, *The Roots of Southern Populism;* and McCurry, *Masters of Small Worlds.* All of these works emphasize that the South's political institutions managed to contain class conflict among whites; but the absence of widespread opposition to planter power in electoral politics did not eliminate resentment of individual planters or a social structure that favored planters' interests.

59. *State* v. *Perry,* 1868, Criminal Action Papers, Granville County.

60. Ibid. For background on George Vann, see *State* v. *Vann,* 1867, and *State* v. *Horner,* 1867, both in Criminal Action Papers, Granville County. Biracial cooperation in theft and the black market was not unusual during the war or in the years immediately afterward. See William A. Philpott to Zebulon B. Vance, 3 Oct. 1864, Vance Papers, for evidence of such activities within Granville County. See also Bolton, *Poor Whites of the Antebellum South,* 46–51, 107–10; Bynum, "War within a War" and *Unruly Women,* 47, 122–25; and Escott, *Many Excellent People,* 77.

61. *State* v. *Perry,* 1868, Criminal Action Papers, Granville County.

62. Ibid. Common whites often drew a distinction between themselves, who lived primarily on their own labor, and wealthy whites, who lived primarily on the labor of others. For instance, one common white woman of Wake County drew society into three classes according to their relationship to labor: slaveholders who had enough labor without hiring it, nonslaveholders who had to rely on their own labor or hire it, and the poorest whites who "never did work." See Nancy P. Richardson to Zebulon B. Vance, 1 Nov. 1864, Vance Papers. Emancipation did not necessarily change this outlook, particularly when the wealthy still benefited from African Americans' labor. See also McCurry, *Masters of Small Worlds,* 47–48.

63. For background on Charles Cole's father, Barzillius L. Cole, see U.S. Bureau of the Census, Population Schedule, 1850, 171; and Tax Lists, 1856, 1859, 1867, 1872, Granville County. The "Constitution and By-Laws of the Granville Grays" lists Barzillius Cole as one of its members. For Charles B. Cole, see Tax List, 1872, Granville County.

64. For the Klan's ties to the Democratic party, see Silas Curtis et al. to William W. Holden, 11 Oct. 1868, Holden Papers. For background on Cole's political career, see *State* v. *Jones and Cole,* 1875, and *State* v. *Blow and Britt,* 1875, both in Criminal Action Papers, Granville County. See also Tourgée, *A Fool's Errand;* and Trelease, *White Terror.*

65. *State* v. *Jones and Cole,* 1875, and *State* v. *Blow and Britt,* 1875, both in Criminal Action Papers, Granville County. See also Tourgée, *A Fool's Errand,* 331–33.

66. Quoted in Rawick, *The American Slave*, 14:15.

67. Bercaw, "The Politics of Household," chap. 5; Crouch and Madaras, "Reconstructing Black Families"; Foner, *Reconstruction*, 88; Frankel, "Freedom's Women"; and Schwalm, "The Meaning of Freedom," 344–48. Between 1865 and 1887 there were twenty-four suits in the local court charging physical abuse, abandonment, or bigamy; most were filed against men. See Criminal Action Papers, Granville County.

68. *State v. Henderson*, 1883, Criminal Action Papers, Granville County. For a similar case, see *State v. Moore*, 1869, Criminal Action Papers, Granville County. Mann, in "Slavery, Sharecropping, and Sexual Inequality," maintains that black men assumed patriarchal power over women after the war; see also Bynum, "Reshaping the Bonds of Womanhood." Frankel, in "Freedom's Women," takes a more subtle approach to black men's assertions of authority within their families, pointing out that the notion of "patriarchy" misrepresents their power in southern society. As she argues, African-American men could never be patriarchs in the same way that elite white or even poor white men could because they lacked both the material resources and the ideological authority, in the form of white skin, necessary to assume that role.

69. *State v. Lawrence*, 1882, Criminal Action Papers, Granville County.

70. *State v. Mabrey*, 64 N.C. 592 (1870); *State v. Oliver*, 70 N.C. 60 (1874). See also *State v. Mabrey*, #9,616, and *State v. Oliver*, #10,815, both in Supreme Court Original Cases, NCDAH.

71. *State v. Lawrence*, 1882, and *State v. Henderson*, 1883, both in Criminal Action Papers, Granville County. In *Heroes of Their Own Lives*, Gordon comments on how domestic violence was not the result of dysfunctional households but rather embedded in the power relationships of what was considered a "normal" family. For discussions of domestic violence, see also Pleck, "Wife Beating in Nineteenth-Century America" and *Domestic Tyranny*; and Nadelhaft, "Wife Torture."

72. *State v. Burwell*, 1880, Criminal Action Papers, Granville County.

73. *State v. Rhodes*, 61 N.C. 453 (1868).

74. *State v. Lawrence*, 1882, Criminal Action Papers, Granville County.

75. *State v. Burwell*, 1880, Criminal Action Papers, Granville County. In "Smiling through Her Tears," Censer argues that antebellum white women also had to conform to the court's vision of victimized womanhood to obtain divorces.

76. *State v. Rhodes*, 61 N.C. 453 (1868).

Chapter 5: "Privilege" and "Protection"

1. Quote from *State v. Noblin*, 1870, Criminal Action Papers, Granville County. Edwards, "Sexual Violence, Gender, Reconstruction, and the Extension of Patriarchy." See also Clinton, "Reconstructing Freedwomen" and "Bloody Terrain"; and Rosen, "Interracial Rape and the Politics of Reconstruction."

2. Hamilton, *The Correspondence of Jonathan Worth*, 2:1082; Stafford quoted in Escott, *Many Excellent People*, 22. For references to the "better class," see, for instance, Hamilton, *The Correspondence of Jonathan Worth*, 2:1257. The attitude was widespread among conservatives; see, for instance, Escott, *Many Excellent People*, 85–112; McCurry, *Masters of Small Worlds*, 247–51; and Olsen, "An Incongruous Presence," 167.

3. For these racialized images, see Jordan, *White over Black*. For a discussion of the way race and class mixed to cast African Americans as permanent dependents, see chapter 2. See also Fields, *Slavery and Freedom on the Middle Ground;* and T. Holt, "'An Empire over the Mind'" and *The Problem of Freedom*.

4. Quotes from Hamilton, *The Papers of Thomas Ruffin*, 4:63; and Hamilton, *The Correspondence of Jonathan Worth*, 2:1156. Ruffin also argued that the Constitutional Convention had no power because it had been called by military authority in violation of the existing state constitution and the powers vested in the people, since many voters had been disqualified under the president's provisions; see Hamilton, *The Papers of Thomas Ruffin*, 4:62–71. Edward Conigland was so taken with Ruffin's arguments against the constitution that he wrote immediately asking Ruffin for permission to submit the letter for duplication in the *Wilmington Journal* and later sent it to the *Raleigh Sentinel* as well; see Hamilton, *The Papers of Thomas Ruffin*, 4:72–73, 77–78. For opposition to the apportionment system, see Hamilton, *The Papers of Thomas Ruffin*, 4:61–62. For arguments critical of the conservative position, see *North Carolina Standard*, 30 May 1866, 8 Aug. 1866, and 22 Aug. 1866. For an overview of the debate in North Carolina, see Escott, *Many Excellent People*, 105–12. See also Perman, *Reunion without Compromise*.

5. Quotes on Worth's racial views from Hamilton, *The Correspondence of Jonathan Worth*, 2:875, 1095; and on the Cooper-Daniel case from Gov. Jonathan Worth to Pres. Andrew Johnson, 31 Dec. 1867, 9, Worth, Governor's Letter Book, 1867–68. See the introduction for an extended analysis of the Cooper-Daniel case. For the intransigence of North Carolina conservatives under Johnson's Reconstruction plan, see, for instance, Escott, *Many Excellent People*, 85–135; Evans, *Ballots and Fence Rails*, 61–102; and H. Raper, *William W. Holden*, 59–85.

6. Quotes from Hamilton, *The Papers of Thomas Ruffin*, 4:63; and *Raleigh Sentinel*, 29 Aug. 1865. See also Hamilton, *The Papers of Thomas Ruffin*, 4:76–77, 132–34; and Escott, *Many Excellent People*, 106–9, 113–35. In fact, Ruffin was completely incapable of grasping the idea that freedpeople were separate from their masters' households. He argued against apportionment on a white basis, maintaining that all blacks should be included for the same reason that white women and children were. Although permanently disfranchised, African Americans, white women, and white children "are as much bound by the laws that may be made and therefore, as much interested in them as the white men." Yet, while white women had delegates "who are their neighbors, know their wants and condition and sympathise with them both

in their wants and wishes" to represent their interests, African Americans did not. Including them in the apportionment would give former slaveholders, who knew the interests of their black neighbors best, the ability to represent freedpeople in the same way that men represented women. Hamilton, *The Papers of Thomas Ruffin*, 4:64.

7. Quotes from Hamilton, *The Correspondence of Jonathan Worth*, 2:1156, 860. Others echoed these fears; see, for instance, Hamilton, *The Correspondence of Jonathan Worth*, 2:1045. Escott, in *Many Excellent People*, underscores elite white distrust of both poor whites and blacks as well as their enduring fear of biracial alliances in his analysis of nineteenth-century North Carolina politics. See also Goodwyn, *The Democratic Promise;* Kousser, *The Shaping of Southern Politics;* Robinson, "Beyond the Realm of Social Consensus"; and Woodward, *Origins of the New South*.

8. Hamilton, *The Correspondence of Jonathan Worth*, 2:1004, 1048; see also 2:1215. One of Worth's correspondents called a Republican leader one of the "*blackest* radicals" in the state, referring not to his skin color, but to his politics (2:953).

9. For warnings that conservatives would provoke the North's wrath, see *North Carolina Standard*, 26 Sept. 1866 and 3 Oct. 1866. Conservatives refused to heed the advice of even longtime friends. Writing from Washington, D.C., Benjamin F. Hedrick, a confidant of Governor Worth, advised him of the rising antagonism toward conservative policies; see, for instance, Hamilton, *The Correspondence of Jonathan Worth*, 2:903. See also Escott, *Many Excellent People*, 104–5.

10. For evidence of biracial collaboration during and immediately after the war, see chapter 4, note 60.

11. *Wilmington Herald*, 10 June 1865, reprinted from the *Raleigh Progress*. For the persistence of tensions among whites in postwar North Carolina politics, see Escott, *Many Excellent People*, 136–70; and Olsen, "An Incongruous Presence." See also Hyman, *The Anti-Redeemers*. William W. Holden was particularly critical of elite white conservative rule and published numerous articles on the subject as editor of the *North Carolina Standard*.

12. Quotes from *Wilmington Herald*, 9 June 1865. The *Raleigh Sentinel's* reports of the legislative debates over the Black Code give the moderates' position. See also R. Alexander, *North Carolina Faces the Freedman*, 39–51; and T. B. Wilson, *The Black Codes of the South*, 96–115. For moderate support for the notion of equal civil rights and an expanded social role for African Americans, see, for instance, *Raleigh Sentinel*, 8 Aug. 1865; *North Carolina Standard*, 14 Feb. 1866, 10 Oct. 1866; and *Wilmington Herald*, 17 July 1865, 30 Jan. 1866, 6 Mar. 1866. The *Wilmington Herald*, however, remained opposed to enfranchising blacks; see, for instance, 8 July 1865 and 27 July 1865. For Holden's initial opposition to universal manhood suffrage, see his address to the 1866 freedmen's convention in the *North Carolina Standard*, 17 Oct. 1866; see also 3 Oct. 1866 and 10 Oct. 1866. In the 1880s, he renounced his support of civil and political rights for African Americans.

13. Quotes from *Wilmington Herald*, 9 June 1865. This distinction between civil and political rights, common to both the North and the South, came up regularly in debates over the status of freedpeople; see, for instance, *North Carolina Standard*, 14 Feb. 1866; and *Wilmington Herald*, 17 July 1865. Moderates assumed that suffrage should be "earned" through intelligence or possession of property; see *Raleigh Sentinel*, 8 Aug. 1865; *Wilmington Herald*, 14 July 1865; *Raleigh Journal of Freedom*, 30 Sept. 1865. For similar debates within the national Republican party, see Foner, *Reconstruction*, 239–61. For white North Carolina Republicans' tenuous commitment to racial equality, see Olsen, "An Incongruous Presence," 165.

14. Quotes from Tourgée, *A Fool's Errand*, 166; and *Raleigh Journal of Freedom*, 7 Oct. 1865. See also Olsen, *A Carpetbagger's Crusade;* and Tourgée, *The Invisible Empire*, 15–20. For "radical" Republicans generally, see Evans, *Ballots and Fence Rails*, 105–27; and Foner, *Reconstruction*, 228–39.

15. These points are most fully elaborated in T. Holt, "'An Empire over the Mind'" and *The Problem of Freedom*.

16. Hamilton, *The Correspondence of Jonathan Worth*, 2:902, 903. For Hedrick's position on slavery, see Hamilton, "Benjamin Sherwood Hedrick." Hamilton, a conservative apologist and racial reactionary, approves of Hedrick's opposition to slavery precisely because it was "not based upon moral grounds nor did the solicitude for the negro have anything to do with it." Rather, Hedrick and others like him thought "the wrong of slavery was not to the slave, but to the non-slaveholder" (5–6). See also Powell, *Dictionary of North Carolina Biography*, 3:95.

17. There were, however, important differences in strategy among African Americans. Conservatives, for instance, advocated hard work and cooperation with southern whites, while shunning political rights, property redistribution, and other more militant claims that radical leaders supported. Many black leaders fell out somewhere between the two poles, with moderates emphasizing civil and political rights, but not the economic issues supported by poorer blacks in rural areas. For discussions of these issues, see R. Alexander, *North Carolina Faces the Freedmen*, 15–20; Foner, *Reconstruction*, 110–19; T. Holt, *Black over White;* and Reidy, *From Slavery to Agrarian Capitalism*, 179–80, 192–99, 208–9.

18. Quotes from *North Carolina Faces the Freedmen*, 80; and *Raleigh Semi-Weekly Record*, 2 Sept. 1865. The editor of the *Nashville Colored Tennessean* echoed these sentiments, arguing that true freedom was impossible without the public power to protect it; reprinted in the *Raleigh Journal of Freedom*, 30 Sept. 1865.

19. *North Carolina Standard*, 14 Feb. 1866. For black abolitionists, see Horton, "Double Consciousness" in *Free People of Color;* Litwack and Meier, *Black Leaders of the Nineteenth Century;* Martin, *The Mind of Frederick Douglass;* and Nash, *Race and Revolution*, 57–87, 167–201. Frederick Douglass, who believed that the emphasis on racial differences obscured the inclusive brotherhood of man implied in the spirit of natural rights, worked fully within

the ideology of universal humanism, as Waldo Martin has termed it. Other black leaders placed more importance on the distinctive ways race had shaped the history and identity of African Americans. But the basic principles of universal rights still influenced their arguments, even those who advocated emigration. However much race mattered in their social, economic, and political agendas, they still maintained that all people deserved not just freedom from slavery but also the right to determine the course of their own destiny and the shape of the society in which they lived. Few white abolitionists envisioned the kind of racial equality proposed by black leaders, but they too grounded their opposition to slavery in the ideology of universal rights. Yet white abolitionists tended to see grateful, younger siblings who would then follow the lead of their white patrons, rather than claim their own voice and participate on equal footing in the nation's social and political institutions. See C. Hall, "Missionary Stories" and " Competing Masculinities" in *White, Male, and Middle Class*. Nonetheless, the image of brothers and sisters carried very different implications than the dominant southern one of parent and child.

20. Quoted in R. Alexander, *North Carolina Faces the Freedmen*, 91. In North Carolina and across the South, freedpeople used phrases from the Declaration of Independence and imagery from the Revolution to carry their demands for racial equity. The delegates to the 1865 freedmen's convention hailed emancipation as the culmination of the nation's purpose, describing it as "a triumph of just principles, a practical assertion of the fundamental truths laid down in the great charter of Republican liberty, the Declaration of Independence." See *Raleigh Journal of Freedom*, 7 Oct. 1865. In its previous issue, 30 Sept. 1865, the newspaper invoked the Declaration to justify full political rights: "If the Declaration of Independence was not based on a lie," then "one man or class *can't* legislate for another." Often, a copy of the Declaration even graced Union League meetings; see Foner, *Reconstruction*, 283. See also Foner, *Freedom's Lawmakers*, 38, 84, 128, 137.

21. Quotes from the *Augusta Colored American*, 13 Jan. 1866; and R. Alexander, *North Carolina Faces the Freedmen*, 91. For similar renderings of African Americans' place in history, see Foner, *Freedom's Lawmakers*, 36, 39, 40, 60, 106, 108, 110, 156, 201. See also Foner, *Reconstruction*, 288.

22. *Oxford Torchlight*, 8 July 1879. For Fourth of July celebrations in black communities elsewhere in the South, see Reidy, *From Slavery to Agrarian Capitalism*, 179.

23. *State* v. *Hughes et al.*, 1874, Criminal Action Papers, Granville County.

24. Quotes from *Wilmington Herald*, 8 July 1865; Foner, *Reconstruction*, 288; Turner quoted in *Augusta Colored American*, 13 Jan. 1866. Black legislators' opposition to measures disfranchising former Confederates demonstrates their commitment to an inclusive definition of universal rights; see Balanoff, "Negro Legislators in North Carolina," 32–33; Foner, *Reconstruction*, 324; Hume, "Negro Delegates," 141–42; and Perman, *The Road to Redemption*, 36–37. See also Foner, *Freedom's Lawmakers*, 80, 131, 138, 176, 208, 231.

25. Poem quoted in A. Alexander, *Ambiguous Lives,* 140.

26. Quotes from Hodes, "The Sexualization of Reconstruction Politics," 404; and *Augusta Colored American,* 13 Jan. 1866. For similar statements linking manhood and political rights, see Foner, *Freedom's Lawmakers,* 18, 22, 91, 137, 191, 215. First in the abolitionist movement and later during Reconstruction, many black women, in particular, did work to include themselves in the universal brotherhood of man, arguing for greater public rights. They were joined by a few of their male counterparts, most prominently Frederick Douglass. A few southern African American leaders, including Abraham H. Galloway and James E. O'Hara from North Carolina, supported women's rights. Even for those who supported women's rights, however, the issue remained tied to the movement for racial equality. In both the North and the South, the security of racial privilege allowed middle-class white women to see gender as something distinct from race and led them to separate from the men of their communities to agitate for their own rights. Such a strategy made less sense to African-American women because their own well-being so clearly rose and fell with that of the race as a whole. This did not mean, however, that black women remained silent on these issues. As Gilmore shows in *Gender and Jim Crow,* black women actually began mobilizing for equal rights and the vote in North Carolina before white women. But in doing so, they were careful not to jeopardize the political and economic goals of their menfolk. See also Carby, *Reconstructing Womanhood;* Higginbotham, *Righteous Discontent;* Horton, "Freedom's Yoke"; and Martin, *The Mind of Frederick Douglass.* For James E. O'Hara and Abraham H. Galloway, see Foner, *Freedom's Lawmakers,* 81–82, 164.

27. For references to taxes and military service, see *Raleigh Journal of Freedom,* 30 Sept. 1865, 7 Oct. 1865; and *Raleigh Semi-Weekly Record,* 2 Sept. 1865. See also Foner, *Freedom's Lawmakers,* 60, 106, 110, 156 for military service; 36, 40, 201 for labor; and 18 for taxes.

28. Quotes from *Raleigh Journal of Freedom,* 7 Oct. 1865; and R. Alexander, *North Carolina Faces the Freedmen,* 102. See also Foner, *Freedom's Lawmakers,* 88; Petition of the Freedmen in the Trent Settlement to Thaddeus Stevens, in Padgett, "Reconstruction Letters from North Carolina: Part 1," 185–87.

29. Quote from *Raleigh Journal of Freedom,* 14 Oct. 1865.

30. Quotes from Moses M. Hester et al. to William W. Holden, 9 Oct. 1868, and Silas L. Curtis et al. to William W. Holden, 11 Oct. 1868, both in Holden Papers. Hodes, in "The Sexualization of Reconstruction Politics," also argues that the Klan targeted households, raped women, and sexually mutilated black men specifically to "unman" black men and thus push them out of the political arena. Contemporary and secondary accounts not only testify to the role of the Klan and other vigilante actions against African Americans in destroying the Republican party but also emphasize that it sought to do so by targeting and destroying black households; see Evans, *Ballots and Fence Rails,* 69–73; Olsen, "The Ku Klux Klan"; *Testimony Taken by the Joint Select Committee to Inquire into the Condition of Affairs in the Late Insurrectionary States;* Tourgée, *The Invisible Empire;* and Trelease, *White Terror.*

31. Petition by thirty-four Halifax County freedmen to Elihu Benjamin Washburne, in Padgett, "Reconstruction Letters from North Carolina: Part 4," 395–96. For African-American emigration from the South, see Cohen, *At Freedom's Edge;* Painter, *Exodusters;* and Reidy, *From Slavery to Agrarian Capitalism,* 181–84, 230–32.

32. John W. Johnson to Curtis H. Brogden, 1876, Curtis H. Brogden, Governor's Papers, NCDAH. For Granville County's black military company, see *State* v. *Hughes et al.,* 1874, Criminal Action Papers, Granville County; and *Oxford Torchlight,* 1 Apr. 1879. For black militias elsewhere, see Evans, *Ballots and Fence Rails,* 101–2, 138–39; Foner, *Freedom's Lawmakers,* 119, 131, 223; and Reidy, *From Slavery to Agrarian Capitalism,* 205, 219.

33. Bardaglio, "Rape and the Law in the Old South"; Bynum, *Unruly Women,* 117–18; Johnson, *Ante-Bellum North Carolina,* 508–10. For discussions of vigilante justice and rape, see J. Hall, "'The Mind That Burns in Each Body'" and *Revolt against Chivalry;* Williamson, *The Crucible of Race;* and Wyatt-Brown, *Southern Honor.*

34. For the rarity of rape cases, see Bynum, *Unruly Women,* 117; and Johnson, *Ante-Bellum North Carolina,* 658. While twenty-four cases in a twenty-year period may not seem like an overwhelming number, it was a dramatic change from the antebellum period. See *State* v. *Parker,* 1866, *State* v. *Cato,* 1868, *State* v. *Puryear et al.,* 1869, *State* v. *Ragland,* 1869, *State* v. *Noblin,* 1870, *State* v. *Baird,* 1872, *State* v. *Allen,* 1873, *State* v. *Dalby,* 1873, *State* v. *Wilson,* 1874, *State* v. *Adcock,* 1875, *State* v. *Stewart,* 1876, *State* v. *Wilkerson,* 1876, *State* v. *Burton,* 1876, *State* v. *Regan,* 1878, *State* v. *Allen,* 1882, *State* v. *Johnson,* 1882, *State* v. *Burton,* 1882, *State* v. *Peace,* 1883, *State* v. *Wilkerson,* 1883, *State* v. *Humphries,* 1885, *State* v. *Bass,* 1885, *State* v. *Jones,* 1886, *State* v. *Adkins,* 1887, and *State* v. *Blackwell,* 1887, all in Criminal Action Papers, Granville County. Local courts elsewhere duplicated the pattern; see Criminal Action Papers, 1865–90, Edgecombe County, NCDAH; and Criminal Action Papers, 1865–90, Orange County. These cases, moreover, underrepresent resistance to sexual assault, since they include only those cases in which the official charge was rape or attempted rape or where sexual assault was specifically mentioned in the complaint or testimony. They do not include cases dismissed by justices or those that involved sexual assault but were tried as simple assault. Many other incidents also went unreported. No doubt poor white and black women hesitated to submit to the ordeal of a trial, at which their actions and intentions would be treated with skepticism, if not open hostility. Some may have preferred to resolve the matter within their communities, without state interference. For a discussion of this point, see Rapport, "The Freedmen's Bureau as a Legal Agent for Black Men and Women in Georgia," 39–41. Like women today, many postbellum Granville women might have been reluctant to prosecute those men most likely to assault them—friends and relatives. Indeed, they could not prosecute either husbands or fathers. Marital rape was unheard of and North Carolina did not pass a law prohibiting incest until 1879. See *Laws and Resolutions of North Carolina* (1879), chap. 16. See also Bardaglio, "'An Outrage upon Nature.'"

35. Hodes, "Wartime Dialogues on Illicit Sex" and "The Sexualization of Reconstruction Politics"; Rosen, "Race, Gender, and the Politics of Rape" and "Struggles over 'Freedom.'"

36. Two sexual assault cases were listed as affray and assault; see *State* v. *Ragland*, 1869, and *State* v. *Puryear et al.*, 1869, both in Criminal Action Papers, Granville County. These two cases just happened to have testimony attached; no doubt many other assault cases also involved sexual violence. Excluding domestic violence cases, there were fifty-two cases involving male-on-female violence between 1865 and 1887; see Criminal Action Papers, Granville County.

37. Quotes from Andrews, *The South since the War*, 177; and *State* v. *Rhodes*, 61 N.C. 453 (1868). For the importance of class distinctions in determining attitudes toward southern women, see Bynum, *Unruly Women;* Fox-Genovese, *Within the Plantation Household*, 192–241; and McCurry, *Masters of Small Worlds*, 121–28. For similar attitudes in the North, see Stansell, *City of Women*.

38. Petition for Clemency for William Somerville, May 5–10, 1869, Holden Papers. As the petitioners explained, a majority of the jury had favored acquittal. Unable to sway the others, however, those who favored Somerville finally accepted a compromise, reducing the initial rape charge to attempted rape instead.

39. The *National Republican* article was reprinted in the *Oxford Torchlight*, 23 Sept. 1879. See also *State* v. *Barnett*, 1879, Criminal Action Papers, Granville County. For the racial distinctions of whites, northern and southern, see Carby, *Reconstructing Womanhood;* Frankel, "Freedom's Women"; J. Hall, "'The Mind That Burns in Each Body'"; hooks, *Ain't I a Woman*, 27–34; Hunter, "Household Workers in the Making"; D. White, *Ar'n't I a Woman?* 27–61; and Rosen, "Rape and the Politics of Gender and Race."

40. *Oxford Torchlight*, 23 Sept. 1879.

41. *State* v. *Peace*, 1883, Criminal Action Papers, Granville County; *Oxford Torchlight*, 25 Nov. 1879.

42. *State* v. *Brooks*, 76 N.C. 1 (1877). The Supreme Court generally lessened the burden of proof for women, loosening evidentiary standards for penetration, allowing for women's emotional state in questioning, tightening its treatment of cases involving girls under the age of consent, and applying far stricter standards to men in determining their intent, particularly when they were black; see *State* v. *Hodges*, 61 N.C. 231 (1867); *State* v. *Storkey*, 63 N.C. 7 (1868); *State* v. *Hargrave*, 65 N.C. 466 (1871); *State* v. *Johnson*, 67 N.C. 55 (1872); *State* v. *Neely*, 74 N.C. 425 (1876); *State* v. *Johnston*, 76 N.C. 209 (1877); *State* v. *Laxton*, 78 N.C. 564 (1878); *State* v. *Dancy*, 78 N.C. 437 (1878); *State* v. *Dancy*, 83 N.C. 608 (1880); *State* v. *Staton*, 88 N.C. 654 (1883); *State* v. *Mitchell*, 89 N.C. 521 (1883); and *State* v. *Long*, 93 N.C. 543 (1885). See the final section of this chapter for a discussion of the standards applied in determining intent and their racial implications. For the kind of scrutiny women generally received in rape cases, see, for instance, *State* v. *Marshall*, 61 N.C. 49 (1866); and *State* v. *Daniel*, 87 N.C. 507 (1882).

43. *State* v. *Stewart*, 1876, Criminal Action Papers, Granville County.

44. *State* v. *Puryear,* 1869, and *State* v. *Bragg,* 1872, both in Criminal Action Papers, Granville County.

45. *State* v. *Stewart,* 1876, Criminal Action Papers, Granville County.

46. *State* v. *Allen,* 1882, and *State* v. *Puryear,* 1869, both in Criminal Action Papers, Granville County.

47. *State* v. *Stewart,* 1876, Criminal Action Papers, Granville County.

48. *State* v. *Puryear,* 1869, *State* v. *Stewart,* 1876, *State* v. *Allen,* 1882, and *State* v. *Bragg,* 1872, all in Criminal Action Papers, Granville County.

49. *Oxford Torchlight,* 25 Jan. 1876; see also *Oxford Torchlight,* 23 Sept. 1879.

50. *Laws and Resolutions of North Carolina* (1879), chap. 156. For slander cases in Granville County, see *State* v. *Richmond,* 1888, and *State* v. *Davis,* 1886, both in Criminal Action Papers, Granville County. See also A. King, "Constructing Gender."

51. *State* v. *Regan,* 1878, Criminal Action Papers, Granville County; *Oxford Torchlight,* 12 Mar. 1878 and 30 Apr. 1878.

52. *State* v. *Regan,* 1878, Criminal Action Papers, Granville County; *Oxford Torchlight,* 12 Mar. 1878 and 30 Apr. 1878.

53. *State* v. *Boothe and Oakley,* 1875, Criminal Action Papers, Granville County. They pled guilty to the charges; see *State* v. *Boothe and Oakley,* Apr. Term 1876, Superior Court Minutes, Granville County, NCDAH. See also *State* v. *Webb et al.,* 1875, Criminal Action Papers, Granville County. The charivari, a southern custom that can be traced back to medieval Europe, is a communal, ritualized form of discipline for someone who had deviated from accepted community norms in some way. The victim is serenaded with music and singing, sometimes tarred and feathered, and occasionally ridden out of the community. See, for instance, Wyatt-Brown, *Southern Honor,* 435–61.

54. The defendants entered a guilty plea and the judgment was suspended on payment of costs; see *State* v. *Webb et al.,* July Term 1875, Superior Court Minutes, Granville County. For discussions of the different sexual standards applied to men and women as well as those applied to women of different classes, see Bardaglio, *Reconstructing the Household;* and Bynum, *Unruly Women.* See also Gilfoyle, *City of Eros;* Smith-Rosenberg, *Disorderly Conduct;* and Stansell, *City of Women.*

55. *State* v. *Bass [alias Chavis],* 1885, Criminal Action Papers, Granville County; for verdict and sentence see *State* v. *Bass [alias Chavis],* Sept. Term 1885, Superior Court Minutes, Granville County. See also *State* v. *Baird,* 1872, *State* v. *Johnson,* 1882, *State* v. *Jones,* 1886, *State* v. *Blackwell,* 1887, and *State* v. *Adkins,* 1887, all in Criminal Action Papers, Granville County. John Jones was sentenced to five years in the state penitentiary; see *State* v. *Jones,* Spring Term 1885, Superior Court Minutes, Granville County. Such treatment of black-male-on-white-female rape was not uncommon; see Bardaglio, "Rape and the Law in the Old South."

56. *Raleigh Journal of Freedom,* 14 Oct. 1865.

57. *State* v. *Cooper,* 1864–67, Criminal Actions Concerning Slaves and Free Persons of Color, Granville County. For men's names on cases of sexual vi-

olence, see *State* v. *Adcock*, 1875, and *State* v. *Blackwell*, 1887, both in Criminal Action Papers, Granville County.

58. *State* v. *Baird*, 1872, and *State* v. *Allen*, 1873, both in Criminal Actions Papers, Granville County.

59. *State* v. *Peace*, 1883, Criminal Action Papers, Granville County.

60. Ibid.; *State* v. *Overby*, 1883, Criminal Action Papers, Granville County. The grand jury, however, did not indict Overby.

61. *State* v. *Peace*, 1883, Criminal Action Papers, Granville County. In her testimony, Martha Overby's mother labels her daughter's experience rape, but her description suggests that she treated it otherwise at the time. Beyond the difficulties of explaining her ideas about sexuality and marriage, Martha Overby could not even sue for breach of promise. In 1877, the North Carolina Supreme Court had declared that a breach of promise to marry did not constitute fraud; see *Moore* v. *Mullen*, 77 N.C. 327 (1877). Minow's analysis of the limits of legal categories in *Making All the Difference* speaks directly to Martha Overby's and other poor white and black women's dilemmas. As she argues, the law is preoccupied with static categories, "ready to contain whatever new problem may arise" (8). These categories rest on concepts of difference that treat as "marginal" and "inferior" "any person who does not fit the normal model of the autonomous, competent individual" (10). Marked by multiple differences, African-American and poor white women did not even fit into the already limited categories assigned to women.

62. *Laws of North Carolina* (1876–77), constitution, art. 4, sec. 27, and chap. 154; *Laws and Resolutions of North Carolina* (1879), chap. 92; *Public and Private Laws of North Carolina* (1889), chap. 504. See also Escott, *Many Excellent People*, 166–70; and Perman, *The Road to Redemption*, 193–220.

63. Quotes from *State* v. *Mitchell*, 1877, Criminal Action Papers, Granville County; and *Oxford Torchlight*, 20 July 1880.

64. Bardaglio, *Reconstructing the Household*. See also Grossberg, *Governing the Hearth*.

65. Quotes from *State* v. *Oliver*, 70 N.C. 60 (1874); and *State* v. *Pettie*, 80 N.C. 367 (1879). The cases dealing with domestic issues are too numerous to list here; for representative cases that extended the court's control over the private sphere, see, for instance, *Beard* v. *Hudson*, 61 N.C. 180 (1867); *State* v. *Rhodes*, 61 N.C. 453 (1868); *State* v. *Harris*, 63 N.C. 1 (1868); *Stout* v. *Woody*, 63 N.C. 37 (1868); *State* v. *Hairston and Williams*, 63 N.C. 451 (1869); *State* v. *Reinhardt and Love*, 63 N.C. 547 (1869); *Biggs* v. *Harris*, 64 N.C. 413 (1870); *State* v. *Mabrey*, 64 N.C. 592 (1870); *State* v. *Adams and Reeves*, 65 N.C. 537 (1871); *State* v. *Brown*, 67 N.C. 470 (1872); *Mitchell* v. *Mitchell*, 67 N.C. 307 (1872); *State* v. *Alford*, 68 N.C. 322 (1873); *Horne* v. *Horne*, 72 N.C. 530 (1875); *Thompson* v. *Thompson*, 72 N.C. 32 (1874); *Long* v. *Long*, 77 N.C. 304 (1877); *State* v. *Shaft*, 78 N.C. 464 (1878); *State* v. *Keesler*, 78 N.C. 469 (1879); *Miller* v. *Miller*, 78 N.C. 102 (1878); *Webber* v. *Webber*, 79 N.C. 572 (1878); *Scoggins* v. *Scoggins*, 80 N.C. 319 (1879); *Muse* v. *Muse*, 84 N.C. 35 (1881); *White* v.

White, 61 N.C. 453 (1868); *State* v. *Huntley,* 91 N.C. 617 (1884); *State* v. *Edens,* 95 N.C. 693 (1886); and *Johnson* v. *Allen,* 100 N.C. 131 (1888). The court, however, kept itself out of the issue of child abuse; see *State* v. *Jones,* 95 N.C. 588 (1886).

66. *Taylor* v. *Taylor,* 76 N.C. 433 (1877).

67. *The Matter of Frank Bumpass and Ella Lumsford, Matt Lumsford, and Rosa Lumsford,* 1881, Apprentice Bonds, Granville County.

68. *State* v. *Neely,* 74 N.C. 425 (1876).

69. Ibid. The state supreme court later stepped back from this extreme stance and overturned *Neely* in *State* v. *Massey,* 86 N.C. 658 (1882). The following year, however, the court returned to a position close to that of *Neely* in *State* v. *Mitchell,* 89 N.C. 521 (1883). Both *Massey* and *Mitchell,* moreover, suggest the extent to which the lower courts determined cases according to the principle set out in *Neely.*

Chapter 6: The "Best Men"

1. *State* v. *Taborn,* May Term 1887, Superior Court Minutes, Granville County. For the fire, see *Oxford Torchlight,* 15 Mar. 1887.

2. The Granville County Knights of Labor left no sources and the *Oxford Torchlight* rarely mentioned the order except to ridicule it. In this chapter I have pieced the organization's story together from various local sources and two revealing letters written to the *Journal of United Labor* (the official publication of the national Knights of Labor) by Robert Cohen, the white masterworkman of the black local. By bringing the presence of the Knights into focus, Cohen's letters provide the framework necessary to fit together the remaining pieces of the story. These dramatic events in Granville County defy traditional historical narratives that, following the lead of Rayford Logan in *The Negro in American Life and Thought,* define the 1880s as the "nadir" of southern history and focus on either Reconstruction or Populism. Other historians have begun to explore the intervening years, picking up on the insights of Woodward, in *The Strange Career of Jim Crow,* Goodwyn, in "Populist Dreams and Negro Rights," and Kousser, in *The Shaping of Southern Politics.* Studies of the southern Knights of Labor have pointed to the importance of these years; see Gould, "The Strike of 1887"; Kahn, "The Knights of Labor and the Southern Black Worker"; Kessler, "The Organization of Negroes in the Knights of Labor"; McLaurin, *The Knights of Labor in the South* and "The Knights of Labor in North Carolina Politics"; McMath, "Southern White Farmers and the Organization of Black Farm Workers"; and Rachleff, *Black Labor in the South.* Other historians have looked back to the 1880s for the roots of Populism; see Goodwyn, *The Democratic Promise;* Hahn, *The Roots of Souther Populism;* and McMath, "Sandy Land and Hogs in the Timber." A few studies, such as Greenwood's *Bittersweet Legacy,* are beginning to treat the late nineteenth century as a syncretic whole. Scholars approaching the period from the perspective of women have also emphasized the importance of the

1880s for the black community; see Gilmore, *Gender and Jim Crow;* and Higginbotham, *Righteous Discontent.*

3. Silas L. Curtis et al. to William W. Holden, 11 Oct. 1868. See also Moses M. Hester et al. to William W. Holden, 9 Oct. 1868, Holden Papers.

4. Quotes from James A. Bullock to R. W. Lassiter, 22 Mar. 1869, and Silas Curtis et al. to William W. Holden, 11 Aug. 1869, both in Holden Papers; Frank McGhee quoted in B. White, *In Search of Kith and Kin,* 34. See also W. A. Johnson et al. to William W. Holden, 18 Aug. 1869, Holden Papers.

5. *Oxford Torchlight,* 14 Nov. 1876, 21 Nov. 1876, 5 Dec. 1876, 19 Dec. 1876, 2 Jan. 1877, 9 Jan. 1877, and 20 Feb. 1877.

6. Quote from Anderson, *Race and Politics in North Carolina,* 4. For border changes, see Carlson, "Homeplace and Tobaccoland," 77. Many Democrats within Granville opposed the creation of Vance County precisely because they feared it would undermine the local party; see *Oxford Torchlight,* 18 Jan. 1881, 25 Jan. 1881, 29 Mar. 1881, 19 Apr. 1881, and 17 May 1881; and *Granville Free Lance,* 21 Jan. 1881, 4 Feb. 1881, and 15 Apr. 1881.

7. Quote from *North Carolina Standard,* 24 Oct. 1866. As Olsen notes in "An Incongruous Presence," white Republicans "were likely to have been Whigs or Douglas Democrats, opponents of secession, outspoken critics of the Confederacy, leaders in the peace movement, and/or advocates of democratic reform" (164). For tensions within the Democratic party, see *Oxford Torchlight,* 30 Oct. 1877, 18 June 1878, and 7 Sept. 1880; and *Granville Free Lance,* 22 Feb. 1878, 22 Mar. 1878, and 5 Apr. 1878. The proliferation of independent candidates who broke away from the Democratic party suggest the political consequences of these tensions. For enduring conflicts among whites that continued to plague Democrats after they seized control of southern state governments, see Escott, *Many Excellent People,* 136–95; Hyman, *The Anti-Redeemers;* and Perman, *The Road to Redemption.*

8. The *Raleigh Sentinel* quoted in Perman, *The Road to Redemption,* 123. For efforts of the Democrats across the South to address apathy and get out the vote, see Perman, *The Road to Redemption,* 125–31, 149–77. For white apathy within Granville County, see *Granville Free Lance,* 5 Nov. 1880 and 10 Nov. 1882.

9. Quotes from *Oxford Torchlight,* 30 Apr. 1878; see also 26 Mar. 1878, 9 Apr. 1878, 11 June 1878, and 13 July 1886.

10. Quote from *Oxford Torchlight,* 24 Aug. 1880; the writer was protesting taxes the legislature placed on tobacco manufacturing and peddling in its previous session. Statistics from Tilley, *The Bright Tobacco Industry,* 547. For the commercialization of southern agriculture and the declining economic conditions of whites across the South, see Escott, *Many Excellent People,* 172–79, 220–40; Ford, "Rednecks and Merchants"; Goodwyn, *Democratic Promise;* Hahn, *The Roots of Southern Populism,* 137–203; and Hyman, *The Anti-Redeemers,* 10–16, 205–7.

11. See Tilley, *The Bright Tobacco Industry,* 346–95, for the geographic expansion of bright tobacco culture; 234–36 for the change to once-a-year

marketing. This change to a short marketing period began in the mid-1890s at the behest of Bright Belt farmers, like those in Granville County, who felt threatened by farmers in eastern North Carolina, where tobacco matured earlier and could be marketed earlier as well. For typical fears of competition, see *Oxford Torchlight*, 9 Mar. 1886 and 15 Feb. 1887.

12. Quote from Bureau of Labor Statistics, *Thirteenth Annual Report* (1899), 42. Tilley calls the period from 1865 to 1885 "The Era of Small Scale Manufacturing"; afterward, as she argues, large-scale manufacturing took over; see *The Bright Tobacco Industry*, 489–544. For other complaints from farmers about price-fixing and the American Tobacco Company, see Bureau of Labor Statistics, *Fifth Annual Report* (1891), 82; and Bureau of Labor Statistics, *Seventh Annual Report* (1893), 74. For the trial in Granville County, see *State* v. *Currin and Others*, 1890, Criminal Action Papers, Granville County. The American Tobacco Company was broken up under the Sherman Anti-Trust Act.

13. Figures from U.S. Bureau of the Census, Agricultural Schedules, 1880, 1990, Population Schedules, 1880, 1900. For laborers' problems with irregular employment, see Bureau of Labor Statistics, *First Annual Report* (1887), 77–80. For the drop in wage rates, see annual reports of the Bureau of Labor Statistics (1887–1900).

14. U.S. Bureau of the Census, Agricultural Schedules, 1870, 1880, Population Schedules, 1870, 1880, 1900.

15. Quote from Bureau of Labor Statistics, *First Annual Report* (1887), 108. The annual reports of the Bureau of Labor Statistics (1887–1900) are filled with similar comments. This same bias was evident in the *Raleigh Progressive Farmer*, the official newspaper of the Farmer's Alliance. The newspaper devoted most of its space to the mortgage system, which farm owners increasingly relied on to obtain funds to plant their crops, which often resulted in the loss of their lands. Its calls for self-sufficiency also applied primarily to farm owners, who were able to select their crop mix. But the newspaper was only minimally concerned with tenants, whom it tended to lump together with wage laborers in the category "farm labor." The distinction is most clear in the newspaper's summary of Leonidas L. Polk's address to the Inter State Convention of Farmers; see *Raleigh Progressive Farmer*, 12 Jan. 1888; see also 17 Feb. 1886, 24 Feb. 1886, 3 Mar. 1886, 10 Mar. 1886, 17 Mar. 1886, 24 Mar. 1886, 14 Apr. 1886, and 14 July 1886. For similar sentiments, see *Oxford Torchlight*, 17 Feb. 1886, 9 Mar. 1886, and 30 Mar. 1886.

16. Bureau of Labor Statistics, *First Annual Report* (1887), 97. Mortgage figures from U.S. Bureau of the Census, Population Schedule, 1900.

17. Quote from Bureau of Labor Statistics, *First Annual Report* (1887), 105. For the tenor of complaints, see the annual reports of the Bureau of Labor Statistics (1887–1900). For population statistics, see *Twelfth Census of the United States*, 1:32. The population did decline between 1880 and 1890 (from 31,286 to 24,484), but that was because a sizeable portion of Granville was cut off in 1881 to create Vance County.

18. See *Oxford Torchlight,* 17 Feb. 1885, 24 Feb. 1885, 3 Mar. 1885, 17 Mar. 1885, 14 Apr. 1885, 16 Mar. 1886, 4 Jan. 1887, 25 Jan. 1887, 1 Feb. 1887, and 6 Oct. 1887; *Raleigh Progressive Farmer,* 10 Nov. 1886. For opposition to Democratic tax policies, see *Oxford Torchlight,* 24 Aug. 1880. For common whites' opposition to Democratic economic policies generally, see Escott, *Many Excellent People,* 188–92; and Hyman, *The Anti-Redeemers.* See also R. Brown, "The Southern Range"; Durrill, "Producing Poverty"; Hahn, *The Roots of Southern Populism;* and McMath, "Sandy Land and Hogs in the Timber."

19. Quotes from *Oxford Torchlight,* 10 Aug. 1886 and 2 Nov. 1886; see also 9 Nov. 1886, 16 Nov. 1886, 30 Nov. 1886, and 7 Dec. 1886.

20. Quotes from *Oxford Torchlight,* 4 Jan. 1887; Howell quoted in *Oxford Public Ledger,* 22 July 1890. See also *Oxford Torchlight,* 25 Jan. 1877 and 1 Feb. 1887. Granville County Stock Law Petitions, Boxes 17 and 18, 1887, General Assembly Session Records, NCDAH. The *Oxford Torchlight* later withdrew its support of the stock law when it became apparent that the political repercussions would be more severe than originally anticipated; see the 10 Aug. 1886 issue.

21. Arnold quoted in Foner, *Freedom's Lawmakers,* 10. For similar complaints by black leaders elsewhere in the South, see 18, 23, 80–81, 193, 196, 216. *Oxford Torchlight* reports also highlight these issues; see 14 July 1874, 1 Aug. 1876, 22 Aug. 1876, 3 Oct. 1876, 10 Oct. 1876, 25 June 1878, 6 Aug. 1878, 6 June 1880, 14 Sept. 1880, and 21 Sept. 1880. See also Foner, *Reconstruction,* 346–64, 539–53; Greenwood, *Bittersweet Legacy,* 81–88; Olsen, "An Incongruous Presence"; Perman, *The Road to Redemption,* 22–56, 135–48; Reidy, *From Slavery to Agrarian Capitalism,* 186–214; and Robinson, "Plans Dat Comed from God."

22. R. W. Lassiter quoted in Perman, *The Road to Redemption,* 33; *Oxford Torchlight,* 6 May 1879. For the Republicans' support for internal improvements, see Foner, *Reconstruction,* 298–99, 379–92; and Perman, *The Road to Redemption,* 32–34. For open collaboration between North Carolina Republicans and Democrats on commercial development, see Perman, *The Road to Redemption,* 67–76. Woodward's *Origins of the New South* is the classic statement of the rise of a business and commercial elite within the South; see also Ayers, *The Promise of the New South.* During Granville's 1879 municipal election, the *Oxford Torchlight* supported a "railroad ticket," composed of Republicans and Democrats committed to building up rail transportation; see 22 Apr. 1879 and 29 Apr. 1879. For a harmony of interests between elite white Republicans and Democrats on the issue of commercial development, see Durrill, "Producing Poverty"; Escott, *Many Excellent People,* 196–219; Foner, *Reconstruction,* 210–14; and Reidy, *From Slavery to Agrarian Capitalism,* 189–90, 215–41, 247. For collaboration within Granville County, see *Oxford Torchlight,* 8 June 1875, 15 June 1875, 18 Mar. 1879, and 17 Feb. 1880. For articles arguing that internal improvements were in the public interest, see *Oxford Torchlight,* 24 Feb. 1874, 12 May 1874, 29 Sept. 1874, 3 Nov. 1874, 18 May 1875, 18 Mar. 1879, 1 Apr. 1879, 15 Apr. 1879, 6 May 1879, 20 Jan. 1880, 24

Feb. 1880, 3 Aug. 1880, 10 Aug. 1880, 8 Feb. 1881, 24 May 1881, 7 June 1881, 16 Aug. 1881, and 8 June 1886. Other articles focused on the ways internal improvements would boost Oxford's economy, but always contained the implicit assumption that Oxford's commercial success was in everyone's interests. Virtually every issue of the *Oxford Torchlight* and the *Granville Free Lance* carried an article promoting internal improvements.

23. Articles in the *Oxford Torchlight* portrayed the first railroad scheme as very popular; see 8 June 1875, 4 Mar. 1879, 25 Mar. 1879, 22 Apr. 1879, and 16 Sept. 1879. Buried amidst the enthusiasm were reports that several townships voted against taxes for the project; see 13 May 1879 and 16 Aug. 1881. Apparently, some African Americans in Oxford organized their own group to support the railroad; see *Granville Free Lance*, 21 Mar. 1879 and 28 Mar. 1879. But some black leaders elsewhere in the South began openly criticizing Republicans for funding internal improvements while ignoring African Americans' economic problems; see Foner, *Freedom's Lawmakers*, 80–81. For growing opposition among whites to Republican support for economic development and the growing tax burden, see Foner, *Reconstruction*, 512–63; Olsen, "An Incongruous Presence," 175–78; Perman, *The Road to Redemption*, 221–36; and Thornton, "Fiscal Policy and the Failure of Radical Reconstruction in the Lower South." Later, common whites would criticize Redeemer governments on exactly the same grounds; see Hyman, *The Anti-Redeemers*, 98–123.

24. For figures on black landownership, see S. Holt, "A Time to Plant," 88. There were 2,258 African-American adult males aged twenty-one and older in the county in 1900; see U.S. Bureau of the Census, *Twelfth Census of the United States*, vol. 1, Population, part 2, 196. Of course, black women also owned land. But, assuming that African-American men over age twenty were more likely to be household heads, this comparison gives a rough idea of how many households owned land. Between 1880 and 1900, the African-American population of Granville dropped from 17,679 to 11,887. U.S. Bureau of the Census, *Twelfth Census of the United States*, vol. 1, Population, part 1, 550. The largest decline, between 1880 and 1890, from 17,679 to 12,360, was not because of emigration, but because a large section of Granville was cut off in 1881 to create Vance County. Reports of out-migration proliferated during the 1880s in the *Oxford Torchlight;* see 20 Jan. 1880, 10 Feb. 1880, 12 Jan. 1886, 16 Mar. 1886, and 5 July 1887; see also *Raleigh Progressive Farmer,* 17 Mar. 1886 and 24 Mar. 1886. For figures on property ownership in black landowning households, see S. Holt, "A Time to Plant," 240, 242–43.

25. Divisiveness within the party suggests dissatisfaction; see, for instance, *Oxford Torchlight,* 3 Oct. 1876 and 24 Oct. 1876. Evans, in *Ballots and Fence Rails,* 156–66, also points out that by the 1870s the Republican party offered little but offices, and even those began to disappear once conservative Democrats seized control of the state government. For disillusionment among blacks with the Republican party in particular and party politics in general,

see Escott, *Many Excellent People*, 184–85; and Greenwood, *Bittersweet Legacy*, 72–74. Many historians have concluded that the Republican party ultimately ignored African Americans' most pressing economic and political concerns; see Evans, *Ballots and Fence Rails;* Foner, *Reconstruction;* T. Holt, *Black over White;* Perman, *The Road to Redemption*, 22–56; and Reidy, *From Slavery to Agrarian Capitalism*, 186–214.

26. For the organization of the Oxford Knights, see *Journal of United Labor*, 10 June 1886, 2094, and 10 Aug. 1886, 2141. Garlock, in *Guide to the Local Assemblies of the Knights of Labor*, 357, identifies Local 7478 as black and Local 8127 as white. Because the Granville County Knights of Labor left no written records, there are no membership lists, minutes from meetings, or information about the activities of the locals. Although an extremely unreliable source for accurate information about the Knights, the *Oxford Torchlight*, 13 July 1886, attributed 150 members to the black local. If correct, then a majority of the black membership would have been wage laborers because there were not enough skilled artisans, professionals, merchants, and propertyholders in Oxford's black community to account for the majority of the membership. The white local likely had quite a few poor members as well. According to McLaurin, in "The Knights of Labor in North Carolina Politics," "the Knights enjoyed their most spectacular growth in the summer and fall of 1886" (299). Kahn, in "The Knights of Labor and the Southern Black Worker," 53–54, notes that Raleigh Knights sent organizers into other North Carolina cities and recruited members through newspaper advertisements and circulars during 1885 and 1886. The organization of the Oxford Knights probably resulted from these efforts.

27. For profiles of the business community and occupational structure in Oxford, see *Chataigne's North Carolina State Directory and Gazetteer, 1883–84*, 351–56; *Branson's North Carolina Business Directory for 1884*, 330–36; *Branson's North Carolina Business Directory, 1890*, 311–17; and *Branson's Business Directory, 1896*, 295–300. See also U.S. Bureau of the Census, Population Schedule, 1880. In *The Bright Tobacco Industry*, 213, 260, Tilley describes Oxford as a small marketing town with little local manufacturing. For revealing discussions of the town's lack of industry, see also *Oxford Torchlight*, 21 June 1881, 28 June 1881, 5 July 1881, 12 July 1881, and 2 Aug. 1881.

28. For planters who lived in town, see M. Brown, "The Architecture of Granville County," 199–205. For an example of the mobility of workers, see *State* v. *Landing*, 1888, Criminal Action Papers, Durham County, NCDAH; *State* v. *Hopkins*, 1887, Criminal Action Papers, Granville County; and B. White, *In Search of Kith and Kin*, 52–55.

29. For the political platform of the North Carolina Knights, see McLaurin, "The Knights of Labor in North Carolina Politics," 302–3. For the Oxford municipal election, see *Oxford Torchlight*, 4 May 1886; and *Journal of United Labor*, 11 June 1887, 2422–23. W. F. Rogers, who was elected mayor, was a Democrat who became a Knight. The *Oxford Torchlight* did not identify Rogers as a Knight in its report on 4 May 1886 of the election. But Rob-

ert Cohen identified the 1886 mayor as a Knight in his 11 June 1887 letter, so presumably Rogers declared himself a Knight soon after he took office, if not at the time of his election. Rogers, moreover, was able to attract a large portion of the African-American vote, which suggests that he was already a very different kind of Democratic candidate. In the largest turnout for a municipal election in that decade, Rogers received 230 votes, while the Republican candidate received only 1 vote. By January 1887, Rogers was elected to the State Executive Board of the Knights of Labor at the North Carolina State Assembly meeting; see *Journal of United Labor,* 2 Apr. 1887, 2339. The *Oxford Torchlight* did not identify any Knights of Labor candidates in Granville County in the fall 1886 election, but in other parts of the state—most notably in the Fourth Congressional District, which included Raleigh and surrounding counties—the Knights and the Republican party combined forces to defeat the Democrats; see McLaurin, "The Knights of Labor in North Carolina Politics," 301–5. Given the dissatisfaction among Granville Democrats with their party, the identification of the Knights with the Republicans may have helped county Republicans in this election. Moreover, many of the independent candidates may well have been Knights. For the 1886 elections, see *Oxford Torchlight,* 19 Oct. 1886, 26 Oct. 1886, 2 Nov. 1886, 9 Nov. 1886, 16 Nov. 1886, and 30 Nov. 1886. No doubt the bad crop that year accentuated economic complaints in the countryside and put independent candidates over the edge; on 11 August 1886 the *Raleigh Progressive Farmer* reported that Granville farmers were plowing their tobacco under and planting peas and corn in its place to avoid a total loss.

Given the county's political history and economic structure, politics provided a much stronger basis for a biracial, cross-class alliance than common labor-related concerns. The focus on politics, moreover, was common to the Knights at this time, particularly in the South; see Fink, *Workingman's Democracy;* Kahn, "The Knights of Labor and the Southern Black Worker"; McLaurin, "The Knights of Labor in North Carolina Politics" and *The Knights of Labor in the South;* and Rachleff, *Black Labor in the South.* Local opposition to centralization in the tobacco industry may have also facilitated the local alliance. In *A Generation of Boomers,* for instance, Stromquist argues that the Knights of Labor were able to build a cross-class alliance in midwestern towns economically dependent on the railroads where the local elite joined railroad workers in opposing the arbitrary power wielded by the railroad companies. Merchants in Oxford who were as dependent on the rapidly consolidating tobacco-manufacturing firms as midwestern merchants were on the railroads also may have found the Knights' petty producer rhetoric attractive. For a similar coalition among Independents and disaffected Republicans and Democrats, see Foner, *Freedom's Lawmakers,* 77–78.

30. McGhee quoted in B. White, *In Search of Kith and Kin,* 34. Other historians have also argued that some Democrats grudgingly accepted black suffrage and directed their efforts toward influencing how African Americans would vote. See, for instance, Perman, *The Road to Redemption,* 16–20,

57–67; and Reidy, *From Slavery to Agrarian Capitalism,* 199. As Gilmore argues in *Gender and Jim Crow,* a new generation of North Carolina Democrats, who came of age in the late 1880s, launched the state's disfranchisement campaign.

31. *Oxford Torchlight,* 11 July 1876. For similar references, see, for instance, *Oxford Torchlight,* 17 July 1874, 2 May 1876, 4 July 1876, 15 Aug. 1876, 22 Aug. 1876, 29 Aug. 1876, 5 Sept. 1876, 12 Sept. 1876, 19 Sept. 1876, 26 Sept. 1876, 10 Oct. 1876, 31 Oct. 1876, 4 June 1878, 11 June 1878, 25 June 1878, 2 July 1878, 9 July 1878, 26 July 1878, 8 June 1880, 22 June 1880, 31 Aug. 1880, 5 Oct. 1880, and 11 Apr. 1882. For the participatory nature of Republican gatherings and African Americans' approach to politics in particular, see E. Brown, "To Catch a Vision of Freedom"; Foner, "Black Reconstruction Leaders at the Grass Roots."

32. Quotes from *Oxford Torchlight,* 11 July 1876 and 29 Aug. 1876; and *State v. Neely,* 74 N.C. (1876) 425. See chapter 5 for an analysis of this case. For similar references, see *Oxford Torchlight,* 17 July 1874, 15 Aug. 1876, 29 Aug. 1876, 5 Sept. 1876, 26 Sept. 1876, 19 Feb. 1878, 4 June 1878, 25 June 1878, 9 July 1878, 26 July 1878, and 3 Dec. 1878.

33. *Oxford Torchlight,* 28 Sept. 1880, 6 Jan. 1880, 9 July 1878, 26 July 1878, and 1 Aug. 1876. The *Granville Free Lance* also portrayed the Republican party as exclusively black; see, for instance, 22 Mar. 1878. For other *Oxford Torchlight* references to the biracial character of the local Republican party, see, for instance, 4 July 1876, 15 July 1876, 29 Aug. 1876, and 1 Oct. 1878. For other *Oxford Torchlight* depictions of white Republicans as race traitors, see, for instance, 5 Oct. 1880 and 12 Oct. 1880.

34. *Oxford Torchlight,* 4 June 1878. These were the images picked up and promoted by the Dunning school; see, for instance, Hamilton, *Reconstruction in North Carolina.* For assertions that whites actually controlled the party, see also *Oxford Torchlight,* 1 Aug. 1876, 17 Oct. 1876, 23 Jan. 1878, 13 Feb. 1878, 20 Feb. 1878, 26 Feb. 1878, 12 Mar. 1878, 30 Apr. 1878, 14 May 1878, 11 June 1878, 2 July 1878, 8 June 1880, 28 Sept. 1880, 12 Oct. 1880, and 17 Aug. 1886; and *Granville Free Lance,* 7 July 1882. To underscore the point that African Americans lacked the capacity for political leadership, the editors of the *Oxford Torchlight* also regularly ridiculed the ignorance of politically prominent blacks; see, for instance, 2 May 1876, 18 July 1876, 22 Aug. 1876, 19 Sept. 1876, 12 Dec. 1876, and 19 Oct. 1880. For discussions of such Democratic characterizations of the Republican party, see Olsen, "An Incongruous Presence," 171–72; and Reidy, *From Slavery to Agrarian Capitalism,* 198.

35. For *Oxford Torchlight* allegations that local Republican leaders were driven by greed and self-interest, see, for instance, 2 May 1876, 1 Aug. 1876, 29 Aug. 1876, 12 Sept. 1876, 17 Oct. 1876, 24 Oct. 1876, 28 Nov. 1876, 2 Jan. 1877, 22 Jan. 1878, 19 Feb. 1878, 12 Mar. 1878, 16 July 1878, 23 July 1878, 22 June 1880, 17 Aug. 1880, 14 Sept. 1880, 12 Oct. 1880, and 16 Nov. 1880. Not stopping with local leaders, articles in the newspaper portrayed the entire party in this way as well; see, for instance, 3 Oct. 1876, 10 Oct. 1876,

2 Jan. 1877, 9 Jan. 1877, 12 Mar. 1878, 9 July 1878, 6 May 1879, 17 Feb. 1880, 2 Mar. 1880, 9 Mar. 1880, 16 Mar. 1880, 30 Mar. 1880, 6 Apr. 1880, 13 Apr. 1880, 27 Apr. 1880, 4 May 1880, 25 May 1880, 15 June 1880, 29 June 1880, 13 July 1880, 17 Aug. 1880, 14 Sept. 1880, 16 Nov. 1880, and 27 July 1886.

36. *Oxford Torchlight,* 20 June 1876. For the Kinton affair, see 12 Sept. 1876 and 19 Sept. 1876. For *Oxford Torchlight* allegations of Republican mismanagement of local finances, see, for instance, 4 Aug. 1874, 11 Apr. 1876, 25 Apr. 1876, 2 May 1876, 9 May 1876, 16 May 1876, 15 Aug. 1876, 29 Aug. 1876, 10 Oct. 1876, 17 Oct. 1876, 24 Oct. 1876, 28 Nov. 1876, 30 Jan. 1877, 13 Nov. 1877, 20 Nov. 1877, 19 Feb. 1878, 5 Mar. 1878, 30 Apr. 1878, 1 Oct. 1878, 3 Dec. 1878, 13 Apr. 1880, and 17 Aug. 1880.

37. *Oxford Torchlight,* 12 Sept. 1876 and 20 June 1876.

38. *Oxford Torchlight,* 26 Mar. 1878, 12 Nov. 1878, and 15 Jan. 1878. With few exceptions, both the *Oxford Torchlight* and the *Granville Free Lance* heaped hyperbolic praise on Democrats; for examples see *Oxford Torchlight,* 18 Apr. 1876, 6 Aug. 1878, 24 Aug. 1880, 14 Sept. 1880, 5 Oct. 1880, 26 Apr. 1881, 6 Jan. 1885, and 26 Oct. 1886; and *Granville Free Lance,* 3 May 1878.

39. *Oxford Torchlight,* 14 Sept. 1880, 24 Feb. 1880, and 9 Apr. 1878. For references to "gentlemen," "best citizens," "right men," and "best men," see 18 Apr. 1878, 16 July 1878, 6 Aug. 1878, 22 Apr. 1879, 4 May 1880, 20 July 1880, 7 Sept. 1880, 18 Apr. 1882, 6 Jan. 1885, and 26 Oct. 1886. For other invocations of the Democrats' manliness, see, for instance, *Oxford Torchlight,* 21 Nov. 1876, 6 Feb. 1877, 22 June 1880, and 26 Oct. 1886; and *Granville Free Lance,* 25 June 1880. For Republican leaders as women, see *Oxford Torchlight,* 5 Oct. 1880.

40. William H. Gregory, "The Alexander Family of North Carolina," Gregory Papers.

41. *Oxford Torchlight,* 18 July 1876 and 5 Jan. 1886. By implication, the newspaper's "blackening" of the Republican party made the Democratic party "white." Other articles also explicitly referred to the Democrats as the party of white men; see, for instance, 25 July 1876, 30 Apr. 1886, 23 July 1886, 27 July 1886, and 16 Nov. 1886.

42. *Oxford Torchlight,* 5 Oct. 1880 and 13 July 1880. For similar connections between business and politics, see also *Oxford Torchlight,* 31 Aug. 1880, 26 Apr. 1881, 17 May 1881, and 11 May 1886. The emphasis on property ownership and material possessions also came out in the insistence that only Democratic candidates could fairly represent the "tax payers" and "property holders" of the county; see, for instance, 30 Apr. 1878 and 9 Jan. 1877. In its 14 January 1879 issue, the newspaper went one step further, returning to the conservative arguments of the late 1860s and arguing that property ownership should be a prerequisite for political participation.

43. *Oxford Torchlight,* 5 Oct. 1880, 23 Mar. 1886, and 4 June 1878. See also *Granville Free Lance,* 10 May 1878 and 25 June 1880.

44. *Oxford Torchlight,* 4 Aug. 1874, 11 May 1875, 22 June 1875, and 6 July 1875. For the Democratic mayor's many accomplishments, see 9 Nov.

1875. For *Oxford Torchlight* articles applauding the competence of Democratic officeholders generally, see 12 Aug. 1879, 24 Feb. 1880, 7 Sept. 1880, 14 Sept. 1880, 21 Sept. 1880, 28 Sept. 1880, 17 May 1881, and 26 Oct. 1886.

45. *Oxford Torchlight,* 3 Mar. 1874, 18 Apr. 1876, and 9 May 1876. For similar articles presenting Democrats as public servants, see, for instance, 18 July 1876 and 30 Apr. 1878. For Democrats passing themselves off as "citizens' candidates" in the municipal elections, see 19 Apr. 1881 and 18 Apr. 1882.

46. *Oxford Torchlight,* 11 June 1878, 9 July 1878, and 12 Oct. 1886. The editors of the newspaper regularly tried to convince black voters that the Democrats, not the Republicans, had their interests at heart; see, for instance, 29 Aug. 1876, 19 Sept. 1876, 10 Oct. 1876, 17 Oct. 1876, 23 Jan. 1877, 20 Feb. 1877, 11 June 1878, 9 July 1878, 23 July 1878, 6 Aug. 1878, 26 Nov. 1878, 28 Sept. 1880, 7 June 1881, 28 Mar. 1882, 11 Apr. 1882, and 13 Jan. 1885. The editors of the *Oxford Torchlight* emphasized the Democrats' concern for African Americans by charging that white Republican leaders ignored their black constituency; see, for instance, 1 Aug. 1876, 29 Aug. 1876, 3 Oct. 1876, 10 Oct. 1876, 5 Dec. 1876, 26 Feb. 1878, 12 Mar. 1878, 7 May 1878, 14 May 1878, 23 July 1878, 8 July 1879, 8 June 1880, 22 June 1880, 27 July 1880, 17 Aug. 1880, 31 Aug. 1880, 14 Sept. 1880, 28 Sept. 1880, 28 Mar. 1882, and 10 Aug. 1886. The editors of the *Oxford Torchlight* insisted that the Republicans treated African Americans like slaves and that blacks would become "men" only if they joined the Democrats; see, for instance, 3 Oct. 1876, 12 Mar. 1878, 30 Apr. 1878, 23 July 1878, and 8 July 1879; see also *Granville Free Lance,* 3 May 1878. Indeed, the editors tried to create the illusion of a mass exodus from the Republican party with continual reports of African Americans who had joined the Democrats or advocated that others do so; see, for instance, *Oxford Torchlight,* 22 Aug. 1876, 29 Aug. 1876, 19 Sept. 1876, 10 Oct. 1876, 9 Jan. 1877, 14 May 1878, 11 June 1878, 23 July 1878, 24 Aug. 1880, and 17 Aug. 1886. See also Escott, *Many Excellent People,* 171–95; Greenwood, *Bittersweet Legacy,* 72–74; and Reidy, *From Slavery to Agrarian Capitalism,* 190.

47. *Oxford Torchlight,* 29 June 1880 and 29 Aug. 1876.

48. *Oxford Torchlight,* 11 July 1876. See also 22 Aug. 1876 and 31 Oct. 1876. There is far less information about the Republican party because the local newspapers that supported it did not survive as the *Oxford Torchlight* did. But, for all their biases, the articles in the *Oxford Torchlight* are still revealing. For the elite orientation of white Republican leaders in the 1870s, see Evans, *Ballots and Fence Rails,* 150–75; Perman, *The Road to Redemption,* 87–107; and Olsen, "An Incongruous Presence." The contrast with many African-American leaders is striking; see, for instance, Balanoff, "Negro Legislators in the North Carolina General Assembly"; Hume, "Black and Tan Constitutional Conventions"; and F. Logan, "Black and Republican." The distance between white Republicans and black laborers and tenants was even wider; see Foner, *Nothing but Freedom,* 74–110, and *Reconstruction,* 374–79; T. Holt, *Black over White;* Reidy, *From Slavery to Agrarian Capitalism,* 161–214; and Saville, *The Work of Reconstruction,* 143–95.

49. *Oxford Torchlight,* 3 Oct. 1876 and 20 July 1880. See also 31 Oct. 1876. For opposition to these ideals of respectability, see Foner, *Freedom's Lawmakers,* 215. For divisions among North Carolina black leaders about how best to proceed in this increasingly hostile political environment, see Anderson, *Race and Politics in North Carolina;* and Escott, *Many Excellent People,* 181–84. The comments of black leaders in Granville parallel a development noted by Greenwood in *Bittersweet Legacy,* 81–88; she argues that by the 1880s a group of educated and professional blacks in Charlotte began to identify themselves as the "better class" and to distinguish themselves from poorer blacks. See also Gatewood, *Aristocrats of Color;* Gilmore, *Gender and Jim Crow;* Higginbotham, *Righteous Discontent;* and Painter, "Martin R. Delany."

50. *Oxford Torchlight,* 24 Oct. 1876. In *The Road to Redemption,* 22–56, Perman argues that after 1868, the Centrists gained control of the Republican party, moving it in a more conservative direction through the support of internal improvements and the development of business and commerce. Given this direction, divisions would develop between the party's leaders and its rank and file.

51. For the ideology of the Knights, see Fink, *Workingman's Democracy;* and Rachleff, *Black Labor in the South.* For the Republican party, see Foner, *Free Soil, Free Labor, Free Men.*

52. *Oxford Torchlight,* 18 May 1886.

53. Racial tensions in the southern Knights of Labor are well documented; see Gould, "The Strike of 1887"; Kahn, "The Knights of Labor and the Southern Black Worker"; McLaurin, "The Knights of Labor in North Carolina Politics" and *The Knights of Labor in the South;* and Rachleff, *Black Labor in the South.* For critiques highlighting the conservative implications of the tradition of labor and political protest on which the Knights' drew, see chapter 2. See also S. Levine, *Labor's True Woman;* McCurry, *Masters of Small Worlds;* MacLean, *Behind the Mask of Chivalry;* Roediger, *The Wages of Whiteness;* Saxon, *The Rise and Fall of the White Republic;* and Stansell, *City of Women.*

54. *Oxford Torchlight,* 18 May 1886; Cohen quoted in *Journal of United Labor,* 11 June 1887, 2422–23. In Oxford, as elsewhere in the South, white Knights occupied the most prominent leadership positions. Apparently, even the masterworkman of the black local, Robert Cohen, was white. Only one black man, Henderson Cogwell, won election to office, but it seems he failed to post bond because the office was filled by a white man; see *Oxford Torchlight,* 3 May 1887 and 10 May 1887. Henderson Cogwell is identified as a Knight in the testimony of *State* v. *Hopkins,* 1887, Criminal Action Papers, Granville County. Cogwell was an established carpenter; W. F. Rogers, Oxford's mayor in 1886, was a hardware merchant. The background of leaders in other southern Knights of Labor locals was similar; see Gould, "The Strike of 1887," 49–50; and McLaurin, *The Knights of Labor in the South,* 151–55. The term "better classes" comes from Greenwood, *Bittersweet Legacy.* See also Gilmore, *Gender and Jim Crow.*

55. Cohen quoted in *Journal of United Labor,* 10–25 Oct. 1886, 2185; *Oxford Torchlight,* 18 May 1886 and 25 May 1886; Cohen quoted in *Journal of United Labor,* 11 June 1887, 2422–23. See also *Oxford Torchlight,* 27 July 1886.

56. *Oxford Torchlight,* 16 Feb. 1886; see also 9 Mar. 1886, 23 Mar. 1886, 30 Mar. 1886, 27 Apr. 1886, 11 May 1886, 18 May 1886, 22 June 1886, 3 Aug. 1886, 24 Aug. 1886, 14 Sept. 1886, 21 Sept. 1886, 19 Oct. 1886, 4 Jan. 1886, 1 Feb. 1886, 3 May 1886, 24 May 1886, 21 June 1886, 6 Oct. 1886, and 16 Nov. 1887.

57. *Journal of United Labor,* 11 June 1887, 2422–23; *Oxford Torchlight,* 24 May 1887.

58. See, for instance, *Oxford Torchlight,* 2 Nov. 1886.

59. *Oxford Torchlight,* 19 Apr. 1881.

60. The only documentation of the case appears in the Superior Court Minutes, Granville County; see *State* v. *Taborn,* May Term 1887, Superior Court Minutes, Granville County. See also *Oxford Torchlight,* 15 Mar. 1887 and 17 May 1887.

61. *Oxford Torchlight,* 22 Mar. 1887. See also 15 Mar. 1887. For African Americans' identification with black criminals as people who were also marginalized from political and legal processes, see Du Bois, *The Souls of Black Folk,* 199–201; and Ayers, *Vengeance and Justice,* 141–265.

62. *Oxford Torchlight,* 5 Jan. 1886. For the 1881 lynching, see *Granville Free Lance,* 2 Dec. 1881. For articles about lynching and black-on-white crime, see *Oxford Torchlight,* 6 Jan. 1885, 18 May 1886, 15 June 1886, 13 July 1886, 21 Sept. 1886, 17 May 1887, and 31 May 1887. See Escott, *Many Excellent People,* 185–88, for the increasingly virulent racist articles in North Carolina newspapers at this time. For additional examples, see *Raleigh Progressive Farmer,* 3 Mar. 1886, 10 Mar. 1886, 2 June 1887, 20 Oct. 1887, and 24 Nov. 1887.

63. *Oxford Torchlight,* 15 Mar. 1887.

64. *Oxford Torchlight,* 22 Mar. 1887. See also 15 Mar. 1887.

65. *Oxford Torchlight,* 12 Apr. 1887. See also 22 Mar. 1887.

66. *Journal of United Labor,* 11 June 1887, 2422–23.

67. Cohen quoted in *Journal of United Labor,* 11 June 1887, 2422–23.

68. *Oxford Torchlight,* 22 Mar. 1887. See also 15 Mar. 1887, 17 Mar. 1887, 24 May 1887, and 21 June 1887.

69. *Oxford Torchlight,* 26 Apr. 1887 and 17 May 1887; *State* v. *Hopkins,* 1887, and *State* v. *Hopkins and Lockett,* 1887, both in Criminal Action Papers, Granville County.

70. *State* v. *Hopkins,* 1887, Criminal Action Papers, Granville County. See also *State* v. *Hopkins and Lockett,* 1887, Criminal Action Papers, Granville County. Witnesses generally received less than ten dollars from the county as reimbursement for their time and travel. For instance, in an unnamed case in 1874, the highest amount paid for service as a witness was fourteen dollars and most received sums under ten dollars; see Criminal Action Papers, Granville County.

71. *State* v. *Hopkins,* 1887, Criminal Action Papers, Granville County. See also *State* v. *Hopkins and Lockett,* May Term 1887, and *State* v. *Hopkins, Lockett,*

and Taborn, Sept. Term 1887, both in Superior Court Minutes, Granville County; *State* v. *Hopkins and Lockett,* 1887, Criminal Action Papers, Granville County; and *State* v. *Cook and Landing,* 1888, Criminal Action Papers, Durham County.

72. *State* v. *Hopkins,* 1887, Criminal Action Papers, Granville County. The testimony in this case also reveals that W. F. Rogers visited Hopkins in jail and brought him whiskey.

73. *Oxford Torchlight,* 4 Apr. 1888 and 29 Feb. 1888. See also *State* v. *Hopkins, Lockett, and Taborn,* Sept. Term 1887, and *State* v. *Hopkins,* Dec. Term 1887, both in Superior Court Minutes, Granville County; and *State* v. *Cook and Landing,* 1888, Criminal Action Papers, Durham County.

74. *Oxford Torchlight,* 17 May 1887.

75. *Oxford Torchlight,* 31 May 1887 and 24 May 1887. See also Massur, *Rites of Execution.*

76. *Oxford Torchlight,* 21 June 1887.

77. For violence directed at the Knights in the 1887 municipal election, see *Journal of United Labor,* 11 June 1887, 2422–23; *State* v. *Parham,* two counts of assault with a deadly weapon, one against Robert Cohen and the other against Mack O'Day, 1887, Criminal Action Papers, Granville County; and *State* v. *Cohen,* May Term 1887, Superior Court Minutes, Granville County.

78. *State* v. *Taborn,* May Term 1887, Superior Court Minutes, Granville County. Lee Pool had run for town commissioner in 1878 and 1881; Sandy Parham, whose name appeared repeatedly in connection with the Republican party during the 1870s and 1880s, had run for town commissioner in 1878 and 1886; see *Oxford Torchlight,* 7 May 1878, 10 May 1881, and 4 May 1886. Of the six other jury members who could be identified, all were black and all owned significant amounts of property. Seven of the eight owned land, ranging from three-quarters of an acre to twenty-four acres; the top landowner, Sandy Parham, held three town lots worth $850. The one juror who did not own land possessed $189 in livestock and tools in 1886. The other jurors also owned significant amounts of moveable property, ranging from $25 to $910 in 1885 and from $87 to $910 in 1886. See Tax Lists, 1885–86, Granville County; and U.S. Bureau of the Census, Population Schedule, 1880.

79. *State* v. *Taborn,* May Term 1887, Superior Court Minutes, Granville County; *Oxford Torchlight,* 17 May 1887. Previous sexual violence cases had focused on the rights of African-American and poor white women to protection against sexual attacks, not the rights of alleged attackers to a fair trial. While Belle Booth's case differed from these because she was an elite white woman, it was similar in the sense that she, like the other women, brought charges against an unattached poor man like Albert Taborn. Neither African Americans nor common whites made any attempt to heroize the men who attacked poor white and black women. To the contrary, prosecution of these men formed part of a larger struggle to empower black and common white men to protect their female relatives and to claim privileges of womanhood for black and common white women. Considering the weak case

presented on Taborn's behalf, to declare Taborn innocent would be to give him the benefit of the doubt and to establish a potentially dangerous precedent, jeopardizing the efforts of poor whites and African Americans to obtain convictions themselves, while also reinforcing Democratic propaganda that all black men were irresponsible. Thus, whereas African Americans equated Taborn's acquittal with victory for those of their race and class, others believed it could potentially undermine their political power.

80. *Oxford Torchlight,* 17 May 1887 and 21 June 1887.

81. The *Oxford Torchlight* does not mention the local Knights after June 1887. For W. F. Rogers's refusal to testify, see *State* v. *Cook and Landing,* 1888, Criminal Action Papers, Durham County.

82. Democratic County Commissioners cut Oxford Township in two to create Salem Township, with the line running straight through the town of Oxford. While no explanation was given, the intent was clear. See *Oxford Torchlight,* 9 May 1888. Later, the Farmers' Alliance and Populist party attracted many black members. In fact, W. A. Patillo, the state lecturer and organizer of the Colored Farmers' National Alliance of North Carolina, lived in Granville County; see, for instance, W. A. Patillo to Elias Carr, 20 Apr. 1891, W. A. Patillo to Elias Carr, 2 May 1891, and W. A. Patillo to Elias Carr, 12 May 1891, all in Elias Carr Papers, Collection 160, East Carolina Manuscript Collection, J. Y. Joyner Library, East Carolina University, Greenville. But the Alliance focused exclusively on the interests of landholding farmers and renters with a good deal of independence over their farming operations, not tenants and wage laborers. To counter the fluctuating tobacco market and the monopoly practices of the American Tobacco Company, the Alliance organized cooperative tobacco factories and a cooperative tobacco warehouse with the goal of increasing the prices they received for their crop by severing their dependence on the American Tobacco Company. Instead of selling to American, Granville farmers would sell to Alliance factories through the Alliance warehouse, which would also eliminate the high fees farmers paid at private warehouses. To fund these projects the Alliance chartered a joint stock company, presided over by some of the county's wealthiest planters. For them, the company was probably as much a profit-making enterprise as it was an expression of cooperative solidarity with their brothers and sisters of the Alliance. The warehouse, moreover, did not serve the poorest farmers, since only Alliance members could use it. The tobacco factories also were intended to make money for Alliance members, not for the wage laborers who worked in them. Indeed, the Alliance subsumed tenants' and laborers' interests under those of landlords in the same way the Democratic party had. For instance, the *Raleigh Progressive Farmer,* in its 7 February 1887 issue, insisted that interests of farmers and laborers were "identical" and that "whatever benefits one will benefit the other." For the history of the Alliance in Granville County, see Rivers, "Entrepreneurs and Reformers at a Country Crossroads"; and Tilley, *The Bright Tobacco Industry,* 413. For class divisions within the Granville Alliance, see also Lewis Spaugh to Elias Carr,

12 Sept. 1889, Carr Papers. Given the economic policies of the Alliance and its strong connection with the Democratic party, it is no wonder that its political offshoot, the Populist party, enjoyed limited success in Granville County. With poor African Americans and whites only nominally committed to the party, it simply could not sustain the violent campaign mounted against it. In the *Granville County Reformer* the county Populist party announced that "We hold the Truth to be Self-Evident, that All Men are Created Equal," but these words rang hollow to poor county residents. Carlson, "Homeplace and Tobaccoland," 77.

83. *Oxford Torchlight,* 6 Dec. 1887.

84. Connor and Poe, *The Life and Speeches of Charles Brantley Aycock,* 229, 230, 232. For an illuminating discussion of this process, see Gilmore, *Gender and Jim Crow.*

Bibliography

Archival and Manuscript Collections

Apprentice Bonds, Granville County. North Carolina Division of Archives and History. Raleigh.

Bastardy Bonds, Granville County. North Carolina Division of Archives and History. Raleigh.

Brogden, Curtis H. Governor's Papers. North Carolina Division of Archives and History. Raleigh.

Bullock, John. Papers. Special Collections Library. Duke University. Durham.

Caldwell, Tod R. Governor's Papers. North Carolina Division of Archives and History. Raleigh.

Carr, Elias. Papers. Collection 160. East Carolina Manuscript Collection. J. Y. Joyner Library. East Carolina University. Greenville, N.C.

Civil Action Papers, Granville County. North Carolina Division of Archives and History. Raleigh.

Criminal Action Papers, Durham County. North Carolina Division of Archives and History. Raleigh.

Criminal Action Papers, Edgecombe County. North Carolina Division of Archives and History. Raleigh.

Criminal Action Papers, Granville County. North Carolina Division of Archives and History. Raleigh.

Criminal Action Papers, Orange County. North Carolina Division of Archives and History. Raleigh.

Criminal Actions Concerning Slaves and Free Persons of Color, Granville County. North Carolina Division of Archives and History. Raleigh.

Divorce Records, Granville County. North Carolina Division of Archives and History. Raleigh.

Election Records, Granville County. North Carolina Division of Archives and History. Raleigh.

Federal Writers' Project Records. Southern Historical Collection. University of North Carolina at Chapel Hill.

Fleming, M. B. Papers. Special Collections Library. Duke University. Durham.

General Assembly Session Records. North Carolina Division of Archives and History. Raleigh.

Granville County Account Books. Miscellaneous Books, 1860–92. Southern Historical Collection. University of North Carolina at Chapel Hill.

Gregory, William H. Papers. Special Collections Library. Duke University. Durham.

Hargrove, Elizabeth R. Papers. Special Collections Library. Duke University. Durham.

Holden, William W. Papers. North Carolina Division of Archives and History. Raleigh.

Horner, James H. Papers. Special Collections Library. Duke University. Durham.

Independent Order of the Good Templars, Grand Lodge of North Carolina, Health Seat Lodge, No. 40, Papers. Special Collections Library. Duke University. Durham.

Jones, Henry W. Papers. Special Collections Library. Duke University. Durham.

Marriages of Free People, Granville County. North Carolina Division of Archives and History. Raleigh.

Miscellaneous Records, Granville County. North Carolina Division of Archives and History. Raleigh.

Records of the Adjutant General's Office. RG 94. National Archives. Washington, D.C.

Records of the Assistant Commissioner for the State of North Carolina. Records of the U.S. Bureau of Refugees, Freedmen, and Abandoned Lands. RG 105. National Archives Microfilm Publication M843.

Records of the Pension Bureau. RG 15. National Archives. Washington, D.C.

Records of the U.S. Army Continental Commands. RG 393. National Archives. Washington, D.C.

Records of the U.S. Bureau of Refugees, Freedmen, and Abandoned Lands. RG 105. National Archives. Washington, D.C.

Schenck, David. Papers. North Carolina Division of Archives and History. Raleigh.

Shotwell, Bettie. Papers. Special Collections Library. Duke University. Durham.

Superior Court Minutes, Granville County. North Carolina Division of Archives and History. Raleigh.

Supreme Court Original Cases, 1800–1900. North Carolina Division of Archives and History. Raleigh.

Tax Lists, Granville County. North Carolina Division of Archives and History. Raleigh.

Vance, Zebulon B. Governor's Papers. North Carolina Division of Archives and History. Raleigh.

Wills, Granville County. North Carolina Division of Archives and History. Raleigh.

Worth, Jonathan. Governor's Letter Book. 1865–67, 1867–68. North Carolina Division of Archives and History. Raleigh.

———. Governor's Papers. North Carolina Division of Archives and History. Raleigh.

Government Documents

Bureau of Labor Statistics of the State of North Carolina. Annual Reports. 1887–1900.

Journal of the Convention of the State of North Carolina at Its Session of 1865. Raleigh, 1865.

Laws and Resolutions of the State of North Carolina Passed by the General Assembly at Its Session 1873–74. Raleigh, 1874.

Laws and Resolutions of the State of North Carolina Passed by the General Assembly at Its Session 1874–75. Raleigh, 1875.

Laws and Resolutions of the State of North Carolina, Passed by the General Assembly at Its Session of 1879. Raleigh, 1879.

Laws and Resolutions of the State of North Carolina, Passed by the General Assembly at Its Special Session of 1880. Raleigh, 1880.

Laws and Resolutions of the State of North Carolina, Passed by the General Assembly at Its Session of 1881. Raleigh, 1881.

Laws and Resolutions of the State of North Carolina, Passed by the General Assembly at Its Session of 1883. Raleigh, 1883.

Laws and Resolutions of the State of North Carolina, Passed by the General Assembly at Its Session of 1885. Raleigh, 1885.

Laws and Resolutions of the State of North Carolina Passed by the General Assembly at Its Session of 1887. Raleigh, 1887.

Laws and Resolutions of the State of North Carolina, Passed by the General Assembly at Its Session of 1889. Raleigh, 1889.

Laws and Resolutions Passed by the General Assembly of the State of North Carolina, at the Special Session . . . of July, 1868. Raleigh, 1868.

Ordinances Passed by the North Carolina State Convention at the Sessions of 1865–66. Raleigh, 1867.

North Carolina Reports: Cases at Law Argued and Determined in the Supreme Court of North Carolina. 1812–90.

Public Laws and Resolutions . . . of the State of North Carolina Passed by the General Assembly at the Session of 1872–73. Raleigh, 1873.

Public Laws of the State of North Carolina, Passed by the General Assembly at Its Session 1868–69. Raleigh, 1869.

Public Laws of the State of North Carolina, Passed by the General Assembly at Its Session 1869–70. Raleigh, 1870.

Public Laws of the State of North Carolina Passed by the General Assembly at Its Session 1870–71. Raleigh, 1871.

Public Laws of the State of North Carolina, Passed by the General Assembly at Its Session 1871–72. Raleigh, 1872.

Public Laws of the State of North Carolina Passed by the General Assembly at Its Sessions, 1876–77. Raleigh, 1877.

Public Laws of the State of North Carolina, Passed by the General Assembly at the Session of 1866. Raleigh, 1866.

Public Laws of the State of North Carolina Passed by the General Assembly at the Sessions of 1866–67. Raleigh, 1867.

Testimony Taken by the Joint Select Committee to Inquire into the Condition of Affairs in the Late Insurrectionary States. Vols. 1–13. Washington, D.C.: GPO, 1872.

U.S. Bureau of the Census. *Historical Statistics of the United States, Colonial Times to 1870, Bicentennial Edition.* Part 1. Washington, D.C.: GPO, 1975.

———. Manuscript Records. Population and Agriculture Schedules, 1850, 1860, 1870, 1880, 1900. Granville County, N.C.

———. *Twelfth Census of the United States, Taken in the Year 1900.* Washington, D.C.: GPO, 1901.

Newspapers and Journals

Augusta Colored American
Charlotte Democrat
Daily Charlotte Observer
Granville Free Lance (Oxford, N.C.)
Journal of United Labor (Philadelphia)
Newbern Daily Journal of Commerce
Newbernian
New Bern Times
New York Tribune
North Carolina Standard (Raleigh)
Oxford Leader
Oxford Public Ledger
Oxford Torchlight
Raleigh Blasting-Powder
Raleigh Daily Record
Raleigh Gazette
Raleigh Journal of Freedom
Raleigh Progressive Farmer
Raleigh Semi-Weekly Record
Raleigh Sentinel
Raleigh Weekly Republican
Tarboro Southerner
Warrenton Gazette
Wilmington Herald

Books, Articles, and Other Published Materials

Alexander, Adele Logan. *Ambiguous Lives: Free Women of Color in Rural Georgia, 1789–1879.* Fayetteville: University of Arkansas Press, 1991.

Alexander, Roberta Sue. *North Carolina Faces the Freedmen: Race Relations during Presidential Reconstruction, 1865–67.* Durham: Duke University Press, 1985.

Anderson, Eric. *Race and Politics in North Carolina, 1872–1901.* Baton Rouge: Louisiana State University Press, 1981.

Andrews, Sidney. *The South since the War: As Shown by Fourteen Weeks of Travel and Observation in Georgia and the Carolinas.* Boston: Ticknor and Fields, 1866.

Applewhite, Marjorie Mendenhall. "Sharecropper and Tenant in the Courts of North Carolina." *North Carolina Historical Review* 31 (Apr. 1954): 134–49.

Ashe, Samuel A., Stephen B. Weeks, and Charles L. Van Noppen, eds. *Biographical History of North Carolina from Colonial Times to the Present.* 8 vols. Greensboro: Charles L. Van Noppen, 1905–17.

Auman, William T. "Neighbor against Neighbor: The Inner Civil War in the Randolph County Area of Confederate North Carolina." *North Carolina Historical Review* 61 (Jan. 1984): 60–90.

Auslander, Leora. "Feminist Theory and Social History: Explorations in the Politics of Identity." *Radical History Review* 54 (Fall 1992): 158–72.

Ayers, Edward L. *The Promise of the New South: Life after Reconstruction.* New York: Oxford University Press, 1992.

———. *Vengeance and Justice: Crime and Punishment in the Nineteenth Century American South.* New York: Oxford University Press, 1984.

———. "The World the Liberal Capitalists Made." *Reviews in American History* 19 (June 1991): 193–99.

Bailyn, Bernard. "The Challenge of Modern Historiography." *American Historical Review* 87 (Feb. 1982): 1–24.

Balanoff, Elizabeth. "Negro Legislators in the North Carolina General Assembly, July 1868–February 1872." *North Carolina Historical Review* 49 (Jan. 1972): 21–32.

Bardaglio, Peter W. "'An Outrage upon Nature': Incest and the Law in the Nineteenth-Century South." In *In Joy and in Sorrow: Women, Family, and Marriage in the Victorian South, 1830–1900,* ed. Carol Bleser. 32–51. New York: Oxford University Press, 1991.

———. "Rape and the Law in the Old South: 'Calculated to Excite Indignation in Every Heart.'" *Journal of Southern History* 60 (Nov. 1994): 749–72.

———. *Reconstructing the Household: Families, Sex, and the Law in the Nineteenth-Century South.* Chapel Hill: University of North Carolina Press, 1995.

Bardolph, Richard. "Inconstant Rebels: Desertion of North Carolina Troops in the Civil War." *North Carolina Historical Review* 41 (Apr. 1964): 163–89.

Baron, Ava, ed. *Work Engendered: Toward a New History of American Labor.* Ithaca: Cornell University Press, 1991.

Bellows, Barbara L. "'My Children, Gentlemen, Are My Own': Poor Women, the Urban Elite, and the Bonds of Obligation in Antebellum Charleston." In *The Web of Southern Social Relations: Women, Family, and Education,* ed. Walter J. Fraser Jr., R. Frank Saunders Jr., and Jon L. Wakelyn. 52–71. Athens: University of Georgia Press, 1985.

Bender, Thomas. "Wholes and Parts: The Need for Synthesis in American History." *Journal of American History* 73 (June 1986): 120–36.

Bennett, Judith M. "Feminism and History." *Gender and History* 1 (Autumn 1989): 251–72.

Berlin, Ira. *Slaves without Masters: The Free Negro in the Antebellum South*. New York: Pantheon, 1974.

Berlin, Ira, Barbara J. Fields, Thavolia Glymph, Joseph P. Reidy, and Leslie S. Rowland, eds. *Freedom: A Documentary History of Emancipation, 1861–1867*. Series 1, vol. 1, *The Destruction of Slavery*. New York: Cambridge University Press, 1985.

Berlin, Ira, Thavolia Glymph, Steven F. Miller, Joseph P. Reidy, Leslie S. Rowland, and Julie Saville, eds. *Freedom: A Documentary History of Emancipation, 1861–1867*. Series 1, vol. 3, *The Wartime Genesis of Free Labor: The Lower South*. New York: Cambridge University Press, 1991.

Berlin, Ira, Steven F. Miller, Joseph P. Reidy, and Leslie S. Rowland, eds. *Freedom: A Documentary History of Emancipation, 1861–1867*. Series 1, vol. 2, *The Wartime Genesis of Free Labor: The Upper South*. New York: Cambridge University Press, 1993.

Berlin, Ira, Steven F. Miller, and Leslie S. Rowland, eds. "Afro-American Families in the Transition from Slavery to Freedom." *Radical History Review* 42 (Fall 1988): 89–121.

Berlin, Ira, Joseph P. Reidy, and Leslie S. Rowland, eds. *Freedom: A Documentary History of Emancipation, 1861–1867*. Series 2, *The Black Military Experience*. New York: Cambridge University Press, 1982.

Billings, Dwight B., Jr. *Planters and the Making of a "New South": Class, Politics, and Development in North Carolina, 1865–1900*. Chapel Hill: University of North Carolina Press, 1979.

Bishir, Catherine W. *North Carolina Architecture*. Chapel Hill: Published for the Historic Preservation Foundation of North Carolina, Inc. by the University of North Carolina Press, 1990.

Blassingame, John W. *The Slave Community: Plantation Life in the Antebellum South*. New York: Oxford University Press, 1972.

Bleser, Carol, and Frederick Heath. "The Clays of Alabama: The Impact of the Civil War on a Southern Marriage." In *In Joy and in Sorrow: Women, Family, and Marriage in the Victorian South, 1830–1900*, ed. Carol Bleser. 135–53. New York: Oxford University Press, 1991.

Blewett, Mary H. *Men, Women, and Work: Class, Gender, and Protest in the New England Shoe Industry, 1780–1910*. Urbana: University of Illinois Press, 1988.

Bloch, Ruth. "The Gendered Meanings of Virtue in Revolutionary America." *Signs* 13 (Autumn 1987): 37–58.

Bode, Frederick A., and Donald E. Ginter. *Farm Tenancy and the Census in Antebellum Georgia*. Athens: University of Georgia Press, 1986.

Bolton, Charles C. *Poor Whites of the Antebellum South: Tenants and Laborers in Central North Carolina and Northeast Mississippi*. Durham: Duke University Press, 1994.

Boydston, Jeanne. *Home and Work: Housework, Wages, and the Ideology of Labor in the Early Republic*. New York: Oxford University Press, 1990.

Bradley, Frances Sage, and Margaretta A. Williamson. *Rural Children in Selected Counties of North Carolina*. Washington, D.C.: GPO, 1918; rpt., New York: Negro Universities Press, 1969.

Branson's Business Directory, 1896. Raleigh, 1896.

Branson's North Carolina Business Directory, 1890. Raleigh, 1889.

Branson's North Carolina Business Directory for 1884. Raleigh, 1884.

Brown, Elsa Barkley. "African-American Women's Quilting: A Framework for Conceptualizing and Teaching African-American Women's History." *Signs* 14 (Summer 1989): 921–29.

———. "Polyrhythms and Improvisation: Lessons for Women's History." *History Workshop Journal* 31 (Spring 1991): 85–90.

———. "'What Has Happened Here': The Politics of Difference in Women's History and Feminist Politics." *Feminist Studies* 18 (Summer 1992): 295–312.

———. "Womanist Consciousness: Maggie Lena Walker and the Independent Order of Saint Luke." *Signs* 14 (Spring 1989): 610–33.

Brown, Marvin A. "The Architecture of Granville County." In *Heritage and Homesteads: The History and Architecture of Granville County, North Carolina.* 163–232. Oxford: Granville County Historical Society, 1988.

———. "Inventory of Buildings." In *Heritage and Homesteads: The History and Architecture of Granville County, North Carolina.* 233–469. Oxford: Granville County Historical Society, 1988.

Bryant, Jonathan M. "'We Have No Chance of Justice before the Courts': The Freedmen's Struggle for Power in Greene County, Georgia, 1865–1874." In *Georgia in Black and White: Explorations in the Race Relations of a Southern State, 1865–1950,* ed. John C. Inscoe. 13–37. Athens: University of Georgia Press, 1994.

Burnham, Margaret. "An Impossible Marriage: Slave Law and Family Law." *Law and Inequality* 5 (July 1987): 187–225.

Burr, Virginia Ingraham, ed. *The Secret Eye: The Journal of Gertrude Clanton Thomas, 1848–1889.* Chapel Hill: University of North Carolina Press, 1990.

———. "A Woman Made to Suffer and Be Strong: Ella Gertrude Clanton Thomas, 1834–1907." In *In Joy and in Sorrow: Women, Family, and Marriage in the Victorian South, 1830–1900,* ed. Carol Bleser. 215–32. New York: Oxford University Press, 1991.

Burton, Orville Vernon. *In My Father's House Are Many Mansions: Family and Community in Edgefield, South Carolina.* Chapel Hill: University of North Carolina Press, 1985.

Bynum, Victoria. "On the Lowest Rung: Court Control over Poor White and Free Black Women." *Southern Exposure* 12 (Nov.–Dec. 1984): 40–44.

———. "Reshaping the Bonds of Womanhood: Divorce in Reconstruction North Carolina." In *Divided Houses: Gender and the Civil War,* ed. Catherine Clinton and Nina Silber. 320–33. New York: Oxford University Press, 1992.

———. *Unruly Women: The Politics of Social and Sexual Control in the Old South.* Chapel Hill: University of North Carolina Press, 1992.

———. "'War within a War': Women's Participation in the Revolt of the North Carolina Piedmont, 1863–1865." *Frontiers* 9, no. 3 (1987): 43–49.

Carby, Hazel. *Reconstructing Womanhood: The Emergence of the Afro-American Woman Novelist.* New York: Oxford University Press, 1987.

Carlson, Andrew J. "Homeplace and Tobaccoland: A History of Granville County." 1–160. In *Heritage and Homesteads: The History and Architecture of Granville County North Carolina.* Oxford: Granville County Historical Society, 1988.

"Catalog of Horner School, Oxford, N.C., A Classical, Mathematical, Scientific, and Military Academy, 1882–1883." Raleigh, 1883.

Cecil-Fronsman, Bill. *Common Whites: Class and Culture in Antebellum North Carolina.* Lexington: University Press of Kentucky, 1992.

Censer, Jane Turner. "A Changing World of Work: North Carolina Elite Women, 1865–1895." *North Carolina Historical Review* 73 (Jan. 1996): 28–55.

———. *North Carolina Planters and Their Children, 1800–1860.* Baton Rouge: Louisiana State University Press, 1984.

———. "'Smiling through Her Tears': Ante-Bellum Southern Women and Divorce." *American Journal of Legal History* 25 (Jan. 1982): 114–34.

Chataigne's North Carolina State Directory and Gazetteer, 1883–1884. Raleigh, 1883.

Clinton, Catherine. "Bloody Terrain: Freedwomen, Sexuality, and Violence during Reconstruction." *Georgia Historical Quarterly* 76 (Summer 1992): 310–32.

———. "Caught in the Web of the Big House: Women and Slavery." In *The Web of Southern Social Relations: Women, Family, and Education,* ed. Walter J. Fraser Jr., R. Frank Saunders Jr., and Jon L. Wakelyn. 19–34. Athens: University of Georgia Press, 1985.

———. *The Plantation Mistress: Woman's World in the Old South.* New York: Pantheon Books, 1982.

———. "Reconstructing Freedwomen." In *Divided Houses: Gender and the Civil War,* ed. Catherine Clinton and Nina Silber. 306–19. New York: Oxford University Press, 1992.

Cohen, William. *At Freedom's Edge: Black Mobility and the Southern White Quest for Racial Control, 1861–1915.* Baton Rouge: Louisiana State University Press, 1991.

Collins, Patricia Hill. *Black Feminist Thought: Knowledge, Consciousness, and the Politics of Empowerment.* Boston: Unwin Hyman, 1990.

Connor, R. D. W., and Clarence Poe. *The Life and Speeches of Charles Brantley Aycock.* New York: Doubleday, Page, 1912.

"Constitution and By-Laws of the Granville Grays, Approved February, 1885." Oxford, N.C., 1885.

Cott, Nancy F. *The Bonds of Womanhood: "Woman's Sphere" in New England, 1780–1835.* New Haven: Yale University Press, 1977.

———. "Giving Character to Our Whole Civil Polity: Marriage and the Public Order in the Late Nineteenth Century." In *U.S. History as Women's History: New Feminist Essays,* ed. Linda K. Kerber, Alice Kessler-Harris, and Kathryn Kish Sklar. 107–21. Chapel Hill: University of North Carolina Press, 1995.

———. "On Men's History and Women's History." In *Meanings for Manhood: Construction of Masculinity in Victorian America,* ed. Mark Carnes and Clyde Griffin. 205–11. Chicago: University of Chicago Press, 1990.

Crouch, Barry A., and Larry Madaras. "Reconstructing Black Families: Perspectives from the Texas Freedmen's Bureau Records." *Prologue* 18 (Summer 1986): 109–22.

Culclasure, Scott P. "'I Have Killed a Damned Dog': Murder by a Poor White in the Antebellum South." *North Carolina Historical Review* 70 (Jan. 1993): 13–39.

Cullen, Jim. "'I's a Man Now': Gender and African American Men." In *Divided Houses: Gender and the Civil War*, ed. Catherine Clinton and Nina Silber. 76–91. New York: Oxford University Press, 1992.

Daniel, Pete. *Breaking the Land: The Transformation of Cotton, Tobacco, and Rice Cultures since 1880.* Urbana: University of Illinois Press, 1985.

———. *The Shadow of Slavery: Peonage in the South, 1901–1960.* Lexington: University of Kentucky Press, 1978.

Davidoff, Leonore, and Catherine Hall. *Family Fortunes: Men and Women of the English Middle Class, 1780–1850.* Chicago: University of Chicago Press, 1980.

Davis, Angela. "Reflections on the Black Woman's Role in the Community of Slaves." *Black Scholar* 3 (Dec. 1981): 3–15.

———. *Women, Race, and Class.* New York: Random House, 1981.

Dennett, John Richard. *The South as It Is, 1865–1866.* New York: Viking Press, 1965; rpt., Athens: University of Georgia Press, 1986.

Dittmer, John. "The Education of Henry McNeal Turner." In *Black Leaders of the Nineteenth Century*, ed. Leon Litwack and August Meier. 253–72. Urbana: University of Illinois Press, 1988.

Dublin, Thomas. *Women at Work: The Transformation of Work and Community in Lowell, Massachusetts, 1826–1860.* New York: Columbia University Press, 1979.

Du Bois, W. E. B. *Black Reconstruction: An Essay toward a History of the Part Which Black Folk Played in the Attempt to Reconstruct Democracy in America, 1860–1880.* New York: Russell and Russell, 1935.

———. *The Souls of Black Folk.* New York: Signet, 1969.

Durrill, Wayne K. "Producing Poverty: Local Government and Economic Development in a New South County, 1874–1884." *Journal of American History* 71 (Mar. 1985): 764–81.

———. *War of Another Kind: A Southern Community in the Great Rebellion.* New York: Oxford University Press, 1990.

Edwards, Laura F. "Sexual Violence, Gender, Reconstruction, and the Extension of Patriarchy in Granville County, North Carolina." *North Carolina Historical Review* 68 (July 1991): 237–60.

Elkins, Stanley. *Slavery: A Problem in American Institutional and Intellectual Life.* Chicago: University of Chicago Press, 1959.

Elliott, Mrs. Sarah. *Days Long Ago: A Novelette.* Raleigh: Uzzell and Wiley, 1881. Copy in the North Carolina Collection, University of North Carolina at Chapel Hill.

———. *Mrs. Elliott's Housewife, Containing Practical Receipts in Cookery.* New York: Hurd and Houghton, 1870; Cambridge: Riverside Press, 1872. Copy in the North Carolina Collection, University of North Carolina at Chapel Hill.

Escott, Paul D. *Many Excellent People: Power and Privilege in North Carolina, 1850–1900.* Chapel Hill: University of North Carolina Press, 1985.

———. "The Moral Economy of the Crowd in Confederate North Carolina." *Maryland Historian* 13 (Spring–Summer 1982): 1–18.

———. "Poverty and Governmental Aid for the Poor in Confederate North Carolina." *North Carolina Historical Review* 61 (Oct. 1984): 462–80.

Evans, William McKee. *Ballots and Fence Rails: Reconstruction on the Lower Cape Fear.* Chapel Hill: University of North Carolina Press, 1966.

Faue, Elizabeth. *Community of Suffering and Struggle: Women, Men, and the Labor Movement in Minneapolis, 1915–1945.* Chapel Hill: University of North Carolina Press, 1991.

Faust, Drew Gilpin. "Altars of Sacrifice: Confederate Women and Narratives of War." *Journal of American History* 76 (Mar. 1990): 1200–1228.

———. *A Sacred Circle: The Dilemma of the Intellectual in the Old South, 1840–1860.* Baltimore: Johns Hopkins University Press, 1977.

———. "'Trying to Do a Man's Business': Slavery, Violence, and Gender in the American Civil War." *Gender and History* 4 (Summer 1992): 197–214.

Fields, Barbara J. "The Advent of Capitalist Agriculture: The New South in a Bourgeois World." In *Essays on the Postbellum Southern Economy,* ed. Thavolia Glymph and John J. Kushma. 73–94. College Station: Texas A&M Press for the University of Texas at Arlington, 1985.

———. "Ideology and Race in American History." In *Region, Race, and Reconstruction: Essays in Honor of C. Vann Woodward,* ed. J. Morgan Kousser and James M. McPherson. 143–77. New York: Oxford University Press, 1982.

———. *Slavery and Freedom on the Middle Ground: Maryland during the Nineteenth Century.* New Haven: Yale University Press, 1985.

———. "Slavery, Race, and Ideology in the United States of America." *New Left Review,* no. 181 (May–June 1990): 95–118.

Fink, Leon. *Workingman's Democracy: The Knights of Labor and American Politics.* Urbana: University of Illinois Press, 1983.

Fitzgerald, Michael W. *The Union League Movement in the Deep South: Politics and Agricultural Change during Reconstruction.* Baton Rouge: Louisiana State University Press, 1989.

Flynt, J. Wayne. "Folks like Us: The Southern Poor White Family, 1865–1935." In *The Web of Southern Social Relations: Women, Family, and Education,* ed. Walter J. Fraser Jr., R. Frank Saunders Jr., and Jon L. Wakelyn. 225–44. Athens: University of Georgia Press, 1985.

Foner, Eric. "Black Reconstruction Leaders at the Grass Roots." In *Black Leaders of the Nineteenth Century,* ed. Leon Litwack and August Meier. 219–34. Urbana: University of Illinois Press, 1988.

———. *Freedom's Lawmakers: A Directory of Black Officeholders during Reconstruction.* New York: Oxford University Press, 1993.

———. *Free Soil, Free Labor, Free Men: The Ideology of the Republican Party before the Civil War.* New York: Oxford, 1970.

———. *Nothing but Freedom: Emancipation and Its Legacy.* Baton Rouge: Louisiana State University Press, 1983.

———. *Politics and Ideology in the Age of the Civil War.* New York: Oxford, 1980.
———. *Reconstruction: America's Unfinished Revolution.* New York: Harper and Row, 1988.
Ford, Lacy K., Jr. *Origins of Southern Radicalism: The South Carolina Upcountry, 1800–1860.* New York: Oxford University Press, 1988.
———. "Rednecks and Merchants: Economic Development and Social Tensions in the South Carolina Upcountry, 1865–1900." *Journal of American History* 71 (Sept. 1984): 294–318.
Foster, Gaines M. *Ghosts of the Confederacy: Defeat, the Lost Cause, and the Emergence of the New South, 1865–1913.* New York: Oxford University Press, 1987.
Fox-Genovese, Elizabeth. *Feminism without Illusions: A Critique of Individualism.* Chapel Hill: University of North Carolina Press, 1991.
———. *Within the Plantation Household: Women in the Old South.* Chapel Hill: University of North Carolina Press, 1988.
Frankenburg, Ruth. *White Women, Race Matters: The Social Construction of Whiteness.* Minneapolis: University of Minnesota Press, 1993.
Franklin, John Hope. *The Free Negro in North Carolina, 1790–1860.* Chapel Hill: University of North Carolina Press, 1943; rpt., New York: Russell and Russell, 1969.
Fraser, Nancy. *Unruly Practices: Power, Discourse, and Gender in Contemporary Social Theory.* Minneapolis: University of Minnesota Press, 1989.
Frederickson, George. *The Black Image in the White Mind: The Debate on Afro-American Character and Destiny, 1817–1914.* New York: Harper and Row, 1971.
Frederickson, Mary. E. "'Each One Is Dependent on the Other': Southern Churchwomen, Racial Reform, and the Process of Transformation, 1880–1940." In *Visible Women: New Essays on American Activism,* ed. Nancy A. Hewitt and Suzanne Lebsock. 296–324. Urbana: University of Illinois Press, 1993.
———. *The Enclosed Garden: Women and Community in the Evangelical South, 1830–1900.* Chapel Hill: University of North Carolina Press, 1985.
Garlock, Jonathan. *Guide to the Local Assemblies of the Knights of Labor.* Westport, Conn.: Greenwood Press, 1982.
Gatewood, William B. *Aristocrats of Color: The Black Elite, 1880–1920.* Bloomington: Indiana University Press, 1990.
Genovese, Eugene D. *The Political Economy of Slavery: Studies in the Economy and Society of the Slave South.* New York: Pantheon Books, 1965.
———. *Roll, Jordan, Roll: The World the Slaves Made.* New York: Vintage Books, 1976.
———. *The Slaveholders' Dilemma: Freedom and Progress in Southern Conservative Thought, 1820–1860.* Columbia: University of South Carolina Press, 1992.
———. *The World the Slaveholders Made: Two Essays in Interpretation.* New York: Pantheon Books, 1969.
Genovese, Eugene D., and Elizabeth Fox-Genovese. "The Divine Sanction of Social Order: Religious Foundations of the Southern Slaveholders' World View." *Journal of the American Academy of Religion* 55 (Summer 1987): 211–33.

———. *Fruits of Merchant Capital: Slavery and Bourgeois Property in the Rise and Expansion of Capitalism*. New York: Oxford University Press, 1983.

———. "The Political Crisis of Social History: A Marxian Perspective." *Journal of Social History* 10 (Winter 1976): 205–20.

———. "The Social Thought of the Antebellum Southern Divines." In *Looking South: Chapters in the Story of an American Region*, ed. Winifred B. Moore Jr. and Joseph F. Tripp. 31–40. New York: Greenwood Press, 1989.

Giddings, Paula. *When and Where I Enter: The Impact of Black Women on Race and Sex in America*. New York: Bantam, 1984.

Gilfoyle, Timothy J. *City of Eros: New York City, Prostitution, and the Commercialization of Sex, 1820–1920*. New York: Norton, 1992.

Gilmore, Glenda Elizabeth. *Gender and Jim Crow: Women and the Politics of White Supremacy in North Carolina, 1896–1920*. Chapel Hill: University of North Carolina Press, 1996.

Glassie, Henry. *Folk Housing in Middle Virginia: A Structural Analysis of Historic Artifacts*. Knoxville: University of Tennessee Press, 1975.

Glymph, Thavolia. "Freedpeople and Ex-Masters: Shaping a New Order in the Postbellum South, 1865–1868." In *Essays on the Postbellum Southern Economy*, ed. Thavolia Glymph and John J. Kushma. 48–72. College Station: Texas A&M Press for the University of Texas at Arlington, 1985.

Glymph, Thavolia, and John J. Kushma, eds. *Essays on the Postbellum Southern Economy*. College Station: Texas A&M Press for the University of Texas at Arlington, 1985.

Goodwyn, Lawrence C. *The Democratic Promise*. New York: Oxford University Press, 1976.

———. "Populist Dreams and Negro Rights: East Texas as a Case Study." *American Historical Review* 76 (Dec. 1971): 1435–56.

Gordon, Linda. "Black and White Visions of Welfare Reform: Women's Welfare Activism, 1890–1945." *Journal of American History* 78 (Sept. 1991): 539–50.

———. *Heroes of Their Own Lives: The Politics and History of Family Violence*. New York: Viking, 1988.

———. "Social Insurance and Public Assistance: The Influence of Gender in Welfare Thought in the United States, 1890–1935." *American Historical Review* 97 (Feb. 1992): 19–54.

Gorn, Elliott J. "'Gouge and Bite, Pull Hair and Scratch': The Social Significance of Fighting in the Southern Backcountry." *American Historical Review* 90 (Feb. 1985): 18–43.

Gould, Jeffrey. "The Strike of 1887: Louisiana Sugar War." *Southern Exposure* 12 (Nov.–Dec. 1984): 45–55.

Greenwood, Janette Thomas. *Bittersweet Legacy: The Black and White "Better Classes" in Charlotte, 1850–1910*. Chapel Hill: University of North Carolina Press, 1994.

Grossberg, Michael. *Governing the Hearth: Law and the Family in Nineteenth-Century America*. Chapel Hill: University of North Carolina Press, 1985.

Grubb, Alan. "House and Home in the Victorian South: The Cookbook as

Guide." In *In Joy and in Sorrow: Women, Family, and Marriage in the Victorian South, 1830–1900,* ed. Carol Bleser. 154–75. New York: Oxford University Press, 1991.

Gutman, Herbert G. *The Black Family in Slavery and Freedom, 1750–1925.* New York: Pantheon Books, 1976.

———. "Work, Culture, and Society in Industrializing America, 1815–1919." 3–78. In *Work, Culture, and Society in Industrializing America.* New York: Knopf, 1976.

Hagood, Margaret Jarman. *Mothers of the South: Portraiture of the White Tenant Farm Woman.* Chapel Hill: University of North Carolina Press, 1939; rpt., New York: Greenwood Press, 1969.

Hahn, Steven. "Common Right and Commonwealth: The Stock-Law Struggle and the Roots of Southern Populism." In *Region, Race, and Reconstruction: Essays in Honor of C. Vann Woodward,* ed. J. Morgan Kousser and James M. McPherson. 51–88. New York: Oxford University Press, 1982.

———. "A Response: Common Cents or Historical Sense?" *Journal of Southern History* 59 (May 1993): 243–58.

———. *The Roots of Southern Populism: Yeoman Farmers and the Transformation of the Georgia Upcountry, 1850–1890.* New York: Oxford University Press, 1983.

Hall, Catherine. *White, Male, and Middle Class: Explorations in Feminism and History.* New York: Routledge, 1992.

Hall, Jacquelyn Dowd. "'The Mind That Burns in Each Body': Women, Rape, and Racial Violence." In *Powers of Desire: The Politics of Sexuality,* ed. Ann Snitow, Christine Stansell, and Sharon Thompson. 328–49. New York: Monthly Review Press, 1983.

———. "O. Delight Smith's Progressive Era: Labor, Feminism, and Reform in the Urban South." In *Visible Women: New Essays on American Activism,* ed. Nancy A. Hewitt and Suzanne Lebsock. 166–98. Urbana: University of Illinois Press, 1993.

———. "Private Eyes, Public Women: Images of Class and Sex in the Urban South, Atlanta, Georgia, 1913–1915." In *Work Engendered: Toward a New History of American Labor,* ed. Ava Baron. 243–72. Ithaca: Cornell University Press, 1991.

———. *Revolt against Chivalry: Jessie Daniel Ames and the Women's Campaign against Lynching.* Rev. ed. New York: Columbia University Press, 1993.

Hall, Jacquelyn Dowd, James Leloudis, Robert Korstad, Mary Murphy, LuAnn Jones, and Christopher Daly. *Like a Family: The Making of a Southern Cotton Mill World.* Chapel Hill: University of North Carolina Press, 1987.

Halttunen, Karen. *Confidence Men and Painted Women: A Study of Middle-Class Culture in America, 1830–1870.* New Haven: Yale University Press, 1982.

Hamilton, J. G. DeRoulhac. "Benjamin Sherwood Hedrick." *James Sprunt Historical Publications* 10, no. 1 (1910): 5–42.

———, ed. *The Correspondence of Jonathan Worth.* Raleigh: North Carolina Historical Commission and Edwards and Broughton Printing, 1909.

———. *North Carolina Biography.* Vol. 4 of *A History of North Carolina.* Chicago: Lewis, 1919.

——. *North Carolina since 1860*. Vol. 3 of *A History of North Carolina*. Chicago: Lewis, 1919.

——, ed. *The Papers of Thomas Ruffin*. Raleigh: North Carolina Historical Commission and Edwards and Broughton Printing, 1920.

——. *Reconstruction in North Carolina*. New York: Columbia University Press, 1914.

Hartog, Hendrik. "Marital Exits and Marital Expectations in Nineteenth Century American." *Georgetown Law Journal* 80 (Oct. 1991): 95–129.

Hawkesworth, Mary E. "Knowers, Knowing, Known: Feminist Theory and Claims of Truth." *Signs* 14 (Spring 1989): 533–57.

Hewitt, Nancy A. "Beyond the Search for Sisterhood: American Women's History in the 1980s." *Social History* 10 (Oct. 1985): 229–321.

——. "Compounding Differences." *Feminist Studies* 18 (Summer 1992): 313–26.

——. "In Pursuit of Power: The Political Economy of Women's Activism in Twentieth-Century Tampa." In *Visible Women: New Essays on American Activism*, ed. Nancy A. Hewitt and Suzanne Lebsock. 199–222. Urbana: University of Illinois Press, 1993.

——. "Reflections from a Departing Editor: Recasting Issues of Marginality." *Gender and History* 4 (Summer 1992): 3–9.

Higginbotham, Evelyn Brooks. "African-American Women's History and the Metalanguage of Race." *Signs* 17 (Winter 1992): 251–74.

——. *Righteous Discontent: The Women's Movement in the Black Baptist Church, 1880–1920*. Cambridge, Mass.: Harvard University Press, 1993.

Higham, John. "Multiculturalism and Universalism: A History and Critique." *American Quarterly* 45 (June 1993): 195–219.

Hine, Darlene Clark. "Rape and the Inner Lives of Black Women in the Middle West." *Signs* 14 (Summer 1989): 912–20.

Hodes, Martha. "The Sexualization of Reconstruction Politics: White Women and Black Men in the South after the Civil War." *Journal of the History of Sexuality* 3, no. 3 (1993): 402–17.

——. "Wartime Dialogues on Illicit Sex: White Women and Black Men." In *Divided Houses: Gender and the Civil War*, ed. Catherine Clinton and Nina Silber. 230–42. New York: Oxford University Press, 1992.

Holt, Sharon Ann. "Making Freedom Pay: Freedpeople Working for Themselves, North Carolina, 1865–1900." *Journal of Southern History* 60 (May 1994): 229–62.

Holt, Thomas C. *Black over White: Negro Political Leadership in South Carolina during Reconstruction*. Urbana: University of Illinois Press, 1977.

——. "'An Empire over the Mind': Emancipation, Race, and Ideology in the British West Indies and the American South." In *Region, Race, and Reconstruction: Essays in Honor of C. Vann Woodward*, ed. J. Morgan Kousser and James M. McPherson. 283–313. New York: Oxford University Press, 1982.

——. *The Problem of Freedom: Race, Labor, and Politics in Jamaica and Britain*. Baltimore: Johns Hopkins University Press, 1992.

hooks, bell. *Ain't I a Woman: Black Women and Feminism*. Boston: South End Press, 1981.

Horner, J. H. "Patent Plant-Bed Burner, and Its Application to Curing Tobacco in Barns, Patented by J.H. Horner, Oxford, N.C., July 28th, 1885, no. 323, 151." N.p.: [1885]. Copy in the North Carolina Collection, University of North Carolina at Chapel Hill.

"Horner Military School, Annual Catalog, 1905." Charlotte, 1905. Copy in the North Carolina Collection, University of North Carolina at Chapel Hill.

"Horner Military School, Annual Catalog, 1906." Raleigh, n.d. Copy in the North Carolina Collection, University of North Carolina at Chapel Hill.

"Horner School, Oxford, North Carolina." N.p.: [1879]. Copy in the North Carolina Collection, University of North Carolina at Chapel Hill.

Horton, James Oliver. "Freedom's Yoke: Gender Conventions among Antebellum Free Blacks." *Feminist Studies* 12 (Spring 1986): 51–76.

———. *Free People of Color: Inside the African American Community.* Washington, D.C.: Smithsonian Institution Press, 1993.

Horton, James Oliver, and Lois E. Horton. *Black Bostonians: Family Life and Community Struggle in the Antebellum North.* New York: Holmes and Meier, 1979.

Hull, Gloria T., Patricia Bell Scott, and Barbara Smith, eds., *All the Women Are White, All the Blacks Are Men, but Some of Us Are Brave: Black Women's Studies.* Old Westbury, N.Y.: Feminist Press, 1982.

Hume, Richard L. "Negro Delegates to the State Constitutional Conventions of 1867–69." In *Southern Black Leaders of the Reconstruction Era,* ed. Howard N. Rabinowitz. 129–53. Urbana: University of Illinois Press, 1982.

Hunter, Captain J. B. "Useful Information Concerning Yellow Tobacco and Other Crops, as Told by Fifty of the Most Successful Farmers of Granville County, North Carolina." Oxford, N.C., 1880. Copy in the North Carolina Collection, University of North Carolina at Chapel Hill.

Hunter, Tera W. "Domination and Resistance: The Politics of Wage Household Labor in New South Atlanta." *Labor History* 34 (Spring–Summer 1993): 205–20.

Hyman, Michael R. *The Anti-Redeemers: Hill-Country Political Dissenters in the Lower South from Redemption to Populism.* Baton Rouge: Louisiana State University Press, 1990.

Inscoe, John. *Mountain Masters, Slavery, and the Sectional Crisis in Western North Carolina.* Knoxville: University of Tennessee Press, 1989.

Isaac, Rhys. *The Transformation of Virginia, 1740–1790.* Chapel Hill: University of North Carolina Press, 1982.

Jahn, Raymond, ed. *Tobacco Dictionary.* New York: Philosophical Library, 1954.

Janiewski, Dolores E. *Sisterhood Denied: Race, Gender, and Class in a New South Community.* Philadelphia: Temple University Press, 1985.

Jaynes, Gerald David. *Branches without Roots: Genesis of the Black Working Class in the American South, 1862–1882.* New York: Oxford University Press, 1986.

Jellison, Katherine. *Entitled to Power: Farm Women and Technology, 1913–1963.* Chapel Hill: University of North Carolina Press, 1993.

Jennings, Thelma. "'Us Colored Women Had to Go through a Plenty': Sexual Exploitation of African American Slave Women." *Journal of Women's History* 1 (Winter 1990): 45–74.

Jensen, Joan. *Loosening the Bonds: Mid-Atlantic Farm Women: 1750–1850.* New Haven: Yale University Press, 1986.

Johnson, Guion Griffis. *Ante-Bellum North Carolina: A Social History.* Chapel Hill: University of North Carolina Press, 1937.

Jones, Jacqueline. *Labor of Love, Labor of Sorrow: Black Women, Work, and the Family from Slavery to the Present.* New York: Basic Books, 1985.

Jordan, Winthrop. *White over Black: American Attitudes toward the Negro, 1580–1812.* Chapel Hill: University of North Carolina Press, 1968.

Joyner, Charles. *Down by the Riverside: A South Carolina Slave Community.* Urbana: University of Illinois Press, 1984.

Judt, Tony. "A Clown in Regal Purple: Social History and the Historians." *History Workshop Journal* (Spring 1979): 66–94.

Kahn, Kenneth. "The Knights of Labor and the Southern Black Worker." *Labor History* 18 (Winter 1977): 47–70.

Kantor, Shawn Everett, and J. Morgan Kousser. "Common Sense of Commonwealth?: The Fence Law and Institutional Change in the Postbellum South." *Journal of Southern History* 59 (May 1993): 201–42.

———. "Rejoinder: Two Visions of History." *Journal of Southern History* 59 (May 1993): 259–66.

Karlsen, Carol F. *The Devil in the Shape of a Woman: Witchcraft in Colonial New England.* New York: Norton, 1987.

Keller, Morton. *Affairs of State: Public Life in Late Nineteenth Century America.* Cambridge, Mass.: Belknap Press of Harvard University Press, 1977.

Kenzer, Robert C. *Kinship and Neighborhood in a Southern Community: Orange County, North Carolina, 1849–1881.* Knoxville: University of Tennessee Press, 1987.

Kerber, Linda K. "The Paradox of Women's Citizenship in the Early Republic: The Case of *Martin vs. Massachusetts,* 1805." *American Historical Review* 97 (Apr. 1992): 349–78.

———. "Separate Spheres, Female Worlds, Woman's Place: The Rhetoric of Women's History." *Journal of American History* 75 (June 1988): 9–39.

———. *Women of the Republic: Intellect and Ideology in Revolutionary America.* Chapel Hill: University of North Carolina Press, 1980.

Kessler, Sidney H. "The Organization of Negroes in the Knights of Labor." *Journal of Negro History* 37 (July 1952): 248–76.

Kessler-Harris, Alice. *A Woman's Wage: Historical Meanings and Social Consequences.* Lexington: University of Kentucky Press, 1990.

King, Andrew J. "Constructing Gender: Sexual Slander in Nineteenth-Century America." *Law and History Review* 13 (Spring 1995): 63–110.

King, J. Crawford. "The Closing of the Southern Range: An Exploratory Essay." *Journal of Southern History* 48 (Feb. 1982): 53–70.

Kousser, J. Morgan. *The Shaping of Southern Politics: Suffrage Restriction and the Establishment of the One-Party South, 1880–1910.* New Haven: Yale University Press, 1974.

Kulik, Gary, ed. Special issue on multiculturalism. *American Quarterly* 45 (June 1993).

Landes, Joan B. *Women and the Public Sphere in the Age of the French Revolution.* Ithaca: Cornell University Press, 1988.

Lebsock, Suzanne. *The Free Women of Petersburg: Status and Culture in a Southern Town, 1784–1860.* New York: Norton, 1984.

———. "Radical Reconstruction and the Property Rights of Southern Women." *Journal of Southern History* 43 (May 1977): 195–216.

———. "Woman Suffrage and White Supremacy: A Virginia Case Study." In *Visible Women: New Essays on American Activism,* ed. Nancy A. Hewitt and Suzanne Lebsock. 62–100. Urbana: University of Illinois Press, 1993.

Levine, Lawrence. *Black Culture and Black Consciousness: Afro-American Folk Thought from Slavery to Freedom.* New York: Oxford University Press, 1977.

Levine, Susan. *Labor's True Woman: Carpet Weavers, Industrialization, and Labor Reform in the Gilded Age.* Philadelphia: Temple University Press, 1984.

Litwack, Leon. *Been in the Storm So Long: The Aftermath of Slavery.* New York: Knopf, 1979.

———. *North of Slavery: The Negro in the Free States, 1790–1860.* Chicago: University of Chicago Press, 1961.

Litwack, Leon, and August Meier, eds. *Black Leaders of the Nineteenth Century.* Urbana: University of Illinois Press, 1988.

Logan, Frenise A. "Black and Republican: Vicissitudes of a Minority Twice Over in the North Carolina House of Representatives, 1876–1877." *North Carolina Historical Review* 61 (July 1984): 311–46.

Logan, Rayford W. *The Negro in American Life and Thought: The Nadir.* New York: Collier, 1954.

MacLean, Nancy. *Behind the Mask of Chivalry: The Making of the Second Ku Klux Klan.* New York: Oxford University Press, 1994.

Maddex, Jack P., Jr. "Proslavery Millennialism: Social Eschatology in Antebellum Southern Calvinism." *American Quarterly* 31 (Spring 1979): 46–48.

———. "'The Southern Apostasy' Revisited: The Significance of Proslavery Christianity." *Marxist Perspectives* 2 (Fall 1979): 132–41.

Malone, Ann Patton. *Sweet Chariot: Slave Family and Household Structure in Nineteenth-Century Louisiana.* Chapel Hill: University of North Carolina Press, 1992.

Mann, Susan A. "Slavery, Sharecropping, and Sexual Inequality." *Signs* 14 (Summer 1989): 774–99.

Martin, Waldo. *The Mind of Frederick Douglass.* Chapel Hill: University of North Carolina Press, 1984.

Mascia-Lees, Frances E., Patricia Sharpe, and Colleen Ballerina Cohen. "The Postmodernist Turn in Anthropology: Cautions from a Feminist Perspective." *Signs* 15 (Autumn 1989): 7–33.

Massur, Louis P. *Rites of Execution: Capital Punishment and the Transformation of American Culture, 1776–1865.* New York: Oxford University Press, 1989.

Mathews, Donald G. *Religion in the Old South.* Chicago: University of Chicago Press, 1977.

McCoy, Drew R. *The Elusive Republic: Political Economy in Jeffersonian America.* Chapel Hill: University of North Carolina Press, 1980.

McCurry, Stephanie. *Masters of Small Worlds: Yeoman Households, Gender Relations, and the Political Culture of the Antebellum South Carolina Low Country.* New York: Oxford University Press, 1995.

———. "The Politics of Yeoman Households in South Carolina." In *Divided Houses: Gender and the Civil War,* ed. Catherine Clinton and Nina Silber. 22–38. New York: Oxford University Press, 1992.

———. "The Two Faces of Republicanism: Gender and Proslavery Politics in Antebellum South Carolina." *Journal of American History* 78 (Mar. 1992): 1245–64.

McDonald, Forrest, and Grady McWhiney. "The Antebellum Southern Herdsman: A Reinterpretation." *Journal of Southern History* 41 (May 1975): 147–66.

McKenzie, Robert Tracy. "Postbellum Tenancy in Fayette County, Tennessee: Its Implications for Economic Development and Persistent Black Poverty." *Agricultural History* 61 (Spring 1987): 16–33.

McLaurin, Melton. *Celia, a Slave.* Athens: University of Georgia Press, 1991.

———. "The Knights of Labor in North Carolina Politics." *North Carolina Historical Review* 49 (July 1972): 298–315.

———. *The Knights of Labor in the South.* Westport, Conn.: Greenwood Press, 1984.

McMath, Robert C., Jr. "Sandy Land and Hogs in the Timber: (Agri)cultural Origins of the Farmers' Alliance in Texas." In *The Countryside in the Age of Capitalist Transformation: Essays in the Social History of Rural America,* ed. Steven Hahn and Jonathan Prude. 205–29. Chapel Hill: University of North Carolina Press, 1985.

———. "Southern White Farmers and the Organization of Black Farm Workers: A North Carolina Document." *Labor History* 18 (Winter 1977): 115–19.

McMillen, Sally G. *Motherhood in the Old South: Pregnancy, Childbirth, and Infant Rearing.* Baton Rouge: Louisiana State University Press, 1990.

Minow, Martha. *Making All the Difference: Inclusion, Exclusion, and American Law.* Ithaca: Cornell University Press, 1990.

Modleski, Tania. *Feminism without Women: Culture and Criticism in a "Postfeminist" Age.* New York: Routledge, 1991.

Mohanty, Chandra Talpade. "Cartographies of Struggle: Third World Women and the Politics of Feminism." In *Third World Women and the Politics of Feminism,* ed. Chandra Talpade Mohanty, Ann Russo, and Lourdes Torres. 1–47. Bloomington: Indiana University Press, 1991.

———. "Under Western Eyes: Feminist Scholarship and Colonial Discourses." In *Third World Women and the Politics of Feminism,* ed. Chandra Talpade Mohanty, Ann Russo, and Lourdes Torres. 51–80. Bloomington: Indiana University Press, 1991.

Monkkonen, Eric. "The Dangers of Synthesis." *American Historical Review* 91 (Dec. 1986): 1146–57.

Montgomery, David. *Beyond Equality: Labor and the Radical Republicans, 1862–1872.* New York: Knopf, 1967.

———. *Citizen Worker: The Experience of Workers in the United States with Democracy and the Free Market during the Nineteenth Century.* New York: Cambridge University Press, 1993.

———. *The Fall of the House of Labor: The Workplace, the State, and American Labor Activism, 1865–1925.* New York: Cambridge University Press, 1987.

Moraga, Cherríe, and Gloria Anzaldúa, eds. *This Bridge Called My Back: Writings by Radical Women of Color.* Watertown, Mass.: Persephone Press, 1981.

Morgan, Edmund. *American Slavery, American Freedom: The Ordeal of Colonial Virginia.* New York: Norton, 1975.

Moss, Alfred. "Alexander Crummell: Black Nationalist and Apostle of Western Civilization." In *Black Leaders of the Nineteenth Century,* ed. Leon Litwack and August Meier. 237–51. Urbana: University of Illinois Press, 1988.

Muhlenfield, Elisabeth. *Mary Boykin Chesnut: A Biography.* Baton Rouge: Louisiana State University Press, 1981.

Nadelhaft, Jerome. "Wife Torture: A Known Phenomenon in Nineteenth-Century America." *Journal of American Culture* 10 (Fall 1987): 39–59.

Nash, Gary. *Forging Freedom: The Formation of Philadelphia's Black Community, 1720–1840.* Cambridge, Mass.: Harvard University Press, 1988.

———. *Race and Revolution.* Madison: Madison House, 1990.

Nash, Gary, and Jean R. Soderlund. *Freedom by Degrees: Emancipation in Pennsylvania and Its Aftermath.* New York: Oxford University Press, 1991.

Newman, Louise, Joan Williams, Lise Vogel, and Judith Newton. "Theoretical and Methodological Dialogue on the Writing of Women's History." *Journal of Women's History* 2 (Winter 1991): 58–108.

Nicholson, Linda, ed. *Feminism/Postmodernism.* New York: Routledge, 1990.

———. *Gender and History: The Limits of Social Theory in the Age of the Family.* New York: Columbia University Press, 1986.

Nieman, Donald G. "Black Political Power and Criminal Justice: Washington County, Texas, 1868–1884." *Journal of Southern History* 55 (Aug. 1989): 391–420.

———. *To Set the Law in Motion: The Freedmen's Bureau and the Legal Rights of Blacks, 1865–1868.* Millwood, N.Y.: KTO Press, 1979.

Oakes, James. "The Political Significance of Slave Resistance." *History Workshop* 22 (Autumn 1986): 89–107.

———. "The Present Becomes the Past: The Planter Class in the Postbellum South." In *New Perspectives on Race and Slavery in America,* ed. Robert H. Abzug and Stephen E. Maizlish. 149–63. Lexington: University of Kentucky Press, 1986.

———. *Slavery and Freedom: An Interpretation of the Old South.* New York: Knopf, 1990.

O'Brien, Gail. *The Legal Fraternity and the Making of a New South Community.* Athens: University of Georgia Press, 1986.

Olsen, Otto H. *A Carpetbagger's Crusade: The Life of Albion Winegar Tourgée.* Baltimore: Johns Hopkins University Press, 1965.

———. "An Incongruous Presence." In *Reconstruction and Redemption in the*

South, ed. Otto H. Olsen. 156–201. Baton Rouge: Louisiana State University Press, 1980.

——————."The Ku Klux Klan: A Study in Reconstruction Politics and Propaganda." *North Carolina Historical Review* 39 (Summer 1962): 340–62.

Osterweis, Rollin G. *The Myth of the Lost Cause, 1865–1900.* Hamden, Conn.: Archon Books, 1973.

Ownby, Ted. *Subduing Satan: Religion, Recreation, and Manhood in the Rural South, 1865–1920.* Chapel Hill: University of North Carolina Press, 1990.

Padgett, James A. "Reconstruction Letters from North Carolina: Part 1, Letters to Thaddeus Stevens." *North Carolina Historical Review* 18 (Apr. 1941): 171–95.

——————. "Reconstruction Letters from North Carolina: Part 4, Letters to Elihu Benjamin Washburne." *North Carolina Historical Review* 18 (Oct. 1941): 395–96.

Painter, Nell Irvin. *Exodusters: Black Migration to Kansas after Reconstruction.* New York: Knopf, 1976.

——————. "The Journal of Gertrude Clanton Thomas: An Educated White Woman in the Eras of Slavery, War, and Reconstruction." Introduction to *The Secret Eye: The Journal of Gertrude Clanton Thomas, 1848–1889,* ed. Virginia Ingraham Burr. 1–67. Chapel Hill: University of North Carolina Press, 1990.

——————. "Martin R. Delany: Elitism and Black Nationalism." In *Black Leaders of the Nineteenth Century,* ed. Leon Litwack and August Meier. 149–71. Urbana: University of Illinois Press, 1988.

——————. "Of *Lily,* Linda Brent, and Freud: A Non-Exceptionalist Approach to Race, Class, and Gender in the Slaveholding South." *Georgia Historical Quarterly* 76 (Summer 1992): 241–59.

——————. "'Social Equality,' Miscegenation, and the Maintenance of Power." In *The Evolution of Southern Culture,* ed. Numan B. Bartley. 47–67. Athens: University of Georgia Press, 1988.

Pateman, Carole. *The Sexual Contract.* Stanford: Stanford University Press, 1988.

Paul, Hiram. *History of the Town of Durham.* Raleigh: Edwards, Broughton, 1884.

Perman, Michael. *Reunion without Compromise: The South and Reconstruction, 1865–1868.* New York: Cambridge University Press, 1973.

——————. *The Road to Redemption: Southern Politics, 1869–1879.* Chapel Hill: University of North Carolina Press, 1984.

Pitkin, Hanna Fenichel. *Fortune Is a Woman: Gender and Politics in the Thought of Niccolo Machiavelli.* Berkeley: University of California Press, 1984.

Pleck, Elizabeth. *Domestic Tyranny: The Making of Social Policy against Family Violence from Colonial Times to the Present.* New York: Oxford University Press, 1987.

——————. "Wife Beating in Nineteenth-Century America." *Victimology* 4, no. 1 (1979): 60–74.

Poovey, Mary. *Uneven Developments: The Ideological Work of Gender in Mid-Victorian England.* Chicago: University of Chicago Press, 1988.

Powell, William S. *Dictionary of North Carolina Biography.* 5 vols. to date. Chapel Hill: University of North Carolina Press, 1979–.

———. *When the Past Refused to Die.* Durham: Moore Publishing, 1977.

Rable, George C. *Civil Wars: Women and the Crisis of Southern Nationalism.* Urbana: University of Illinois Press, 1989.

Raboteau, Albert J. *Slave Religion: The "Invisible Institution" in the Antebellum South.* New York: Oxford University Press, 1978.

Rachleff, Peter J. *Black Labor in the South: Richmond, Virginia, 1865–1890.* Philadelphia: Temple University Press, 1984.

Ransom, Roger L., and Richard Sutch. *One Kind of Freedom: The Economic Consequences of Emancipation.* New York: Cambridge University Press, 1977.

Raper, Arthur. *Preface to Peasantry: A Tale of Two Black Belt Counties.* Chapel Hill: University of North Carolina Press, 1936; rpt., New York: Athenaeum, 1968.

Raper, Horace W. *William W. Holden: North Carolina's Political Enigma.* Chapel Hill: University of North Carolina Press, 1985.

Rapport, Sara. "The Freedmen's Bureau as a Legal Agent for Black Men and Women in Georgia: 1865–1868." *Georgia Historical Quarterly* 73 (Spring 1989): 26–53.

Rawick, George, ed. *The American Slave: A Composite Autobiography.* Series 2, vols. 14–15. Westport, Conn.: Greenwood Press, 1972.

Reid, Richard. "A Test Case of the 'Crying Evil': Desertion among North Carolina Troops during the Civil War." *North Carolina Historical Review* 58 (July 1981): 243–62.

Reid, Whitelaw. *After the War: A Southern Tour, May 1, 1865, to May 1, 1866.* Cincinnati: Moore, Wilstach, and Baldwin, 1866.

Reidy, Joseph P. "Aaron A. Bradley: Voice of Black Labor in the Georgia Lowcountry." In *Southern Black Leaders of the Reconstruction Era,* ed. Howard N. Rabinowitz. 281–308. Urbana: University of Illinois Press, 1982.

———. *From Slavery to Agrarian Capitalism in the Cotton Plantation South: Central Georgia, 1800–1880.* Chapel Hill: University of North Carolina Press, 1992.

Riley, Denise. *Am I That Name?: Feminism and the Category of 'Women' in History.* Minneapolis: University of Minnesota Press, 1988.

Robert, Joseph C. *The Tobacco Kingdom: Plantation, Market, and Factory in Virginia and North Carolina, 1800–1860.* Durham: Duke University Press, 1938.

Roberts, John W. *From Trickster to Badman: The Black Folk Hero in Slavery and Freedom.* Philadelphia: University of Pennsylvania Press, 1989.

Robinson, Armstead. "Beyond the Realm of Social Consensus: New Meanings of Reconstruction for American History." *Journal of American History* 68 (May 1981): 276–97.

———. "Plans Dat Comed from God: Institution Building and the Emergence of Black Leadership in Reconstruction Memphis, 1865–1880." In

Toward a New South?: Studies in Post-Civil War Southern Communities, ed. Orville Vernon Burton and Robert C. McMath. 71–102. Westport, Conn.: Greenwood Press, 1982.

Rodgers, Daniel T. "Republicanism: The Career of a Concept." *Journal of American History* 79 (June 1992): 11–38.

Roediger, David R. *Towards the Abolition of Whiteness: Essays on Race, Politics, and Working Class History.* New York: Verso, 1994.

———. *The Wages of Whiteness: Race and the Making of the American Working Class.* New York: Verso, 1991.

Rogers, William Warren, Jr. *Black Belt Scalawag: Charles Hays and the Southern Republicans in the Era of Reconstruction.* Athens: University of Georgia Press, 1993.

Rose, Willie Lee. *Rehearsal for Reconstruction: The Port Royal Experiment.* New York: Knopf, 1964.

Roydhouse, Marion W. "Bridging Chasms: Community and the Southern YWCA." In *Visible Women: New Essays on American Activism,* ed. Nancy A. Hewitt and Suzanne Lebsock. 270–95. Urbana: University of Illinois Press, 1993.

Ryan, Mary P. *The Cradle of the Middle Class: The Family in Oneida County, New York, 1790–1865.* New York: Cambridge University Press, 1981.

———. *Women in Public: Between Banners and Ballots, 1825–1880.* Baltimore: Johns Hopkins University Press, 1990.

Salinger, Sharon V. *"To Serve Well and Faithfully": Labor and Indentured Servants in Pennsylvania, 1682–1800.* New York: Cambridge University Press, 1987.

Salmon, Marylynn. *Women and the Law of Property in Early America.* Chapel Hill: University of North Carolina Press, 1986.

Saville, Julie. *The Work of Reconstruction: From Slave to Wage Laborer in South Carolina, 1860–1870.* New York: Cambridge University Press, 1994.

Saxton, Alexander. *The Rise and Fall of the White Republic: Class Politics and Mass Culture in Nineteenth-Century America.* New York: Verso, 1990.

Scott, Anne Firor. *The Southern Lady: From Pedestal to Politics, 1830–1930.* Chicago: University of Chicago Press, 1970.

Scott, Joan Wallach. *Gender and the Politics of History.* New York: Columbia University Press, 1988.

Scott, Rebecca. "The Battle over the Child: Child Apprenticeship and the Freedmen's Bureau in North Carolina." *Prologue* 10 (Summer 1978): 101–13.

Senechal, Roberta. *The Sociogenesis of a Race Riot: Springfield, Illinois, in 1908.* Urbana: University of Illinois Press, 1990.

Shalhope, Robert E. "Republicanism and Early American Historiography." *William and Mary Quarterly* 39 (Apr. 1982): 334–56.

———. "Toward a Republican Synthesis." *William and Mary Quarterly* 29 (Jan. 1972): 49–80.

Shifflett, Crandall. *Coal Towns: Life, Work, and Culture in Company Towns of Southern Appalachia, 1880–1960.* Knoxville: University of Tennessee Press, 1991.

———. *Patronage and Poverty in the Tobacco South: Louisa County Virginia, 1860–1900.* Knoxville: University of Tennessee Press, 1982.

Silber, Nina. *The Romance of Reunion: Northerners and the South, 1865–1900.* Chapel Hill: University of North Carolina Press, 1993.

Sims, Anastasia. "'The Sword of the Spirit': The WCTU and Moral Reform in North Carolina, 1883–1933." *North Carolina Historical Review* 64 (Oct. 1987): 394–415.

Smith, Barbara, ed. *Home Girls: A Black Feminist Anthology.* New York: Kitchen Table–Women of Color Press, 1983.

Smith-Rosenberg, Carroll. "Dis-Covering the Subject of the 'Great Constitutional Discussion,' 1786–1789." *Journal of American History* 79 (Dec. 1992): 841–73.

———. *Disorderly Conduct: Visions of Gender in Victorian America.* New York: Knopf, 1985.

Snay, Mitchell. "American Thought and Southern Distinctiveness: The Southern Clergy and the Sanctification of Slavery." *Civil War History* 35 (Dec. 1989): 311–28.

Sommerville, Diane Miller. "The Rape Myth in the Old South Reconsidered." *Journal of Southern History* 61 (Aug. 1995): 481–518.

Stanley, Amy Dru. "Beggars Can't Be Choosers: Compulsion and Contract in Postbellum America." *Journal of American History* 78 (Mar. 1992): 1265–93.

Stansell, Christine. *City of Women: Sex and Class in New York, 1789–1860.* Urbana: University of Illinois Press, 1987.

Stearns, Peter. "Social and Political History." *Journal of Social History* 16 (Spring 1983): 3–6.

Steinfeld, Robert J. *The Invention of Free Labor: The Employment Relation in English and American Law and Culture, 1350–1870.* Chapel Hill: University of North Carolina Press, 1991.

Strickland, John Scott. "Traditional Culture and Moral Economy: Social and Economic Change in the South Carolina Low Country, 1865–1900." In *The Countryside in the Age of Capitalist Transformation: Essays in the Social History of Rural America,* ed. Steven Hahn and Jonathan Prude. 141–78. Chapel Hill: University of North Carolina Press, 1985.

Stromquist, Shelton. *A Generation of Boomers: The Pattern of Railroad Labor Conflict in Nineteenth-Century America.* Urbana: University of Illinois Press, 1987.

Stuckey, Sterling. "A Last Stern Struggle: Henry Highland Garnet and Liberation Theory." In *Black Leaders of the Nineteenth Century,* ed. Leon Litwack and August Meier. 129–47. Urbana: University of Illinois Press, 1988.

Swift, Zephaniah. *A System of Laws of the State of Connecticut.* 2 vols. Windham, Conn., 1795.

Tate, Claudia. *Domestic Allegories of Political Desire: The Black Heroine's Text at the Turn of the Century.* New York: Oxford University Press, 1992.

Thomas, Mary Martha. *The New Woman in Alabama: Social Reforms and Suffrage, 1890–1920.* Tuscaloosa: University of Alabama Press, 1992.

Thompson, E. P. "Time, Work-Discipline, and Industrial Capitalism." *Past and Present* 38 (Dec. 1967): 56–97.

Thornton, J. Mills, III. "Fiscal Policy and the Failure of Radical Reconstruction in the Lower South." In *Region, Race, and Reconstruction: Essays in Honor of C. Vann Woodward*, ed. J. Morgan Kousser and James M. McPherson. 349–94. New York: Oxford University Press, 1982.

———. *Politics and Power in a Slave Society: Alabama, 1800–1860*. Baton Rouge: Louisiana State University Press, 1978.

Tilley, Nannie May. *The Bright Tobacco Industry, 1860–1929*. Chapel Hill: University of North Carolina Press, 1967.

Tise, Larry E. *Proslavery: A History of the Defense of Slavery in America*. Athens: University of Georgia Press, 1987.

Tomlins, Christopher L. *Law, Labor, and Ideology in the Early American Republic*. New York: Cambridge University Press, 1993.

Tourgée, Albion W. *A Fool's Errand*. New York: Fords, Howard, and Hulbert, 1879; rpt., New York: Harper and Row, 1966.

———. *The Invisible Empire*. New York: Fords, Howard, and Hulbert, 1880; rpt., Baton Rouge: Louisiana State University Press, 1989.

Trelease, Allen W. *The North Carolina Railroad, 1849–1871, and the Modernization of North Carolina*. Chapel Hill: University of North Carolina Press, 1991.

———. *White Terror: The Ku Klux Klan Conspiracy and Southern Reconstruction*. New York: Harper and Row, 1971.

Tushnet, Mark V. *The American Law of Slavery, 1810–1860: Consideration of Humanity and Interest*. Princeton: Princeton University Press, 1981.

Ulrich, Laurel Thatcher. *Good Wives: Image and Reality in the Lives of Women in Northern New England, 1650–1750*. New York: Oxford University Press, 1983.

———. *A Midwife's Tale: The Life of Martha Ballard, Based on Her Diary, 1785–1812*. New York: Knopf, 1990.

Vlach, John Michael. *Back of the Big House: The Architecture of Plantation Slavery*. Chapel Hill: University of North Carolina Press, 1993.

Walters, Ronald G. *The Antislavery Appeal: American Abolitionism after 1830*. Baltimore: Johns Hopkins University Press, 1976.

Watson, Harry L. "Conflict and Collaboration: Yeomen, Slaveholders, and Politics in the Antebellum South." *Social History* 10 (Oct. 1985): 273–98.

———. *Jacksonian Politics and Community Conflict: The Emergence of the Second American Party System in Cumberland County, North Carolina*. Baton Rouge: Louisiana State University Press, 1981.

Wayne, Michael. *The Reshaping of Plantation Society: The Natchez District, 1860–1880*. Baton Rouge: Louisiana State University Press, 1983.

Wedell, Marsha. *Elite Women and the Reform Impulse in Memphis, 1875–1915*. Knoxville: University of Tennessee Press, 1991.

Weiner, Jonathan. "AHR Forum: Class Structure and Economic Development in the American South, 1865–1955." *American Historical Review* 84 (Oct. 1979): 970–1006.

———. *Social Origins of the New South, 1860–1885.* Baton Rouge: Louisiana State University Press, 1978.

Wheeler, Marjorie Spruill. *New Women of the New South: The Leaders of the Woman Suffrage Movement in the Southern States.* New York: Oxford University Press, 1993.

White, Barnetta McGhee. *In Search of Kith and Kin.* Baltimore: Gateway Press, 1986.

White, Deborah Gray. *Ar'n't I a Woman: Female Slaves in the Plantation South.* New York: Norton, 1985.

White, Shane. *Somewhat More Independent: The End of Slavery in New York City, 1770–1810.* Athens: University of Georgia Press, 1991.

White, William Wallace. *Diary, 1857–1910.* Birmingham: Leonard Henderson White, n.d. Copy in the North Carolina Collection, University of North Carolina at Chapel Hill.

Whites, LeeAnn. *The Civil War as a Crisis in Gender: Augusta, Georgia, 1860–1890.* Athens: University of Georgia Press, 1995.

———. "The Civil War as a Crisis in Gender." In *Divided Houses: Gender and the Civil War,* ed. Catherine Clinton and Nina Silber. 3–21. New York: Oxford University Press, 1992.

———. "Rebecca Latimer Felton and the Problem of 'Protection' in the New South." In *Visible Women: New Essays on American Activism,* ed. Nancy A. Hewitt and Suzanne Lebsock. 41–61. Urbana: University of Illinois Press, 1993.

Wilentz, Sean. *Chants Democratic: New York City and the Rise of the American Working Class, 1788–1850.* New York: Oxford, 1984.

Wiley, Bell Irvin. *Confederate Women.* Westport, Conn.: Greenwood Press, 1975.

Williams, Michael Ann. *Homeplace: The Social Use and Meaning of the Folk Dwelling in Southwestern North Carolina.* Athens: University of Georgia Press, 1991.

Williams, Patricia J. *The Alchemy of Race and Rights.* Cambridge, Mass.: Harvard University Press, 1991.

Williamson, Joel. *The Crucible of Race: Black-White Relations in the American South since Emancipation.* New York: Oxford University Press, 1984.

Wilson, Charles Reagan. *Baptized in Blood: The Religion of the Lost Cause, 1865–1920.* Athens: University of Georgia Press, 1980.

Wilson, Joan Hoff. *Law, Gender, and Injustice: A Legal History of U.S. Women.* New York: New York University Press, 1991.

Wilson, Theodore Brantner. *The Black Codes of the South.* University: University of Alabama Press, 1965.

Winters, Donald L. "The Agricultural Ladder in Southern Agriculture: Tennessee, 1850–1870." *Agricultural History* 61 (Summer 1987): 36–52.

Woodman, Harold D. *King Cotton and His Retainers: Financing and Marketing the Cotton Crop of the South, 1800–1925.* Lexington: University of Kentucky Press, 1968.

———. *New South, New Law: The Legal Foundations of Credit and Labor Relations in the Postbellum Agricultural South.* Baton Rouge: Louisiana State University Press, 1995.

————. "Post–Civil War Southern Agriculture and the Law." *Agricultural History* 53 (Jan. 1979): 319–37.

————. "Reconstruction of the Cotton Plantation in the New South." In *Essays on the Postbellum Southern Economy,* ed. Thavolia Glymph and John J. Kushma. 95–119. College Station: Texas A&M Press for the University of Texas at Arlington, 1985.

————. "Sequel to Slavery: The New History Views the Postbellum South." *Journal of Southern History* 48 (Nov. 1977): 523–54.

Woodward, C. Vann. *Origins of the New South, 1877–1913.* Baton Rouge: Louisiana State University Press, 1951.

————. *The Strange Career of Jim Crow.* 3d rev. ed. New York: Oxford University Press, 1974.

————. *Tom Watson: Agrarian Rebel.* New York: Macmillan, 1938.

Wriggins, Jennifer. "Rape, Racism, and the Law." *Harvard Women's Law Journal* 6 (Spring 1983): 103–41.

Wright, Gavin. *Old South, New South: Revolutions in the Southern Economy since the Civil War.* New York: Basic Books, 1986.

Wyatt-Brown, Bertram. *Southern Honor: Ethics and Behavior in the Old South.* New York: Oxford University Press, 1982.

Yearns, W. Buck, and John G. Barrett. *North Carolina Civil War Documentary.* Chapel Hill: University of North Carolina Press, 1980.

York, Brantley. *The Autobiography of Brantley York.* Durham: Seeman Printery, 1910.

Unpublished Papers and Dissertations

Bercaw, Nancy. "Defeat from Within: Planter Women and the Politics of Household in the Civil War Delta." Paper presented at the annual meeting of the Southern Historical Association, Orlando, Nov. 1993.

————. "The Politics of Household: Domestic Battlegrounds in the Transition from Slavery to Freedom in the Yazoo-Mississippi Delta, 1850–1860." Ph.D. diss., University of Pennsylvania, 1996.

Brown, Elsa Barkley. "To Catch a Vision of Freedom." Paper presented at the Social History Seminar, Newberry Library, Chicago, Oct. 1991.

————. "Uncle Ned's Children: Negotiating Community and Freedom in Postemancipation Richmond, Virginia." Ph.D. diss., Kent State University, 1994.

Brown, R. Ben. "The Southern Range: A Study in Nineteenth Century Law and Society." Ph.D. diss., University of Michigan, 1993.

Cole, Stephanie. "Servants and Slaves: Domestic Service in the Border Cities, 1800–1850." Ph.D. diss., University of Florida, 1994.

Emory, Samuel Thomas. "Bright Tobacco in the Agriculture, Industry, and Foreign Trade of North Carolina." Ph.D. diss., University of Chicago, 1939.

Frankel, Noralee. "Freedom's Women: African-American Women in Mississippi, 1860–1870." Ms.

Hewitt, Nancy. "The Right Chemistry: Recasting Questions of Gender, Race, and Class." Paper presented at the Newberry Seminar in American Social History, Newberry Library, Chicago, Mar. 1991.

Hodes, Martha. "Sex across the Color Line: White Women and Black Men in the Nineteenth Century South." Ph.D. diss., Princeton University, 1991.

Holt, Sharon Ann. "A Time to Plant: The Economic Lives of Freedpeople in Granville County, North Carolina, 1865–1900." Ph.D. diss., University of Pennsylvania, 1991.

Hume, Richard L. "Black and Tan Constitutional Conventions of 1867–1869 in Ten Former Confederate States: A Study of Their Membership." Ph.D. diss., University of Washington, 1969.

Hunter, Tera W. "Household Workers in the Making: Afro-American Women in Atlanta and the New South, 1861 to 1920." Ph.D. diss., Yale University, 1990.

Rivers, Francis J. "Entrepreneurs and Reformers at a Country Crossroads: Granville County, North Carolina, and the Crop-Lien System." Senior thesis, Duke University, 1983.

Rosen, Hannah. "Interracial Rape and the Politics of Reconstruction." Paper presented at the National Graduate Women's Studies Conference, Ann Arbor, 1990.

———. "Race, Gender, and the Politics of Rape in the Post-Emancipation South." Ph.D. diss. in progress, University of Chicago.

———. "Rape as Reality, Rape as Fiction: Rape Law and Ideology in the Antebellum South." Ms., History Department, University of Chicago, 1989.

———. "Struggles over 'Freedom': Sexual Violence during the Memphis Riot of 1866." Paper presented at the Berkshire Conferemóe of Women Historians, Poughkeepsie, N.Y., June 1993.

Schwalm, Leslie Ann. "The Meaning of Freedom: AfricIn-American Women and Their Transition from Slavery to Freedom in Lowcountry South Carolina." Ph.D. diss., University of Wisconsin, 1991.

Index

Abolitionists, 190, 192, 194, 316*n19*

Adultery, 57–58, 60, 208–9

African Americans: views of and efforts of to obtain civil and political rights, 13–16, 192–98, 218, 244–45, 246, 252, 260*n22*, 269*n58*, 316*n17*, 317*n20;* and marriage, 18–19, 31–32, 34, 36–40, 45–47, 54–60, 62, 63, 64–65, 269–70*n60*, 273*nn79, 80*, 274*n86;* and labor relations, 19, 66–67, 77–80, 82–83, 85–87, 88, 89, 90–100, 102–6, 175, 286*n50*, 288–89*n61;* 310–11*n46;* and gender ideology, 20–21, 22–23, 145–47, 210–11, 214–17, 229, 238–39, 243–44, 250–51; conflicts between men and women, 21, 62, 63, 105, 178–82, 211–13, 313*n68;* and Knights of Labor, 22, 218–19, 240–42, 246–48, 250–51, 252; and parental rights, 39, 40–44, 47–53, 104–5, 272–73*n77;* and local courts, 49–50, 53–54, 63–64, 96–98, 184–85, 198–200, 213–14, 244–45, 272*n76;* and extended family ties, 59–60; economic position of, 66, 83, 87–88, 151, 158–61, 166–67, 168–70, 222–25, 228; and property, 90, 91–92, 124–25, 147–48, 157, 168–69, 225–26, 228; and ideology of merit, 110–11, 123–24, 125, 143–44, 230, 233–34, 235–37, 239–40, 253–54, 333*n49;* houses of, 137–39, 158, 159, 307*n28;* and party politics, 170, 172–73, 177, 197, 219–21, 226–28, 231–32, 233, 237–40, 251–52, 253–54, 327*n23;* whites' views of, 185–86, 187–88, 189–90, 191–92, 216–17, 245–46, 247, 250, 253–54, 280–81*n25*, 288*n59;* militia companies of, 194, 198; and the Ku Klux Klan, 197, 220, 225, 227; and

emigration, 197–98, 228. *See also* Free Blacks; Servants; Slavery; Slaves; Wage Laborers

—Men: in the U.S. Army, 47, 166–67, 171; as laborers, 83, 86, 93–94, 97–100, 103–4, 175; whites' views of, 95–96, 173–77, 233–34; and manhood, 114–15, 161–62, 166–73, 177–80, 205; views of and efforts of to obtain civil and political rights, 195–98, 210–13, 216–17, 219–21, 239–40, 250–51; mentioned, 209

—Women: views of and efforts of to obtain civil and political rights, 15–16, 21, 178–82, 184–85, 195–97, 198–200, 210, 211–13, 318*n26*, 319*n34*, 322*n61;* and disfranchisement, 23; as laborers, 87, 102–3, 104, 117–18, 148–52, 156–57, 177–78, 284*n46;* whites' views of, 134–35, 202–3, 301*n56;* and womanhood, 147–61, 167–68

Agricultural ladder, 91–92

Alabama, 145, 194, 195

Albert (last name unknown), 83

Allen, Adline, 211

Allen, Jack, 205–6

Allen, Martha, 177–78

Allen, Warren, 93–94, 97, 99, 100, 103

Allen, William, 99, 145, 146, 171–72

Ambrose, Harriet, 42–44, 47

American Tobacco Company, 223–24

Amis, Frances, 87, 88, 153, 154

Ancrum, Edward, 170

Andrews, Sidney, 77, 201

Antebellum South, the: conservative political ideology of, 3–4, 10–12, 13, 18–19, 39–40, 75, 312*n58*. *See also* Free Blacks; Slavery; Slaves

Apprenticeship, 39, 43–44, 47–53, 54,

LAURA F. EDWARDS has written articles on women's history, southern history, and legal history. She is an assistant professor at the University of South Florida.

Books in the Series
Women in American History

Babe: The Life and Legend of Babe Didrikson Zaharias *Susan E. Cayleff*

Writing Out My Heart: Selections from the Journal of Frances E. Willard, 1855–96 *Carolyn De Swarte Gifford*

U.S. Women in Struggle: A *Feminist Studies* Anthology *Edited by Claire Goldberg Moses and Heidi Hartmann*

In a Generous Spirit: A First-Person Biography of Myra Page *Christina Looper Baker*

Mining Cultures: Men, Women, and Leisure in Butte, 1914–41 *Mary Murphy*

Gendered Strife and Confusion: The Political Culture of Reconstruction *Laura F. Edwards*